Compliant Rebels

Seventeen million people have died in civil wars, and rebel violence has disrupted the lives of millions more. In a fascinating contribution to the active literature on civil wars, this book finds that some contemporary rebel groups actually comply with international law amid the brutality of civil conflicts around the world. Rather than celebrating the existence of compliant rebels, the author traces the cause of this phenomenon and argues that compliant rebels emerge when rebel groups seek legitimacy in the eyes of domestic and international audiences that care about humanitarian consequences and human rights. By examining rebel groups' different behaviors, such as civilian killing, child soldiering, and allowing access to detention centers, *Compliant Rebels* offers key messages and policy lessons about engaging rebel groups with an eye toward reducing civilian suffering in war zones.

Hyeran Jo is an assistant professor of political science at Texas A&M University. Her primary research topics are the role of international organizations and non-state actors in contemporary world politics, and she has published articles in various academic journals including the *British Journal of Political Science* and the *Journal of Conflict Resolution.*

Problems of International Politics

Series Editors

Keith Darden, *American University*
Ian Shapiro, *Yale University*

The series seeks manuscripts central to the understanding of international politics that will be empirically rich and conceptually innovative. It is interested in works that illuminate the evolving character of nation-states within the international system. It sets out three broad areas for investigation: (1) identity, security, and conflict; (2) democracy; and (3) justice and distribution.

Titles in the Series

Şener Aktürk, *Regimes of Ethnicity and Nationhood in Germany, Russia, and Turkey*
Séverine Autesserre, *Peaceland: Conflict Resolution and the Everyday Politics of International Intervention*
Lisa Baldez, *Defying Convention: US Resistance to the UN Treaty on Women's Rights*
Henry E. Hale, *Patronal Politics: Eurasian Regime Dynamics in Comparative Perspective*
Donald Horowitz, *Constitutional Change and Democracy in Indonesia*
Adria K. Lawrence, *Imperial Rule and the Politics of Nationalism: Anti-Colonial Protest in the French Empire*
Steven Levitsky and Lucan A. Way, *Competitive Authoritarianism: Hybrid Regimes after the Cold War*
Tarek Masoud, *Counting Islam: Religion, Class, and Elections in Egypt*
Shaul Mishal and Ori Goldberg, *Understanding Shiite Leadership: The Art of the Middle Ground in Iran and Lebanon*
Harris Mylonas, *The Politics of Nation-Building: Making Co-Nationals, Refugees, and Minorities*

Compliant Rebels

Rebel Groups and International Law in World Politics

HYERAN JO

Department of Political Science
Texas A&M University

This material is based upon work supported by the National Science Foundation under grant number SES #1260218. Any opinions, findings, and conclusions or recommendations expressed in this material are those of the author and do not necessarily reflect the views of the National Science Foundation.

CAMBRIDGE
UNIVERSITY PRESS

CAMBRIDGE
UNIVERSITY PRESS

University Printing House, Cambridge CB2 8BS, United Kingdom

Cambridge University Press is part of the University of Cambridge.

It furthers the University's mission by disseminating knowledge in the pursuit of education, learning and research at the highest international levels of excellence.

www.cambridge.org
Information on this title: www.cambridge.org/9781107110045

First published 2015

A catalogue record for this publication is available from the British Library

ISBN 978-1-107-11004-5 Hardback

Dedicated to my parents

Contents

Tables and Illustrations

TABLES

BOXES

FIGURES

MAPS

Acknowledgments

This book focuses on rebel groups and why they might choose to comply with the international laws of war. I have written this book not to celebrate the compliant rebels, but to understand why compliant rebels emerge. When I first floated the idea to study this topic to my colleague, Jon Bond, he asked, "Aren't rebel groups, by definition, not compliant?" This puzzle is why I have been interested in this question. In general, rebel groups are non-conformists. When do they conform to existing rules? How do rebel groups move from non-compliance to compliance? What are the motivations and political processes that produce compliant rebels?

As it turned out, the answer to these questions can be found only in an interdisciplinary endeavor engaging not only politics, but also economics, sociology, and law. I had to understand legal foundations that governed rebel groups, dig deeper into the social relationships between rebels and ordinary people around them, analyze the financial portfolios of rebel groups to figure out how they support their warfare, and discover how savvy and uncanny some rebel leaders are in advertising their compliance with the international laws of war.

This inquiry has not always been objective. Although I tried to keep my hat as a political scientist I sometimes found the task challenging and realized that one cannot be entirely impassionate while studying this topic of rebel violence. Many stories I read during my research reminded me how brutal humans can be to each other. I cannot imagine what life would be like for a 12-year-old boy with an amputated arm between rebel and government fighting in the Democratic Republic of the Congo (DCR). I also shudder when I remember a story about a young boy in Uganda who was instructed by the rebels to, "First, kill your family." Also ingrained in my memory are the old pictures of the Korean War where the same ethnic

Koreans killed each other for accusing each other of being "rebels" – although, the Korean War is often classified as a civil war.

Four people, especially, have shaped my thinking and influenced my experience on this topic: James Morrow at the University of Michigan, Beth Simmons at Harvard, Quan Li at Texas A&M University, and Jongryn Mo at Yonsei University. They have been my intellectual beacons during my formative years as a scholar. The book idea germinated from my collaboration with Jim on his project on the laws of war, and his continuing engagement with this line of inquiry shaped this book. Beth has given me invaluable vision and advice on pursuing this topic, let alone the detailed comments on the book manuscript. Quan and Jongryn have been my good mentors both at personal and professional levels.

I am grateful for policymakers and practitioners who shared their time and views: Olivier Bangerter (Humanitarian Policy Team at Federal Department of Foreign Affairs, Switzerland), Claude Bruderlein (Harvard Kennedy School), Howard Buffett (Buffett Foundation), Gerard McHugh (formerly at UNOCHA), Andrew Natsosis (formerly at USAID), Simar Singh (Conflict Dynamics International), David Tuck (ICRC), Carole Frampton-de Tscharner (Geneva Call), Stuart Maslan (Geneva Academy), Audrey Palama (ICRC), Linda Potet (Mercy Corps), Carrie Grunloh (USAID), Jonathan Somer (Persona Grata Consulting), Chris Tomlinson (Associated Press), and Alec Wargo (United Nations). My discussions with them pushed me to do a reality check of my academic work and to find a practical value to my otherwise pedantic exercise.

Additionally, many in academia encouraged this project and sharpened my thinking. Special thanks to Sara Mitchell, Reyko Huang, and Nisha Fazal for reading the full manuscript and participating in my book workshop. Sara helped me to grow professionally over the years from my graduate years through programs such as the Journeys of World Politics and the Visions in Methodology conference. Nisha spurred my interests in this topic and gave me useful feedback, for example, by using my related work at her graduate seminar at Columbia University. Reyko and I shared many conversations on rebel groups, and I thank her for being a great sounding board for me.

Many others, too, helped me to improve the quality of the book. Thanks to George Edwards for walking me through the book publishing process and giving me the book's title; and Matt Fuhrmann for his comments on policy aspects. I would also like to thank my colleagues Kim Hill and Judy Bear for reading some chapters. Many others have engaged in the intellectual discussions about this book at various stages: Tanja Börzel, Terry Chapman, Robert Chesney, William Clark, Dara Cohen, Mike Findley, Benjamin Fordham, Kristian Gleditsch, Valerie Hudson, Simon Hug, Jennifer Keister, Robert Keohane, Heike Krieger, Maria Escobar-Lemmon, Giovanni Mantilla, Steve

Ratner, Thomas Risse, Idean Salehyan, Ian Shapiro, Kathryn Sikkink, Sandesh Sivakumaran, Jessica Weeks, and Reed Wood.

This book is a product of many collaborative works. Chapter 5, on civilian killing, benefited from a collaborative project with Beth Simmons. Chapter 7, on detention visits, draws on the materials developed in collaboration with my graduate students Catarina Thomson and Kate Bryant. My Rebel Groups and International Law research team deserves special mention: Josiah Barrett, Yvette Isidori, Dillon Lucas, Erin Mitchell, Carly Potz-Nielsen, Mitch Radtke, Kade Rhodes, Grant Schauer, Kaitlyn Simpson, Katie Walantas, Wendy Wang, and Clay Webb. My professional editor, Paul Morsink, made this book more accessible to readers.

This research benefited from institutional support from the Law and Social Sciences Program at the National Science Foundation (NSF) (SES # 1260218); the Scowcroft Institute of International Affairs at the Bush School of Government and Public Policy; the Buffett Foundation; the Center for Conflict and Development; and the College of Liberal Arts at Texas A&M University. Marjorie Zatz, the Program Officer at the NSF, funded this research with enthusiasm. I also thank Ed Price and Howard Buffett for sharing their experience in the DRC, as well as for sharing their passions about the issues of conflict and development. I particularly wish to thank John Haslam of Cambridge University Press for seeing the value of this book project.

This is an academic book, but the writing process has also been a personal journey. This book would have not been possible without the support of my family. My husband was with me throughout the ups and downs of the writing process. I cannot thank him enough for engineering my life for the better. I also thank my in-laws for their tireless guidance and advice. My son Dureh, who while in my womb, had to read many horrible stories of war with me. His happy smile has the magic to erase all the images of troubling episodes of rebel violence I read while working on this book. Dureh is a little rebel who still teaches me a lot of lessons about compliance and defiance. My brother and sisters always gave me emotional support when I needed it. Lastly, I thank my parents. They have always, without fail, had the patience to wait. I dedicate this book to them.

Rebel Group Abbreviations

Readers will find that the book usually refers to rebel group names in English with their most frequently used abbreviations (e.g., Kurdistan Workers' Party (PKK)). The following abbreviations provide a list of alternate names, both in English and in their native language, along with their abbreviations:

ABSDF	All Burma Students' Democratic Front (Myanmar)
ABSU	All Bodo Students' Union (India)
ADF	Allied Democratic Forces (Uganda)
AFDL	Alliance of Democratic Forces for the Liberation of Congo-Zaire (Democratic Republic of the Congo)
AFRC	Armed Forces Revolutionary Council (Sierra Leone)
AMB	Al-Majd Brigades/Al-Aqsa Martyrs Brigades (Israel)
ANM	Arab Nationalist Movement (Israel)
AQAP	Al-Qaeda in the Arabian Peninsula (Yemen)
AQIM	Al-Qaeda in the Islamic Maghreb (Algeria, Mauritania)
ARDUF	Afar Revolutionary Democratic Union Front (Ethiopia)
ARIF	Arakan Rohingya Islamic Front (Myanmar)
ARS/UIC	Alliance for the Re-liberation of Somalia/Union of Islamic Courts (Somalia)
ATNMC	Alliance touarègue du Nord-Mali pour le changement (*North Mali Tuareg Alliance for Change*) (Mali)
ATTF	All Tripura Tiger Force (India)
BDK	Bundu dia Kongo (*Kingdom of Kongo*) (Democratic Republic of the Congo)
BdSF/NDFB	Bodo Security Force/National Democratic Front of Bodoland (India)

BLA	Baluchistan Liberation Army (Pakistan)
BMA	Burmese Muslim Association (Myanmar)
BRA	Bougainville Republican Army (Papua New Guinea)
CNDD	Conseil national pour la défense de la démocratie (*National Council for the Defense of Democracy*) (Burundi)
CNDD-FDD	Conseil national pour la défense de la démocratie–Forces pour la défense de la démocratie (*National Council for the Defense of Democracy–Forces for the Defense of Democracy*) (Burundi)
CNDP	Congrès national pour la défense du peuple (*National Congress for the Defense of the People*) (Democratic Republic of the Congo)
CNR	Conseil national de redressement du Tchad (*National Council of Chadian Recovery*) (Chad)
CPI-Maoist	Communist Party of India-Maoist (India)
CPJP	Convention of Patriots for Justice and Peace (Central African Republic)
CPN-M/UPF	Communist Party of Nepal-Maoist/United People's Front (Nepal)
CPP	Communist Party of the Philippines (Philippines)
CRA	Coordination de la résistance armée (*Coordination of the Armed Resistance* (Niger)
CSNPD	Comité de sursaut national pour la paix et la démocratie (*Committee of National Revival for Peace and Democracy*) (Chad)
DHD-BW	Dima Halim Daogah–Black Widow (India)
DKBA	Democratic Buddhist Karen Army (Myanmar)
EIJM	Eritrean Islamic Jihad Movement (Eritrea)
ELN	Ejército de Liberación Nacional (*National Liberation Army*) (Colombia)
EPL	Ejército Popular de Liberación (*Popular Liberation Army*) (Colombia)
EPLF	Eritrean People's Liberation Front (Ethiopia)
EPR	Ejército Popular Revolucionario (*Popular Revolutionary Army*) (Mexico)
EPRDF	Ethiopian People's Revolutionary Democratic Front (Ethiopia)
ETA	Euskadi Ta Askatasuna (*Basque Homeland and Freedom*) (Spain)
EZLN	Ejército Zapatista de Liberación Nacional (*Zapatista Army of National Liberation*) (Mexico)
FAFN	Forces armées des forces nouvelles (*Armed Forces of the New Forces*) (Côte d'Ivoire)

FARC	Fuerzas Armadas Revolucionarias de Colombia (*Revolutionary Armed Forces of Colombia*) (Colombia)
FARF	Forces armées pour la république fédérale (*Armed Forces for a Federal Republic*) (Chad)
FDLR	Forces démocratiques de libération du Rwanda (*Democratic Forces for the Liberation of Rwanda*) (Rwanda)
FDN/Contras	Fuerza Democrática Nicaragüense–Contras (*Nicaraguan Democratic Force–Contras*) (Nicaragua)
FDR	Front démocratique du renouveau (*Democratic Front for Renewal*) (Niger)
FDSI-CI	Forces de défense et de sécurité impartiales de Côte d'Ivoire (*Defense Forces and Impartial Security of the Ivory Coast*) (Côte d'Ivoire)
FDU	Forces démocratiques unies (*United Democratic Forces*) (Congo–Brazzaville)
FIAA	Front islamique arabe de l'Azawad (*Arab Islamic Front of Azawad*) (Mali)
FIS	Front islamique du salut (*Islamic Salvation Front*) (Algeria)
FLAA	Front de libération de l'Aïr et l'Azaouad (*Aïr and Azawad Liberation Front*) (Niger)
FLEC	Frente para a Libertação do Enclave de Cabinda (*Front for the Liberation of the Enclave of Cabinda*) (Angola)
FLEC-FAC	Frente para a Libertação do Enclave de Cabinda–Forças Armadas de Cabinda (*Front for the Liberation of the Enclave of Cabinda–Armed Forces of Cabinda*) (Angola)
FLRN	Front pour la libération et la reconstruction nationales (*Revolutionary Front for the Liberation of Haiti*) (Haiti)
FMLN	Frente Farabundo Martí para la Liberación Nacional (*Farabundo Martí National Liberation Front*) (El Salvador)
FNI	Front des nationalistes et intégrationnistes (*Nationalist and Integrationist Front*) (Democratic Republic of the Congo)
FNT	Front national tchadien (*National Front of Chad*) (Chad)
FPR	Front patriotique rwandais (*Rwandan Patriotic Front*) (Rwanda)
FRCI	Forces républicaines de Côte d'Ivoire (*Republican Forces of Côte d'Ivoire*) (Côte d'Ivoire)

FRUD	Front pour la restauration de l'unité et de la démocratie (*Front for the Restoration of Unity and Democracy*) (Djibouti)
FRUD–AD	Front pour la restauration de l'unité et de la démocratie–Ahmed Dini (*Front for the Restoration of Unity and Democracy–Ahmed Dini*) (Djibouti)
FUCD	Front uni pour le changement démocratique au Tchad (*United Front for Democratic Change in Chad*) (Chad)
FUNCINPEC	Front uni national pour un Cambodge indépendant, neutre, pacifique, et coopératif (*National United Front for an Independent, Neutral, Peaceful, and Cooperative Cambodia*) (Cambodia)
FUNCINPEC/ANS	Front uni national pour un Cambodge indépendant, neutre, pacifique, et coopératif/Armée nationale Sihanoukiste (*National United Front for an Independent, Neutral, Peaceful, and Cooperative Cambodia/Sihanoukist National Army* (Cambodia, Vietnam)
GAM	Gerakan Aceh Merdeka (*Free Aceh Movement*) (Indonesia)
GIA	Groupe islamique armé (*Armed Islamic Group*) (Algeria)
IGLF	Issa and Gurgura Liberation Front (Ethiopia)
IMU	Islamic Movement of Uzbekistan (Tajikistan)
INPFL	Independent National Patriotic Front of Liberia (Liberia)
ISI	Islamic State of Iraq (Iraq)
JEM	Justice and Equality Movement (Sudan)
JIG	Jihad Islamic Group (Uzbekistan)
JSS/SB	Jana Samhati Samiti/Shanti Bahini (Bangladesh)
JVP	Janathā Vimukthi Peramuṇa (*People's Liberation Front*) (Sri Lanka)
KCP	Kangleipak Communist Party (India)
KDP/PDK	Kurdistan Democratic Party/Partiya Demokrat a Kurdistanê (Iraq)
KDPI	Partiya Demokrat a Kurdistan–Îran (*Kurdish Democratic Party of Iran*) (Iran)
KIO	Kachin Independence Organization (Myanmar)
KLA	Kosovo Liberation Army (*Ushtria Çlirimtare e Kosovës*) (Yugoslavia)
KNF	Kuki National Front (India)
KNPP	Karenni National Progressive Party (Myanmar)
KNU	Karen National Union (Myanmar)

KPNLF	Khmer People's National Liberation Front (Cambodia, Vietnam)
LRA	Lord's Resistance Army (Uganda)
LRM	Lao Resistance Movement (Laos)
LTTE	Liberation Tigers of Tamil Eelam (Sri Lanka)
LURD	Liberians United for Reconciliation and Democracy (Liberia)
MCC	Maoist Communist Centre of India (India)
MDD[-FANT]	Mouvement pour la démocratie et le développement–Forces armeés nationale du Tchad (*Movement for Democracy and Development–National Armed Forces of Chad*) (Chad)
MDJT	Mouvement pour la démocratie et la justice au Tchad (*Movement for Democracy and Justice in Chad*) (Chad)
MEK	Mujahadeen-e-Khalq (*People's Mojahedin of Iran*) (Iran)
MFDC	Mouvement des forces démocratiques de la Casamance (*Movement of Democratic Forces of Casamance*) (Senegal)
MILF	Moro Islamic Liberation Front (Philippines)
MJP	Mouvement pour la justice et la paix (*Movement for Justice and Peace*) (Côte d'Ivoire)
MKP	Maoist Komünist Partisi (*Maoist Communist Party*) (Turkey)
MLC	Mouvement de libération du Congo (*Movement for the Liberation of Congo*) (Democratic Republic of the Congo, Zimbabwe, Angola, Namibia, Chad)
MNDAA	Myanmar National Democratic Alliance Army (Myanmar)
MNJ	Mouvement des Nigériens pour la justice (*Nigerien's Movement for Justice*) (Niger)
MNLF	Moro National Liberation Front (Philippines)
MNLF-HM	Moro National Liberation Front–Habier Malik (Philippines)
MNLF-NM	Moro National Liberation Front–Nur Misuari (Philippines)
MODEL	Movement for Democracy in Liberia (Liberia)
MPA	Mouvement populaire Anjouanais (*Anjouan People's Movement*) (Comoros)
MPA	Mouvement populaire de l'Azaouad (*Azawad People's Movement*) (Mali)
MPCI	Mouvement patriotique de Côte d'Ivoire (*Patriotic Movement of Côte d'Ivoire*) (Côte d'Ivoire)

MPIGO	Mouvement populaire ivoirien du Grand Ouest (*Ivorian Popular Movement of the Great West*) (Côte d'Ivoire)
MPS	Mouvement patriotique du salut (*Patriotic Salvation Movement*) (Chad)
MQM	Muttahida Qaumi Movement (Pakistan)
MRTA	Movimiento Revolucionario Túpac Amaru (*Túpac Amaru Revolutionary Movement*) (Peru)
MTA	Mong Tai Army (Myanmar)
NDFB-RD	National Democratic Front of Bodoland–Ranjan Daimary (India)
NDPVF	Niger Delta People's Volunteer Force (Nigeria)
NLFT	National Liberation Front of Tripura (India)
NMSP	New Mon State Party (Myanmar)
NPFL	National Patriotic Front of Liberia (Liberia)
NRF	National Redemption Front (Sudan)
NSCN	Nationalist Socialist Council of Nagaland (India)
NSCN-K	National Socialist Council of Nagaland–Khaplang (India)
NTC	National Transitional Council of Libya (Libya)
OLF	Oromo Liberation Front (Ethiopia)
ONLF	Ogaden National Liberation Front (Ethiopia)
OPON	Otryad Politsii Osobogo Naznacheniya (*Special Purpose Police Unit*) (Azerbaijan)
Palipehutu-FNL	Parti pour la libération du peuple hutu–Forces nationales de liberation (*Party for the Liberation of the Hutu People–National Forces of Liberation* (Burundi)
PDK	Party of Democratic Kampuchea (Cambodia)
PFLP	Popular Front for the Liberation of Palestine (Israel)
PFNR	Popular Front for National Renaissance (Chad)
PIJ	Palestinian Islamic Jihad (Israel)
PIRA/IRA	Provisional Irish Republican Army/ Irish Republican Army (United Kingdom)
PJAK	Partiya Jiyana Azad a Kurdistanê (*Party of Free Life of Kurdistan*) (Iran)
PKK/Kadek	Partiya Karkerên Kurdistan/Kongreya Azadi Demokrasiya (*Kurdistan Workers' Party/Congress for Freedom and Democracy in Kurdistan*) (Turkey)
PLA	People's Liberation Army (India)
PLO	Palestine Liberation Organization (Israel)
PNA	Palestinian National Authority (Israel)
PREPAK	People's Revolutionary Party of Kangleipak (India)
PUK	Patriotic Union of Kurdistan (Iraq)
PULF	People's United Liberation Front (India)

PWG	People's War Group (India)
RAFD	Rassemblement des forces démocratiques au Tchad (*Rally of Democratic Forces of Chad*) (Chad)
RCD	Rassemblement congolais pour la démocratie (*Rally for Congolese Democracy*) (Congo/Zaire, Zimbabwe, Angola, Namibia, Chad)
RFDG	Rassemblement des forces démocratiques de Guinée (*Rally of Democratic Forces of Guinea*) (Guinea)
RIRA	Real Irish Republican Army (United Kingdom)
RJF	Reform and Jihad Front (Iraq)
RSO	Rohingya Solidarity Organisation (Myanmar)
RUF	Revolutionary United Front (Sierra Leone)
SCIRI	Supreme Council for the Islamic Revolution in Iraq (Iraq)
SL	Sendero Luminoso (*Shining Path*) (Peru)
SSA-S	Shan State Army–South (Myanmar)
SLM/A	Sudan Liberation Movement/Army (Sudan)
SLM/A-MM	Sudan Liberation Movement/Army–Minni Minnawi (Sudan)
SNM	Somali National Movement (Somalia)
SPLM	Sudan People's Liberation Movement (Sudan)
SPLM/A-N	Sudan People's Liberation Movement/Army–North (Sudan)
SPM	Somali Patriotic Movement (Somalia)
SRRC	Somalia Reconciliation and Restoration Council (Somalia)
SSLM/A	South Sudan Liberation Movement/Army (Sudan)
SSPP	Shan State Progress Party (Myanmar)
TNSM	Tehreek-e-Nafaz-e-Shariat-e-Mohammadi (*Movement for the Enforcement of Islamic Law*) (Pakistan)
TTP	Tehrik-i-Taliban Pakistan (*Student Movement of Pakistan*) (Pakistan)
UCK	Ushtria Çlirimtare e Kombëtare (*National Liberation Army*) (Macedonia)
UFDD	Union of Forces for Democracy and Development (Chad)
UFDR	Union des forces démocratiques pour le rassemblement (*Union of Democratic Forces for Unity*) (Central African Republic)
UFR	Union des forces de résistance (*Union of the Forces of Resistance*) (Chad)
UFRA	Union des forces de la résistance armée (*Union of Forces of Armed Resistance*) (Niger)

UIFSA	United Islamic Front for the Salvation of Afghanistan (Afghanistan)
ULFA	United Liberation Front of Asom (India)
UNITA	União Nacional para a Independência Total de Angola (*National Union for the Total Independence of Angola*) (Angola, Cuba, Namibia)
UNLF	United National Liberation Front (India)
UNLF	Uganda National Liberation Front (Uganda)
UPA	Uganda People's Army (Uganda)
URNG	Unidad Revolucionaria Nacional Guatemalteca (*Guatemalan National Revolutionary Unity*) (Guatemala)
USC	United Somali Congress (Somalia)
UTO	United Tajik Opposition (Tajikistan, Russia, Uzbekistan)
UWSA	United Wa State Army (Myanmar)
WNBF	West Nile Bank Front (Uganda)
WSB	West Side Boys (Sierra Leone)

Legal Instruments

The following lists the legal instruments cited or referenced in *Compliant Rebels* with regard to international humanitarian law, organized according to the human rights issue addressed. This list is not exhaustive, but purports to enumerate important legal milestones for each issue discussed in Chapters 5, 6 and 7.

CHAPTER 5. CIVILIAN KILLING

St. Petersburg Declaration (1868)
Geneva Conventions I–IV (1949)
Additional Protocols I and II to the Geneva Conventions (1977)
Rome Statute (1998)

CHAPTER 6. CHILD SOLDIERING

Additional Protocol II to the Geneva Conventions (1977)
Cape Town Principles (1977)
Convention on the Rights of the Child (1989)
Paris Principles (1991)
Rome Statute (1998)
Optional Protocol to the Convention on the Rights of the Child on the Involvement of Children in Armed Conflict (2000)

CHAPTER 7. DETENTION ACCESS

Common Article 3 to the Geneva Conventions I–IV (1949)
International Covenant on Civil and Political Rights (1966)
Additional Protocol II to the Geneva Conventions (1977)

PART I

PUZZLE OF COMPLIANT REBELS

1

Introduction

> Bearing in mind that the Frente Farabundo Martí para la Liberacion Nacional has the capacity and the will and assumes the commitment to respect the inherent attributes of the human person . . .
>
> San José Agreement between El Salvador and the Farabundo Martí National Liberation Front (FMLN), 26 July 1990[1]

> First, kill your family.
>
> A unit commander of the Lord's Resistance Army (LRA)[2]

> I hacked the woman on the back of her neck and on her breast with a machete. I hacked the child on his neck and on his side. One of them begged me not to do it, but Kabila told me to do it or he would kill me, so I hacked him as well and cut off his head.
>
> A Revolutionary United Front (RUF) child soldier as a witness at the Special Court for Sierra Leone[3]

During a decade of armed struggle between 1981 and 1991, the Farabundo Martí National Liberation Front (FMLN) in El Salvador maintained good relations with civilians, refrained from using child soldiers, and did not mistreat enemy government soldiers. Nor was this the result of mere happenstance. In *Legitimacy of Our Methods of Struggle*,[4] published in 1988, the Salvadoran rebel political–military organization described their ways of waging warfare against the government as being consistent with international humanitarian norms. In 1990, the group then signed the San José Agreement

[1] The San José agreement between El Salvador and the Frente Farabundo Martí para la Liberacion Nacional, signed by both sides on July 26, 1990. UN Doc. A/44/971-S/21541 (August 16, 1990), Annex.

[2] Re-quoted from Eichstaedt (2009).

[3] Sesay, Alpha, "Former Child Soldier Describes the Atrocities Committed by the RUF and the AFRC," Summary from Charles Taylor at the Special Court for Sierra Leone (May 5, 2008).

[4] FMLN (1988).

with the government, reiterating their commitment to human rights, and laying the groundwork for the peace agreement in 1992.[5] The rebel group subsequently developed itself into a viable political party – a party that exists to this day.[6]

To be sure, during the years of armed struggle, the FMLN *did* commit a number of human rights violations, and these were documented in the Truth Commission Report to the United Nations published in March 1993. The list of violations includes kidnappings, abductions, and extra-judicial killings of government sympathizers. However, this list pales when compared with the long list of massacres and other grave human rights violations perpetrated by government forces. In the UN Commission's report it is clearly noted that the vast majority of abuses during El Salvador's civil war were committed by members of the Salvadoran military.[7]

The FMLN's largely compliant behavior is in stark contrast to the behavior of other notoriously violent rebel groups, such as the Revolutionary United Front (RUF) in Sierra Leone, known for killing and maiming civilians and government soldiers between 1991 and 1999.[8] During its three-week "Operation No Living Thing" in January 1999, for example, the RUF captured Freetown, the capital of Sierra Leone, and brutally massacred 6,000 people using axes, machetes, and knives.[9] The Lord's Resistance Army (LRA) in Uganda, one of the continent's "oldest, most violent, and persistent armed groups,"[10] recruited children by abduction and used girl soldiers as sex slaves.[11]

Neither of these groups fared well once fighting ended. The RUF participated in post-conflict elections held in 2001, but garnered just 2 percent of the popular vote. In 2009, three senior RUF commanders, Issa Hassan Sesay, Morris Kallon, and Augustine Gbao, were found guilty of war crimes and crimes against humanity by the Special Court for Sierra Leone, an international tribunal established in 2002.[12] For his part, the LRA's leader, Joseph Kony, has been indicted by the International Criminal Court (ICC), but is still at large, refusing to surrender. After several military offensives by the Ugandan Government, the LRA lost its base in northern Uganda and now roams the Central African Republic (CAR) in small numbers, still committing atrocities.

These contrasting cases encapsulate the puzzle of this book. Why is it that the FMLN made a formal commitment to "respect human persons," while the LRA and the RUF showed such extreme disrespect for human life? More

[5] Acuña (1995); Doyle *et al.* (1997); and Clapham (2006). [6] Alvarez (2010).

[7] Betancur *et al.* (1993).

[8] The atrocities of the RUF have been extensively documented, including by the Truth and Reconciliation Commission of Sierra Leone, available at: www.sierraleonetrc.org. See also Reno (2011); Scheffer (2013).

[9] Gberie (2005). [10] US Department of State (2012). [11] Allen and Vlassenroot (2010).

[12] Special Court for Sierra Leone (2009); and Iliopoulos (2009).

generally, why do some rebel groups comply with international standards of conduct in warfare, while others do not? Are rebel groups aware of international standards? When and why do they make conscious efforts to abide by international rules? These are the series of questions this book seeks to answer.

I provide an explanation for why compliant rebels sometimes emerge amid the brutality of civil conflicts. The central thesis of the book is that legitimacy-seeking rebel groups are more likely to comply with international law than legitimacy-indifferent groups. Rebel groups that have a focus on political programs, groups that forge deep social relations, and groups that have human rights-conscious external sponsorship are those that are likely to exhibit international law compliance. In contrast, rebel groups that privilege military gains, have no social ties with their domestic constituencies, or have human rights-disregarding external sponsors will show little respect for international standards of warfare. In the pursuit of political legitimacy during armed struggles, some rebel groups come to know and care about international standards of behavior in making their political survival strategies. They then favor relatively humane methods of warfare, and avoid methods that are considered to be inhumane.

The task of this introductory chapter is to explicate this puzzle of *rebel compliance* and to give a short answer to the puzzle. I explain why we want to investigate the phenomenon of rebels conforming to international humanitarian and human rights rules. I then lay out the logic of rebel compliance – detailing the underlying assumptions and expectations about the nature of civil war and rebellion that lead legitimacy-seeking rebels to comply. The next section provides the conceptual terrain of this book. It explores the key concepts – legitimacy and compliance – in greater depth, along with the operational measures used to ascertain and quantify rebel compliance. I end the chapter with a brief summary of the book's central findings, together with a discussion of the potential impacts that these findings may have in academic research and policy circles.

THE PUZZLE OF REBEL COMPLIANCE

This book will present a study of contemporary rebellion. Specifically, it is about rebel groups and their decision to conform to existing norms of restraint in warfare. International law is generally considered *weak*, whereas rebel groups' incentives to violate rules and norms are usually *strong*. International law differs in significant ways from domestic law. For one thing, there is no world police and no world court. The presence and reach of Interpol are minimal, and the jurisdictional reach of the International Court of Justice or the ICC is limited.

In contrast to the fragile force of international law, the incentives of rebel groups to violate the rules of war seem powerful. It is not apparent why any rebel group would want to abide by – let alone genuinely care about – international law when taking up arms to fight against a government opponent. In what is often an asymmetric conflict facing a strong opponent (i.e., national army), how and why would a compliant rebel group emerge? That is the central question I wish to unravel in this book. Its central exploration will be to find the conditions in which rebel groups try to conform to international norms and their motivations to do so.

The puzzle of rebel compliance comes in several layers. One layer lies in the strategic and military considerations of rebel groups. What is not obvious about law-abiding rebels is that, even as they rebel against the national government, they choose to abide by international rules, at least in some respects. Yet international humanitarian or human rights norms often contradict the logic of violence to which rebel groups usually adhere. These norms prohibit the sort of actions that often serve the strategic interests of rebel groups – the sort of actions that may, at times, give them a competitive advantage over government forces.

For instance, rebels may want to respond to troop shortages by recruiting child soldiers to their ranks, or they might feel the need to kill civilians to root out government sympathizers. Also, in some cases "international standards" may be against the rebels' ideological or religious stance whereby they consider some civilians as enemies. Extremist jihadist groups may see adherents of other religions as enemies, and groups subscribing to extreme versions of Marxism may see wealthy civilians as enemies. Given these military or ideological constraints, how can we make sense of rebel compliance? Why would rebels ignore military incentives and/or ideological considerations and comply with international rules and norms?

The other layer of the puzzle comes from the fact that rebel groups have played little role in creating international law. Nor have they ever been signatories to international treaties and conventions, such as the Geneva Conventions. Why would rebel groups follow rules they neither created nor signed on to? Although rebel groups do have obligations under international law even without consent,[13] it is intriguing to observe that some groups voluntarily submit themselves to those rules. Also, international law governing non-state actors, including rebel group members, is less precise than laws governing states. With weakly binding rules without much consent, little precision in rules, and weak enforcement power behind these rules, rebel compliance provides a hard test of international law. This inherent limitation by design creates a theoretical puzzle. Again: why do some rebel groups comply?

I want to note that this question regarding rebel compliance is slightly different from the question of why some groups denounce or renounce violence, although the two are connected. History has witnessed some groups

[13] See Clapham (2010) and Sivakumaran (2012) on the rebel groups' obligations in international law.

publicly vowing to reject the use of violence. A famous example is the case of Al Gama'ah al-Islamiyah in Egypt. The leadership denounced violence in 1997 – the very violence they had relied on for a decade – and issued a fatwā (a formal judgment stemming from Islamic law) to this effect from prison.[14] This abrupt shift from violence to non-violence may sometimes be one part of the story of compliant rebels, as some groups decide to comply and then move to seek political solutions by abandoning violence altogether. However, from the perspective of armed groups' general strategy, exercising restraint while continuing an armed struggle is a different sort of commitment than the wholesale rejection of violent methods. The difference between "constrained violence" and "no violence" is a subtle one, but the former allows the use of violence, while the latter does not allow it. For its part, this book will focus on the question of rebel compliance and leave the task of researching the non-violence question to other scholars.[15]

At a more fundamental level, the question of compliance is central to political science, and specifically to questions of authority, norms, regulations, and violence. Why do political actors accept and respect certain forms of political authority? Why do political actors follow norms? How do political actors respond to regulations and laws? What makes political actors resort to violence with or without restraint? With this puzzle of rebel compliance in mind, this book will also touch upon these fundamental questions of law and order.

RELEVANCE

Solving the puzzle of rebel compliance is important because of its practical relevance for international peace. If we can understand the conditions under which rebels respect humanitarian and human rights law, then we can leverage this knowledge to reduce the number of instances of unconstrained violence. Since the very foundation of humanitarian law is based on human dignity, rebels changing their behavior to conform to international standards of restraint would mean less unchecked violence in the world and less civilian suffering.

In formulating foreign policy and designing interventions, the large volumes of policy-related works focus on military interventions, but little attention has been given to the diplomacy dimension of rebel engagement, such as having dialog, persuasion, and negotiation. This book will make the point that a proper understanding of which armed groups can be successfully engaged and how we

[14] See the group's writing translated in al-Gama'ah al-Islamiyah (2014). Also see discussions on the group in Bukay (2004); Blaydes and Rubin (2008); Jackson (2009).

[15] Whether non-violence pays is a heated debate. Chenoweth and Stephan (2012), for instance, find that non-violence is an effective strategy of civil movements, while Thomas (2014) finds that terrorist tactics are more effective in extracting concessions out of governments (at least in the African conflicts she studied).

can make sense of their motivations could play a crucial role in helping to devise effective foreign policy in conflict zones.

Rebel violence is one of the pressing issues of our time. By definition, rebel groups are perpetrators of violence. Rebel groups are armed organizations that fight against a government in an internal armed conflict in order to advance their political and/or military agenda.[16] They resort to violence to attain their objectives in opposing central governments. When the violence is directed toward civilians, it causes a tremendous amount of suffering to civilian populations. Some 17 million people worldwide have perished in the crossfire of governments and rebels over the past five decades.[17] About 60 out of 300 rebel groups around the world are still using child soldiers.[18] And only 30 percent of rebel groups have opened themselves to allow the International Committee of the Red Cross (ICRC) to monitor their detention centers at some point during their armed struggle.[19] As for the detainees held by other rebel groups, their fates are unknown. Reporting on human rights abuses is improving over time with the growth of human rights monitors such as the Human Rights Watch. However, in some cases, rebel violence becomes even more intractable and complex because of rebel group rivalries, the degeneration of rebels into criminal gangs, and long-running rebellions that continuously fail to reach stable and peaceful solutions.

The examination of rebel compliance has implications for contemporary foreign policy, especially with regard to the possibility of engaging rebel groups constructively in talks and negotiations of various kinds. Rebel engagement has always been a foreign policy option. However, this option has almost always languished under a cloud of uncertainty and skepticism. Skeptics may argue that there is no science to deciding which groups are worth engaging with, or to predicting the likelihood of success. Going a step further, some might even suggest that brutal, unconstrained wars that violate norms and laws may actually shorten the overall length of conflicts. Also, rebel engagement is a highly unpopular option for some political regimes that are loathe to confer any legitimacy on rebel groups. This is especially the case when advocates of engagement are unable to provide any solid guidance or reassurance regarding the likelihood of success. All of which explains why, in most situations, hardline policies such as military offensives or economic sanctions tend to be preferred by policymakers.

Yet this is precisely where a study such as this of rebel compliance can make a significant contribution. If we know which rebel groups are predisposed to

[16] For a taxonomy of rebel groups and discussion of terminology, see Clapham (2006: 288); also see Sobek and Payne (2010). This definition excludes paramilitary groups (e.g., Autodefensas Unidas de Colombia, Kamajors in Sierra Leone, Ninjas in Congo Brazzaville) from the scope of my study.

[17] This is an approximate figure that appears in Laitin (2007) and Regan (2008).

[18] de la Sabliere (2012).

[19] Jo and Thomson (2013). This amounts to forty-seven rebel groups out of 251 groups.

comply with international rules, we can target these groups and selectively engage them for the purpose of reducing human suffering in conflict zones. With new information and insights in play, it certainly becomes harder to reject out-of-hand the option of talking to rebel groups, especially when there appears to be a real possibility of lessening civilian suffering. From the perspective of civilians and many conflict victims, a rebellion adhering to the principles of international humanitarian law may be far better than a short but extremely brutal war. Taking on the question of how best to intervene in cases of egregious human rights abuses in civil conflicts, this book will demonstrate that international law matters to some rebel groups, and that nurturing this interest in international law can be a catalyst for change.

REBEL GROUPS MEET INTERNATIONAL LAW

Rather than being wars between states, most wars today are internal conflicts where a government is fighting a single rebel group or multiple groups.[20] In 2012, there were thirty-two active armed conflicts worldwide, all of which were internal conflicts.[21] Today about 300 rebel groups are operating worldwide. And yet, while ample research exists regarding violence committed by governments, research on rebel violence and their compliance behaviors related to international law is relatively scant and unhelpful in answering the important foreign policy questions of our day.

This book's inquiry focuses on rebel groups active in civil conflicts between 1989 and 2009. This period is marked by the end the Cold War, the rise of human rights movements, and the normative changes that have unfolded since the fourth Geneva Convention and the Additional Protocol. The end the Cold War is important as it connects with significant changes in the nature of rebellions. During the Cold War period, most rebel groups were characterized by their commitment to the anti-colonial struggle, to liberation movements in the 1950s and 1960s, and then to Marxist–Leninist movements in the 1970s and 1980s.[22] The rise of human rights movements is important due to the fact that human rights norms became global.

The post-Cold War period has observed the proliferation of new norms and legal codifications, arising partly out of the brutal experiences of many conflicts and massacres. During this period, more and more rebel groups have actively sought to interact with humanitarian and human rights organizations to vie for resources or to de-list themselves from the list of shame. At the same time, some rebel group leaders have been indicted or sentenced by international courts

[20] Under international law, civil wars are called "armed conflicts not of an international character." Armed conflicts were traditionally between or among states. *Internal conflicts, civil wars*, and *armed conflicts not of an international character* – all three terms will be used interchangeably in this book.

[21] Themner and Wallensteen (2012).

[22] See Reno (2011) for the history of rebel groups, especially in the African context.

under new accountability norms.[23] In this way, international law is developing to take into account the consequences of violence in internal conflicts.[24] These are the legal, political, and normative environments in which contemporary rebel groups are operating.

International law, as related to the context of civil conflicts, has undergone developments over time. The Geneva Conventions and the Additional Protocol of 1977 advanced the consensus on laws pertaining to conflicts of a non-international character.[25] In addition to these legal instruments, the institutional landscape for international law has changed too. Several ad hoc international war crimes tribunals have been operating in the world's most atrocious conflicts in Cambodia, Rwanda, Sierra Leone, and Yugoslavia for the past two decades. In 1998, the Rome Statute established the ICC, a permanent international judicial body that can prosecute war crimes, crimes against humanity, and genocide. These institutional landmarks were accompanied by normative changes on the global level. International humanitarian organizations provided services for victims of conflicts and promoted international humanitarian law. Human rights organizations around the world named and shamed perpetrators of violence and atrocities. These humanitarian and human rights workers, which I would call "agents of international law," brought about the normative changes on the international legal scene.

Among many topics of international law, three areas – humanitarian law, human rights law, and criminal law – are particularly relevant to rebel groups or the members of rebel groups.[26] Note that I mention "members of rebel groups" here. As rebel groups are armed organizations, most of the accountability rests with the superior command, according to the command responsibility principle. So, in most cases, rebel group leaders would be responsible for inciting unconstrained violence.

The first relevant body of law is international humanitarian law. This body of law, sometimes called *the law of war* or *jus in bello*, regulates conduct in warfare. In international humanitarian law, legal instruments such as Common Article 3 of the Geneva Conventions[27] are particularly applicable. These

[23] Sikkink (2011) terms this "justice cascade."

[24] See Sivakumaran (2012) for a comprehensive review of law pertaining to non-international armed conflicts.

[25] The term "conflicts of non-international character" is often used in the legal literature. The term is equivalent to "civil conflicts" in this book.

[26] See in particular Zegveld (2002); Clapham (2006); Sassoli (2010); and Sivakumaran (2012) for discussion of international law applicable to rebel groups. Scheffer (2013) calls for collecting the common areas of these three laws and calling it "atrocity law" as it is applicable to civil conflict situations. Atrocity law would be the collection of laws that cover war crimes or crimes against humanity during wartime and peacetime, in addition to a legal means for justice in those cases. I agree that atrocity law is a useful category, but in this book I follow the traditional classification of the topical issues in international law.

[27] The Geneva Conventions specify prescriptions and proscriptions of the laws of war (Roberts and Guelff 2000).

instruments lay out minimum standards of restraint for warring parties in internal conflicts, as well as major legal principles such as the principle of distinction between combatants and non-combatants.

Second, international human rights law is relevant to civil wars since victims in conflict zones have basic human rights – from the right to life to the right to food. In international human rights law, the specific norms and principles are enshrined in agreements such as the Convention on the Rights of the Child and its Optional Protocol, and the Convention against Torture.

Third, international criminal law is relevant. Some of the crimes committed by rebel groups are of an international nature, such as crimes against humanity and war crimes, and rebel groups are subject to international criminal law.[28] The Rome Statute is particularly relevant in the context of rebel violence. The Statute specifies the types of crimes that fall under the ICC's jurisdiction, namely, war crimes, crimes against humanity, and genocide.[29] Along with international humanitarian and human rights law, international criminal law defines the rights and obligations of rebel groups in civil wars.

Contemporary rebellion is markedly different than war and rebellion as they have traditionally been understood. Historically, most rebel groups were part of national liberation movements driven by the demand for independence from colonial powers in the early twentieth century or motivated by leftist ideology during the Cold War period. The picture of today's rebel groups is diverse and ranges from terrorist organizations such as Al-Qaeda (who use extreme tactics such as suicide bombings or the destruction of targets with symbolic value),[30] to warlords in Afghanistan (whose goal is to profit regionally and to debase the central government), to organizations that focus on social movements and engage in armed struggle on a small scale, such as the Zapatistas in Mexico. Regionally, rebel groups are clustered mostly in Africa due to heavy internal fighting in countries that are part of the Great Lakes region. At the same time, rebel movements are common in Asia and the Middle East, too.

Recent rebel movements, like many other phenomena these days, are globalized in their scope and aims. Some facets of globalization, such as the spread of small arms or connections among terrorist groups, do not bode well for world peace. Other facets of globalization, however, such as increased global awareness of conflicts and rebel groups' growing engagement with the international community, may bode well for the future and work to our advantage. Today's rebel groups also interact with international organizations, which are increasingly becoming important players in conflict zones.

[28] Cassesse (2008). [29] Schabas (2011).

[30] The central difference between rebel groups and terrorist organizations is the extent and nature of their military operations (rebel groups having military operations, whereas terrorists exclusively rely on covert operations) and territorial control (rebel groups having territorial control, terrorists do not). See Cronin (2011) for more on this distinction. Also see Chapter 2 of this book.

New trends have emerged with the development of technology as well. For example, the leaders of the March 23 Movement (M23), a rebel group in the DRC, were following the tweets of key political actors in the United States (e.g., President Obama, *Washington Post* columnists) and tracking the international community's reaction to their violations of international law (e.g., United Nations (UN) Human Rights Committee).[31] This global landscape of rebellion is new and creates more points of contact than ever before for today's rebel groups to interface with international rules and norms.

Traditionally, international law "belonged" rightfully to states. But rebel groups are now players on the international legal scene. Some groups make unilateral declarations to abide by humanitarian law. During the recent civil war in Libya, for instance, the National Transitional Council (NTC) in 2011 declared that "its policies strictly adhere to the Geneva Convention relative to the treatment of prisoners of war."[32] Other rebel groups choose to forge international agreements with international organizations. For example, in 2009, the Moro Islamic Liberation Front (MILF) in the Philippines signed an Action Plan with the UN Special Representative Office of Children and Armed Conflict to stop using child soldiers.[33] Some rebel groups have their own courts, such as the People's Court established by the Communist Party of Nepal-Maoist (CPN-M).[34] Other groups have an internal code of conduct consistent with international humanitarian rules. The Kosovo Liberation Army (KLA), for example, had standing orders in 1998 that included several points regarding the treatment of civilians and the detention of non-combatants.[35] These examples illustrate that rebel groups *are* aware of laws and legal frameworks, and sometimes strive to make the point that they want to abide by international standards.

At the same time, the members of rebel groups have obligations under international law.[36] The Common Article 3 of the Geneva Conventions as well as Additional Protocol II lay out the obligations both for governments and also for non-state armed groups engaged in internal conflicts. Regardless of their consent to be bound, rebel group leaders are subject to the core obligations of international humanitarian law, such as the prohibitions against committing "violence to life and person, in particular, murder of all kinds, mutilation, cruel treatment and torture," and against "outrages upon personal dignity, in particular humiliating and degrading treatment."[37] Whether rebel groups acknowledge these obligations and attempt to abide by them is an empirical question that the subsequent chapters of this book will address.

[31] The twitter network of M23 was followed by the author and the snapshots are on file with the author. Also see Fisher (2012).

[32] Sivakumaran (2011: 8). [33] Watchlist (2013). [34] Kleffner (2012).

[35] Weinstein (2006); Bangerter (2012). [36] Clapham (2010); Dabone (2011).

[37] Common Article 3, subparagraphs (a) and (c).

Several caveats are in order when examining rebel groups' conduct in relation to international law. It is important to note that international law as it applies to rebel groups is not as definite and explicit as the law governing states. Legal rules pertaining to rebel groups are often vague and implicit. For example, which legal principles may be applied to armed conflicts of a non-international character is still a matter of dispute.[38] Also, in this area of law, there is intense debate about whether rebels or terrorists are to be considered lawful combatants and treated as such,[39] which would, among other things, confer upon captured rebels the rights of prisoners of war under the Geneva Conventions.[40] States have invested in developing humanitarian law for more than a century now, so laws involving states are clearer than the laws that govern rebel groups. In this sense, international law is "in the making" with respect to rebel groups, and this is what makes this topic interesting.

In relation to the norms regarding rebel groups, I also want to note that human rights norms have never been entirely clear, unproblematic, and coherent. They are profoundly politically contested.[41] For example, in some cultures, particularly in Muslim countries, children over 15 are considered to be adults, and Western norms prohibiting children under 18 from serving in the military are not well accepted in those societies. The prohibition against killing innocent civilians is more universally accepted, but in practice, rebel groups sometimes justify attacks on civilians with the argument that these civilians were supporting the government and therefore can be classified as enemy combatants. This lack of clarity in legal norms and the associated high level of political contestation bring into focus the theoretical puzzle to which we have already alluded: why do some rebel groups choose to adhere to these sometimes amorphous and often contested norms?

THE ARGUMENT

My argument, in brief, is that compliant rebels emerge when they seek legitimacy. *And not just any kind of legitimacy.* The legitimacy rebel groups seek is typically politically situated and audience-specific. Compliant rebels are those that want to enhance the "legitimacy" of their own organization and movement in the eyes of key political "audiences" that care about values consistent with international law at domestic and international "levels."

The first part of the argument concerns the nature of rebel "legitimacy." The legitimacy rebel groups seek to establish is not necessarily the

[38] Clapham (2006); Alston *et al.* (2007).

[39] See *Hamdan* v. *Rumsfeld* 548 US 557 (2006), for example, as well as legal issues related to Guantanamo detainees.

[40] Henckaerts and Doswald-Beck (2005); Ratner (2011).

[41] I thank Roger Haydon for this point.

legitimacy of the "rules," but the legitimacy of their "own organization or movement." Rebel groups might recognize the inherent value of international law and the legitimacy of the rules themselves, but I argue that the law's political and instrumental value is also a great motivator for some rebel groups that attempt to comply.[42] In some situations, rebel groups voluntarily comply because their local norms are consistent with global norms. At other times, rebel groups strategically decide to comply, despite the cost of doing so, to enhance the legitimacy of their armed struggle. This utilitarian compliance – compliance behavior resulting from instrumental calculations – has political value to it, and I call this "strategic legitimacy."

The second part of my argument addresses the question of "audience." The critical question is: in whose eyes do rebel groups want to establish legitimacy? Legitimacy needs an audience. One cannot establish legitimacy by itself, in a vacuum. Invariably, there is an intended audience, and a rebel group's goal is to have the core audience recognize its viability and authority. It therefore seems important for us to identify these key audiences and know who they are. The nature and characteristics of these core constituencies will matter in understanding how rebel groups forge their military strategies and, in general, think about compliance with international law. For their part, rebel audiences and supporters may or may not care about rebel groups' compliance. Some will, and these relatively international law-conscious constituencies are the ones that may at times have a certain degree of leverage with regard to inducing rebel compliance. If rebel groups are dependent on particular political audiences that have preferences for human rights and humanitarian rules, we can expect that rebel groups will be more likely to exercise restraint in their armed struggle.

The third part of my argument pertains to the level at which rebel groups can be expected to seek legitimacy. As discussed in the previous section, the global environment is important as well as the rebels' home base. In any given situation, the balance between international and domestic legitimacy-seeking will be determined by the extent of a group's reliance on each type of support, specifically whether the rebel movement is more reliant on domestic support or foreign support. Although support is not equivalent to legitimacy, support is often an integral part of legitimacy. The fact that a rebel group is supported by some sponsor means that they have acquired some level of legitimacy or approval from that sponsor.

International legitimacy is particularly important to contemporary rebels. Rebel groups are increasingly aware of international sentiments in part because their political survival often hinges on the amount of legitimacy and support they can garner.[43] It is no coincidence that a third of 100 prominent rebel

42 In this regard, my argument is different from Franck's argument that most nations follow international law because they think the law itself is legitimate. See Franck (1990).

43 See Byman *et al.* (2001); Boot (2013); Salehyan *et al.* (2014) for the dependence of rebels on foreign state support.

groups have established their own "foreign affairs department" and now conduct their own diplomacy.[44] Taking advantage of the Internet, many rebel groups now appear on YouTube reporting the opposing government's human rights violations, on Twitter following the UN Human Rights Committee or the ICC, or on Facebook to post updates about their military or political victories.[45] A growing number of rebel groups also forge commitments with respect to human rights in peace agreements, or by engaging the United Nations, or by declaring their intentions to comply with the Geneva Conventions to the International Committee or the Red Cross.[46] International backing can also work as a good bargaining chip when a rebel group negotiates with a government.[47]

However, international legitimacy is usually not the end goal sought by most rebels. International support is valuable to the extent that it buys domestic legitimacy. Garnering domestic support to become a viable political entity is important for certain rebel groups that want to impose their political program or revolutionary vision. Domestic populations are usually the main source of recruits to sustain a rebellion, the main source of food and logistical support, and the ultimate guarantor of a rebel group's power on its home turf. To be sure, some groups impose order by force, but even these groups depend on some level of domestic support to be successful.

Substantively, my argument regarding legitimacy and compliance draws on one or two strands of prior research. Extant studies on legitimacy within authoritarian political regimes and on the legitimacy of political actors challenging the hierarchical political order are relevant to my thinking about rebel legitimacy and compliance. Scholars such as Wedeen have studied how authoritarian legitimacy is formed and sustained, and how the achievement of even a semblance of legitimacy generates an effective form of power, creating obedience and inducing complicity.[48] Wedeen's work is particularly relevant to the study of rebel groups, because many rebel groups operate in authoritarian states and try to establish their own legitimacy in the context of authoritarian systems. Scott's study on peasant movements is also relevant as it deals with the question of how lowly peasants establish their own legitimacy via "everyday resistance" in the form of foot-dragging, pilfering, feigned ignorance, slander, arson, sabotage, etc.[49] His work sheds light on how marginalized rebel groups strive to find their political place. Similar to the research of Wedeen and Scott, my work shares

[44] The Karen National Union (KNU) sent their diplomatic corps to the United Nations to present their positions. Also notable is the use of social media by rebel groups. Al-Shabaab in Somalia sent out their messages via Twitter, and M23, a rebel group in DRC, conducted their public relations campaign using Facebook. Although both social media uses were eventually suspended because of their potential ramifications, these examples illustrate the desire of rebel groups to reach out for support and attention.

[45] See Mattiaci and Jones (2014). [46] Bell (2008); Sivakumaran (2012). [47] Kelman (2001).

[48] Wedeen (1999). [49] Scott (1984, 1990).

the core message that political actors deficient in initial legitimacy may seek to obtain what they lack, and that this legitimacy-seeking behavior will have implications for their eventual political behavior and for their relationships with other political actors.

ASSUMPTIONS

My argument about legitimacy and compliant rebels builds on several working assumptions that I want to lay bare in this section. These assumptions mostly concern the nature of rebellion: what rebels are fighting for; how they support and sustain their rebellion; and what their relationships are with their core political constituencies. Unpacking these assumptions, and then developing an explanation for rebel compliance using these building blocks, is an important first step toward solving the puzzle that is at the heart of this book's inquiry.

The first working assumption is that *civil wars are more than armed conflicts* (Assumption 1). I conceptualize civil war as being a struggle for political legitimacy as much as it is an armed conflict for military victory. Some scholars focus exclusively on the military dimension. Military strategies and battle outcomes are, of course, important, but the choice of military tactics and strategies largely occurs in the context of pursuing political goals. I start from Clausewitz's well-known maxim that "war is politics by other means," noting that armed conflicts are political acts as much as they are military ones. The extent to which rebel groups overtly engage in politics will, of course, vary from case to case, but I assume that rebel groups in civil wars are no exception to the general principle that particular actions are chosen in relation to larger political goals. I also agree with Hannah Arendt's insight: "Violence, being instrumental by nature, is rational to the extent that it is effective in reaching the end that must justify it."[50] In varying degrees, rebel violence arises for the purpose of achieving political goals. In the eyes of the rebels, if not others, violent means are justified, even compelled, by the end they have in sight.

The second assumption is that *rebel groups want to survive in order to attain their goal*, be it political autonomy or subversion of the existing government (Assumption 2). Some rebel groups prioritize their military survival and therefore favor ruling by force like "roving bandits";[51] others want to survive both politically and militarily, and therefore make it a priority to appeal to potential constituencies at home and abroad. In determining whether or not to comply with international law, rebel groups will typically weigh their options and consider how much compliant actions will contribute to their ultimate goal of survival.

[50] Arendt (1970: 79). [51] Olson (2000).

The third assumption is that *rebellion needs resources and support* (Assumption 3). Like any other political activity, rebel groups need material and non-material support to sustain their movement. They need new recruits to fight for their cause, and arms and ammunition to confront government military forces. Some groups also need sponsors that can provide political support. To certain rebel groups, the key supporters will be mainly domestic civilians or international actors. For others, the main lifeline may be natural resources. This variation in rebel groups' support base will be the point of departure for the analysis and argument that follow.

The fourth assumption is that the *preferences and values of key rebel audiences matter* in understanding rebel compliance (Assumption 4). A rebel movement never exists in complete isolation; its operations necessarily take it beyond itself and involve interfacing with a political and social context. Most rebel groups have some level of interest in forging relations with civilians and outside supporters to garner support. And what these audiences want finally matters as much as what rebel groups want. Indeed, what these audiences want can sometimes strongly influence what rebel groups do and how they behave with respect to international law. Civilians involved in ethnic conflict, for example, might want to offer their help voluntarily to rebel movements. In those cases, the "help" might violate international law, yet the rebel group receiving it might not think twice about the violation. In cases where globally dispersed supporters have strong views about respecting human rights, on the other hand, a rebel group may be influenced to reject actions that are strategically expedient, but not acceptable.

The fifth working assumption is that *rebel compliance is costly* in many cases (Assumption 5). In numerous situations, it is easy and expedient for rebel groups to violate international humanitarian and human rights rules. To uphold international standards, the rebel leadership has to take steps to enforce rules against harassing civilians and other abusive behavior. Sanctioning its own soldiers might hurt the group's morale. Issuing prohibitions on looting, for instance, will take away the material incentives that some rebel soldiers may have for joining the group and staying with it. Similarly, a rebel group's use of anti-personnel landmines – in areas where civilians are likely to be harmed – may provide it with a modest tactical advantage and some sense of security in its fight against better-equipped and more mobile government forces. Rebel leadership may realize that banning the use of landmines will therefore be tactically dangerous and also unpopular with their rank-and-file fighters. When a conflict is asymmetric, as in civil wars, it is easy to resort to whatever methods of war appear immediately effective, even if they involve some violation of international laws.

The last assumption brings us back to the central puzzle of this book: if it is costly to comply with international rules, why would some rebel groups do so? Here, thinking about the potential benefits of complying is the key to solving the puzzle of rebel compliance. I reason that, in the scales of decision making, legitimacy is the key driver that puts weight on the compliance side for some rebel groups. When the time comes to compare the benefits and costs of compliance, if rebel groups see the prospect of achieving political gains by complying, they are more likely to change their overall behavior from non-compliance to compliance. I explore this logic more fully in the following section.

THE LOGIC OF COMPLIANT REBELS

The working assumptions described in the previous section highlighted central features of civil conflicts and rebel groups. With these assumptions in mind, how do we make sense of compliant rebels? The legitimacy concerns and political ambitions of rebel groups (Assumption 1) will be crucially counterbalanced against strategic and military considerations because compliance is in general costly (Assumption 5). When the pursuit of legitimacy can aid the overall sustainability or success of rebellion (Assumption 2), compliant rebels may arise. In this utilitarian calculation, rebel groups are strategic actors that care about the consequences of their actions and about their interactions with other key stakeholders. In weighing their goals and the likely consequences of their specific actions, rebel groups will comply to the extent that compliance will not damage their rebellion and rather help in some way (Assumption 3).

The interaction with other political actors is important, as a rebel group's legitimacy will usually be determined via the perceptions and actions of other actors. Key actors include potential supporters at home and abroad: domestic populations of co-ethnics, diaspora populations, foreign state sponsors, or other rebel networks. Rebel groups' pursuit of legitimacy will be undertaken and navigated vis-à-vis these potential supporters. At the same time, not all actual or potential supporters will matter in inducing compliance (Assumption 4). Not every supporter of rebellion will care and invest in international law compliance. Co-ethnics abroad may or may not care about supporting a legitimate insurgency at home rather than funneling support to a group branded as a "terrorist" entity. Some foreign sponsors of rebellions may not care about how rebels behave and may instead care exclusively about their chances of winning power. In these circumstances, international law violations that result in significant numbers of innocent civilian casualties might not be avoidable.

The balance between the domestic and international legitimacy considerations depends on which one is more important to the rebel group for garnering support and survival (Assumption 2). For rebel groups that largely rely on a domestic population for support, foreign preferences will not matter much. By the similar logic, for rebel groups that exclusively rely on outside support for arms and ammunition, satisfying foreign demands will be a top priority.

Consequently, I expect that compliant rebels will emerge when rebel groups seek legitimacy in the eyes of core constituencies that care about behaviors consistent with international norms. If rebel groups seek to achieve legitimacy in the eyes of key audiences with preferences for rules consistent with international standards, then we are likely to see rebel compliance. Note that this conclusion crucially relies on the previously discussed assumptions about the goals of rebellion and the importance of the surrounding political environment. If compliance were not costly, rebel compliance would no longer be a puzzle, and if we assumed that rebel movements could sustain themselves without any interaction with domestic and international actors, then legitimacy – and whether or not to pursue it – would not be a part of rebels' calculus in deciding whether or not to comply with international law.

Because of my emphasis on the potentially strategic value of compliance, I can characterize my theory as the "strategic legitimacy theory of rebel compliance." It is "strategic" in the sense that I focus on rebels' interactions with the government they oppose, as well as with domestic and international constituencies. At its core, the theory is about utilitarian compliance because rebel groups expect to gain something from compliant behavior. In this strategic calculation, rebel groups do not make their decisions on their own, but in the context of a larger political environment and as a result of interactions with their core political constituencies.

In this theory of strategic legitimacy, the instrumental value of promoting legitimacy is important for rebel group compliance. In some cases, rebel groups may comply simply because their local norms or organizational norms *already* coincide with international law. However, in most cases where rebel groups experience a shift from non-compliance to compliance, my theory expects that rebel groups will gradually come to see the value of complying. In this scenario, what makes a rebel group turn the corner and start pursuing legitimacy is not necessarily a moral or philosophical epiphany about the moral character of human rights violations. Moral values can be one part of the calculation on the part of rebel groups about whether to comply or not, but my theory suggests that the instrumental value of compliance plays an important role.

The role of national governments cannot be missed in completing the story of compliant rebels. As a main antagonist in the story of rebellion, the government assumes many roles. In some cases, would-be rebel groups may be sufficiently appeased by the government to engage in negotiations and other efforts to achieve peaceful change; a conflict may never even get to the stage of armed rebellion. In dealing with already emerged rebel groups, governments will sometimes concede some amount of political space within which the rebel groups are allowed to operate. In these instances, the government can play the role of facilitator and help to produce compliant rebels. On the other hand, wittingly or unwittingly, governments can also be a force against compliance.

Feeling threatened, a government can ban rebel groups' political activities and engage in repressive actions that have the effect of creating a breeding ground for extremists.[52] A threatened government can also play a stern gatekeeper role and thwart the efforts of well-intentioned international actors that want to enter rebel zones for humanitarian purposes.[53] Military actions by the government can also often create situations that increase the likelihood of rebels violating humanitarian rules. For example, a cycle of reciprocal, tit-for-tat killings may take hold, with both sides feeling justified in their actions, even when these involve clear humanitarian violations.

The life cycle of rebellion is also important to consider if we try to determine when rebel compliance may be observed. Adapting what we know about the life cycle of terrorism,[54] I suggest that the life of a rebel group moves through four stages: (1) incubation: the conception and development stage where networking and recruitment occur; (2) strategic violence: the commercialization stage where appeals to key constituents and targeted audiences (funders and sympathizers) occur; (3) political violence: the growth stage where violence takes on a more political tone; and (4) political transformation: the stability stage where a rebel group develops itself into more of a political–military organization than an armed group. Rebel groups may seek legitimacy at all stages, but in different degrees. My theory of strategic legitimacy would predict that rebel groups are more likely to develop the urgency of pursuing legitimacy in the latter part of the life cycle. This is because key audiences play a critical role in the success and failure of rebellion as rebel movements mature, and as possible final outcomes of rebellion come into focus.

At this point, I want to be more explicit and precise about what my core argument entails. First, my main claim is probabilistic. I claim that rebel groups that seek legitimacy are more "likely" to try to comply with humanitarian rules "compared with" legitimacy-indifferent groups. Second, related to the first point, I do not claim that legitimacy-seeking groups are always rule-compliant. Depending on the particular interaction patterns that exist with key political audiences and the circumstances in which rebel groups find themselves, legitimacy-seeking rebels may sometimes violate international rules. Short-term military and strategic incentives may blind legitimacy-seeking groups to their long-term goals. In this regard, is important to note that my main claim should be seen as a theoretical claim about a general trend, not as a hard-and-fast prediction about rebel group decision making in all cases or for a specific case. Understanding the particular circumstances that can discourage compliance in the case of groups that are generally

52 See Staniland (2012b) for governments' varied reactions to rebellion.

53 Jo and Thomson (2013) present evidence for this in the context of detention visits by the ICRC.

54 Donohue and Cristal (2012). Also see Herbst (2004) for the distinction between "nascent" and "mature" rebels.

legitimacy-seeking is an important part of the puzzle that will occupy us in the rest of this book.

It is also important to recognize what my theory *does* offer. My theory is primarily designed to explain the association between legitimacy-seeking and rebel compliance with international norms and laws. Although the theory is not designed to provide a dynamic explanation laying out the explicit causal pathways leading from legitimacy-seeking behavior to compliance, the theory has the potential to shed light on key drivers of change within rebel groups. My theory recognizes the fluidity of legitimacy-seeking characteristics and the fact that, over time and over the course of the organizational life of a rebel group, the importance of those characteristics can change as well, motivating or discouraging rebel compliance.

ALTERNATIVE EXPLANATIONS

Three alternative and potentially competing arguments can be considered in response to my strategic legitimacy theory: I will label them as: (1) the military–tactical considerations argument; (2) the structural argument regarding capacity; and (3) the argument for the centrality of ideology. In what follows, I will introduce each argument and examine its validity relative to my strategic legitimacy theory.

The first alternative explanation for rebel group violence emphasizes the paramount importance of military and tactical considerations. Those who favor this view may hold that armed groups' behaviors, including compliance and non-compliance, are primarily dictated by military and strategic factors. This argument shares my third assumption that rebel groups want to win the civil conflict in which they are engaged, but ignores my first assumption that civil wars are always more than just a military contest. If rebel groups ignore political legitimacy and care only about military victories, they might win the battles, but they will never win the war. The military–tactical considerations argument has the hardest time explaining rebel groups' restraint: the decision not to use a particular tactic when it would be tactically or strategically advantageous to do so. In contrast, my theory is designed to provide an explanation for the phenomenon of compliant rebels.

The second alternative explanation is the structural argument regarding capacity. This line of argument holds that compliant rebels emerge because they "can," having strong organizational structures with effective command and control. However, the capacity argument ignores the importance of willingness and motivation. Capacity is necessary, but not sufficient to make a rebel group change course and begin to comply with international law. Rebel motivation is just as important as what rebels can do. Even if rebel groups have the capacity to comply, their behavior will not change unless they have the willingness to comply, and the necessary leadership and initiative to turn this willingness into disciplined action.

Another alternative explanation for compliant rebels focuses on ideology.[55] It is plausible to think that some rebel groups comply not necessarily because of international law, but because of their own social or organizational norms. Social science research shows that congruence between societal values and law is important if there is to be lasting rule adherence over time.[56] When social norms are consistent with international standards, a group's ideology – not international law – may be the main driver of compliance.

Whether the centrality of ideology argument becomes an alternative to my legitimacy-focused argument depends on how we define ideology. If we define ideology narrowly as a summary of a group's dogmatic beliefs (e.g., Marxism or Jihadism), then we might be able to distinguish the role of ideology from the role of legitimacy-seeking. We could find out what those dogmatic beliefs state with regard to international law compliance and assess the independent impact of those beliefs on rebel compliance. However, if we define ideology broadly to include all "political programs"[57] and political ideas, legitimacy-seeking will be part of a rebel group's ideology.

Here, we also have to think about where laws come from. In general, law is an outgrowth of social norms, and international law is no exception. Some rebel groups may be motivated by a moral sense of what is wrong and what is right.[58] If we take this naturalist view of law, maybe it just so happens that the ideology of some rebel groups is consistent with international law.[59] On the other hand, when a group's ideology coincides with international law, this may attest to the hidden effect of international law. In other words, it is possible that international law as a social custom already influenced the development of rebel groups' social norms and their ideology. In this process of social norms affecting international law and international law consolidating those social norms, it will be difficult to disentangle the effect of international law from social norms as they are already fused together.

In response to this potential rival argument regarding the ideology broadly defined, I want to point out that my argument is *consistent* with such argument, particularly for the emphasis on the social bases of rebellion.[60]

[55] For a recent review of the literature on rebellion and ideology, see Sanín and Wood (2014).

[56] Tyler (2010).

[57] This broad view of ideology is consistent with Sanín's and Wood's definition (2014: 215): "a more or less systematic set of ideas that includes the identification of a referent group (a class, ethnic, or other social group), an enunciation of the grievances or challenges that the group confronts, the identification of objectives on behalf of that group (political change or defense against its threat), and a (perhaps vaguely defined) program of action."

[58] Wood (2003) shows this role of ideology in the case of the FMLN in El Salvador.

[59] For example, if secessionist rebel groups protect their co-ethnics, they may do so for strategic reasons (because they depend on these core supporters), or because they sincerely believe that protecting them is the right thing to do. In fact, the origin of some aspects of international law goes back to customary international law, and the custom of distinguishing combatants from non-combatants constitutes a key part of the protection norm.

[60] Staniland (2012a).

My legitimacy-focused argument highlights the often neglected connection between political and economic patronage and compliance behavior vis-à-vis international norms. Specifically, rebel groups' political relationships with their sponsors, patrons, and other key audiences are part of the rebel groups' compliance process. The theory of strategic legitimacy thus recognizes that ties with local communities, representation with political parties, and other institutional networks determine the course of rebellion and how rebel groups fight wars.

At this point, I do not want to leave the reader with the mistaken impression that the four arguments discussed in the preceding paragraphs are mutually exclusive or even necessarily antagonistic to each other. These arguments may at times look like rival explanations of rebel group behavior because they do not all share the same assumptions. They may also produce somewhat different expectations. However, I wish to underscore that my theory of legitimacy and compliance does not negate the strategic and structural arguments, but rather *complements* these existing arguments. I acknowledge that rebel groups' military and tactical considerations are generally of the utmost importance. Still, there are circumstances where international law compliance may coincide with military objectives, and where exercising restraint might confer benefits on the political front that outweigh short-term battlefield gains. Also, I concede that organizational capacity is important, though only to the extent that willingness to change allows it to operate. Ideology is also an important part of my rebel compliance story, but since ideological change often happens slowly, and compliance behavior sometimes changes quickly, my theory of strategic legitimacy may provide a better explanation than ideology for rebel compliance.

CONCEPTS AND OPERATIONALIZATION

The preceding theoretical discussion suggests that the related empirical inquiry requires the operationalization of key abstract concepts such as legitimacy and compliance. This section discusses the efforts and challenges of measuring legitimacy and compliance, and the rationale behind adopting particular indicators and measures.

Compliance

Compliance is conceptually defined as conformity to existing rules and norms.[61] Analogously, *rebel compliance* in this book will be defined as rebel groups' behaviors consistent with international rules. One challenge of this book is that I cannot possibly investigate the full range of possible compliance behaviors. International humanitarian law and human rights law cover vast areas, from the

[61] Raustiala and Slaughter (2006).

treatment of civilians to the regulation of methods of warfare. Other areas include prohibitions against the intentional killing of innocent civilians; protection norms for particularly vulnerable persons, such as women and children; and prohibitions against the use of chemical and biological weapons, as well as incendiary devices.

Among the many topics related to compliance, this book focuses on three main issues: violence against civilians, violence against children, and violence against detainees. Specifically, I examine the killing of civilians by rebel groups, the use of child soldiers by rebel groups, and rebel groups' decisions with regard to the ICRC and granting it access to their detention centers.

The choice of these three issues was dictated by the two concerns of salience and clarity. With regard to issue salience, it is widely acknowledged that ordinary civilians, children, and people in detention are the three primary victims of conflicts involving rebel violence. These are the categories of people that are most often exposed to rebel violence and that become victims of rebel non-compliance. In terms of clarity, what matters is that international standards and expectations for the three aforementioned categories of victims are clearly articulated and relatively well established. Customary international law clearly enshrines the principle that a distinction must be made between combatants and non-combatants.[62] With regard to children, international law clearly states that the use of children in war is prohibited.[63] International law also stipulates that persons in detention should be treated humanely,[64] and that warring parties have an obligation to allow visits by humanitarian actors.[65]

The first issue, violence against civilians, has been historically prevalent and at the same time relevant to contemporary humanitarian and security concerns. The treatment of civilians is *the* prime issue in any internal armed conflict. At the same time, it is a dimension of rebel group behavior that often appears highly resistant to international law and norms. I specifically look into the actions of rebel groups that deliberately kill civilians, which is clearly prohibited in international law. Compliance in this area of behavior consists of respecting civilian life and refraining from intentional killing of civilians. Non-compliance will be defined as the indiscriminate and entirely avoidable killing of civilians. These norms are written in the Geneva Conventions, the core document of humanitarian law, and the principle of distinction between combatants and non-combatants is well established in practice and as customary international law.

The second issue concerns violence against children. The particular focus will be the rebel groups' use of child soldiers.[66] The issue of child soldiers has

[62] Henckaerts and Doswald-Beck (2005). Customary international humanitarian law Rules 1–24 cover the treatment of civilians in non-international armed conflicts.

[63] *Ibid.*, Rule 135. [64] *Ibid.*, Rules 118–128. [65] *Ibid.*, Rules 53–56.

[66] Other types of violence against children include killing and maiming, sexual violence, attacks on schools, and abduction. See United Nations (2013a).

recently been the target of intense scrutiny, and the issue is inherently important as child soldiering affects children's security and well-being in conflict-ridden zones. Compliance in this area would involve restraint in using children, to be more exact, youths under the age of 18, in rebel ranks, especially for combat purposes. Non-compliance would entail active use of child soldiers for combat purposes. Extreme non-compliance would be using children as human shields. These prohibitions against child soldiering are written in the Convention on the Rights of the Child, as well as in the recent Paris Commitment. Both legal instruments have received wide support globally and the norm of respecting children's rights is shared across cultures.

The treatment of detainees is the third issue area explored in this book. How detainees are treated is a well-established and highly visible humanitarian issue. Almost every recorded war has involved prisoners and detainees, from the POW camps of the two world wars to the recent Guantanamo prisons. How rebel groups treat government soldiers and civilian detainees has generally not been well documented, however. Given the difficulty of obtaining accurate information about detainee treatment by rebel groups, I instead focus on whether rebel groups grant access to their detention centers and allow visits by the ICRC. The rationale here is that allowing detention visits is compliant behavior that clearly contrasts with its opposite: denying access to the ICRC. The Common Article 3 of the Geneva Convention recommends that the ICRC be allowed to monitor detention centers, and states that access is the first step of compliance that can contribute to the improvement of detainee treatment. Non-compliance in the context of detention visits involves the outright rejection of ICRC visits. Although a denial of access does not necessarily mean that detainees are being badly treated, restricting ICRC access generally corresponds to detainees not receiving the kind of treatment and not enjoying the rights to which they are entitled under international law.

The three aforementioned issues obviously do not constitute an exhaustive list of important areas of inquiry in the area of humanitarian violations.[67] There are other important issues worth considering, such as torture, forced disappearances, rape, use of landmines and small arms, destruction of historical monuments, and arbitrary detention of persons, to name a few.[68] These issues deserve separate and in-depth attention in future research, but for now, I will simply note that many of them are related to the three issues I have chosen to examine here. For example, the use of child soldiers is linked to the small arms issue because the AK-47 rifle is the weapon most frequently used by child soldiers. Similarly, the treatment of civilians is related to sexual violence because rape and sexual abuse often occur in the process of civilian killing.

[67] See Morrow (2007) for the full range of issues in the context of interstate war.

[68] The last two issues, including the issue of rape and forced disappearance, are legal grounds for the ICC to open an investigation, as it did so in the case of Mali on January 16, 2013.

I examine these additional humanitarian issues in Chapter 8 and discuss how my theory can inform our understanding of these phenomena as well.

In analyzing these three issue areas of compliance, I look at rich array of rebel compliance behaviors, creating a typology of rebel compliance. At the basic level, I try to distinguish "compliers" and "non-compliers." As compliance is on a continuous scale, this dichotomy is for empirical convenience, but it will help us to navigate rebel compliance behaviors in a more straightforward fashion. To slice it through time, I distinguish "persistent compliers" and "switchover compliers." Persistent compliers are the rebel groups that comply throughout their rebellion from start to finish. At the other extreme, there will be persistent objectors: rebel groups that never comply during their lifespan. Switchover compliers are the rebel groups that alter their behaviors, from non-compliance to compliance, or from compliance to non-compliance, during their lifespan. This typology of compliance will come in handy when I discuss rebel compliance behaviors throughout the book.

In operationalizing compliance in each issue area, I wear a political scientist's hat. This means that I look at empirical regularities in rebel behavior rather than determining the legal status of each case of compliance or non-compliance. I am not an international law scholar, nor do I have all the circumstantial evidence that would be necessary to make valid judicial determinations. My approach will not be satisfying to legal scholars, but in this book I sacrifice legal specificity in favor of uncovering general patterns and trends. This decision to use a loose definition of compliance stems from the fact that the norms and principles regarding civilian killing, child soldiering, and detention visits are not set in stone and vary in practice. While they are universally accepted, these norms in actual practice present us with numerous challenges. Take, for example, the matter of defining a child as someone under the age of 18. In some cultures, youth over 15 are accepted as adults and assume adult roles when they turn 15. Also, imagine trying to apply this definition of adulthood in societies where there is no reliable birth certification system. In these circumstances, it is extremely difficult, if not impossible, to determine the true status of every case of suspected child soldiering. On the other hand, given the available information, I will subsequently show that it is possible to discern general patterns of child soldiering across rebel groups, as well as changes in child soldiering from year to year. In each chapter, readers will be reminded again of these challenges of measuring rebel compliance and associated efforts to overcome such difficulties.

Legitimacy

The concept of legitimacy is central to the study of politics and social science in general. The study of law, psychology, organizational studies, and sociology – all have dealt with the concept of legitimacy and its effects on social phenomena.[69] Yet legitimacy is often considered an elusive concept in terms of its actual operationalization. This section discusses the definition of legitimacy and develops measures of legitimacy in the context of rebel groups in civil conflicts. Those measures are used throughout the book, and I feel it is important to bring them to the reader's attention and explain how and why they were chosen.

We start by looking at the definition of legitimacy. This book will adopt the traditional definition: the perception that an entity is a viable political entity.[70] Analogously, and more concretely, rebel legitimacy will be defined as "support and recognition that a rebel group is a viable political authority." In this notion of legitimacy, the concepts of legitimacy, support, and recognition are interrelated. Legitimacy is essentially about perception of the viable authority, but in my definition it includes both material and non-material aspects. To rebel groups, the end goal is not necessarily the perception of the core constituencies, but how the perceptions lead to support and recognition. In this respect, my definition of legitimacy is expansive, including elements such as support and recognition. The assumption here is that support and recognition are not forthcoming without the sense of approval or expectation about the viability of authority of a rebel group.

My definition of rebel legitimacy builds on existing definitions of legitimacy, modifying them into the rebel group context. Max Weber's classical definition of legitimacy is often cited: "the basis of every system of authority, and correspondingly of every kind of willingness to obey, is a belief [regarding legitimacy], a belief by virtue of which persons exercising authority are lent prestige."[71] Note that Weber's definition emphasizes that legitimacy is "belief," which may be not easily measurable. Perception is important, but it will often follow with observable phenomena, which is why I emphasize support and recognition as key part of rebel legitimacy.

Lipset's adaptation of this definition to political contexts is particularly useful in thinking about rebel legitimacy: "legitimacy involves the capacity of a political system to engender and maintain the belief that existing political institutions are the most appropriate or proper ones for the society."[72] Lipset's definition of legitimacy was geared toward "state institutions." Rebel groups, by contrast, lack "the capacity of a political system" and therefore have to *create* the belief that their *new* political institutions are proper ones for their society. Building that new perception is never easy and typically takes considerable effort over time. Recognizing rebel groups' status as start-up political entities, legitimacy in this book will be defined primarily in terms of observable indicators that reveal the tendencies of legitimacy motivations.

[69] See Zelditch (2001) and Lamb (2014) for an overview of the concept of legitimacy in the social science literature, and Fabienne (2010) for a discussion of legitimacy in the context of political philosophy. See Beetham (1991) and Gilley (2009) for more recent work in political science.

[70] See below my discussion on Weber's definition. [71] Weber (1964: 382). [72] Lipset (1983: 64).

The degree of legitimacy is usually measured in terms of approval rates expressed as a percentage of the overall population.[73] Such measures of approval rarely exist for rebel groups. A British polling firm, Opinion Research Business (ORB), took a survey in Syria in 2014 and found that the Islamic State of Iraq and the Levant (ISIL) and its goal of creating a pan-Arab Islamic caliphate earned an approval rate of only 4 percent from a sample of 1,014 adults living in twelve of Syria's fourteen provinces.[74] Such efforts to gauge support for rebel groups are still relatively rare, however. In the absence of approval rating data, the task then is to develop some objective indicators that can serve as proxies for popular support and thus for legitimacy.

Another measurement challenge has to do with the multifaceted nature of legitimacy: a challenge taken up by more recently developed measures of legitimacy. In measuring the legitimacy of state institutions in Latin America, for example, Booth and Seligson looked at various levels and types of support.[75] In constructing measures of "state legitimacy," Gilley for his part developed indicators of legitimacy by looking at actions and attitudes regarding views of legality (e.g., importance of laws), views of justification (e.g., political trust), and acts of consent (e.g., election turnout).[76] All these efforts suggest that the operationalization of legitimacy requires understanding the various dimensions of legitimacy in specific political contexts.

Before operationalizing rebel legitimacy in a more concrete fashion, we also have to look into how rebel groups attempt to gain legitimacy. According to Weber's study of legitimacy, the sources of legitimacy are threefold: tradition, charisma, and legality.[77] Rebel groups rarely have a claim to tradition, as their organizational history is almost always just getting started. Unless they are able to make appeals to local traditions or to long-standing ethnic or regional identities and/or traditions, they are bound to be relatively new entities. Legal traditions and documents also rarely help rebel groups establish legitimacy, given that rebellion typically starts from dissent and from breaking with existing authorities. In the absence of these conventional sources of legitimacy, rebel groups have to seek out or somehow create their own sources of legitimacy. To borrow an analogy from marketing, rebel groups have to internally re-brand their legitimacy while reaching out to external networks.[78] The rebel groups' reservoir of possible sources of legitimacy then would include: (1) charismatic leadership; (2) appeals to ethnic traditions; (3) political representation (or elections) to increase the legality of the movement; and (4) international recognition to expand

[73] For discussions of measuring legitimacy at the macro state level, see Weatherford (2002); Gilley (2006).

[74] Jenkins (2014). [75] Booth and Seligson (2009). [76] Gilley (2006). [77] Weber (1964).

[78] Rao *et al.* (2008).

external networks and boost the legality of their organization. Among these sources, representation and international recognition are likely to be associated with strategic compliance specifically targeting domestic and international audiences.

Bearing in mind these sources of legitimacy for rebel groups, my approach is to measure latent variables and consider some legitimacy-enhancing rebel characteristics or activities.[79] The presence of a rebel political wing is one measure I propose in the context of rebel compliance. Political participation has long been considered to be a factor that enhances legitimacy. Rebel groups that have independent political wings (that are not just dominated by the group's military wing) exhibit several legitimacy-seeking characteristics. The first of these is an interest in political representation and participation. Legally allowed rebel political wings are more likely to participate in local and national civic life and elections. The second characteristic is rebel groups' political knowledge. Rebel political wings often have sub-units such as communication departments or human rights divisions to deal with external relations, so they are more likely to develop a sense of what is acceptable and what is not with respect to norms and rules in the international arena.

The second measure of legitimacy I use is rebel groups' desire to secede and specifically whether secession is a core group objective. Groups that aim to establish independent political control and autonomy in their own region are significantly different from other types of group aiming to change or overthrow the central government but not to secede. Because of the often violent reaction from a central government fearing national fragmentation,[80] it is difficult for secessionist groups to garner widespread domestic support at the national level. Secessionists, however, can garner support from their co-ethnics or local supporters, so their compliance will depend on exactly how they forge the relationship with their core domestic audience.

For secessionist groups, it is an uphill battle in the international arena when the currently existing borders are well established and respected under international law. In this respect, international legitimacy or support becomes a very costly asset for groups striving for independence, an asset highly prized when it is obtained.[81] The future prospect of joining the ranks of states and gaining acceptance from peer states can thus be an important motivation for secessionist rebel groups to abide by international law.[82]

My third measure of legitimacy-seeking attributes pertains specifically to audiences abroad. When rebel groups are dependent on external sponsors that care about human rights, they are more likely to comply with international law. One relevant measure here is the number of permanent secretariats of

[79] Bollen (2002).

[80] Walter (2009) considers this reputational concern of governments vis-à-vis separatist groups.

[81] Bloom and Licklider (2007).

[82] In this vein, recent studies also show that secessionist rebels are more likely than other groups to conduct foreign diplomacy by setting up a foreign affairs department. See Huang (2013).

human rights organizations situated in a foreign sponsor's state. Where such permanent secretariats exist, there is a higher likelihood that the advocacy efforts of human rights organizations will be reflected on the external sponsor's foreign policy. I additionally consider the interaction patterns of rebel groups with humanitarian organizations, given that these organizations are often the ones that negotiate with insurgent groups to provide services to victims in conflict zones. The thinking here is that the interaction between rebel groups and international actors is one indication that a rebel group is motivated to seek international legitimacy.

In these indicators of rebel legitimacy I develop and use in this book, readers will see how I strive to distinguish the concept of legitimacy from the notion of compliance. More often than not, the definition of legitimacy includes rule compliance, as being "legitimate" is equated with being "compliant with the law."[83] My defense to the potential conflation between legitimacy and compliance is twofold.[84]

First, legitimacy and compliance have specific meaning in the context of rebel groups in civil wars. Conceptually, they are distinct in the story of rebel groups and international law. Legitimacy is the rebel characteristics that shape the perception of relevant constituencies on the domestic and international level. Compliance, on the other hand, is the behavioral patterns of rebel groups. In effect, I try to distinguish rebel characteristics and behavioral patterns to keep the independent force of legitimacy effect on compliance.

Second, it is important to note the causal arrows between legitimacy and compliance. Legitimacy-seeking characteristics might lead to rebel compliance, as my theory postulates, but compliance does not necessarily lead to legitimacy. Some groups might comply without seeking legitimacy, perhaps out of their own beliefs that it is the right thing to do to respect civilian life. In these circumstances, compliance occurs implicitly and does not circle back to legitimacy. Therefore, the concept and use of legitimacy and compliance in this book assuages the concern of reverse causality, as they have specific meaning and contexts of rebel compliance.

In sum, this book considers legitimacy-seeking rebel groups in relation to three criteria: whether they have prior experience with political parties and local/national elections; whether they aim to establish a new state; and whether they rely on foreign supporters that care about international humanitarian and human rights. Certainly, these are not the only ways to judge rebel groups' legitimacy-seeking characteristics. Still, these measures provide a reliable way to capture whether rebel groups have the willingness and motivation to pursue political legitimacy at home and abroad.

[83] As per the *American Heritage College Dictionary*, 4th edn., p. 792.
[84] I thank Matt Fuhrmann for bringing this point to my attention.

EVIDENCE OF COMPLIANT REBELS

This book presents two central findings. The first finding is that *compliant rebels exist.* Contrary to conventional thinking that rebel groups are only perpetrators of violence, this book presents evidence that changes in rebel behavior are possible and that, in fact, these changes have been actually observed. There is ample evidence that many rebel groups in civil wars are abusers and violators of humanitarian rules. However, some rebel groups *do* follow international norms and exercise restraint. In particular contexts, and under particular conditions, some rebel groups do become aware of international law, commit to international rules, and change their behavior accordingly.

The face of rebel compliance is not uniform. Rebel compliance develops differently across issue areas. Compliant rebels rarely emerge with regard to the prohibition against killing civilians when there are reciprocal killings by the government. Non-compliance also appears to be particularly entrenched in the area of child soldiering. And in general, civil wars that last a long time have a higher likelihood of producing non-compliant rebel groups.

The second finding is that *compliant rebels emerge when they seek legitimacy.* What compliant rebel groups have in common is that, at some point, they decide to seek legitimacy in some fashion. Some rebel groups form political wings early on and start pursuing political agendas that involve conforming to international standards. Other rebel groups gradually develop an affinity to international law recognizing their need for international legitimacy and through interaction with rights-minded international actors. Compliance often starts without any explicit legal commitment, but in some cases compliant rebels arise because of the conscious effort by the group's political wing to exercise restraint or as a result of interaction with international actors.

I arrived at these two findings by gathering systematic data and by testing the idea of legitimacy-based compliance. I specifically examine the records of contemporary rebel groups between 1989 and 2009 using statistical analyses, by tracking down the histories of hundreds of rebel groups, and by talking to many people who have had interactions with rebel groups. The book's quantitative and qualitative analysis will reinforce the view of my strategic legitimacy theory that rebel groups often seek legitimacy not necessarily out of principle alone, but for material and strategic reasons. Evidence shows rebel groups change their behavior from non-compliance to compliance not because they suddenly embrace the values and principles behind international law, but because such change in behavior helps increase their chances of survival and goal attainment.

An example can help illustrate my findings. The Sudan People's Liberation Movement (SPLM) was a rebel group formerly in Sudan (now in South Sudan). The secessionist group started its movement in 1983 and negotiated a

Comprehensive Peace Agreement in 2005, becoming a political party in South Sudan. The rebel group abandoned its tactic of using child soldiers in 2006 in the face of the looming secessionist election and national referendum in 2010. The move to comply with international law came about when the group developed into a viable political institution with a plan for building a new state in South Sudan.[85] The group wanted to shape their reputation and bolster their legitimacy by changing the perceptions of their potential supporters. The Christian community in the United States was the key audience for the SPLM in their fight against the dominantly Muslim Sudanese government.[86]

By contrast, during the early part of its armed rebellion, the SPLM's compliance records were not good.[87] Amnesty International in its 1995 report noted with grave concern that "deliberate attacks [by the SPLM] ... have been ... responsible ... for the destruction of rural communities. Prisoners have been tortured, in some cases to death."[88] More recently, with civil conflict again flaring up, now within South Sudan, the SPLM has returned to using child soldiers.

Looking back over the organization's history, we therefore conclude that the SPLM's decision to comply with international law was a *strategic* move made in pursuit of achieving political *legitimacy* in order to become a new nation in the world. This example supports my strategic legitimacy theory, showing the strategic use of compliance to gain legitimacy. Building on this specific example, this book seeks to establish the general conditions under which these reasons arise and come into focus, such that they are recognized and acted upon.

CONTRIBUTION

This book's unique contribution stems from its in-depth examination of the relationship between rebel groups and international law. Whether or not rebel groups are aware of international law, whether or not and for what reasons they care about complying with international law – this is the central focus of this book. It is a relatively specific and specialized focus, and yet it speaks to several bodies of research in political science and law. Especially relevant are the literatures on political violence and on compliance with international law. By creating a synthesis of these two topics, this book will discover the role of international law in the phenomenon of political violence.

The topic of political violence has produced a vast literature, as it is intertwined with questions about political order and change. This book's contribution lies in the new understanding it provides of rebel violence from

[85] Bixler (2002); Hamberg (2013).
[86] Bob (2005) argues that the SPLM/A's decision was also influenced by its interactions with NGOs.
[87] European Sudanese Public Affairs Council (1998). [88] Amnesty International (1995).

the perspective of international legal compliance. The study of political violence and the study of compliance are intricately related but different. The two are related because they often look the same on a behavioral spectrum. Extreme political violence is often associated with non-compliance with international norms. Low levels of political violence often look like compliance.

The key difference is that compliance can happen amid violence. In fact, that is at the heart of international humanitarian law (or *jus in bello* or the laws of war) – that amid brutality, there are some principles to be kept as part of law compliance. So, political violence against government soldiers is acceptable within the framework of international law. However, even the minimum level of treating innocent civilians inhumanely is a violation of international legal principles. In short, not all political violence will be inconsistent with international law. These are subtle, but important distinctions. Normally in the study of political violence, the consideration of international norms will not be factored in. In my study of compliant rebels, international norms take an important place as an anchor to evaluate wartime violence.

The value of synthesizing the topics of law and violence is twofold. First, from this perspective we will be able to better understand changes in rebel behavior. Previous studies have primarily focused on what causes violence, but my focus is on what inhibits that violence and what factors produce change from unconstrained to constrained violence, in the context of international law. Second, this book will demonstrate that the role of international actors as agents of international law is crucial insofar as their engagement with rebel groups. The later chapters will show that their decisions about *how exactly* to engage with these groups can have a significant impact on rebel group behavior. This book is distinct from other studies of rebel violence with its focus on rebel reactions to international legal norms. Ultimately, this book, I hope, can shed light on how the agents of international law can function and effect change in rebel group behavior with a view to reducing rebel group violence.

Most crucially, this book tries to bridge perspectives in international relations and international law. For understanding rebel group behavior, bridging perspectives is beneficial in at least two respects. It brings more empirical evidence to the attention of international legal scholars while at the same time underscoring the functions and mechanisms of international legal rules and norms, which are increasingly investigated by political scientists. This marriage of international law and international relations gives me a unique perspective to inquire into rebel violence – the role of international norms and agents of international law in conflict zones.

The focus on norms and laws can shed light on the deeper dynamics shaping rebel group behavior. As an outgrowth of social norms, laws usually reflect social values and establish common ground with regard to what is accepted and what is not.[89] These important contextual legal factors are often neglected when

[89] Morrow (2007); Simmons (2010).

scholars zoom in on strategic and military matters. In general, political scientists have a tendency to underestimate the influence of norms and laws. International relations scholars in particular, especially those who view matters of *Realpolitik* as the core of the discipline, tend to focus on strategic concerns and military imperatives and little else. In the following chapters, I acknowledge the importance of strategic and military calculations, but also show that there are situations where these calculations are compatible with the conditions that make rebel groups comply with existing international norms.

For their part, political science methods and perspectives can bring new bodies of evidence and insight to international legal scholarship. The two disciplines favor different modes of inquiry. The main emphasis in international law is on the legal reasoning behind relevant rules and principles, often overlooking the actual practices and behaviors of non-state armed groups. The methods used in political science can provide systematically collected empirical evidence that is often lacking in international legal scholarship. Some legal scholars have already noted a gradual trend in compliance studies in international law toward including such evidence. For example, Howse and Teitel argue that "the notion of rule compliance is much too narrow an angle of vision to comprehend international law's normative effects." They therefore try to redirect the attention of their colleagues in international legal studies to "the actual behavioral effects of rules."[90] This is the paradigm I adopt in this book as I inquire into how rebel groups take up particular rules and connect them to specific actions.

For the study of politics in general, this book sheds new light on issues and questions that preoccupy political scientists: questions of order, violence, peace, justice, and legitimacy. The theory of rebel compliance brings up questions from political philosophy regarding political legitimacy – the sources and consequences of legitimacy. Also, the topic engages important questions in comparative politics about political parties, political violence, and ultimately the question of political order.

Beyond making a contribution to academic understanding of political order and violence, this book has several policy aims. I hope to provide a useful and informative typology of rebel group aims and motivations for policymakers and practitioners. The findings and resources presented in this book can serve as a knowledge base and can also provide policymakers and practitioners with helpful conceptual infrastructure for training and application in the field.

THE ROAD AHEAD

The book is organized as follows. Chapter 2 provides background and describes the scope of the inquiry. It offers a more precise working definition of rebel groups and delves into important details of international legal standards related

[90] Howse and Teitel (2010: 128).

to rebel groups. Building on this background, Chapter 3 explicates my theory of rebel compliance and offers a legitimacy-based argument of compliance. I explain why the legitimacy motivation of rebel groups is important in understanding their compliance behavior. Specifically, I discuss what political legitimacy means to rebel groups, how rebels seek legitimacy, and how the search for legitimacy shapes and constrains rebel behaviors.

Chapter 4 serves as a bridge from theory to empirics. In this chapter, I discuss general patterns gleaned from the Rebel Groups and International Law (RGIL) database and explain how I link my theoretical concepts to empirical measures. The following three chapters, Chapters 5, 6, and 7, are the core empirical chapters of this book. These chapters examine the nexus between the pursuit of legitimacy and compliance behaviors in the three key issue areas of humanitarian compliance: civilian killing, child soldiering, and detention access. Each chapter is organized in a similar fashion. First, I introduce the status of norms regarding a given issue. Next, I discuss theoretical expectations couched in the specific issue area, overview the available data, and show my statistical findings. Finally, in each issue area, I illustrate the link between compliance and legitimacy-seeking behavior through one or more case studies. In all three chapters, I spend time investigating the motivations and behaviors of rebel groups complying with international law.

Chapter 8 takes stock of the empirical findings presented in the preceding three chapters and discusses other applicable issues, such as the use of landmines or sexual violence. The book's final chapter, Chapter 9, summarizes key findings and discusses the policy option of humanitarian engagement targeting legitimacy-seeking rebel groups. In this last chapter, I also pose questions that invite the reader to work with the book's theory and evidence using historical examples. In closing the book, I discuss what this work means broadly for the future development of international norms and human security in the coming decades.

2

Background

In this chapter, we will examine several facts as a background to help us understand compliant rebels. The background information will guide us through the detailed argument in the next chapter (Chapter 3), as well as subsequent chapters on empirical evidence of compliant rebels (Chapters 5–7). To set the scope of this book, I will first define "rebel group" as a unit of analysis. I will also address the historical and recent developments in international law regarding rebel groups. International law was mainly developed to govern the relations of states in an international system. To develop the proper understanding of the conditions surrounding rebel group compliance with international norms, we must address whether rebel groups are even aware of rules and norms of international law, and whether they are bound by international law. The working definition of a rebel group as well as the development of international law will fill in the information for the twin parts of this book's subtitle: "rebel groups" and "international law."

DEFINING REBEL GROUPS

Thus far, I have not explicitly engaged readers for a discussion of what a rebel group is. This section will provide the discussion on what I set out to study (and what I do not). I first define a rebel group, and then distinguish a rebel group from a terrorist organization – the category commonly mixed in common parlance. Lastly, I examine what it means to study rebel groups at a group-level rather than at an individual-level. Since I study rebel compliance as a group phenomenon, I will discuss the ramifications of simplifying individual rebel members into a group.

What is a Rebel Group?

Rebel groups are military organizations that fight against a central government. They engage in armed confrontations with the central government, often using violent means. They usually fight for independence of a territory, political autonomy, or greater rights for minority or ethnic groups.

The term "rebel group" takes on a number of different names according to the various contexts and connotations through which it is referenced. Those terms include "insurgents," "guerillas," "non-state armed groups," "armed opposition groups," "freedom fighters," and "parties to an internal armed conflict." Some terms, such as non-state armed groups, are more neutral than others. Substitute terms like "liberation army" and "freedom fighters" are typically used by the rebels themselves as a means to celebrate their cause. The term "armed opposition group" is frequently employed to maintain neutrality in a discussion involving rebel groups, particularly in international legal literature.

In this book, I chose to use the term *rebel groups* to make the point that the legal status of rebel groups under international law is not as established as that of national governments. Also, this book will use the term "rebel groups" exclusively to highlight the fact that these groups are fighting government forces inciting rebellion, and to remind us that they usually "rebel" against a set of existing norms, potentially including international rules.

Rebels and Terrorists

The conceptual overlap between the term "rebel group" and "terrorists" is particularly noteworthy, as the distinction defines the scope of inquiry in this book. There are some overlaps between terrorists and rebel groups. The designation of a terrorist group is often politically determined, motivated by national governments to brand the opposition as such or by international pressure to do so.[1] The branding is often the consequence of groups exercising terror tactics such as suicide bombing or targeting civilian facilities to get their messages through when other tactics have not yielded results. Rebel groups are defined by their fight against their governments, not necessarily by the means of fighting, but in the course of rebellion, some rebel groups decide to employ terrorist tactics instead of direct military confrontations with the government forces. This produces the overlap between terrorist groups and rebel groups.

To explore the definitional boundary between the terms in a more systematic way, I compare two databases – one for terrorists (Global Terrorism Database: GTD) and the other for rebel groups (Non-State Actor: NSA dataset).[2] A comparison of the GTD and NSA list reveals substantial overlaps between terrorist groups and rebel groups as summarized in Figure 2.1. In the first category, about 100 rebel groups are classified as both terrorists and rebel groups. In the second category, another 100 or so are classified solely as rebel groups. In the third category, some 400 groups are classified as solely as terrorist

[1] Beck and Miner (2013). [2] Cunningham *et al.* (2013).

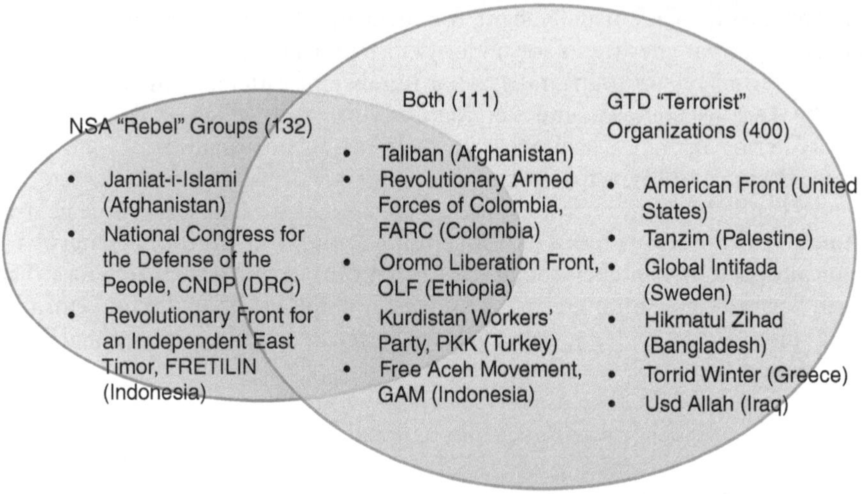

FIGURE 2.1 Rebels and terrorists: examples of rebel groups and terrorist organizations

groups. Note that most of these groups are domestic terrorist groups or often sets of individuals.

The examples in Figure 2.1 set the background as to what this book will cover and what it will *not* cover. This book will examine some rebel groups that are branded as terrorists. These include groups such as the Kurdistan Workers' Party (PKK) in Turkey or the Taliban in Afghanistan, which rebelled against their own governments but have also used terror tactics in the midst of their armed struggles. What this book will not cover is the category of small domestic terrorist groups. Those groups usually focus on narrow policies other than the matters on the structure of the government or territorial changes within a nation. These are important sets of actors to consider humanitarian consequences, but it is beyond the scope of this study as this book primarily concerns the political interactions between organized armed groups and national governments.

In addition to excluding domestic terrorists, this book will also prelude groups that have championed their cause exclusively through peaceful means. Rather than exhibiting resistance in the form of demonstrations, rebel groups in this book engage in direct hostilities and launch military attacks on governments. This means that rebel groups will often have a difficult time in using restraints in fighting an enemy that is often militarily stronger than itself. This very fact of belligerency on the part of rebel groups sets the puzzle of rebel compliance: why violent rebels might have an incentive to refrain from unconstrained violence.

Rebels as "Groups"

I want to emphasize that this book's focus is on rebels as "groups." The book will examine the group-level decision rather than the individual-level decision. I will not attempt to explain the psychologically deviant behaviors of an individual soldier, but rather the policies that rebel group leaders determine for the rest of the group. The primary reason for this is that in terms of international legal responsibility, attribution of crimes or command responsibility is important. When a lower-ranking soldier commits a crime out of psychological impulse, it does not become an international crime. However, when a rebel group's leadership issues orders to massacre a village, its crime is certainly attributable to the rebel leadership and thus subject to the crimes against humanity under international law. This focus on rebel groups is not to disparage the importance of individual responsibility or individual-level explanations for compliance or non-compliance, but to take into account the group dynamics within rebel groups in civil conflicts.

Different rebel groups will have varying degrees of organizational discipline, so we will observe the sometimes low or high level of violations of the laws of war. This organizational requirement also sets the scope of rebel groups that I examine in this book. My analysis will deal with rebel groups with a certain level of organizational structure and exclude small or inactive rebel groups that do not exhibit any organizational characteristics.

Because of this focus, the book will discuss rebel groups *as if* they operated as a single, cohesive entity. However, I fully note that rebel groups function as a collection of individuals with varying interests and actions. A rebel group does not represent the ideas of one person, but rather those of an organization composed of members who each take varying positions, such as a commander or rank-and-file soldier. At the helm of these groups lies rebel leadership whose command varies across different levels of authority. Some rebel groups feature strong individual leaders, as in the case of Joseph Kony (LRA in Uganda), Foday Sankoh (RUF in Sierra Leone), or John Garang (SPLM/A in Sudan). In other instances, authority may be more dispersed and decentralized. A rebel group's organizational structure will have implications for behavior regarding human rights in rebel groups. Depending on its level of authority, rebel leadership can order and incite rebel soldiers to commit violations of the laws of war. In many past instances of genocide, rebel leaders played a central role in inciting the violence leading up to these acts through political propaganda.[3] For example, the cult Joseph Kony created using child soldiers or the use of drugs in killing and maiming ordinary people condoned by Sankoh provide a few additional examples of behavior affected by the presence of a strong rebel leader.

Related to activities conducted by individual members of a rebel group, lower-level violations of international standards can occur without orders. An

[3] Valentino (2004).

individual soldier may violate policies put in place by rebel leadership. In response to these situations, rebel group leadership may take a wide range of action, be it overlooking abuses, punishing transgressions, or prosecuting violations through the group's own court system.[4] Sanctions and punishments are often meted out as a way of disciplining its soldiers, but psychological stress or wartime fatigue can also generate violations at the level of rank-and-file soldiers. These individual behaviors, unaffected by central rebel leadership, will not be covered in this book. Take the example of activity by the Karen National Union (KNU) in Myanmar. The group's central committee prohibits the use of child soldiers as a matter of policy, but in times of troop shortages, lower-ranking commanders often scramble to fulfill their personnel needs by recruiting children. This type of organizational behavior of child soldier use within an organization can be explained, but a rebel soldier acting on impulse and committing the murder of a civilian will not be explained in this book. It is because in these cases of violations committed purely by individuals, legal accountability cannot be traced back to rebel leadership. It is my intention to examine the political behaviors of rebel groups in regard to international law, not to provide psychological explanations for deviant individual behaviors in war and conflict.

As previous research shows, knowledge of the hierarchy commanding rebel organizations lies at the center of any complete understanding of rebel group behavior.[5] Although this book focuses primarily on the violation of laws of war at the organizational level, I pay special attention to what individual components of rebel groups can do to generate violence or exercise restraint. The centralization of command structure and internal codes of conduct, for instance, will matter. So, too, will the type of responses rebel leadership administers to lower-ranking violations. This book will pay particular attention to these political decisions made by rebel groups, in order to investigate how considerations regarding international law affect the group's decision-making calculus.

The nature of rebel groups' organizational structures is also fluid, leading to further variability among group behavior. Political circumstances often determine the formation of a group or coalition.[6] Likewise, it often forces an existing group to splinter into two or more groups. The Sudan Liberation Army (SLA) in Darfur, Sudan, for instance, underwent a number of splits, resulting in the creation of new sub-groups such as the SLA-Minnawi, SLA-Unity, SLA-Abdesh-Shafi, SLA-Free Will, and SLA-AW (Abdel Wahid). This splintering creates additional problems in detecting clear patterns of rebel group violence among the various factions. These conditions, inherent to rebel organizational structures, play a large role in understanding rebel compliance. In sum, rebel groups cannot be viewed in their actions as a single, unified actor. Although treated as one entity, these groups are often composed of many factions that

[4] Sivakumaran (2009). [5] Weinstein (2006). [6] See Christia (2012) for rebel alliances.

strongly determine various characteristics affecting compliance behavior, such as leadership's control over its soldiers or interfactional struggles. This complexity will underpin the analysis in the following chapters.

REBEL GROUPS IN INTERNATIONAL LAW

This section explores international law as it relates to rebel groups. This background information is necessary as this book tries to link rebel group politics and international law. The discussion will open with a brief history on the international legal developments concerning rebel groups. The history will lead to the recent examples where rebel group leaders were indicted within the reach of international law, dovetailed with my observations on the central trends in the legal developments. Next, I will consider whether rebel groups are bound by international law, and whether they are aware of international law. The answer will be yes and yes. All these facts will move us forward in establishing the theory of rebel compliance in the subsequent chapter.

Brief History

Although the idea of military honor or mercy has been around for many centuries, the idea of regulating the terms of warfare with respect for humanity is a little more than a century old.[7] The first developments in international humanitarian law governing the conditions of war among nation-states did not come about until the late 1800s with the advent of the Hague Conventions. Before then, civilians bore the brunt of the violence in ancient and medieval wars, and nations of early modern times did not give serious thought to exercising restraint in warfare. During this period, however, Henri Dunant began pioneering standards of warfare after witnessing the events of the battle of Solferino. His efforts gave birth to the ICRC, an institution expressly purposed to aid in the development of international law related to the conduct of war.

Following the establishment of the ICRC, the international community installed a long list of legal instruments that attempted to codify a consensus among states, while ending a century-long experience of brutal conflicts. The Hague Conventions established the first regulations on the development and use of certain types of weaponry. In the wake of two world wars that revealed man's capacity for violence, particularly in the case of the use of chemical weapons, the Holocaust, and air bombings, world leaders negotiated and forged the four Geneva Conventions. These agreements outlined the essential elements of humane conduct in war, building today's present conception of humane warfare. Some of the most notable of these included the idea that civilians as non-combatants should be spared, that certain weapons cannot be used, and

[7] See Kinsella (2011) for helpful history of the idea of distinguishing civilians from combatants.

that the wounded and the prisoners of war should be treated humanely. The four Geneva Conventions laid out all these principles and crafted them as the core legal instruments for regulating warfare.

Decades later, the international community strengthened the Conventions by adopting the two Additional Protocols. These additions extended standards on the humane conduct of war to internal armed conflicts in response to the rising number of liberation movements and civil conflicts around the world in the 1960s and 1970s. This is particularly when rebel groups came to the forefront on the scene of international legal developments. Before the 1950s, rebel groups existed, but they were not in the realm of international law in a strict sense. Rebellions had existed for centuries as a challenge to existing authorities, but they were not governed by international rules or norms. The idea of considering rebel groups as subjects in international law appeared in *The Law of Nations* in 1758, a work by Emerich de Vattel, but the idea was not seriously considered until the 1960s and 1970s.

The parallel development of an international judicial authority and expanded legal coverage under international humanitarian law resulted from the tide of democratization and the rise of non-governmental organizations (NGOs) that spurred human rights movements around the world. This evolution in international humanitarian standards conferred specific rights to potential victims of abuse through a number of universal principles, such as the idea that torture cannot be tolerated as specified in the Convention against Torture (CAT), or the notion that children should be protected as detailed in the Convention on the Rights of the Child (CRC).

These developments repeatedly remind us that individuals, including individuals partaking in rebellion, *are* part of international law. Also, those developments highlight the connection between potential victims, or those most vulnerable to abuse, such as prisoners, women, children, and war victims, and thereby the relevancy of human rights law in conflict situations.[8] Fostered by norm entrepreneurs, these changing legal landscapes facing human rights and humanitarian matters have been characterized as "justice cascades" where the demand for "justice" ensured accountability for past crimes, which fostered global trend "cascades" reverberating from the international to the domestic arena, and vice versa.[9]

Recent Examples

The reach of international justice has included rebel group leaders on its indicted list, showing that they are no longer immune to the jurisdiction of international law. International justice has been done mostly in the case of government leaders, with examples being the trials of former Bosnian Serb leaders Radovan Karadžić and Ratko Mladić at the International Criminal

[8] Sivakumaran (2012). [9] Sikkink (2011).

Tribunal for Yugoslavia (ICTY) and that of Kang Kek Iew at the Special Tribunal for Cambodia.[10] However, recent examples show that rebel leaders cannot totally escape the force of international justice. The Special Court for Sierra Leone not only tried Charles Taylor for assisting RUF activities, but the Court also tried the leaders of the RUF for their war crimes and crimes against humanity.

The Rome Statute of 1998 provided another major development in the coverage of international humanitarian law concerning rebel groups. The Statute contains one of the most revolutionary ideas in modern legal thought: to expand criminal jurisdiction over high-level government officials who commit atrocities as well as rebel perpetrators. More importantly, the Statute established the ICC, a permanent institution with the authority to investigate and prosecute international crimes irrespective of the considerations of states parties. Unlike the implementation mechanisms existing under other human rights agreements, the ICC has the capacity to deliver direct enforcement.[11] It can investigate, try, and sentence government officials or rebel group leadership if an incident meets certain admissibility and jurisdictional requirements, although the Court must rely upon the cooperation of member states for capturing perpetrators.

As at December 2013, more than ten rebel group leaders faced the ICC under current investigations. The current and preliminary investigations altogether cover about fifteen rebel groups out of some 100 rebel groups in the world. The current cases were brought to the ICC either by state referral or on the prosecutor's own initiation and preliminary investigation, often launched by petitions from civil society. This means that not all rebel group leaders who are perpetrators in the world are going to be tried at the ICC. Only some rebel leaders that meet jurisdictional standards of the ICC (e.g., crimes committed after 2002) and that are not adequately tried at domestic courts (according to the complementarity principle) will be tried at the ICC.[12]

Out of the eight cases on the current ICC docket, five implicate rebel group leaders involved with the conflicts in the DRC, Sudan, Uganda, the CAR, and Mali.[13] Among the eleven cases currently undergoing preliminary examinations,[14] four involve members of active rebel groups operating in Afghanistan, Colombia, Georgia, and Nigeria. The ICC rendered its first decision on Thomas Lubanga, former leader of the Union of Congolese Patriots (UPC), in March 2012 for recruiting and using child soldiers in hostilities during the 2002 conflict in the DRC. This present line-up of ICC cases displays the reach of international justice as it expands into the dynamics of internal conflict. These instances

[10] For the discussion of the domestic and international trials of heads of state and their implications, see Sikkink (2011).

[11] Bassiouni (2012). [12] Schabas (2011).

[13] The situation in Kenya and the Ivory Coast concerned election violence, whereas Libya's situation resulted in warrants against three individuals from the ruling Qaddafi regime.

[14] The legal criteria include: (1) gravity of the situation; (2) admissibility; and (3) interests of justice.

TABLE 2.1 *ICC cases involving rebel groups**

On the docket		
State (situations and country in question)	**Non-state actors Indicted rebel group leaders**	**Status**
Democratic Republic of the Congo	UPC (Thomas Lubanga) FRPI (Germain Katanga) FNI (Ngudjolo Chui) CNDP (Bosco Ntaganda) FDLR (Callixte Mbarushimana)	Investigation Lubanga Decision (March 2012)
Uganda	LRA (Joseph Kony, Vincent Otti, Okot Odhiambo, Dominic Ongwen, Raska Lukwiya)	Investigation
Sudan	URF (Abu Garda) JEM (Abakaer Nourain) SLA-Unity (Jerbo Jamus)	Investigation
Central African Republic	MLC (Jean-Pierre Bemba Gombo)	Investigation
Kenya	None	Pre-trial
Côte d'Ivoire	None	Pre-trial
Libya	None	Pre-trial
Mali	Tuareg rebels	Pre-trial

Preliminary examinations		
State	**Non-state actors Armed groups under scrutiny**	**Under examination**
Afghanistan	Taliban and other insurgent groups	Under examination
Colombia	FARC, ELN, and paramilitary groups	Under examination
Comoros	None	Under examination
Georgia	South Ossetian forces	Under examination
Guinea	None	Under examination
Honduras	None	Under examination
Korea	None	Under examination
Nigeria	Boko Haram, MEND, other gangs and militias	Under examination
Iraq	None	Case dropped
Palestine	None	Case dropped
Venezuela	None	Case dropped

* The information in the table is valid as at December 2013.

Source: International Criminal Court.

of ICC cases show that rebel groups can no longer presume impunity for their actions under evolving prosecutorial pressures, and that rebel groups are exposed to the development of international law.

Trends

Several notable trends arose through the development of international standards and practices. The first trend is *legalization.* The world community responded to instances of brutality by thinking back on what should have been done, leading to ideas in legal texts with more detail and sophistication. This has not erased the historical tension between lofty ideas and brutal reality. Rather, it reflects the general notion that at the very least wars should be fought with restraint. Rebel groups are part of this legalization trend. Some groups have made commitments to international law by declaring their intentions to abide by existing humanitarian rules or by signing agreements with the government, the United Nations or NGOs. This commitment issue is further discussed in Chapter 4.

The second trend is *acceptance.* The ratification of humanitarian and human rights laws brought countries of all stripes together. The Geneva Convention now boasts 170 signatories among the world's 200 countries, and other human rights legal instruments, such as the CAT and CRC, have received consensus from more than the majority of world members with some variations. This near universal accord indicates that the normative environments for respecting humanitarian and human rights of today remains relatively strong compared with other historical periods. Rebel groups cannot escape this development in human rights. While states have the primary responsibilities as negotiators and signers of those treaties, rebels also have to pay attention to the development either to demand political, social, or economic rights from states, or to interact with outside actors for earning external political support in building a nation or creating its own political authority.

The third trend is the *inclusion of private actors* in international law. Traditionally, international law has long been a body of law regulated primarily by the interactions between sovereign nations or states. This is no longer the case. Non-state actors, such as rebel groups, multinational firms or international organizations, are very much in the picture of contemporary legal developments.[15] Especially in an era dominated by civil rather than international conflicts, rebel groups are now subject to the normative development of the international legal scene.

Are Rebel Groups Bound by International Law?

The question of whether rebel groups are bound by international law is relevant to the discussion of compliant rebels. If rebel groups are not bound, they have

[15] Clapham (2006).

nothing with which to comply and they would be free to roam outside the realm of international law. Rebel groups *are* bound by some precepts of international law. Rebel groups may not access the full rights and obligations nations enjoy as the core subjects of public international law. However, rebel groups do maintain some rights and obligations according to international humanitarian and human rights law.[16] As individuals under the international legal system, rebel group members are obliged to abide by the principles of distinction and should not kill innocent civilians. The Common Article 3 of the Geneva Conventions, as well as the Additional Protocol II, for instance, apply directly to rebel groups. At the intersection of human rights and humanitarian law, clear prohibitions exist and are binding on rebel groups, such as prohibitions on committing mass atrocities or violating human life and dignity.

The legal theories and empirical examples support the view that rebel groups are bound by international law.[17] Rebel groups that explicitly consent to international norms and standards are without a doubt bound by international law. When Nelson Mandela's African National Congress (ANC) publicly filed its consent to abide by the Geneva Conventions in 1983, the group showed clear intent to follow international rules by binding itself to the baseline norms. The Ejército de Liberación Nacional (ELN) in Colombia made a similar show of consent when signing the Gates of Heaven agreement with the Colombian Government and civil society, which secured the group's commitment and legal bindings as a result. In more recent cases, as when more than forty rebel groups signed the Deed of Commitment to eradicate the use of anti-personnel mines, or about a dozen rebel groups signed Action Plans with United Nations agencies, groups signal clear intent to be bound by international standards. The commitment issued by the NTC in Libya, in their fight against the Qaddafi regime, in August 2011, is also telling:

> Libya is a Party to all four 1949 Geneva Conventions and to both 1977 Additional Protocols. As such, we recognize that in the conduct of hostilities, we are bound by Common Article 3 to the four Geneva Conventions and to the provisions of Additional Protocol II Relating to the Protection of Victims of Non-International Armed Conflicts, as are the Qadhafi regime's forces.[18]

As the above examples show, legal commitments indicate the will and motivation to abide by global rules even if the rebel groups in question fail to express explicit consent to international agreements.

Even rebel groups without consent, however, carry obligations to abide by some humanitarian law. Since one key source of international law is customary international law – often established by *opinion juris* and persistent practice, rebel groups without consent are bound by international law in a customary sense. The prevention of genocide, now accepted as a global norm, for example,

[16] Alston and Goodman (2012).
[17] For legal theories of rebel groups and international law binding-ness, see Sivakumaran (2012).
[18] National Transitional Council (2011).

clearly applies to rebel groups. The nature of international law-making restricts the participatory rights of rebel groups. Rebel groups do not take part in negotiating international laws and do not have institutional means to ratify the laws. Their obligations derive from being under the authority of a state party or by issue of the laws being natural laws applicable to all subjects of international politics.

The rights of rebel groups are less clear than the obligations imposed on them. The obligations of rebel groups are more clearly stated than the rights of rebel groups in international law. For example, to what extent human rights law applies to rebel groups' obligations is subject to debate. National governments carry many of these obligations, such as the obligation to respect the pursuit of political and civil rights, or the responsibility to pay due diligence to promote economic and social rights. Whether rebel groups enjoy these rights is less clear in international law.[19]

The force of international law binding-ness on rebel groups is a weaker one than domestic legal binding-ness. The binding-ness under international law differs from that under domestic legal systems. This difference stems from the nature of international politics and the sovereign states that compose it. Binding-ness in international law is looser than in the domestic context due to the absence of a strong enforcement system. In domestic legal arenas, enforcement by police and courts provides clear regulations. However, in the international legal arena, there is no world police or world court with authority equivalent to that of domestic enforcement bodies. This looser notion of binding-ness in international law creates a complex political problem as it relates to rebel groups.

The weak binding-ness of international law might eclipse the class of rebel groups that persistently object to international humanitarian law. These "persistent objectors" often defy existing norms and continue to wage their rebellions without exercising any restraints. This declared refusal to comply will be substantively different from the practical failure to comply, as the former upsets the normative order while the latter necessarily does not.[20] Typically, rebels of this nature view international law as a purely Western institution, and their fundamental rejection of the law's values complicate any effort to induce compliance.[21]

The open defiance situation is especially acute in the case of rebel groups operating under some strands of Islamic law. Although Islamic law and international humanitarian law share some conceptions of civilian protection, some variants of Islamic law still differ on the interpretation of what constitutes enemies, the role of children, or the enforcement of justice.[22] Consider the remark by Dokku Umarov, the president of the Chechen independence

[19] Clapham (2010); Dabone (2011).

[20] See Scott (1990: 203–206), on this distinction between a "practical failure to comply" and a "declared refusal to comply" in the context of the resistance by the politically weak.

[21] Bangerter (2011). [22] Modirzadeh (2006); Van Engeland-Nourai (2010); Bassiouni (2013).

movement, in 2007: "We, Mujahideen, reject any laws, rules and establishments that do not come from Allah ... I reject all *kafir* [infidel] laws established in the world."[23]

In the case of other objecting groups, rebels may conclude that abiding by international standards may be against their cause or jeopardize their strategic advantage. In these situations, binding-ness under international law will not be enough to induce compliance, even when these rebels will be held responsible for their transgressions under the existing international criminal justice system.

Do Rebel Groups Know International Law?

The answer to the question of whether rebel groups are aware of international law serves as an important basis for the discussion of compliant rebels. If the members of rebel groups consciously acquire knowledge of international law and strive to abide by its rules, then that should later serve as strong evidence that international law reaches rebel groups for the purpose of compliance. Although knowledge and awareness are not sufficient for the condition of compliance, they can be the first step.

Many rebel groups are aware of the international norms, though they may not have perfect knowledge of how the law operates. Some groups may be more aware of their obligations and consequences than others. The groups with political wings may be more attuned to international political developments than groups with military wings only. Also, the groups with political principals or sponsors that promote international norms are likely to know their obligations and think through the consequences of violating them. It is difficult to gauge a rebel group's understanding of international law with exactness, but several indicators may help to shed some light on the issue.

Formal commitments made by rebel groups provide one observable indicator. From the perspective of rebel groups, there are several ways to commit. The first, is to participate in international negotiations as observers. The second, is to publicly express a willingness to abide by international law. The African National Union, for instance, committed itself to the Geneva Conventions by depositing its intentions at the ICRC.[24] A third way is to make agreements with international organizations, such as the United Nations bodies, or with NGOs. As one of the NGOs working on humanitarian issues, the Geneva Call signed Deeds of commitment with rebel groups with the goal of improving compliance. This pattern of commitment is described further in Chapter 4.

Another indicator of rebel knowledge of international law is the presence of a political wing in a rebel group. Well-structured political wings of rebel groups usually include foreign affairs departments, and it is the political wing that

[23] Re-quoted from Bangerter (2011: 381). The remark is translation from the official version of Amir Dokka's statement of declaration of the Caucasian Emirate, November 22, 2007.

[24] Tambo (1980).

usually promotes political goals rather than emphasizing military means only. Political wings may be more sensitive to the political consequences of military campaigns often directed by the military armed wing of rebel groups. Given this institutional structure, it is reasonable to think that the political wing or affiliation with a political party is more likely to be aware of political surroundings internationally. The KNU in Myanmar provides an example of this, as the group's foreign department frequently visited and engaged the United Nations in an effort to connect with the outside world.[25] Although the group's driving motivation has been its desire to disclose suppression of political activity by the Myanmar junta government, the KNU's efforts highlight the fact that groups with international ties are willing to understand and follow procedure dictated by international standards.

Interestingly, the use of social networks has become a strong indicator of a rebel group's familiarity with international norms. While working on this book, I began following some rebel group leaders on social media websites such as Facebook and Twitter. I noticed that the M23 representative of the DRC, Jeannot Ruzima, follows Paul Kagame (Rwandan president, suspected former supporter of M23), Barack Obama, as well as the UN Human Rights Office and the ICC. Al-Shabaab from Somalia has used Facebook, prompting a heated debate on whether social media sites should permit the type of propaganda that the group actively propagated. These examples tell us that politically savvy and resourceful rebel groups see an advantage in reaching out to an international audience, and that they are "aware" that their behaviors are under the radar of international organizations and, more broadly, the international community.

In some cases, rebel groups may develop an understanding of international law through indirect channels or internalize some universal norms regarding the laws of war. Norms that have reached customary status, like the humane treatment of civilians, typically span across all cultures. In Islamic law, for instance, women and children must be spared from intentional acts of violence during times of hostilities. This standard has been cited under international humanitarian law as well as most other domestic systems of law. In international humanitarian law, as well, civilians are protected as long as they do not participate in war efforts. The distinction between participation and non-participation in war efforts can be elusive, as providing food could sometimes be considered war efforts. In civil wars, amid the fight over control and buying loyalty, rebels and governments might not cast the net wide enough to protect every civilian. For these type of cases where the universal norm is also the local norm, a rebel group may comply without any prior consideration of international rules. Without explicit knowledge or recognition of international law, rebel compliance *is* possible.

[25] The official website of the KNU once had a photo of its delegations visiting the United Nations, demonstrating the rebel group's motivation and reach to conduct foreign affairs. The photo is on file with the author.

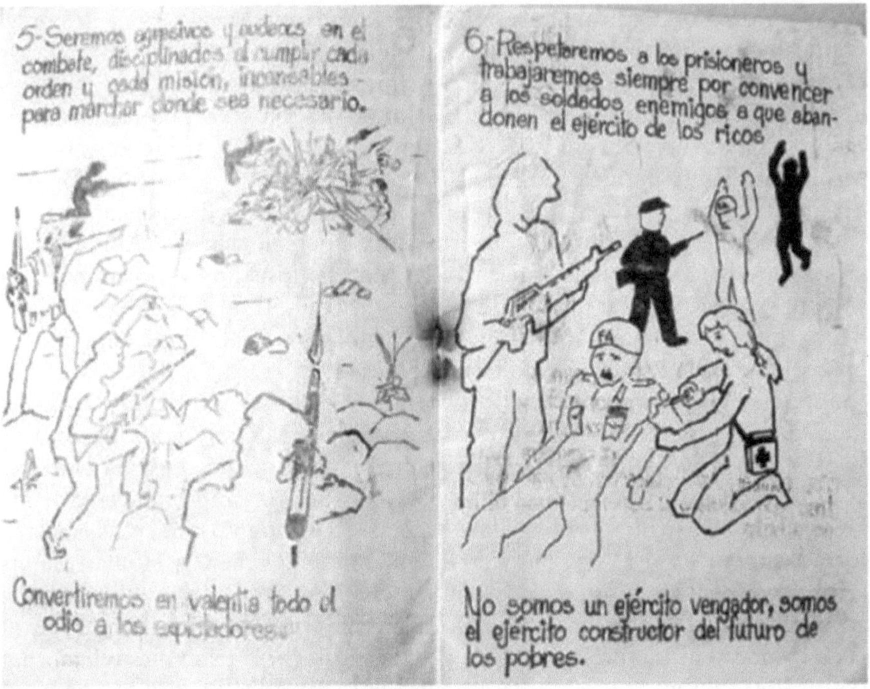

Pages of the FMLN code of conduct from 1985. © Museo de la Palabra y la Imagen, San Salvador

FIGURE 2.2 FMLN's internal code of conduct

Similarly, some rebel groups may maintain an internal code of conduct consistent with humanitarian law, which can be an additional indicator of rebel knowledge of international law. The FMLN in El Salvador is one such example, as illustrated in the group's pamphlet to visualize their internal code of conduct and principles, pictured in Figure 2.2. On this page of the pamphlet issued to the rank-and-file FMLN fighters, the rebel soldiers are encouraged to respect prisoners and to comply with the rules of combat not to "behave like bandits but to build the future of the poor."

Again, knowledge will not convince rebel groups to comply directly. In some cases, knowing is one thing and practice is another. In other cases, compliance might occur implicitly with only tacit knowledge of international law. Some rebel groups might comply not fully realizing that they are doing so. However, the fact that some rebel groups know and commit to international rules serves as a basis that there is awareness among rebel ranks and that some groups recognize the rules. This sets one of the essential background foundations for compliant rebels.

SUMMING UP

This chapter is written as a bridge between the previous introductory chapter and the following theory chapter. We have confirmed that rebel groups are violent *by definition*, as they pursue their political agendas and engage in direct hostilities with the government. They are sometimes labeled as terrorists and engage in group decisions whether to comply with international law or not. We have also discovered that some rebel groups have the capacity to know international law and try to know international standards and sometimes conform to them by making commitments.

The discussion of developments in international law demonstrates two points. One is that rebel groups are part of international law. Not only national governments, but also rebel groups are subject to international law as they are part of the norm development. The second point is about the nature of the norm growth. Normative growth in international law regarding rebel groups originated from developments in international politics, the increasing respect for human rights and humanitarian causes on the global scale. It has been accompanied by the active role of international actors that worked as norm entrepreneurs worldwide. In short, rebel groups cannot escape the reality and development of international law and politics, and, as the subsequent discussions will show, some rebel groups will feel the pressure while others will not.

The violent nature of rebellion begs the question of *why* rebel groups may commit and eventually comply with international law. Chapter 3 delves into this question of the core calculation behind compliance decisions in a more systematic fashion, building arguments over a series of assumptions, our prior understanding of rebel groups, and the realities of warfare.

3

A Theory of Rebel Compliance

The previous chapters have set the background for understanding why a rebel group complies with international norms. Building on that background information, this chapter develops an explanation of how rebel groups' political motivations affect their compliance behaviors. The theoretical development will require an in-depth examination of the nature of rebellion and the political environment for rebel movements. The inquiry will demand attention to rebel groups' awareness of international standards and norms, along with the matter of how and through which channels of influence rebel groups change their behavior from non-compliance to compliance.

I propose a *legitimacy-based theory of rebel compliance*. The main argument of this book is that rebel groups' compliance with international law can be best understood by looking at their motivation for political legitimacy. More specifically, rebel groups with legitimacy-seeking characteristics are more likely to comply with international norms than their legitimacy-indifferent counterparts. Legitimacy-seeking rebel groups usually have political constituencies toward whom rebel movements seek recognition and support. If those domestic and international constituencies have leverage and influence over rebel groups, and if they have human rights or humanitarian concerns, rebel sponsors will influence rebel groups' decisions about how to wage their armed struggles.

In contrast, legitimacy-indifferent groups will have little to no political motivation to appeal to domestic and international constituencies. They may be less interested in building a social base among domestic constituencies or establishing networks with external sponsors that care about human rights. With little interest and need for such domestic and international legitimacy, legitimacy-indifferent rebel groups are more likely to take the route of non-compliance. At its core, the theory presents a *rebel constituency mechanism* where the nature, preference, and leverage of rebel constituencies can influence how rebels behave. Specific channels and the magnitude of influence will be discussed throughout this chapter.

Military and strategic incentives always complicate rebel groups' calculus of compliance. For instance, a tactical need may occasionally lead a legitimacy-seeking group to disregard and violate international norms. However, over the longer term, legitimacy-seeking groups are those for whom the perceived benefits of gaining political legitimacy outweigh occasional military reasons for violating international rules. In this sense, compliance becomes part of a group's overall military strategy, and conforming to international rules becomes a tactic of this strategy. Gains from this "strategic legitimacy" can sometimes help rebel groups win the conflict. The legitimacy is strategically formed because rebel groups develop their sense of legitimacy in an environment where they have to create appeals to their rebellion. Exercising restraint *becomes* strategic because rebel groups make those calculations in the light of their goals to win the civil war.

In what follows, I unpack and explicate the relationship between rebels' legitimacy-seeking motivations and their compliance behaviors. My theoretical analysis of rebel compliance starts with some premises about the nature of civil wars and the motivations of rebel groups to incite rebellion. I use these premises as building blocks to construct my explanation for rebel compliance. Then, I examine the main decision calculus of rebel groups in deciding on compliance and non-compliance in the light of rebel groups' political strategies and social environments. Here, I explain why the understanding of legitimacy is essential in discerning rebel groups' compliance behaviors. In particular, I discuss what legitimacy means to rebels and what particular forms of legitimacy are crucial to their political goals. In this discussion, military incentives of rebel groups and the response of opposing governments will figure large in the equation. The analytic framework on the rebel decision calculus will be followed by the delineation of causal mechanisms leading from non-compliance to compliance (or vice versa). Lastly, I consider alternative explanations, demonstrating the value of my strategic legitimacy theory in relation to other potentially competing explanations.

PREMISES

I start my theory of rebel compliance with five premises.[1] The premises include assumptions about: (1) the political nature of civil conflicts; (2) the organizational goals of rebel groups; (3) the economic structure of rebellion; (4) the rebel groups' key audiences; and (5) the costliness of rebel compliance. With these assumptions about rebel movements and their political environments, we will be able to proceed to the in-depth analysis of rebel behaviors.

[1] Readers will find an analogous summary in the Introduction under the section titled "Assumptions."

Premise (1): Political Nature of Civil Conflicts

Every rebellion starts with a political reason – whether to subvert the government or to capture a part of territory. What rebels want may differ depending on the causes and sources of their motivations for rebellion. Depending on their social, political, and historical circumstances, rebel groups' demands may range from land reform, to economic development, to wealth-sharing, to power-sharing, or to regime change.[2]

My focus on the political aspects of civil conflicts may be apparent to some people. But I want to note that many explanations for civil wars come from the assumption that military aspects are dominant. The common assumption in this literature is that civil wars are generated by opposition "armed" movements with "military" confrontations with the government.[3] Relaxing the assumption that civil conflicts are primarily armed military struggles, my assumption emphasizes "political" aspects of civil conflicts. Rebel groups want not only military victories against governments, but want to satisfy their political demands as well. If we start with the assumption that civil conflicts are predominantly military confrontations, then we will ignore crucial aspects of many rebel movements that are politically motivated with differing degrees and spectrums.[4]

In fact, many studies of civil war recognize these political aspects of rebellion. In his famous treatise *Why Men Rebel*, Ted Gurr identified three political sources of rebellion: popular discontent, utility of collective action, and government reactions. Recently, Cederman *et al.* convincingly showed how political and economic inequalities can ignite ethnic civil conflicts.[5] This recognition of the *political* motivations of rebel groups is the starting point of my theory. Resources, economics, and military victories will certainly matter to rebel groups, but it is ultimately the political goal that compels them to comply with international law.

The assumption about rebel motivations taps into the nature of civil conflicts. Internal fighting between existing government and rebel groups arises from political disagreements over territory, ideology, political autonomy, or

[2] Demands for infrastructure improvements are not rare, either. Education, health, potable water, roads, electricity, and telecommunication facilities are all often on the rebels' development agenda. Sometimes, big demands such as changes to the national constitution involve basic questions of political and social order. These are the list of things that rebels want and desire in civil conflicts. See the discussion in Hazen (2013) on rebel motivations in various cases.

[3] Take the definition of civil wars in Doyle and Sambanis (2006). A civil war is an armed conflict that meets the following criteria: (a) the war has caused more than 1,000 battle deaths; (b) the war represented a challenge to the sovereignty of an internationally recognized state; (c) the war occurred within the recognized boundary of that state; (d) the war involved the state as one of the principal combatants; and (e) the rebels were able to mount an organized military opposition to the state and to inflict significant casualties on the state. These criteria mainly focus on military aspects of civil wars, and do not necessarily consider political motivations of rebellion.

[4] On the emphasis on the political and social aspects of insurgencies, see Tarrow (2007).

[5] Cederman *et al.* (2013).

some other issue. The assumption about rebel objectives does not mean that all rebel groups seek political goals. They will do so in differing degrees with diverse political agendas. Some groups might have an intrinsic motivation to self-profiteer, and these rebel leaderships might themselves degenerate into little more than criminal gangs. However, many rebellions start with a political grievance about acquiring independence with new territory, achieving more autonomy, eliminating discriminations, or changing policies and regimes. This focus on political goals of rebellion is the starting point of my inquiry into rebel compliance.

Premise (2): Rebel Groups as Organizations

In building the theory of rebel compliance, I assume that rebel groups have the organizational goal to survive in order to attain their political demands. Despite the different political demands, rebel groups share a common endeavor to maintain their organization in order to continue their rebellion. This assumption about organizational goals is important in developing explanations for rebel compliance. For one, organizational decisions are made at the group level within the constraints of rebel goals and motivations. Without this assumption of considering rebel groups as one decision entity, the analysis will have to incorporate individual-level explanations such as psychological factors or leadership uniqueness.

To simplify the analysis, this book assumes away the individual-level differences within a rebel organization and analyzes a rebel group *as if it is one entity with one decision point.*[6] This, however, does not mean that I ignore the organizational structure, leadership fissures, or the problem of command-and-control responsibilities of rebel groups. I consider how these organizational factors lead to more or less rebel compliance as an additional influence in my case studies or statistical analysis. The assumption about the rebel group as a unit of analysis is just for analytical convenience and for abstracting the theory, not to ignore the subtleties that can occur within rebel organizations.

Premise (3): Economic Structure of Rebellion

Mobilization is a key aspect of any political process, especially in the context of social movements and protests.[7] Rebel movements are no exception. Mobilization, recruitment, and garnering support are crucial for any rebel movements in furthering their political and military goals. One of the assumptions that I employ in developing the explanation about rebel

[6] As Weinstein (2006) convincingly showed, individual motivations for killing are different from group-level causes. In a group, leadership gives orders, but sometimes soldiers act on their own impulse. One key difference between group-level violence and individual-level violence is its intention, planning, and systematicity.

[7] Tilly (1978).

compliance is that the composition of rebel resources matters in how rebel groups wage their wars. The economic structure will also potentially affect how rebels behave with respect to international law compliance. The attention to rebel resources has roots in civil war studies, such as the works by Paul Collier or Jeremy Weinstein.[8] Following their observations, one of my assumptions is that economic endowment is one of the important aspects of rebellion, along with the political motivations of rebel groups. Legitimacy-seeking motivation is intrinsically linked to the search for material resources and support.

The primary funding sources and funders usually come from three places: the civilian population, natural resources, and external sponsorship. Besides the three funding sources, rebel groups can muster cash and arms from additional sources. Various kinds of transnational support are available for rebels' funding stream, such as support from religious organizations, NGOs, or terrorist networks. Some groups engage in criminal activities such as piracy or kidnapping for ransom. Other groups can also haphazardly capture arms from fighting with the government. Rebel groups often mix and match the wide range of resources to form their own financial "portfolio" to support their armed movements.

Recognizing the respective role of resources and methods of mobilization is important as they have consequences for rebel motivation and eventual compliance with international law. For example, resource-based groups would lack established relations with civilians, which will have consequences for the treatment of civilians. Those groups will have less regard for civilian life than, say, groups that rely on civilian support. The structure of the support and rebel groups' financial portfolios have important implications for legitimacy-building by rebels. The nature of internal and external sponsors of rebellion will also determine political pressures on rebels. I turn to this discussion next.

Premise (4): Rebels' Social Structure

The fourth premise of the strategic legitimacy theory is that rebel groups establish and manage political and social interactions with key stakeholders. On the domestic level, these stakeholders include the civilian population, which rebels rely upon to fill their ranks or to procure logistical and food support. Often, this population has ethnic or family ties with the rebel soldiers themselves. However, more importantly, the civilian population constitutes the majority of the victims of rebel violence.

On the international level, the actors relevant to rebellion include potential sponsors of rebellion, such as foreign country leaders or diaspora populations.

[8] Collier and Hoeffler (2000); Weinstein (2006). These scholars focused on economic resources and recruitment by establishing the distinction between "greedy" and "grievance" rebels, or between "resource-rich" and "resource-poor" rebels. This is not to say that Collier and Weinstein ignore political aspects, but to say that their emphasis is on the economic roots of rebellion.

Rebel groups conduct diplomacy to further their goals vis-à-vis these potential funders, or to extract resources from diaspora populations. Human rights and humanitarian workers in conflict zones also play an increasingly active role in interacting with rebel groups. Human rights groups often report human rights violations committed by warring parties, while humanitarian organizations primarily distribute humanitarian aid to rebel-controlled zones. With these respective roles, they are part of the international social structure of contemporary rebels.

This assumption about rebels' embeddedness in social and political structures is ignored in the studies that focus on military aspects of civil conflicts. However, it is an important element in building the theoretical connection between legitimacy and compliance. Legitimacy cannot exist without audiences that can perceive and evaluate the right to rule and the viability of a rebel political entity. In this sense, this assumption is at the core of a legitimacy theory that will connect rebel audiences to their impacts on rebels' compliance behaviors.

Premise (5): Costliness of Rebel Compliance

The fifth and final premise in developing explanations for rebel compliance is that compliance is costly for rebel groups. If compliance is not costly, then rebel compliance will no longer be a puzzle. Compliance with international law generally places a premium on exercising restraint. Civil conflicts are asymmetric in nature where governments have more military and political power than rebel groups. In this environment, rebel groups may have a strategic incentive not to exhibit restraint. A willingness to disregard international law may be one of the few advantages that the rebels have over the government. It is with this last premise that I move to the analysis of why some rebel groups might decide to comply despite the costliness of compliance.

CALCULUS OF REBEL COMPLIANCE

How do rebel groups make calculations about whether to comply or not? With the five premises outlined above, I sketch the rebels' compliance calculus in this section. In developing a theory of rebel compliance, I examine the decision where rebels seek political survival within a strategic political environment involving the opposing government and potential compliance constituencies. At the core of my following analysis, rebel groups will weigh the benefits and costs of compliance given their goal of insurgency within the constraints of their military means and political contexts.

In my discussion of rebel compliance, interests, interactions, and institutions together affect the behavior of a rebel entity. Rebel interests in seeking legitimacy are the centerpiece of my argument. The interest component will be shaped by the rebel interactions with the opposing government and relevant domestic and international constituencies. Institutions will also play a critical role in linking legitimacy and compliance, as the political interests and interactions are sometimes constrained or conditioned by institutional settings. In particular, the nature and structure of rebel organizations and the political institutions of the opposing governments play crucial roles in shaping compliant rebels.

With this analytical framework in mind, I now explicate the incentives and disincentives of compliance and explain how the legitimacy factor fits into the picture of rebel compliance.[9] I will start the discussion as to why incentives to violate are strong in civil conflicts, and discuss various reasons for rebel non-compliance. This will set our initial expectations about the difficulty of complying with international rules. Then, I will examine rebels' decision calculus, emphasizing the role of legitimacy in inducing compliance.

Incentives to Violate

Incentives to violate the laws of war are *strong* in civil conflicts. To start, rebel groups take up arms believing that peaceful, lawful solutions are not on the negotiation table. As long as there are no constraining factors, rebel groups are likely to embrace whatever military tools and resources they can get their hands on. The fact that they usually engage in asymmetric warfare, facing a much better armed opponent, makes them all the more likely to use unconventional means and indiscriminate methods of warfare. Also recall that rebels usually wage their wars within their own territory. Unlike foreign forces that can attack and retreat, rebels have to find ways to interact with civilians, and it is in the course of these interactions that violations can occur. Most importantly, rebels fight governments that often fight back viciously against insurgencies that challenge their own regime survival. Governments may engage in various brutal tactics, including starving civilians who allegedly support the rebels.[10] Consequently, rebels operating in those areas often adopt guerrilla tactics with the aim of retaliating against government sympathizers. In these and so many other ways, rebels' military needs put them in a predicament where violations of international norms may seem tactically necessary.

A large part of the incentives for rebel groups' behavior is driven by military, tactical, and strategic considerations. By using child soldiers, rebels can overcome troop shortages.[11] By killing civilians, rebels can demonstrate their military capacity and resolve with a "show of force."[12] Rebel groups lose access to these tactical military advantages when they comply with international standards. These forgone military and tactical benefits will be the main costs

[9] For the wealth of examples and the introductory and comprehensive analysis on the reasons for compliance and non-compliance of rebel groups, see Bangerter (2011). In contrast to his account, my account revolves around the legitimacy–compliance linkage, the core of my theory.

[10] Valentino *et al.* (2006). [11] Singer (2006). [12] Salehyan *et al.* (2014).

and sacrifices of compliant rebels. In some cases, if rebels comply with international rules, they may lose out on an opportunity to retaliate against an opposing government's military actions. Showing restraint can be especially difficult during government military offensives, which may prompt the incentives for reprisal.

These costs of compliance are high for certain types of rebel groups. Consider rebel groups that greatly value the demonstration of power by imposing terror. The RUF in Sierra Leone purposefully resorted to brutal amputations in order to attract foreign attention for their lethality. One RUF soldier told his story as a witness in the Special Court of Sierra Leone: "When we started cutting hands, hardly a day BBC would not talk about us."[13] For these types of group, giving up extreme violence will be costly for their military operation, and under these circumstances it is an easy choice for them to mistreat civilians for the purpose of "demonstrating" their power.

Also consider rebel groups with extreme ideologies that do not share the beliefs underlying international rules. The international conception of civilians includes any non-combatant who does not actively participate in the warfare. Jihadism, on the other hand, has a broad conception of enemies, including civilians with different religions. Whether civilians actively participate in the effort does not matter. Whatever different religion or ideology civilians have, those individuals are regarded as enemies.[14]

The commonality of these two types of rebel group is that they have little regard for political legitimacy vis-à-vis their potential constituencies. The groups' authority comes from showcasing military means and ideological doctrines, not from the approval of respective citizens in rebel-held territory or from the international community. For this class of rebels, violating international rules helps them to advance their short-term goals of increasing international coverage or promoting their ideological agenda.

Training and vetting may be another cost of compliance that increases the incentive to violate. Groups with undisciplined soldiers will generate more violations than groups with careful training and tight discipline. However, enforcing discipline requires effort and doing so may be costly for rebel groups operating within very limited resources. Legitimacy-seeking groups may be willing to bear the cost of discipline. Groups such as the FMLN in El Salvador had an internal code of conduct covering humane treatment of enemy soldiers and refraining from killing innocent civilians. These efforts were generated in the political context of the close rebel–community relations that the FMLN was able to build up during its armed struggle.[15] It is also notable that even notorious groups such as the RUF had some level of discipline in the areas they controlled in order to buy the loyalty of civilians, as noted by the Special Court of the Sierra Leone.[16] These examples illustrate that rebel groups

[13] Sierra Leone Truth and Reconciliation Commission (2004: app. 5, p. 17, para. 91).
[14] Geneva Academy (2013). [15] Wood (2003). [16] Bangerter (2011: 363).

often make efforts to discipline their soldiers once they seek legitimacy in the zones that they control.

Facing a variety of incentives to violate and ignore international law, military and tactical calculations will be at the front and center of rebel groups' thinking. Rebel ideology and organizational structures will condition these decisions too. The next question, then, is whether rebel groups have *any* incentives to tip the decision to comply, rather than violate international law.

Incentives to Comply

Incentives to comply with international humanitarian and human rights standards are generally *weak*. When rebels fight governments in asymmetric power situations, rebels may not care much about international rules. Their priorities will be to win the battles against government forces first. Despite there being little incentive to comply, my legitimacy-based theory of rebel compliance suggests the possibility that some rebels do comply. The rise of such compliant rebels depends on the expected benefits from compliance. Rebels may secure certain political benefits by complying with international law. The conferred benefits depend on the group's political audience. With the presence of an international community particularly concerned about upholding international law, compliance may contribute to the making of rebels' authority to rule. For instance, foreign state sponsors that can sway rebels' decisions about how they wage war might demand that rebels exhibit behaviors in conformity to international standards. Transnational supporters, like NGOs, United Nations agencies, and other international actors, may have some influence over a rebel movement by prompting behavioral changes on the part of rebels.

The expected gains from compliance can be either material or non-material. In some instances, material support in the form of arms, logistics, and money can also tip the military balance in the rebels' favor. Political support, such as receiving official recognition, can help rebels to achieve their ultimate goal of governing part or all of their country, or of achieving independence from the central government. Foreign support focused on humanitarian issues may also substantially bolster a rebel group's cause. Such engagement can lead to the involvement of international actors in the peace processes and give rebel groups resources while bargaining with the government.[17]

Take the example of the NTC, which fought against the Qaddafi regime in the Libyan civil war of 2011. It was no coincidence that the NTC announced their commitment to international law, including their willingness to express their "adherence to the principles of international humanitarian law, minimize the harm to the Libyan people" on August 21, 2011.[18] The announcement came right before the UN General Assembly decided to seat the NTC as the country's

[17] Nilsson (2012). [18] Sivakumaran (2011: 8).

representative at the United Nations on September 16, 2011, with 114 member states in favor and seventeen opposed.[19] Examining the timing, we can interpret the move as the NTC's signal of compliance in expectation of gaining international recognition. Note, however, that the NTC's human rights record was not clean. Some factions of the NTC did not exhibit full compliance, committing some human rights violations such as using torture during the fight in 2011.[20] However, it is important to note the potential strategic calculation the NTC made: the group might have expected benefits from gaining international recognition, and they knew that one of the strategic moves was to adhere to international law.

At times, compliance with international law can help rebels to garner voluntary civilian support. With civilian support, rebels may gain access to logistical knowledge that may help them foil government attacks or mount a successful offensive campaign. With the help of international backers that are concerned with development or humanitarian issues, rebels can get closer to domestic legitimacy, demonstrating that they have the credentials to govern with international resources while governments are not able to provide adequate public services such as hospitals or education. Rebels can use coercion to maintain civilian support. But this coercive strategy is usually shown among rebels who are dependent on international backers who do not care about civilian treatment, or groups that do not have deep social relations with civilians. This absence of care in international legitimacy or domestic legitimacy can lead to non-compliance with international standards.

In some cases, the incentives to comply grow as the option for non-compliance becomes unpalatable. Rebels sometimes have to pay for their bad actions. They have to take into account the risks associated with committing violations, such as the possibility of sanctions, prosecutions, military action, and shaming. The international community, through the United Nations sanctions committee, for example, imposes some cost for non-compliance. The M23, a rebel group in the DRC, faced UN sanctions and its three key leaders were subject to travel bans and had all their assets frozen. Additionally, the Rome Statute covering war crimes and crimes against humanity grants the ICC the authority to place rebels on trial for violations of international law. The ICC's first decision on Thomas Lubanga, the leader of the UCP in DRC, in 2012, illustrates this possibility of prosecution. As critics note, however, such punishment is rare and the costs facing rebels under sanctions are usually far from severe.

In general, the cost rebels pay through sanctions and prosecution may appear small. In the absence of any military action, travel bans may not spur rebels to alter their behavior, and imprisonment at the ICC in the Netherlands may actually look appealing when compared with running the risk of being killed

[19] For the complexity of legal issues regarding the NTC's recognition, see Talmon (2011). Also see UN General Assembly (2011a).

[20] Amnesty International (2011).

by an opposing government or rival rebel faction. Rebels may be somewhat weakened by humanitarian interventions. But as the case of Rwanda and Yugoslavia attest, those interventions are in many cases unpopular due to the usual norm of respecting sovereignty of nations. Shaming rebel groups by classifying them as terrorist outfits may also impose some cost. Rebel groups are severely limited in their operations after being placed on several international terrorist lists. But the foreign terrorist organizations listed by the United States and the European Union do not cover all delinquent rebel groups, as those listings are the results of national interests.[21] Fear of international repercussions therefore plays some role in a rebel group's decision calculus regarding compliance behavior, but a limited one given the low probability of punishment and generally low costs associated with international action.

The real cost rebel groups should fear will have less to do with the threat of punishment and more to do with the loss of support for their rebellion. Again, this concern is related to the extent to which rebel groups seek legitimacy. Consider the example of the following two groups: the Mujahadeen-e-Khalq (MEK), which has been fighting against the Iranian regime since 1965; and the Liberation Tigers of Tamil Eelam (LTTE), which fought against the Sri Lanka regime from 1983 until 2009. The terrorist designation by the United States cost the MEK critical Western support in fighting the Iranian regime, which was sorely needed, especially for a movement that was operating from outside Iranian territory.[22] The LTTE lost the cash flow of the Tamil diaspora populations abroad, who had thought they were funding a rightful movement not a terrorist outfit.[23] The loss of diaspora support was damaging for the LTTE, and the group had to face decisions about whether to redirect its means of war. Coupled with legitimacy concerns, these costs are real to rebel survival, as they eventually affect the group's ability to fight.

The incentives to comply become stronger when additional structural conditions are met. When capacity helps rebels to enforce the rules consistent with international law, compliance will be easier. The strong command-and-control structure of a rebel organization, coupled with principles aligned with international rules, will be an effective compliance multiplier. Also, when rebel ideologies are in line with international standards without too much discrepancy to resolve, the incentives to comply will be strong. These favorable conditions will be augmented by the rebel groups' legitimacy-seeking characteristics embedded in their own society as well as in the international community.

In summary, the incentive to comply increases in instances where rebel groups seek international and domestic legitimacy in the eyes of political audiences that can support their rebellion. A rebel group that hopes to gain human rights-conscious external support in the future will generally want to

[21] See the analysis by Beck and Miner (2013) for the complexities surrounding the terrorist listings.
[22] MEK was delisted in 2012. See Masters (2014). [23] Fair (2007).

avoid violating international standards in the present. The rebel movement embedded in its society is more likely to have legitimacy at the outset and continue to seek the domestic legitimacy. These incentives to comply link back to the strategic considerations discussed earlier: rebel groups will try to achieve their goals by buying legitimacy through compliance.

Balancing Incentives

How do rebel groups balance two potentially competing incentives: the incentive to comply and the incentive to violate? The possible trade-off between legitimacy gain and military advantage echoes a classical and fundamental tension in international humanitarian law: the tension between compliance and military necessity. By complying, rebels can gain legitimacy, but at the same time they may risk losing a military and tactical advantage. Conversely, by privileging military and tactical considerations, rebels may lose legitimacy, especially if they violate rules and norms. In balancing the two, rebels are likely to choose compliance when the expected legitimacy gain exceeds the expected military advantage.

Note that I use "possible" trade-off rather than "absolute" trade-off between legitimacy gain and military advantage. Rebels do not necessarily lose military advantage by seeking legitimacy. Seeking legitimacy is also a strategic pursuit that can confer military advantage as well in the long term. When people talk about strategic advantage in civil conflicts, they usually have military and tactical advantages in mind, but, in fact, seeking legitimacy can be part of the long-term strategy portfolio of rebel groups. Seeking legitimacy and acting strategically are not at all at odds. To some rebel groups, seeking legitimacy *is* a strategy.

For those groups choosing to prioritize the pursuit of legitimacy, the loss of tactical military advantage is not absolute, and compliance is not completely incompatible with strategic military advantage. In fact, some legitimacy-seeking rebel groups abide by international law and at the same time can gain strategic advantage. Rebels might have to relinquish some tactical options, but in the long run, their overall military and political strategy may benefit from abiding by the law.

One example involves the Movement of Democratic Forces of Casamance (MFDC), a separatist movement to gain the Casamance region in Senegal. Once the group realized that the anti-personnel mines they used had harmed more of their core supporters among the civilian population than government soldiers, they took significant steps to clear anti-personnel landmines in cooperation with external actors.[24] In the MFDC's case, compliance made both strategic and political sense. The mine ban did curtail their ability to fight the government, but the strategic benefit was that they won valuable support from the local

[24] Email interview with Carole Frampton, Geneva Call, April 19, 2013.

populace. In terms of training and vetting as well, the added benefit of internal discipline may make rebel soldiers better fighters against the government, and the resulting increase in compliance may be beneficial in terms of increasing voluntary logistical support from civilians. Because of the paramount importance of sustaining rebellion and ensuring survival, rebels may comply even at the cost of losing some military advantage, especially when breaking laws risks making them outcasts without any support.

Rebels will balance the two competing incentives throughout their life cycle. The potential trade-off between legitimacy gain and military advantage lies at the center of explaining rebel groups' persistent compliance as well as switchover compliance. *Persistent compliance*, a norm-conforming behavior from the start to the end of the rebellion, occurs when rebel groups recognize the benefits afforded by legitimacy at the outset of rebellion. When rebel groups reason that non-compliance does not pay off, they are likely to stick to compliance throughout the duration of rebel movements. *Switchover compliance*, a move from non-compliance to compliance, occurs when the cost of non-compliance starts to outweigh its benefits. When the cost of non-compliance becomes unbearably expensive compared with the cost of compliance, switchover compliant rebels are likely to emerge. In other words, when a rebel group recognizes that the benefits of compliance increase beyond those to be enjoyed on the basis of military advantage alone, we can expect the rebel group to change its behavior from non-compliance to compliance. Theoretically, it is also possible to switch the other way, from compliance to non-compliance. This will occur when the incentive to violate increases because of a change in circumstances such as the intensification of conflicts or failing peace negotiations.

The theory of rebel compliance presented here can thus be said to be based on the notion of "strategic legitimacy." The explanation I offer in this book differs from previous theories in that it dissects the benefit side of compliance. Previous work has focused narrowly on the cost of non-compliance – arguing that the possible punishments associated with the enforcement of international law are so negligible that rebels are not likely to comply in a broad sense. This line of thought typically concludes that because the risk and cost of punishment are limited, no rebel group considers international law in their decision calculus. It is certainly true that punishment and fear of punishment play a central role in inducing compliance. It is also equally plausible to think that rebel groups are rarely deterred by the punishments associated with the enforcement of international law. This view, however, is incomplete in that it ignores the potential benefits actors gain through compliance.

For most rebel groups, there is something to be gained by complying with international law: recognition, legitimacy, and reputation. Recognition provides international credibility around the world, and thus a stronger strategic position for groups in their struggle against an opposing government at home. Legitimacy also gives rebel groups greater authority compared with their national government, especially in instances where the government itself lacks legitimacy to govern. Having a reputation as a complier with international law can earn rebel groups a medal of good citizenship in the long run. The benefit of having a good reputation by exercising restraint has to be weighed against the cost of possibly appearing weak militarily, insofar as choosing this path will likely mean eschewing shows of force. However, such reputation-building can be beneficial, especially when the government's reputation is poor and when rebel groups can generate positive public relations momentum and attract further political support. Given that some parts of the international community care deeply about rebel groups' compliance, legitimacy-seeking rebels can score both material and political points by complying.

Let me summarize the rebel group calculus for compliance decisions. A rebel group's objective function includes consideration of the group's political goals, military imperatives, and strategic demands, together with an evaluation of the risks and consequences of non-compliance. We expect to see compliant and law-abiding rebels when rebel groups clearly see the benefit of compliance, such as a boost in legitimacy. With the expectation of political benefits of domestic or international legitimacy that can aid their military struggle, rebel groups are more likely to comply. If rebels see an incompatibility between legitimacy and military advantage and only see value in short-term tactical benefits, we are likely to observe non-compliance.

CAUSAL MECHANISMS

How rebel groups move from non-compliance to compliance is the central inquiry of this book. I have thus far focused the discussion on connecting legitimacy and compliance, but have yet to specify the causal pathways linking legitimacy and compliance. The first step to establish causality is to provide a plausible theoretical story linking cause and effect. In this book's context, the "cause" will be legitimacy-seeking motivations of rebel groups. The "effect" will be rebel groups' compliance behavior. With the main ingredients of rebels' calculus regarding international law compliance, this section explicates the causal pathways to compliance. The link from cause and effect will not be as clean as in other hard sciences. In an ideal situation, if we press the button of legitimacy, compliance will automatically occur. However, this section will not demonstrate such automaticity. Rather, the pathway from cause to effect will be characterized by the complex social and political interactions between rebel groups and other stakeholders.

During rebellion, rebel groups develop their social and political interactions with their audiences. Among their political audiences, there will be pro-compliance and anti-compliance constituencies. The nature, preferences, and leverage of those constituencies will constrain how rebels devise their legitimization strategies and decide on compliance with international law. I will call this the *rebels' compliance constituency mechanism*.

The term "compliance constituency" was first developed by Miles Kahler in the context of understanding compliance in political contexts.[25] Compliance constituencies are the core audience that can exert influence on rebel compliance behaviors. Xinyuan Dai recently demonstrated that domestic constituencies matter in explaining the weak power of international institutions.[26] Specifically, she showed that the electoral leverage and the informational endowment of domestic constituencies about the policy process matter in eliciting compliance by national governments with respect to international agreements. Analogously, then, in the context of rebel compliance, what leverage pro-compliance constituencies have, what they know about rebel compliance behaviors, and what they prefer, will matter for understanding the causal process of rebel compliance.

Among the political audiences and sponsors of rebels, those who both care about humanitarian consequences and human rights violations and act on them will determine how rebels behave. The magnitude of political influence of those sponsors will also matter. Even if audiences care, rebel groups will have no qualms about mistreating civilians if they think that sponsors have no leverage over them. Therefore, it will be essential to think about the amount of interests in international law compliance as well as the extent to which pro-compliance constituencies can exercise their political and military influences over rebel groups.

This theoretical consideration goes back to the principal–agent theory in political science. In the principal–agent framework, rebels are agents and external sponsors are principals. How principals can engineer agents to do what they want will depend on the commonality of interests between principals and agents, as well as on the influence principals can have over agents.[27] In the context of rebel compliance, how many common interests rebels share with rebel sponsors in terms of international law compliance, and how much influence the sponsors have over rebel groups by supplying arms or withholding support, will define political relations between rebels and compliance constituencies.

Broadly, compliance constituencies include both domestic and international actors who have stakes and interests in civil conflicts and rebel compliance. Specifically, those pro-compliance constituencies encompass civilians who have preferences for law-abiding behaviors at the domestic level, foreign state sponsors under the influence of civil society at the international level, and, finally, domestic and international civil society.

On the domestic level, the preferences of the civilian population with regard to international law could be absent or deeply divided between compliance and non-compliance. Ordinary civilians may not know much about international law. Civilians may care more about who is winning or losing, might simply want to avoid being abused themselves, or not care about other ethnic groups

[25] Kahler (2000). [26] Dai (2005). [27] McCubbins and Kiwiet (1991).

being abused. It is also quite possible that a civilian population could be divided as to rebels' compliance behaviors. Some parts of a domestic population might have values and preferences consistent with international law. As potential victims, they will want rebel groups to comply. These civilians will care about their and their families' survival and well-being, and they are likely to have pro-compliance preferences.

On the other hand, consider a civilian population that sympathizes with the rebel's goals. In the extreme, those civilians might think that rebellion should be successful using *any* military means. They will not be pro-compliance constituencies. These civilian preferences over rebel compliance are important, but merely having preferences will not determine rebel behavior directly. How much sway civilians can have and how rebel groups rely on civilians also matters. In the face of rebel violence, tribal leaders, for example, would be power-holders relative to ordinary civilians. While civilians can be coerced and forcefully recruited or abused by rebel groups, tribal leaders might be necessary for rebel groups to enforce order in rebel-held areas.

On the international level, foreign state sponsors exert their power over rebels abroad. Decisions to aid rebel groups are primarily based on geopolitical reasons: whether a country has a regional ambition to expand influence to other countries, or have strategic interests in foreign countries. In many cases, human rights concerns are not at the forefront of those considerations, but they are part of such decisions. For instance, the federal law in the United States prohibits the country from aiding rebel groups that have been classified as terrorists. Foreign sponsors are influential in determining the fate of rebel groups. They can supply arms, send money, or suspend support to alienate rebel groups.[28]

In some cases, foreign powers can upset the military balance between the government and rebels. When these foreign state sponsors become compliance constituencies, the primary human rights pressure within those countries will come from their own compliance constituencies, such as domestic human rights or humanitarian groups. As noted, the decision to aid rebel groups abroad will be largely determined by geopolitical reasons, but these foreign powers with human rights domestic constituencies will differ from foreign powers that are under no such pressure. By withdrawing existing support or by denying legitimacy to abusive rebel groups, foreign sponsors can wield some power over rebel groups.

The third category of compliance constituencies is what I would call "agents of international law," mainly human rights or humanitarian organizations both at the domestic and international levels. These entities are committed to upholding human rights and mitigating the humanitarian consequences of rebel violence; their preferences are to make civil wars less inhumane. Although they may not have the power necessary to stop wars, they usually

[28] Byman *et al.* (2001).

monitor, encourage, or name-and-shame rebel groups to exercise restraint. The list of agents of international law includes various UN agencies,[29] the Centre for Humanitarian Dialogue, the ICRC, Human Rights Watch, and Amnesty International. The influence of domestic agents of international law is not likely to be strong during civil war periods as domestic civil society has usually been weakened by an already repressive society and conflict. International civil society has more leverage than domestic civil society over distributing resources and conducting diplomacy with rebel groups. These international agents of international law may empower domestic civil society in some cases.[30]

It is worth noting that, in some cases, there may be "anti-compliance constituencies" that actively support violations of international law by rebel groups. These constituencies may perceive that violence pays and they may believe that violence without restraint is one way to reach the status of "viable authority." There are numerous examples of diaspora populations funding rebel groups no matter what atrocities they perpetrate as long as these groups achieve military victory, as in the case of the LTTE. The preferences of these constituencies will differ markedly from those of "pro-compliance constituencies." For "pro-compliance constituencies," civilian abuse hurts a rebel group's prospects of achieving legitimacy. In contrast, for anti-compliance constituencies, civilian abuse may bolster a group's legitimacy. These anti-compliance constituencies will be committed to prevailing militarily by whatever means may be necessary, regardless of international rules.

It is also important to note that not all legitimacy-seeking groups will comply. Some rebel groups may seek legitimacy *through exercising unrestricted violence*. The capability to inflict pain may be translated into the power to rule, one of the requirements to gain legitimacy. For example, the RUF in Sierra Leone attempted to demonstrate to its foreign backers its ability to "kill" and overthrow government forces.[31] Following the group's failed attempts to build relationships with civilians and diasporas, its sole political audience was foreign backers, one of them being Charles Taylor, the president of Liberia, later convicted by the Special Court of Sierra Leone in 2012.[32] It is also important to note that the RUF relied on the diamond and timber trade as well to finance its wars. It was no coincidence that its main method of demonstrating its military capability was through terrorizing civilians. When a rebel group has violence-approving sponsors and exploits natural resources, deliberate and unchecked violations of international law are the predictable outcome.[33] The legitimacy RUF sought was in the eyes of a compliance-disregarding political audience, so their right to rule originated

[29] The list includes UNICEF, UNOCHA, and the UN peacekeeping or observer missions. UNICEF focuses on children's rights; UNOCHA is responsible for distributing humanitarian aid; and the UN peacekeeping department conducts interagency cooperation providing information to other operating agencies regarding rebel movements and their international law violations.

[30] Risse *et al.* (1999). [31] Hovil and Werker (2005). [32] Hazen (2013). [33] Salehyan *et al.* (2014).

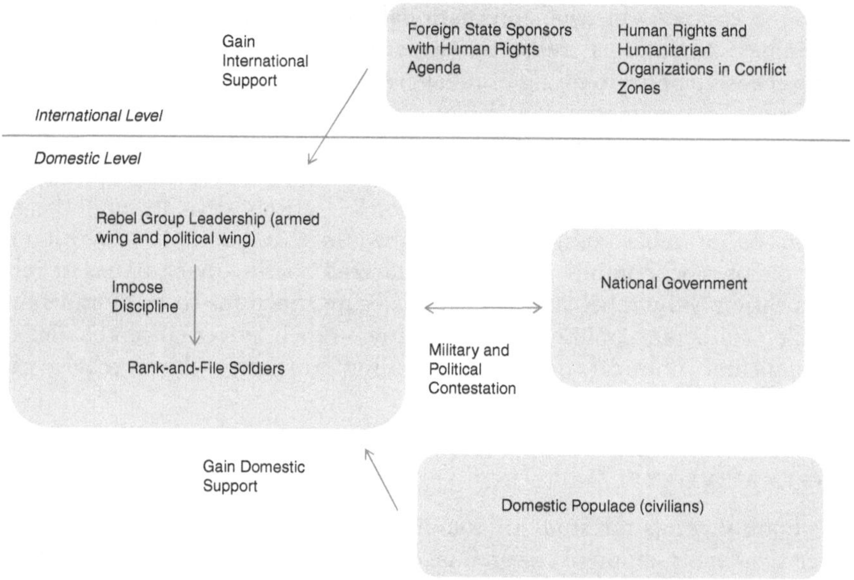

FIGURE 3.1 Rebel groups' compliance constituencies and relationships

from the kind of legitimacy that made the rebel group favor using unrestricted violence. This is why the nature of audience matters in rebel groups' legitimacy-seeking tendencies.

Figure 3.1 shows a constellation of these potential constituencies, along with the interactions that may arise among them in connection with the politics of rebel compliance. In this social and political environment, all rebel groups seek group survival. To survive, they try to find ways to sustain their movements and, through these efforts, establish political relationships with domestic and international actors. The compliance constituencies that provide the most significant and reliable support are likely to have the most influential voices, and these constituencies are the ones rebel groups will try to appease and sustain in order to build legitimacy. In this respect, the preferences, availability, and the political leverage of these compliance constituencies will be crucial with regard to influencing the particular type of legitimacy that rebel groups choose to pursue, as well as how exactly they choose to pursue it.

In examining the political constituencies of rebel groups, as depicted in Figure 3.1, it is important to understand the larger operating environment as a three-way political interaction between rebel groups, the ruling government, and international society. In this scheme, both the ruling government and international society play a critical role in making or breaking rebel compliance; rebel groups do not act alone. Rebellion is largely reactionary, arising in response to developments in the existing political order under a ruling government. Armed struggles, after all, are typically organized in reaction to state repression. On the international level, outside support largely determines whether a rebellion lives or dies. For these reasons, a comprehensive understanding of rebel group behavior cannot be attained by studying rebel organizations in isolation. Rather, such study must take into account relevant interaction among rebels, governments, and international actors, as well as the consequences of this interaction as rebel groups balance military and political realities. These considerations strongly underlie the conception of rebel compliance described in this book. In this picture, the topic of rebel compliance is a multifaceted one involving issues of rebel organization (how rebel commanders delegate functions to local and rank-and-file soldiers), political order (how rebel governance challenges governmental political order), and ruling authority (how rebels gain legitimacy to rule).

ALTERNATIVE EXPLANATIONS

This book presents the study of compliance in the context of rebel violence. Given the long tradition of research on compliance, I stand on the shoulders of giants. Many scholars have put forth explanations concerning why people, institutions, or organizations are rule-compliant. The preceding section has already considered a couple of alternative arguments by way of building a causal story between legitimacy and compliance. This section explores those alternative explanations in more detail and in a more comprehensive fashion. I mainly examine three dominant ways of thinking about rebel compliance: (1) that military advantage is the most important driver for compliance or non-compliance; (2) that capacity is the main determinant of rebel compliance; and (3) that ideology is the key to the explanation of rebel compliance.

Besides the above three potential alternative explanations to rebel compliance, I also examine conventional explanations in compliance literature to assess their applicability to rebel compliance. Existing theories of compliance are also applicable and serve as competing accounts for rebel compliance. The main objective will be to gauge the logic of each explanation and demonstrate why the legitimacy factor might weigh more heavily than other factors.

Since the study of compliance is central to regulatory politics and political institutions, many theories exist. I examine five arguments on compliance, which I will call "the 5 Rs of compliance": retaliation, reciprocity, reputation, ratification, and rule-legitimacy. The first three are from Andrew Guzman's book *How International Law Works*,[34] and the latter two come from additional theories of compliance. The following discussion considers these existing arguments and assesses the logic of those arguments in explaining rebel compliance.

[34] Guzman (2008).

The analysis will show that existing theories are not directly competing explanations for rebel compliance, but that they deserve careful review in order to examine the generalizability of the study of rebel compliance in overall compliance literature. Most of the traditional theories have been developed in the context of state-to-state interactions, and it is important to see the theoretical distinctions between existing theories of compliance and the theory of rebel compliance I propose in this book.

Military Advantage

One potential rival explanation to compliant rebels is that rebels care about military advantage in their compliance decisions. Put simply, rebel groups comply when they see an opportunity for military advantage and they do not comply when they do not see any benefits of military advantage. Despite the parsimonious argument, I see some deficiencies in the logic of this explanation in its assumption and thinking in rebel calculus.

The core assumption behind this explanation is that civil wars are defined as military contestations only. This ignores one of my core assumptions that civil wars are also political contestations that involve a legitimacy battle. It is true that civil wars are after all marked by military confrontations, and that military victory is often needed to gain political control. However, political negotiations and contestations are an important part of the game as well. Many civil wars originate from political grievances, which are expressed in armed opposition movements, so we cannot escape the political reality of civil conflicts. These political processes usually involve winning support from political constituencies and scoring political wins amid military confrontations.

The military advantage explanation also ignores a subtle aspect in the rebel calculus. It is highly plausible to think that compliant rebels will not necessarily sacrifice their potential military advantage to the extent that it would endanger their survival. In particular, long-running rebel actors that rely on the domestic population for potential recruits and voluntary support might gladly bear the cost of disciplining their soldiers to follow the principles of humanitarian law in the prospect of continuing or increased domestic support. These political wins can often be translated into military advantages in the long run. A rebel group's calculus will thus not be a simple military decision, but a more complex decision taking into account its ultimate political success.

Rebel Capacity

Some people might argue that rebel groups comply because they *can*. Certain rebel groups can afford to comply because they have stable and strong command-and-control structures that impose discipline among their members. Under this argument, the capacity of rebel groups should make it easy for them to comply and facilitate compliance within rebel ranks.

One problem with this capacity argument is that the cause (capacity) and effect (compliance) relationships are not clear in some cases. Even with strong discipline, whether the rebel group wants to impose rules consistent with international rules is questionable. Not all internal codes of conduct among rebel groups are consistent with international rules and some may promote rules that are in violation of international customs. In extreme cases, *capacity can cause non-compliance.* Some rebel groups with strong command structures might exploit such strength by imposing rules that can produce atrocious consequences. Well-disciplined soldiers directed by atrocious political programs can wreak as much havoc as rebel soldiers running amok for personal gain. Those ill-intentioned rebel groups can inflict a lot more atrocities responsible for civilian mistreatment. According to this logic, therefore, we cannot expect capable rebels to comply just because they can.

Also, the argument focuses solely on rebel capacity and ignores the *willingness part* of rebel groups in their compliance decisions. Rather, as informed from my theory, when capacity is accompanied by or combined with willingness to comply, compliant rebels are likely. Rebel capacity can facilitate the political goals of rebel groups that strive to be consistent with international rules. Rebel leadership can leverage the rebel political wing to facilitate international involvement. It can garner help within the domestic population to expand more of its political base. In this fashion, rebel capacity can work as the antecedent of willingness and facilitator of legitimacy-seeking characteristics, but it cannot stand alone as an explanation for compliant rebels.

Role of Ideology

Some might put forward an alternative argument focusing on the role of ideology. It is a weighty argument that considers the military and political ideas of rebel groups. Also, it is plausible to think that compliant rebels arise when the rebel group ideology dictates so. In fact, recent trends in rebel research suggest that ideology may play an important role in understanding rebel behavior and organization.[35] However, I am going to argue that ideology may play a role in explaining why some rebel groups are compliant at the outset, but does little to explain "changes" in compliance behavior.

Like legitimacy, ideology is an important part of politics. However, developing a systematic explanation out of ideology appears to be challenging. To make it an explanation, we first have to define ideology. One narrow definition of ideology is the incorporation of rebel doctrines (Maoism, Leninism, etc.). A broader definition of ideology would include political programs as well as religious and ethnic beliefs. For this purpose, Sanin and Wood define the ideology as:

[35] Sanin and Wood (2014).

A more or less systematic set of ideas that includes the identification of a referent group (a class, ethnic, or other social group), an enunciation of the grievances or challenges that the group confronts, the identification of objectives on behalf of that group (political change or defense against its threat), and a (perhaps vaguely defined) program of action.[36]

Following the narrow definition of ideology seems to be too limiting for an explanation. There are not clean-cut categories that can produce meaningful hypotheses or predictions around each category. For one, the Islamist ideology has a lot of variants within it (Jihadism, Sufism, extreme Sunni, etc.), and its practice is subject to interpretation based in many cases on legal opinions (called fatwā) and religious teachings.[37] The way the ideological doctrines are interpreted and put into practice should matter when rebel groups decide to conform to existing rules and norms. How rebel groups interpret the ideology in their political and military circumstances is different across contexts, so it is difficult to paint the systematic picture out of ideology. The second problem with having a narrow definition of ideology is that it cannot explain change adequately. Ideology as a religious doctrine, for instance, is difficult to change in the course of rebel's lifetime, and as a dynamic explanation it can be restrictive.

The broader definition appears to be helpful for the purpose of explaining rebel behavior. It considers the political program of rebel groups as well as their objectives. However, this broader definition comes at a cost that ideology is too broadly defined to be useful in generating concrete explanations. When ideology is defined to include political actions and grievances, as well as objectives, we lose focus in pinpointing which part of ideology is doing the job in producing rebel behavior.

Acknowledging the limitation of ideology as a potential explanation for rebel compliance does not mean that ideology does not matter. Ideology should matter to international law compliance to the extent that it is consistent with international law and to the extent that rebel groups believe in it and practice it in earnest. Ideology can be a good explanation for normative voluntary compliance. When rebel groups normatively exhibit ideas that are consistent with international norms, voluntary compliance is likely. In these cases, we will observe positive coincidences between rebel norms and international norms.

[36] Sanin and Wood (2014: 215).

[37] See Bassiouni and Guellali (2010). Marxism also has a lot of variants under its tree, with various consequences in practice. The Marxism practiced by the FMLN in El Salvador and its belief seems to be different from Maoism practiced and believed by the Naxalites in India in terms of their beliefs about how to treat civilians. Although both emphasized class struggle and the gap between rich and poor, the way each forged their relations with the domestic population appears to have differed greatly in responses to the treatment of civilians. The Maoist rebellion in India is marked by many civilian casualties and heavy use of child soldiers, whereas some variants of the Marxist Sendero Luminoso or the FMLN exercised restraint (see Weinstein 2006).

Retaliation

Fear of retaliation can be a source of any legal compliance. In domestic criminal contexts, the presence of law enforcement officers and the thought of serving life in prison might have deterred many potential perpetrators from committing crimes. In international law, enforcement is weak and the fear of retaliation is likely to be smaller than in domestic contexts. In the case of rebel compliance, the fear of retaliation would hinge on how rebels assess the risk of retaliation by international actors or their key opponents. The risk, in turn, will depend on the magnitude and the likelihood of retaliation: how severe the punishments might be and how frequently they may occur. The risk appears to be small. Economic sanctions based on humanitarian grounds are rare; prosecution possibilities are small, although they are increasing. Rebels' opponents, national governments, rarely retaliate on the ground of human rights violations. Governments engage in military campaigns usually on the ground of national security threats. If the risk of retaliation is not large at domestic and international levels, it cannot be a strong motivator for compliance for rebel groups. The theory of retaliation would therefore expect compliant rebels to be a rare occurrence in the world. Therefore, the explanation that emphasizes retaliation cannot credibly explain why compliant rebels might arise.

Reciprocity

The first dominant explanation for compliance is reciprocity. In the context of rebel compliance, reciprocity will mean that rebels do what the governments do. When governments comply with international rules, rebels are more likely to comply. When governments do not comply, rebels will not comply. The value of reciprocity is central to international cooperation as it has been demonstrated to be the core foundation for international law compliance in the context of interstate relations.[38] The logic of reciprocity lies in the expectation about future interactions. Although this explanation tells us something about patterns of interactions, it does not explain well some situations where governments comply, while rebels do not (or the situations where governments do not comply, when rebels do) in an asymmetric setting.[39] My legitimacy-based theory produces an expectation that those situations can occur during legitimacy battles. When rebels seek legitimacy, they might comply even when governments do not. Compliance in this situation enhances rebels' legitimacy while delegitimizing the opposing government. This does not mean that empirically we will not observe reciprocal patterns, but as a theoretical explanation, reciprocity fails to consider those situations of "battles over legitimacy."

[38] Morrow (2014). [39] See Osiel (2009) on this point.

Reputation

Reputation plays a critical role in many social phenomena, particularly when the main actors are engaged in *repeated* interactions on a specific issue of importance that poses *uncertainty* about the final outcome.[40] The topic of rebel compliance meets these criteria. The issue of rebel compliance is specific enough to be confined to rebels' human rights behaviors and humanitarian violations during *repeated* interaction with the government where the outcome of civil conflicts is quite *uncertain*.

The implication from reputation theories is that rebel groups with long-term visions are more likely to be reputation-builders. Since reputation has many dimensions,[41] the theory also suggests that rebel groups have to balance between a reputation to be militarily strong, on one hand, and a reputation to be compliant, on the other. Some groups give more weight to military prowess, while other groups might sacrifice some military advantage to gain greater political advantage of being compliant by looking into the future.

Conceptually, reputation shares many common features with legitimacy. Both are collective perceptions by others, and involve comparisons and calibrations relative to other referents.[42] Reputation theories can thus greatly inform the question of rebel compliance, in the sense that reputation is part of the causal mechanism in a legitimacy-building process. In essence, legitimacy-seeking rebels will care about their "reputation" of being a "legitimate" entity vis-à-vis their core constituencies. However, the explanations that focus on reputation do not necessarily tell us where reputation comes from. In order to understand why and how rebel groups seek reputation-building, we need to consider factors such as the source of legitimacy. Also, in contrast to reputation-building processes, legitimacy-seeking behavior can be elicited from short-run interactions. The legitimacy-based explanation can explain both short- and long-term rebel groups, therefore providing a better explanation for rebel group compliance relative to reputational theory.

Ratification

Recent theories of compliance by state actors emphasize the role of ratification as the key source of compliance. Ratification is the domestic legal procedure to approve international law and can serve as a powerful tool for compliance with international law for the following reasons. First, ratification is the "explicit expression" of abiding by international rules. Second, ratification generates domestic political momentum to mobilize relevant actors, such as victims and rights activists. Third, ratification is usually followed by "legal reforms" incorporated into domestic law.[43] With these three well-specified causal mechanisms, an explanation hinging on ratification is a compelling theory of compliance for state actors.

[40] Walter (2009). [41] Downs and Jones (2002). [42] Zinko *et al.* (2007). [43] Simmons (2010).

Despite the power of ratification as an explanation for compliance on the part of state actors, whether the explanation is applicable to rebel groups in its entirety is less clear because of the less institutionalized nature of rebel groups relative to state actors. Suppose that some of the legal commitments made by rebel groups are analogous to ratification by state actors. The first mechanism of expression and signal may hold, but whether the expressive commitment will generate compliance is not clear in rebel contexts. There is a question of whether such commitment is genuine or not. Also, capacity problems enter as well, as some rebel groups will be poorly equipped in translating their commitment to compliance.

The second mechanism of generating mobilization is relevant as rebel commitment can lead to more interactions with stakeholders such as international actors or victims. However, whether those actors will have as much political sway as do domestic constituencies in established governments with accountability mechanisms is not clear. The third mechanism of legal reforms will be relevant and analogous, but with little applicability. States can change laws and change political incentives, but rebel groups do not have as strong an institutional capacity as state actors. In the case of rebel groups, they can change their internal code of conduct in line with international law, but the overall expectation is that such changes will not be as sweeping and as comprehensive as the legal reforms of national governments.

The main point of bringing in the ratification argument is that existing compliance theories may have little applicability in the context of rebel compliance. But it is also important to examine the extent to which existing theories can help us to flesh out the nature and mechanisms of rebel compliance.

Rule Legitimacy

As the final explanation for compliance, I consider the argument that focuses on the legitimacy of law. As famously argued in Franck's *The Power of Legitimacy among Nations*, the legitimacy of law draws nations into a "compliance pull" generating voluntary normative compliance.[44] Recent behavioral experiments and regulatory politics also signal the value of rule legitimacy, as in Tom Tyler's work in *Why People Obey the Law*.[45] People obey the law, many experiments show, not because they fear the consequences, but because they view the law or enforcement authority as legitimate. In my book, what generates rebel compliance is not the legitimacy of law itself, but the motivation to generate the legitimacy of its own rebel movement. This is the core difference from the traditional account of international law compliance stemming from the legitimacy of law.

Still, the compliance pull argument has relevance to rebel compliance. Rebel groups might or might not perceive international law as legitimate. If they do

[44] Franck (1990). [45] Tyler (2006).

consider international law as legitimate and say so, they might have an easier time in complying, compared to, say, persistent objectors to international law as a Western product. However, this legal theory does not recognize the political contexts that rebel groups are in. Since the explanation does not consider the nature of civil conflict or how rebel groups are organized, the rule legitimacy theory cannot answer why some rebel groups accept the rules as legitimate while others do not. My theory proposes that rebel groups consider international law as legitimate when they have some expected political gains by complying. So, in my theory, legitimization of rules does not arise naturally, but via the conscious political process of rebellion.

Also, the legal theory of legitimacy diverges in the key expectation about compliance. States participate in the legal process and thus perceive international law as fair, which is why nations obey international law most of the time. This will not be the case of rebel groups that do not participate in the international law-making process and might not regard it as fair since international law is mainly the product of sovereign nations. Then, this argument about international law's legitimacy cannot generate predictions as to why some rebel groups comply while others do not. In this regard, the legal theory is compelling in the context of international law involving states, but when it comes to non-state actors, the theory is less useful.

Taking Stock of Alternative Explanations

The above analysis reveals that some previous explanations are more applicable than others in explaining rebel compliance. Rebel groups comply not because institutional mechanisms assist them in doing so, as these mechanisms do not possess institutional means such as ratification procedures. Additionally, rebel groups do not comply with international standards out of fear of punishment, as international sanctions and prosecutions tend to be weak and rare, although increasing in frequency. While building a reputation through signaling is useful when such labeling helps a rebel group acquire resources, few groups comply solely for the purpose of building a reputation for being nice and good. At the most fundamental level, decisions to comply or not comply are driven by the need to obtain legitimacy – non-material support or material resources to ensure group survival. Lastly, rebels comply not because governments comply. Counterintuitively, compliant rebels can sometimes emerge when the government they oppose does not comply. I would characterize this phenomenon as "negative reciprocity" because rebels will often do exactly what governments do not do, or are unable to do, to boost their legitimacy.

Constructing a theory of compliance is not an easy task. However, in terms of understanding key incentives of core actors, their institutional environments and their interactions with other political actors is at the center of understanding compliance. My legitimacy-based theory of compliance considers those factors in a coherent fashion, starting from the assumptions about rebel motivations and building theoretical expectations, while taking into account other conventional and standard explanations of compliance.

All the existing theories are beneficial to understanding rebel compliance as they inform the theory of rebel compliance in some fashion and suggest alternative pathways or additional factors to consider. However, one common thread identified in the examination of alternative explanations is the value of understanding rebel group motivations to establish and build political legitimacy. The generalizability of this theory beyond rebel groups will depend on whether the key political actor examined is interested in building political legitimacy to a varying degree and whether compliance is one of its end goals. This book leaves this generalization possibility aside, but will rather focus on explaining the rebel compliance in a concrete fashion.

THEORY OF STRATEGIC LEGITIMACY: SUMMARY AND ITS VALUE

This chapter demonstrated that rebel compliance arises out of complex political interactions with opposing governments, outside actors, and civilians. Some rebel groups may not care about international conventions per se, and the rebel leadership may have little reason to listen to what the Geneva Conventions say. These rebel leaders had no hand in negotiating the terms of the treaty and they probably care more about winning their local war than about abstract rules and norms that they may never have heard of anyway. However, it is important to recognize that international law does not operate in a vacuum, but rather within a political context involving compliance constituencies that have preferences and leverages for compliance. Rebel groups that forge political relationships with these pro-compliance constituencies will be more attuned to the humanitarian consequences of civil wars than being squarely focused on military victories at any human cost.

At their core decision calculus, rebel groups will care about international standards when adherence is beneficial for their political survival. When compliance pays off, rebel groups are much more likely to pay attention to international law. The level of reaction to this social pressure will vary among rebel groups depending on their core constituencies and supporters. Groups that rely on civilian support are less likely to abuse civilians, and groups with external patrons that care about human rights records, such as religious or humanitarian organizations, will refrain from committing violence and strive to abide by international standards and norms.

Out of many potential reasons for compliance, I reasoned that legitimacy is the key political dimension separating compliant and non-compliant rebels, as given by the "rebel constituency mechanism" described in this chapter. Legitimacy-seeking rebels are likely to adhere to international rules when such adherence can aid their survival. When a secessionist group has to reach out to international supporters who care about human rights and humanitarian rules, they are more likely to be compelled to rethink their compliance strategy. Conversely, legitimacy-indifferent groups may have no regard for human life and will violate humanitarian rules without restraint. The different survival modes of rebel groups and the varying degrees of their legitimacy-seeking motivations can explain why some rebel groups are compliant and others are not.

With its focus on legitimacy motivation, my theory of rebel compliance generates predictions that rebels comply to increase their chances of political survival. Some legitimacy-seeking rebels might comply at the outset and refrain from civilian abuse out of concern for the well-being of their core constituencies. They might change their behaviors in the course of their rebellion from non-compliance to compliance. Given the life cycle of rebellion from the incubation period to a fully developed politico-military organization, this change is most likely to occur when the rebel organization embraces the value of legitimacy both at home and abroad. The value of strategic legitimacy theory is that it can explain both types of static and dynamic behaviors. In other words, the theory can be fruitfully applied to situations where rebels initially comply and continue to comply, as well as situations where rebels alter their behaviors in midstream.

With these theoretical considerations in mind, the following chapters enter the realm of empirical evidence of compliant rebels. The subsequent chapters will explore whether compliant rebels exist and under what circumstances. Consistent with the theoretical discussions, we will be attentive to the political processes that produce compliant rebels, in particular, whether legitimacy-seeking motivations lead to compliance decisions via rebel constituency mechanisms. In so doing, the empirical chapters will permit readers to consider the following three issues that generate so many victims of rebel violence: civilian killing, child soldiering, and detention visits.

PART II

EVIDENCE OF COMPLIANT REBELS

4

From Theory to Evidence

Previous chapters have introduced the central question of this book on rebel compliance and defined its scope regarding rebel groups and relevant international law. I also have worked through the theory of rebel compliance by considering the central assumptions underlying this book, arguing that rebel groups' legitimacy-seeking motivations matter. Based on these discussions, I will now set the parameters for my empirical inquiry for compliant rebels. This chapter is presented as a bridge between theoretical framework and empirical evidence. Before we dive into the evidence of compliant rebels, I will establish the preliminaries, such as how I actually draw the empirical boundaries to examine the actual behaviors and characteristics of contemporary rebel groups.

At the center of this empirical inquiry is the data from which this book draws its information: the Rebel Groups and International Law (RGIL) database. The database was exclusively built for this book project. It includes both qualitative and quantitative information about rebel groups' institutional and organizational profiles, and their humanitarian and human rights behaviors. General readers will find detailed reporting on each rebel group helpful, and quantitatively inclined readers will have access to the data from which this book draws inference. This chapter is primarily designed to be an introduction to the database. I discuss measures relevant to rebel compliance and present general patterns and trends gleaned from the database. These measures and patterns will be the basis for the recurring theme of legitimacy and compliance throughout the rest of the book. This discussion should provide a helpful segue into the empirical results presented in subsequent chapters.

I shall proceed as follows. The first part introduces the key features of the database. I will then present some patterns about rebel groups' commitment and compliance behaviors with international law. The main part of this chapter is the measurement of legitimacy-seeking motivations by rebel groups. This section will serve as the core of the bridge between the previous theory chapter and the subsequent empirical chapters. The legitimacy-seeking indicators will set the background for developing empirically testable hypotheses, which will then be tested in the subsequent chapters on rebel civilian killing, child soldiering, and detention issues. In part, this section on legitimacy indicators is an extended discussion on the measurement section introduced in Chapter 1, so readers who need a shorter version can go back to the introductory chapter. Lastly, I also add some discussions about the patterns of rebel financing methods, in order to give readers some sense of rebel groups' support base. With the introduction of this book's database and the connection between theory and the empirical domain, I will end the discussion by acknowledging some limitations and drawbacks of the database that readers should be aware of in order to gain a detailed and nuanced understanding of rebel compliance.

REBEL GROUPS AND INTERNATIONAL LAW: A DATABASE

The RGIL database was constructed to better understand rebel groups' practical relations to international law. It is composed of qualitative reports and a quantitative dataset that feature information relevant to rebel groups' commitment to international law and their compliance behaviors with international law. The database presents rebel groups' political and economic surroundings to complete a picture of rebel group compliance. The motivation here is that we cannot fully understand how rebels exercise restraints in conducting their warfare without understanding the political, organizational, and economic environments of rebel groups; for example, the database contains information about how rebel groups finance their wars and what their relationships are with domestic and international constituencies. The key motivation for building the database is to test the theory of strategic legitimacy and compliance, but the database can also be useful for research beyond just rebel groups and rebel groups in areas such as compliance, civil conflicts, and political violence. The database is publicly available on the author's website.

The unique feature of the database is that it includes materials such as a list of legal commitments made by rebel groups and detailed reports on their human rights behavior. The database also accompanies the core dataset that is amenable to quantitative analysis. The qualitative reports and quantitative dataset reflect off one another. Often, the numbers and measures in the quantitative dataset come from the qualitative narratives. The quantitative dataset gives the reader an opportunity to uncover broad trends and patterns. For instance, the summary of international legal instruments relevant to rebel groups will be the basis for the evaluation of compliance, while briefings on the use of child soldiers by each rebel group will serve as the source of quantitative information presented in a numerical format in the dataset. Readers will also get a sense of the state of the research by looking at the links to other datasets and databases related to the topic of rebel groups and international law.

The main sources for the database come from both primary and secondary sources. Primary sources include documents, official websites, or social network sites actually published and managed by rebel groups themselves.[1] Secondary sources include academic sources, journalistic sources, reports by NGOs (e.g., Human Rights Watch), reports produced by international organizations (e.g., truth commission reports), reports from research institutes (e.g., National Consortium for the Study of Terrorism and Responses to Terrorism (START)), and government reports (e.g., US State Department human rights report). My research team strived to rely only on credible resources so as to weed out unsubstantiated information. Readers interested in further details on the database sources should refer to "Notes on Data" in the Appendix.

The RGIL database is an amalgam of existing datasets and new additions. The construction of the quantitative dataset benefited much from previous efforts by civil war scholars. The list of rebel groups started with the Armed Conflict Dataset (ACD), generated by the collaborative effort of the Uppsala Conflict Data Program (UCDP) in Sweden and the International Peace Research Institute (PRIO) in Oslo, Norway.[2] ACD defines civil conflict as "a contested incompatibility that concerns government and/or territory where the use of armed force between two parties, of which at least one is the government of a state, results in at least 25 battle-related deaths."[3] In this dataset, rebel groups are defined as organized oppositions that fight against the government because of political contestation and incompatible goals over territory or policy.[4] Since battle-related deaths include both civilian fatalities as well as military fatalities on either government or rebel side caused by direct military combat,[5] the threshold of twenty-five battle-related deaths will generally exclude inactive rebel groups, groups that do not have the capability to confront the government militarily, and groups that champion their cause exclusively through peaceful means.

The temporal scope of the RGIL database is from 1989 to 2009. The starting point is when the Cold War ends, and the end-point is marked by data availability. The demarcation for starting point is based on the recognition that pre-Cold War rebels are qualitatively different from the post-Cold War rebels.[6] The unit of observation in the RGIL database is the rebel-year. For example, the MFDC in Senegal was actively operating between 1990 and 2003, so it has a total of thirteen observation lines in the RGIL database.[7] Although the MFDC was formed in 1982 and the remnants of the group

[1] What rebel groups actually say and signal to their political audiences is important, and I subject that information to the historical context in weaving the story of compliant rebels.

[2] Gleditsch *et al.* (2002).

[3] UCDP/PRIO Armed Conflict Dataset Codebook, Version 4-2014, available at: www.pcr.uu.se/digitalAssets/124/124920_1codebook_ucdp_prio-armed-conflict-dataset-v4_2014.pdf.

[4] Battle-related deaths include civilian fatalities as well as military fatalities. For more details, see UCDP (2012).

[5] UCDP Battle-Related Deaths Dataset Codebook, Version 5.0-2014 (June 2014), available at: www.pcr.uu.se/digitalAssets/124/124934_1codebook-ucdp-battle-related-deaths-datasets-v.5-2014.pdf.

[6] Kalyvas and Balcells (2010).

[7] UCDP Conflict Encyclopedia, available at: www.ucdp.uu.se/gpdatabase/search.php.

generated low-level conflict until recently even after the peace agreement with the government in 2004, the dataset counts only those active years defined by the ACD, assuming that these are relevant years to examine rebel compliance. Based on this active rebel-year platform being the unit of observation, rebel group characteristics were drawn from the NSA dataset, the most comprehensive dataset on rebel groups to date.[8] Civilian killing records were also added to the RGIL database from the One-Sided Violence (OSV) dataset.[9] Specific details of these datasets are discussed as relevant in the subsequent chapters.

There are several new additions in the RGIL database. One of the signature contributions of the RGIL database is to collect and record comprehensive information about rebel groups' commitment to international law as a stepping stone to compliance. The use of child soldiers by rebel groups is also new, as the cross-rebel comparison has not been done at the global level.[10] The visitation records to rebel detention centers by the ICRC are new as well. Other relevant variables, such as overlap with terrorist lists, were also newly added. With the fusion of existing knowledge and added new features, the RGIL database will contribute to the current inquiry on rebel groups and international law.

REBEL GROUPS' COMMITMENT TO INTERNATIONAL LAW

The RGIL database features a measure of rebel groups' commitment to international law. The main purpose here is to see whether rebel groups are aware of international law. Further, the commitment records can be an indication that rebels consider international law to be legitimate, signaling that their behaviors can be governed by international standards. The secondary goal of collecting the information about rebel groups' legal commitment to international law is to connect the dots between commitment and compliance – a classic topic in both international relations and international law. As we will discover later in this book, commitment to the law transmits a complex picture of behavior that exceeds simply being aware of its provisions. It reaffirms rebel group activities related to international standards, especially when a rebel group makes concrete commitments that extend beyond vague pledges, such as "we respect international humanitarian law."

Conventional wisdom has it that rebels operate outside the scope of international law. In actuality, however, rebels are *part of* international law. While it is true that rebel groups lack the authority to negotiate the terms of international agreements, they commit to existing international law in various ways. Those venues include unilateral declarations where rebel groups

[8] Cunningham *et al.* (2013). [9] Eck and Hultman (2007).

[10] One exception is Lasley (2012), but his sample covers about 100 groups while the RGIL covers about 250 groups. See Beber and Blattman (2013) for African rebel groups' child soldier use.

announce their willingness to abide by international law.[11] Rebel groups can also forge bilateral agreements with governments, international organizations, and NGOs. Commitments may also be made through peace agreements or in rebel groups' internal regulations. Some groups enforce those rules using rebel courts, although whether the system delivers fair justice is debatable in many cases.[12]

The nature of a commitment can vary from the abstract, such as a promise to abide by the Geneva Conventions, to the specific, such as agreeing to a United Nations Action Plan with specific timelines for demobilizing child soldiers. According to the RGIL database, out of 250 rebel groups involved in civil wars between 1990 and 2010, approximately 20 percent expressed commitment in one of the abovementioned forms. Some rebel groups even committed to international law on multiple occasions. The SPLM, for instance, made bilateral agreements with the government of Sudan in 2002, titled the Agreement on the Protection of Civilians and Civilian Facilities, signed the Deed of Commitment with Geneva Call to stop the use of anti-personnel mines in 2009, and concluded with the Action Plan with the United Nations to stop child soldiering in 2012.[13] These multiple legal commitments reveal that some rebel groups are not only aware of the related law, but that these groups consciously and repeatedly commit to respecting international norms. Table 4.1 gives the types of rebel commitment with some examples. Interested readers can consult the Appendix, which gives the more comprehensive list of rebel commitment.

It is also important to note the connection between commitment and compliance. For some rebel groups, there is a link between the two, and for others this link may be absent. Groups that commit to abiding by international law because of reputational concerns are likely to follow through with their commitment, leading to compliance. After MILF signed an Action Plan to stop the use of child soldiers, the group stayed on with its commitment. In contrast, rebel groups that commit for the purpose of attaining short-term material benefit are likely to comply only for a short period or never at all. Once the Forces armées des forces nouvelles (FAFN) in Côte d'Ivoire was taken off the UN's child soldier list, for instance, after it signed the United Nations Action Plan of 2006, the group resumed using child soldiers.[14]

[11] Sometimes, rebel groups privately submit a document to international organizations such as the ICRC instead of making a public announcement. See Sivakumaran (2012).

[12] See Clapham (2006); Ewumbue-Monono (2006); Sassoli (2010); Sivakumaran (2012). The full texts of some of these rebel groups' commitments are available at "Their Words" website, the directory of Armed Non-State Actor Humanitarian Commitments, run by a Swiss NGO, Geneva Call.

[13] Other multiple-committer rebels include CPN-M (Nepal), MILF (Philippines), FMLM (El Salvador), JEM (Sudan), SLM/A (Sudan), PKK (Turkey), and KNPP (Myanmar).

[14] Child Soldiers International (2008c).

TABLE 4.1 *Rebel groups' commitment to international law: types and examples*

Type of legal commitment	Example
Unilateral declaration	Liberation Tigers of Tamil Eelam (LTTE) (Sri Lanka)
Bilateral agreements with government	Revolutionary Armed Forces of Colombia (FARC) (Colombia)
Agreements with international organizations	Convention of Patriots for Justice and Peace (CPJP) (CAR)
Agreements with NGOs	National Council for the Defense of Democracy–Forces for the Defense of Democracy (CNDD-FDD) (Burundi)

REBEL GROUPS' COMPLIANCE WITH INTERNATIONAL LAW

At this point, readers might wonder: how are we to distinguish compliant rebels from their non-compliant counterparts? To identify compliant rebels, the first order of business must be to define and measure compliance. As first introduced in Chapter 1, I define *rebel compliance* as behavioral conformity to international rules and standards by rebel groups in civil conflicts.

At a conceptual level, compliance is on a continuous spectrum, ranging from total non-compliance to perfect compliance. International laws usually define the threshold between non-compliance and compliance, attempting to provide a bright line.[15] But in some cases, the lines for thresholds may not be that bright. For example, international law holds the principle that civilians should be protected as long as they do not participate in war efforts. But in practice, whether rebel soldiers should consider government sympathizers who provide some logistical information as enemy soldiers or as civilians, the law does not provide a clear guideline. As a result, some rebel groups employ expansive definitions of civilians, while others consider civilians narrowly. International law provides principles, but how those principles are applied in combat situations can lack common knowledge about all the contingencies. This normative structure of the standards in law has practical consequences for how rebel groups are aware of, interpret, and practice the law.[16] With these caveats that there might be discrepancies between what the law says and how the law is practiced in mind, I dive into my empirical investigation of rebel compliance.

15 Morrow (2007).

16 See Morrow (2014) for a discussion of shared understanding in laws of war in the context of interstate wars.

General Patterns of Rebel Compliance

Among many international rules that cover a wide range of behaviors, I have decided to focus on three main issues in international humanitarian law: violence against civilians, children, and detainees. The choice of criteria was the saliency of the issues in terms of understanding rebel compliance. Civilians, children, and detainees are the primary victims of conflict that should be protected. Because of this, we want to understand the patterns of when these norms are violated by rebel groups.

The first issue of rebel compliance is the topic of civilian killing, as taken up in Chapter 5. The right to life is the most fundamental basic human rights. The distinction between combatants and non-combatants (i.e., civilians) is a norm that became a customary international rule over time due to its wide acceptance and prevailing practice.[17] In my empirical inquiry into rebel behavior with respect to violence against civilians, I look at the conformity to the no-killing-of-civilians standard by examining the intentional killing of civilians measured in the OSV dataset, which reports the number of civilians killed in each civil war by each respective warring party, including rebel groups.[18]

The data shows that 74 out of 251 contemporary rebel groups between 1989 and 2009 have "directly" and "intentionally" killed civilians at one point in time during their armed struggle. This figure thus excludes *indirect* civilian deaths due to war, famine, or environmental disasters, as well as *unintentional* killing such as collateral casualties. Bearing in mind the inherent difficulties of arriving at these figures in an exact manner, I classified 177 rebel groups as being complier groups, as they are recorded as killing no civilians during their active rebel movements. The other 74 rebel groups are classified as non-compliers, as each group killed approximately 350 civilians on average during their armed struggle.

The second issue of compliance dealt with in this book is the prohibition on the use of child soldiers, as discussed in Chapter 6. The norm of prohibiting the use of child soldiers is a bit more contested than that of the prohibition on civilian killing. For instance, children over 15 are considered an adult in some cultures, while the international legal standard is to regard 18 as the threshold. The majority of countries now use 18 as the conscription threshold in their national armies, while a diminishing number of countries still conscript under-18s for training purposes, but not for combat use.[19] Given these cultural and institutional contexts, I collected information about whether a rebel group used child soldiers or not, the extent of its use, and the recruitment methods. I relied on academic sources such as Lasley (2012) and Beber and Blattman (2013), as well as reports from the United Nations and NGOs such as Child Soldiers International. As it is difficult to know when each rebel group begins and ends child soldiering, this compliance measure does not vary across years, but remains specific to a rebel group.

[17] Henckaerts and Doswald-Beck (2005). [18] Eck and Hultman (2007). [19] Simmons (2010).

In this issue of child soldier use, 77 rebel groups are marked as non-compliers. They are often classified as perpetrators of violence against children by the UN Special Office of Children and Armed Conflict. One hundred and sixty-five groups have not used child soldiers, or at least independent sources could not confirm their use. Child soldiering is geographically concentrated in the DRC, India, Somalia, and Colombia. The distribution of compliers and non-compliers is similar to the civilian killing issue in that compliers comprise about 30 percent of the total, but the geographical concentration is the main difference.

The third issue of rebel compliance is the treatment of detainees, as featured in Chapter 7. Since we cannot reliably measure the compliance record of the treatment condition, I instead examine whether a rebel group has granted access to the ICRC – the only authorized international organization to visit detention centers in conflict zones around the world. The ICRC keeps a confidentiality policy with regard to publishing the detention conditions, so I instead collected the public information about detention access, thinking that the denial of access may approximate to non-compliance.

The records on detention access are from the annual reports of the ICRC dating from 1989 to 2009. Forty-seven rebel groups out of 251 granted full and unfettered access to the ICRC at one point in time during their rebellion. Other conflict years were marked by restrictions on security detainees, or practical difficulties of visiting due to security conditions, and, often, blockage by national governments that did not want the ICRC to interact with their opposing rebel groups. These disruptions in detention visits resulted in a lot of missing-data problems. Because of this, I try to tackle this issue head-on in Chapter 7.

These are very brief overviews of each issue. Readers interested in the details about the data and what these patterns mean are encouraged to proceed to subsequent chapters in addition to the "Notes on Data" in the Appendix for general measurement issues. Each empirical chapter that follows (Chapters 5, 6, and 7) describes more patterns with examples in relation to the strategic legitimacy theory. The stocktaking section in Chapter 8 compares the compliance patterns across the three issue areas and weaves in the connection between legitimacy and compliance in a more close-knit fashion. Additionally, the Appendix details additional information on the patterns and measures of compliance. Measuring compliance is no easy matter, and especially so for rebel groups for which information is not abundant. Due to this, I consider potential biases and errors that come with such measurement efforts.

Typology of Rebel Compliance

The RGIL database is able to assist readers to identify different types of compliance among rebel groups. On a temporal dimension, compliance behaviors of rebel groups can be categorized into two types: persistent compliance and switchover compliance. The main distinction is whether a change of behavior occurs or not. With persistent compliers, there would be no change; with switchover compliers, there will be change.

Persistent compliance occurs when a rebel group exhibits compliant behavior throughout its armed struggle from start to finish. As we will find later in this book, among the groups considered to be in persistent compliance, there exist many conditions inherent in their nature that may bring these rebels into compliance by mere circumstance. For instance, secessionists residing among the domestic population that they aim to one day govern have little reason to antagonize their own civilians in their strongholds. As such, at the outset of hostilities these rebel groups are highly unlikely to violate international norms by destroying civilian life or property, as it would also adversely affect their own aims. This adherence may not necessarily develop with the active intent to abide by international rules, but rather there just happens to be a happy overlap between rebel behavior and the law.

Switchover compliance occurs when rebel groups "switch" from non-compliance to compliance, or in some cases from compliance to non-compliance. According to the legitimacy-based theory of compliance, the change in legitimacy-seeking motivations can induce rebel groups to alter their behaviors during a rebellion. From a policy perspective, instances of switchover compliance generate greater interest than the case of persistent compliers because such changes can come from the intervention of outside actors. Persistent complier or non-complier cases are where policy efforts might not bear fruit, but switchover cases are those where outside diplomatic or military interventions can be most impactful. By disrupting a rebel group's funding structure through sanctions or terminating one of its channels of support, members of the international community can potentially generate switchovers in compliance status.

Consider the issue of civilian killing. Let us say that rebel groups that have not intentionally killed civilians can be classified as compliant. The FMLN in El Salvador is one example of a "persistent complier." The group intentionally refrained from killing civilians throughout the entirety of their armed struggle. Groups that refrain from killing civilians during certain periods of time, typically toward the later stages of rebellion, exhibit "switchover compliance" and are compliant only in times of active restraint. One example of a switchover complier is the National Union for the Total Independence of Angola (UNITA). UNITA's treatment of civilians improved over time in the wake of economic sanctions and other international pressures, so the group can be classified as a "switchover complier."

Figure 4.1 presents the composition of different types of compliers, or groups exhibiting compliant or non-compliant behavior in the issue of civilian killing.[20] The good news is that persistent compliers are in the majority at 51 percent. These

[20] The transition probabilities have been calculated using the STATA program. More detailed information about measurements, as well as types of compliance in other issue areas, is reported in Chapter 8.

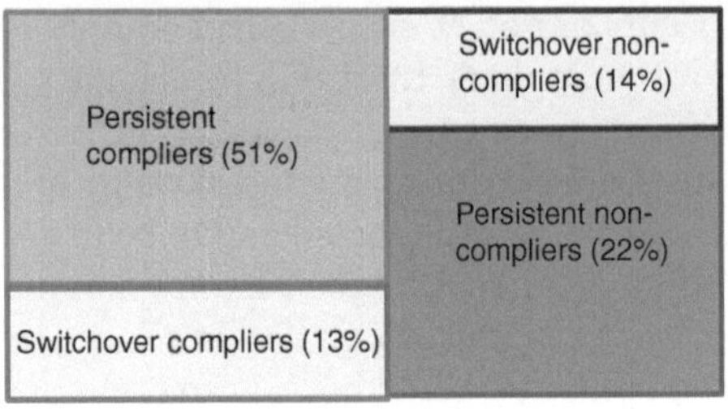

FIGURE 4.1 Types of compliers and non-compliers related to the issue of civilian killing
NB: Compliance is defined as killing no civilians. Non-compliance is defined as a record of some killing. Persistent compliers are those that killed no civilians throughout their armed struggle. Switchover compliers are those that initially killed civilians, but moved to no killing. Switchover non-compliers are those that initially killed no civilians, but later moved to killing. Persistent non-compliers are those that killed civilians throughout their armed struggle.

are rebel groups that did not kill civilians from the start to finish of their rebellion. The bad news is that persistent non-compliers make up almost 22 percent of all rebel groups. The final 30 percent, composed strictly of switchover compliers, sends a positive message to policy prescribers as it suggests that there may be a window in rebel group behavior where influence or other pressures may exact changes. These policy issues are discussed in Chapter 9 in more detail.

Patterns of compliance vary across issue areas. Some rebel groups may comply with one norm by refraining from killing civilians while violating others, for example, by treating detainees harshly or by using child soldiers. Compliance patterns can also vary by time frame. A rebel group may not have started their rebellion by using child soldiers, but the same rebel group may decide to resort to child soldiering when it has a shortage of manpower. Now that we have discussed some of the more important patterns of rebel compliance, I want to turn to exploring the causes behind those patterns.

INDICATORS OF LEGITIMACY-SEEKING REBEL GROUPS

My argument is that the legitimacy-seeking motivations of rebel groups are important determinants of their compliance behaviors. The empirical evidence for the legitimacy-based theory of rebel compliance then requires careful examination of what legitimacy-seeking characteristics are for rebels. How to measure this underlying concept of "legitimacy-seeking motivations" is the challenge I take up in this section.

How do we know whether a rebel group is seeking legitimacy or not? What are the observable characteristics that allow us to make such a distinction? These questions underscore the theoretical challenge of appropriately defining a rebel groups' legitimacy-seeking behaviors and their link to compliance behaviors. I believe the best guide to dispelling the link between legitimacy-seeking behaviors and compliance behaviors lies in a rebel group's governing history and their relationships with core constituencies both at home and abroad.

On an abstract level, legitimacy-seeking rebel groups are the armed opposition groups in civil wars attempting to obtain governing authority in local or national politics.[21] Legitimacy-seeking groups will care about the perception and support from constituencies. They will engage in political activities, building deep social roots in the domestic arena, or forge relationships with external sponsors who care about international law compliance.

Based on these aspects, I focus on these three legitimacy-seeking indicators: (1) the existence of a political wing within a rebel organization; (2) secessionist aims with clear governance objectives in an autonomous region; and (3) foreign support under the influence of human rights groups. The presence of a rebel political wing will generate rebel political activities beyond the military engagement with the government; secessionism will engender the environment where the group forms deep ties with civilians; and foreign support under the influence of human rights groups will make rebel groups conscious of their compliance behavior. In what follows, I identify these three indicators of legitimacy-seeking characteristics and introduce specific measurements of these concepts.

Before I dive into each legitimacy-seeking indicator, I want to clarify one conceptual issue related to measurement. Coming up with these distinctions between legitimacy-seeking and legitimacy-indifferent rebel groups, I note the difference between "having legitimacy" and "seeking legitimacy." Some rebel groups may have legitimacy already by participating in local politics, but these characteristics are also *demonstrated* qualities of legitimacy-seeking characteristics. Without such motivation, rebel groups would not have pursued those political tracts in their rebellion. Also, for these rebel groups, establishing some level of legitimacy is not enough until it achieves its stated goal, be it political autonomy or taking over the central government. Therefore, there will be no clear distinction between "having some level of legitimacy" and "seeking legitimacy" in the case of rebel groups in developing the following measures, although the degree to which legitimacy is desired may vary.

[21] My classification of legitimacy-seeking and legitimacy-indifferent groups shares commonality with existing classifications in its emphasis on political and social constituencies. See Keen (1998) (greed vs. grievance rebel groups); Weinstein (2006) (opportunistic vs. activist rebel groups); Staniland (2012a) (fragmented vs. integrated rebel groups); Stanton (2013) (inclusionary vs. exclusionary rebel groups). It, however, departs from existing classifications in its additional consideration of international legitimacy dimensions of rebellion. The divide between legitimacy-seeking groups and profit-seeking groups is due in part to a disparity in resources and social base, but ultimately rests on the variance in political activities in pursuing domestic and international legitimacy.

Legitimacy-Seeking Indicator (1): Rebel Political Wing

The presence of a rebel political wing provides one indication of a rebel group as being legitimacy-seeking vis-à-vis the domestic populace as well as international audiences. Being involved in the political scene is a characteristic of legitimacy because it demonstrates a history and experience of governance. A militaristic group could still be recognized as viable leaders by a constituency, but the active political component is crucial because of their political capacity to reach out to the domestic constituency and to conduct diplomacy with foreign actors. Moreover, the presence of a political wing indicates a rebel group's awareness of international affairs and norm developments in international law.

Legitimacy-seeking rebel groups are those that take the fight from the battlefield to the political arena, and doing so requires that the group develop the organizational capacity to support political activity. Groups with a political wing typically hold a coherent political vision. In rebel-controlled territories, this vision may actually translate into governing activities, including the administration of social programs like healthcare. Some groups with political wings actually participate in local or national elections, as is the case of Spain's Basque Homeland and Freedom (ETA).[22] These political experiences through election and governance can enhance democratic legitimacy in particular. The fact that rebels have election experience partly indicates that the groups have some popular domestic support.

The influence that a political wing has on the adherence to compliance norms largely depends on how representative a rebel political wing is and how much control the political wing has over its military wing. For instance, Hezbollah's political wing has maintained a strong influence over its military wing. Some rebel groups, like the FLMN in El Salvador, address both military and political concerns through one organization. Other rebel groups have an autonomous political wing structure, such as Sinn Féin and the IRA in Northern Ireland, or a political wing subordinate to military leadership, such as the KLA in Kosovo.[23] These organizational structures affect rebels' level of political and military involvement in rebellion, ultimately influencing their decision on whether to comply with international rules or not.

For a rebel group's political wing to have an impact on that group's compliance with international law, it is critical that the political wing has some control over the group's military wing. A good case in point is the ANC in South Africa. Within the group, decisions made by its political wing were reliably enforced by its military wing. The ANC's military wing, Umkhonto we Sizwe (MK, translated as "Spear of the Nation"), has always

[22] See Sànchez-Cuencaa (2007); Alonso and Reinares (2005) for political activities of ETA. Amaiur, a left-wing separatist Basque coalition and the political wing of ETA, won seven seats (1.4 percent of the vote) in the 2011 general election in Spain. See Economist Intelligence Unit (2013).

[23] Dudouet (2012); also see Weinberg *et al.* (2009).

been under the ANC's political control and subject to its internal mechanisms of accountability.[24]

I adopt a measure from the NSA dataset called "rebel political wing" and "legally allowed political wing" to capture the rebel groups' political activity.[25] The NSA dataset classifies rebel political wing into four categories: no (1), alleged (2), acknowledged (3), and explicit (4); and "legally allowed political wing" into binary categories of yes (1) or no (0). While the presence of a political wing does not guarantee its dominance, the dual nature of military and political wings does provide clues concerning political influence versus military influence. Although the will of the political wing will not always overcome the will of the military wing, I would expect a rebel group's political agenda to exert some influence in the group's overall behavior. Although the drafters of the NSA dataset did not measure the influence of a rebel group's political wing over its military wing, I plan to discuss these detailed political movements in case studies to boost the validity of the measure.

Among 250 rebel groups operating between 1989 and 2009 in the RGIL database, eighty-three groups had a political wing at one point during their armed struggle.[26] Among those eighty-three, forty-three rebel groups enjoyed the status of being legally allowed to have a political wing by the opposing government. This is approximately 30 percent of rebel groups that had a political wing in their organizational structure. Half of those had domestic political constituencies in some fashion by having a political wing that was legally allowed to operate. The examples of rebel groups that have political wing include the KNU in Myanmar, FARC in Colombia, FMLN in El Salvador and UNITA in Angola. It is worth mentioning that the political wing of the KNU had frequent visits to the United Nations, and UNITA in Angola had a political wing that was active in the 1992 elections. These serve as examples of my claim that political wings conduct foreign affairs and participate in elections.

The emergence and growth of rebel political parties also depend on the rebels' relations with the opposing government. For the issues of compliance where governments play active roles as gatekeepers (e.g., allowing aid organizations into rebel-held areas), the legal allowance of a political wing is expected to be a better predictor for compliance behaviors than the mere presence of a rebel political wing. Although governments generally do not want to acknowledge rebel groups as political parties, some do so to reduce the risk of violent resistance.[27] If opposing governments allow a rebel group within the sphere of normal politics and legally recognize the rebels as a party, rebels will then have less incentive to resort to violence unnecessarily. Given rebels' relationship with states, the legitimacy-based theory of compliance predicts that rebels are more likely to comply with international norms when legally permitted to organize a political party.

[24] International Council on Human Rights Policy (2000: 18). [25] Cunningham *et al.* (2013).

[26] I am counting the groups that had political wing explicitly only, leaving out no, alleged, or acknowledged categories.

[27] Gandhi and Lust-Okar (2009).

Legitimacy-Seeking Indicator (2): Secessionist Aims

The second measure of legitimacy-seeking behavior is a rebel group's secessionist aims. As recent literature shows, secessionist rebels desire international legitimacy as they hope to establish a country of their own and place it on the world map.[28] This imperative for a *new* independent country gives them a strong impetus to conduct foreign affairs and reach out to external actors.[29] Non-secessionist rebel groups will also have to earn international legitimacy, but the extent to which they seek out international recognition is not as imperative as it is for secessionist groups. Secessionist groups have to fight against the existing governments. This means that they have to ask the international community to undermine the already established sovereignty of the particular government in the international system. This upsetting of the status quo will be different from gaining "continuing" recognition of the previous political regime.

In addition to this search for international legitimacy, secessionist rebels also pursue domestic legitimacy and may want to abide by international rules to satisfy their domestic constituencies. Rebel groups have to establish legitimacy within their domestic sphere to survive, sustain rebellion, and to win the civil war against the government opposition. Whichever political system the rebels aim at establishing, be it military rule, democracy, or a federalist state, they all have, to some extent, governance aims: that is, to make and implement domestic policies and to conduct diplomacy abroad. Each rebel group will pursue governance aims in varying degrees in different dimensions. Some will want to govern a small pocket of land, achieving political autonomy for its ethnic population; others might want to establish a new national government to govern the entire country. A critical question here is the preference of those who listen to the rebellious cause, how the domestic populace support rebellion, and how civilians perceive their potential to establish authority and rule. The relationship between rebels and the domestic populace provides an important pillar in a rebel group's political experience and the potential to demonstrate political capacity to govern in the future.

The relationship between the domestic populace and rebel groups is a complex subject to study. Rebel group members were part of the domestic populace before they launched their rebellion. New rebel recruits are often from the domestic population, as are their families and relatives. In this tangled social network, the individual preference of the domestic populace with regard to rebel compliance is difficult to pinpoint.[30] Some may want the conflict to end with rebel victory no matter what. Those segments of domestic population will not care much about international human rights standards or international laws of war. Many ordinary people caught in the crossfire between government and rebel forces may want protection for their lives and those of their families. This want will be consistent with international law but to what extent they would sympathize with rebels and in what way they view rebels' legitimacy is difficult to discern in a measurable fashion.

[28] See Fazal (2013). [29] See Huang (2013). [30] I thank Professor Ian Shapiro for this point.

The main difficulty in studying rebel–community relations is the problem of ascertaining the individual preferences of the domestic populace. Many people in the domestic populace would want protection of their right to life – a basic expectation consistent with international human rights norms. However, some people who are politically aligned with secessionist groups may be willing to sacrifice their life for the cause of independence, even if it might mean violation of international standards. Some portions of the domestic populace of the rebel's supporting coalition may want a certain ethnic group to the dominant group in the country, not necessarily caring much about the escalation of conflict or non-compliance with international rules.

Because of the differing opinions, preferences, and attitudes toward rebel compliance among the domestic populace, secessionist aims may produce divergent expectations about rebel groups' compliance with international standards in some instances. As we will later find out, for example, secessionist groups are likely to use child soldiers, in contravention of international law. This is where pursuance of domestic legitimacy can produce non-compliance rather than compliance with international law. This line of reasoning suggests that civilian support can be considered as a legitimacy-seeking indicator, but the interpretation of it should entail careful attention to the preferences of the civilian population.

The consideration of the domestic populace also suggests that my theory of strategic legitimacy is not going to be a blanket statement that legitimacy-seeking rebels will exhibit compliance behaviors no matter what. Legitimacy-seeking rebel groups that care about domestic legitimacy might sometimes violate international laws when the domestic populace may be averse to compliance, privileging winning the war with some human cost. For instance, in populations where the age of majority is 15, they might consider it important to their culture to allow their teenagers to fight, which is contradictory to international norms.

The indicator for secessionist group is from the NSA dataset. In the RGIL database, 57 out of 251 contemporary rebels are secessionist. This number may have been larger for the prior generation of rebel groups between the 1960s and 1980s when independence movements were at their height. Also, if we include groups that seek the political autonomy of a certain region, the number grows to eighty-seven groups. These secessionist movements are worldwide, ranging from Kashmir insurgents in India/Pakistan, Patani insurgents in Thailand, the MFDC in Senegal, and the SPLM in Sudan (now South Sudan).

Some brief examples show the connection between secessionism and compliance with international law. It is notable that the MFDC, fighting for the independence of the Casamance region in Senegal, signed the Deed of Commitment with Geneva Call to stop the use of anti-personnel mines in their struggle, and complied with the commitment.[31] Also, in Sudan, the

[31] Interview with Carole Frampton, 2013.

SPLM signed Operation Lifeline Sudan (OLS) with the United Nations, pledging to respect humanitarian law. Although the aid related to OLS was siphoned off and contributed to the loss of SPLM's domestic legitimacy, such comprehensive commitment was unprecedented at that time, and that type of engagement paved the way for further humanitarian engagement.[32] These examples are also the cases where secessionist groups engaged external actors. This is the legitimacy-seeking indicator I turn to next.

Legitimacy-Seeking Indicator (3): Human Rights-Conscious Foreign Sponsorship

The third legitimacy-seeking indicator of rebel groups is their reliance on external sponsorship, and how that sponsorship is influenced by human rights or humanitarian concerns. Among foreign sponsors there are those that care about human rights or humanitarian issues, who believe they should influence whether rebel groups exercise restraints during their armed struggle. Other foreign sponsors might not care much about human rights or humanitarian consequences. Rebel groups that rely on sponsors that are under pressure from human rights organizations are going to seek legitimacy lest they lose political or military support. According to the measure of foreign state sponsors in the NSA dataset, among the 251 rebel groups that existed between 1990 and 2010, 93 had explicit support from foreign governments, 33 had alleged support, and 119 had no foreign state support. Foreign sponsorship is a substantial portion of rebel groups' support type. Alleged and explicit support cases make up more than half of the rebellions between 1990 and 2010. The supporters range from major powers such as the United States or Germany, to middling ones such as China and India, all the way to small ones such as Rwanda, Sudan, Libya, and Cuba.

In the present era, international organizations as well as domestic human rights groups operate as agents of change, with their ability to interact with rebel groups directly by engagement and negotiation or indirectly by pressuring foreign governments in shaping their foreign policy agenda. Human rights organizations are not supporters of rebels per se, but they are important foreign actors that can influence the compliance behaviors of rebels. Traditionally, international organizations and NGOs have not been recognized as significant sources of influence over rebel group behavior. Not anymore. It is now known that rebel groups understand aid flows from international organizations and NGOs and how they can use them to generate resources, especially as more and more human rights and humanitarian organizations begin operating in various conflict zones across the globe.

Granted, not many international organizations directly engage rebel groups. For instance, among some twenty human rights organizations that have

[32] Washburne (2010).

expertise on child soldier issues, including Save the Children and the International Rescue Committee, only five, including the UN Special Office on Children and Conflict and Geneva Call, directly engage rebel groups for training and negotiation.[33] However, a larger number of organizations must deal indirectly with rebel groups in delivering their human rights or humanitarian goals, whether they like it or not. Médecins sans Frontières, an NGO that cares for the wounded in war-torn regions of the world, published a candid report of field officers negotiating, both implicitly and explicitly, with rebel groups to enable them to operate in conflict zones, especially in rebel-held areas.[34] In some instances, the officers had to take rebel soldiers to their hospitals or pay taxes to rebels in order to tend to civilian victims. Like Médecins sans Frontières, many organizations must face a similar, brutal reality of working with or against rebel groups, which forces many agonizing decisions. It is not their intention to cooperate with rebel groups, but they must make deals with them in order to achieve organizational objectives, such as protecting civilians.

Human rights organizations and humanitarian organizations can operate as agents of international law, prompting changes in rebel behavior. Humanitarian organizations usually differ from human rights organizations by their service roles in conflict zones. For example, groups like Geneva Call have achieved commitments from forty-six rebel groups worldwide not to use anti-personnel mines. However, human rights and humanitarian goals are often blurred in this day and age. For instance, the United Nations sub-body, the Office of the Special Representative of the Secretary-General for Children and Armed Conflict, has engaged rebel groups in Sudan and Yemen to demobilize child soldiers and assist them with reintegration into society. This kind of activity serves dual goals of promoting humanitarian law as well as children's rights in human rights law.

The measure of the number of human rights organizations (HROs) in foreign state sponsors comes from the study on rebel groups' external supporters.[35] The measure counts the number of HRO secretariats in each foreign state sponsor at a certain point in time.[36] The number ranges from zero to seventy-one. The United States houses the largest number of HRO secretariats (seventy-one), providing non-military support to the Jondullah rebellion in Iran or supporting UNITA in Angola at the height of the Cold War under the Reagan Doctrine. At the other end of the spectrum are countries that do not house any HRO secretariats, but support rebel groups abroad. One example is Iran and Syria supporting Hezbollah. As we will see in the subsequent chapters, these foreign influences will have a significant and substantial influence on the

[33] This report on international organizations focusing on the issue of child soldiering is available on the author's project webpage.

[34] Magone *et al.* (2011). [35] Salehyan *et al.* (2014).

[36] The list of 432 HROs is from Murdie and Bhasin (2011). The list includes prominent HROs, such as Human Rights Watch and Amnesty International, and less well-known ones, such as the International Association of Peace Foundations.

behaviors of rebel groups in conformity with international standards of human rights and humanitarian law.

The point is not that the governments with active human rights organizations are under the complete control of the HROs, but that those countries care more about human rights in deciding rebel sponsorship "relative to" the counterpart governments who do not have such human rights constituencies. The influence of human rights organizations is therefore a relative claim, not an absolute one. The comparison here is between rebels getting support from the United States (e.g., Jondullah in Iran) versus rebels who received support from Qaddafi's Libya or/and Charles Taylor's Liberia (e.g., the RUF in Sierra Leone). The claim is not that the US always supports or encourages rebel groups to abide by human rights. Even recognizing the fact that human rights organizations will not dictate the foreign policy goals of a nation, their channel of influence leads us to the expectation that there will be differences in preferences with a nation under human rights influence from one without such influence.

Taking Stock

The three legitimacy-seeking conditions can occur separately or simultaneously. Some rebel groups will focus on political activities by participating in normal political processes, such as elections or policymaking to the extent allowed by the opposing state. Other rebel groups might try to utilize their political wings and activities to establish a lasting connection with civilians.[37]

The presence of one or more legitimacy indicators does not guarantee compliance behaviors by rebel groups. They only serve as predictors of compliance and my hypotheses are probabilistic conjectures. It is also notable that some groups fail to engage external actors despite their legitimacy-seeking records. The PKK in Turkey, for example, sought domestic legitimacy from its population, but nonetheless engaged in many kinds of non-compliance behaviors, as the group relied heavily on funding from the diaspora population in Europe. In the case of the Maoists in Nepal, maintaining governance functions did not guarantee that the group would refrain from committing abuses against the civilian population. The group enjoyed popular support, but committed numerous acts of violence against citizens. These cases

[37] The performance of legitimacy indicators can vary across contexts. For example, the working of legitimacy-seeking characteristics will differ based on the ability of rebel groups to utilize and transmit those characteristics. Rebel groups' military strength, fighting capacity, or the command-and-control structures are mediating variables here. For example, rebel groups that exhibit legitimacy-seeking characteristics will utilize their capability in command-and-control structures to further reduce violence. Rebel groups without legitimacy characteristics may exploit their command-and-control structures to commit more violence. Note that these legitimacy-seeking indicators are not necessary but are sufficient conditions. For example, a rebel group having a governing function does not guarantee the rebel group having legitimacy goals. Also, the more sub-indicators, the more likely the group will be legitimacy-seeking.

may often arise because of temporary military imperatives or because the more extreme factions act on their own impulses rather than follow the party line.

The lesson here is that the theoretical associations do not provide perfect predictors for compliance. Even a rebel group with the seemingly "right" characteristics, possessing all the legitimacy-seeking indicators, may well stumble on the road to non-compliance in practice. However, these associations and likelihoods will reveal what matters in determining oscillations between non-compliance and compliance. Except for some anomaly cases, the guideline of looking at legitimacy-seeking characteristics can usefully be used to inform policy choices and contribute to our understanding of rebel compliance.

To this end, Box 4.1 provides a checklist for rebel groups' legitimacy-seeking characteristics. Note the interrelationships among indicators. Rebel groups with electoral experience are more likely to establish strong embedded relationships with their constituencies (L1 and L2 often go together). Groups that are open to transnational actors, especially religious organizations or diaspora populations, will have close relations with domestic civilians (L2 and L3 often go together).

Note on the Fate of Compliant Rebels

The fate of these legitimacy-seeking rebel groups can be also examined in the RGIL database. Since my argument is that legitimacy-seeking characteristics are

Box 4.1 Checklist: identifying legitimacy-seeking rebel groups

Legitimacy-seeking indicator (1) (L1): engagement in normal politics:

- Does the group have a political wing that has some control over an armed wing?
- Does the group have past political experience in normal politics, such as participating in local elections, to the extent that the national government has allowed this?

Legitimacy-seeking indicator (2) (L2): embedded relations with domestic constituencies:

- Does the group rely on civilians for their voluntary support, not resorting to looting resources?
- Does the group aim at secession or political autonomy of a certain region with governance aims?

Legitimacy-seeking indicator (3) (L3): openness to international constituencies:

- Is the group open to outside actors such as humanitarian organizations?
- Does the group have external sponsors that care about human rights norms?

likely to lead to compliance, it would be instructive to see the patterns as to how these legitimacy-seeking groups end their conflicts. Among forty-three rebel groups with legal political wings, nine signed peace agreements, two signed ceasefire agreements, four resulted in victories, one resulted in defeat, twenty-two remain as low activity rebellions, and seven have not been terminated. Having a legal political wing does not get rebels to the victory line. However, considering the win rate of less than 10 percent (twenty-three rebel groups won out of 251 groups in the dataset), this is not a bad record, indicating that legitimacy-seeking characteristics may not be centrally disadvantaging to rebel groups in general.

Here is the type of conflict resolution among fifty-seven secessionist groups, one of the proxies for governance aims in my legitimacy-seeking indicators: ten signed peace agreements, ten signed ceasefire agreements, seven ended due to a one-sided victory (only the Eritrean People's Liberation Front (EPLF) in Ethiopia achieved victory as a rebel; other cases are victory by government forces), twenty-five remain in low activity, and eleven are not terminated. Secessionist groups have a difficult time achieving victory and are more likely to reach an agreement (peace agreement or ceasefire) or to continue rebellion in some fashion, either at low level or at intense level.

Rebel groups with a foreign state sponsor with civil society influence are more likely to make peace agreements as a means to end the conflict. As detailed in Table 4.2, rebel groups with such sponsors resulted in 27 percent (twenty-five out of ninety-two) making peace agreements. Rebel groups with sponsors under no civil society influence resulted in 14 percent (twenty-three out of 154) signing peace agreements. Legitimacy-seeking rebels are more likely to win (14 percent: thirteen out of ninety-two) compared with the groups without such HRO influence (6 percent: ten out of 154).

TABLE 4.2. *Fate of rebel groups and foreign state sponsorship*

	Rebel groups without foreign state sponsor under HRO influence	Rebel groups with foreign state sponsor under HRO influence	Total
Peace agreements	23	25	48
Ceasefire	9	5	14
Government victory	21	5	26
Rebel victory	10	13	23
Low activity	70	27	97
Not terminated	21	17	38
Total	154	92	246

REBELS AND RESOURCES

Getting material support is part of legitimacy-building. The support for rebels is not the same as conferring legitimacy, but the information on rebel support provides background to what type of support rebel groups can muster. Recall that legitimacy is the perception of relevant political constituencies about the viability of authority or rule. Support is often a necessary part of legitimacy, but not every rebel group that enjoys support has legitimacy. For example, even if a rebel group funds itself sufficiently with natural resources such as diamonds and timber, the group does not have natural constituencies to respond to and, therefore, that particular resource-dependent rebel group will lack legitimacy.

Since the key to the strategic legitimacy theory is the mode of rebel financing and support in relation to key rebel constituencies, I hereby present some patterns related to rebels' resources. With this information, readers will be able to have a general sense of how rebels gain resources and support, and later connect these patterns to compliance behaviors. As the objective of this chapter is to report empirical patterns, this section will focus on the information gleaned from the RGIL database. Readers can find more detailed discussions on theoretical relevance of resources and legitimacy in Chapter 3.

How do rebel groups finance rebellion in general? Every organization needs resources to operate, and rebel organizations are no exception. Rebel groups must pay or feed their soldiers and buy munitions for their fight against an opposing government. Broadly defined, resources in this section are not confined to material support, but include political support as well. Rebel groups can finance their operations through a number of various sources, including natural resources, taxes on the civilian population, monetary or in-kind diaspora support, kidnapping for ransom, extortion, foreign firms, or external state support. Rebels may also receive munitions through the opposing government itself.

Primary resource channels occur at three levels: domestic support, foreign support, and natural resources. Domestic sources typically rely on civilians, often through forcible taxation or recruitment from the civilian pool. Foreign support includes a variety of sources, including support from foreign governments, transnational military and non-military support, as well as diaspora support. The third resource channel – natural resources – relies upon a rebel group's ability to locate and extract natural resources, such as diamonds, gems, or drugs. These financing types are discussed in more detail below before I present the empirical patterns of the rebel groups' financing portfolio.

Domestic Support

Domestic support defines rebel groups' mobilization capability. Rebels' home base provides a strong source of political support and resources. Here is where rebels usually get their recruits, along with any logistical or material support held exclusively by the domestic population. Buying loyalty or garnering allegiance is no easy matter and civilian support can be either forced or voluntary. When rebel groups recruit children into their ranks, for instance, they either forcefully recruit them or convince the community to volunteer their children for the group's cause. Rebels typically receive material support through forceful means, like taxation, while logistical support is most often given voluntarily. Domestic funding sources also include most instances of kidnapping for ransom, although some kidnap cases involve foreign persons. How rebels extract resources from domestic sources varies across groups. The Maoists in Nepal, for example, engaged in taxation, whereas the Revolutionary Armed Forces of Colombia (FARC) relied on kidnapping for ransom. These different modes of extraction will have consequences for the nature of rebel groups' community relations.

Rebels must compete against opposing governments for domestic support, and often the competition is fierce. In some instances, the struggle may become so hostile that rebel groups begin selectively targeting civilians to stave off defection to the opposing government.[38] Some separatist rebels lack any readily accessible broad domestic support and instead attempt to rely upon foreign support on top of the sympathy from their own ethnics. A case in point is Aceh in Indonesia. Its movement for independence never garnered much popularity among the Indonesian population, so the rebellion attempted to appeal to the international community to sustain its activities. As these examples illustrate, domestic support is vital for the success of a rebellion as their rule will eventually be in the rebel groups' domestic political sphere. But not every rebel group enjoys domestic support from civilians, and they often find themselves resorting to extortion and forceful recruitment.

Foreign Support

In this era of global interconnectedness, rebellions have become international affairs. Foreign support comes in various forms, be it military or non-military, and from various sources, such as foreign governments, the diaspora community, or even business firms. The influence of these private and public foreign actors should not be understated, especially when strong regional or global security interests are at stake. Often, such support is large enough to tip a rebellion's balance of power. The well-known business connections maintained by the RUF in Sierra Leone with foreign firms allowed the group to circumvent the travel ban imposed by the United Nations. RUF members invited private businessmen to come to them instead of them flying outside. This circumvention of travel bans allowed the group to secure a vital line of support money from diamond proceeds. In the case of LTTE in Sri Lanka, diaspora support strongly fueled the rebellion's violence before the event of September 11.

[38] Kalyvas (2006).

However, when the group was branded as a terrorist organization after September 11, the diaspora population refrained from supporting direct military actions which had consequences on the course of LTTE movement.[39]

Traditionally, external state support has played an influential role in determining the outcome of armed political opposition. Its importance has been particularly strong in African rebellions, where the widespread presence of rare, precious resources such as diamonds often sustains armed rebellion with the assistance of external influences.[40] It is important, however, to recognize that external or foreign support may take many shapes, and the very *source* of foreign support has consequences on rebel groups' compliance behavior. If rebels rely heavily on foreign supporters that care about human rights (e.g., democratic states under civil society influence), those rebel groups would be more likely to exercise restraints than their counterparts who rely on external sponsors that do not care about international norms (e.g., terrorist networks).

The nature of foreign support also matters, whether it is substantial military support or just verbal sympathy for the rebel cause. The international discussion surrounding sponsors of the Syrian rebels in 2013 highlights this aspect. Some extremist factions of the rebels had received support from various charities across Kuwait, while the United States funneled training and military resources to the Syrian Free Army.[41] As a result, the rebellion has taken on deeply divided nature, from the extreme Syrian factions, such as the Islamic State in Iraq and the Levant (ISIL) and Jabhat al-Nusra, to the more moderate ones, such as Ahrar al-Sham and Jaysh al-Islam. This crosshair state of Syrian rebellion generated much debate on how foreign supporters can create fruitful engagements with rebel groups.[42] At the time of writing (October 2014), the fate of Syrian rebels against the Assad regime is far from certain given the complexity of geopolitics involving the United States, Russia, Saudi Arabia, Qatar, Turkey, and Iran, with the rapid rise of ISIL.

Foreign support may also take the form of non-state transnational support. Transnational support can indicate a broader transnational constituency composed of some combination of overt supporters and idle sympathizers. Such support includes financing by Islamic charities, help by ethnic kin in neighboring regions, or assistance from a distant diaspora. Of the types of transnational support channels, diaspora support has become one of the fastest growing, as large-scale patterns of international migration has resulted in greater funds being sent to countries involved in civil conflict. These remittances are five times larger than the sum of all foreign aid in fragile countries,[43] although it is difficult to estimate how much of these funds are funneled into conflicts and end up in rebel hands. This diverse map of foreign support will be examined further in the subsequent chapters when we connect these funding sources to rebel behaviors.

[39] Fair (2007). [40] Clapham (1998); Boot (2013). [41] Dickinson (2013). [42] Al-Abdeh (2013).
[43] World Bank (2014).

Natural Resources

Rebel-held territory often houses natural resources, such as oil, diamonds, drugs, minerals, and timber, that can provide rebel groups with a lucrative source of financing. Some resources are easier to utilize than others, making them much easier to convert into militant resources. Diamonds can get onto black markets easily, while oil cannot since it requires pipelines and other capital intensive investments. "Conflict/blood diamonds" exploited by UNITA in Angola and the RUF in Sierra Leone provided the groups with a quick and profitable means for financing their operations until international sanctions stepped in and effectively halted the traffic in them. For these reasons of accessibility and extractability, diamonds are classified as lootable natural resources along with timber and drugs, whereas oil and natural gas are classified as unlootable natural resources.[44] Whenever and wherever available, all that rebels require to generate revenue from natural resources is an adequate means for extraction and access to a marketplace.[45] As such, natural resources supply many attractive options for financing since rebels can avoid the potential constraints that may result from relying on domestic or foreign supporters. It allows rebels to generate their own revenues while avoiding the coercive preferences of political principals.

Rebel Groups' Financing Portfolio

How do rebel groups *actually* finance their wars? The RGIL database gives a glimpse of the view on the distribution of resource dependency among rebel groups, as reported in Table 4.3. The resources considered in this table are: domestic support, foreign support, and natural resources. Domestic support is measured with "moderate or high mobilization capacity" – the ability to mobilize personnel – from the NSA dataset.[46] The rationale here is that if a rebel group can mobilize the domestic population at a great level, their domestic source of support is likely to be substantial. Foreign support is measured with "explicit foreign government support," also from NSA. In this scheme, "no support" or "alleged support" cases are sidelined because only explicit support would indicate a significant and ostensible source of foreign funding. Natural resources are measured with the presence of "lootable resources" in civil conflict zones from Fearon's work on natural resources.[47]

These categories are by no means an exhaustive list of rebel groups' financing methods. As explained above, we could alternatively look at diaspora support, support from rebel-terrorist networks, and contributions from religious affiliations, etc. Also, the natural resources can be further broken down to different types of resources such as oil, drugs, timber, or gems. With the caveat that the distribution relies on specific measurement and that the list is non-exhaustive, I examine broad patterns of rebel financing.

[44] Ross (2004). [45] Hazen (2013). [46] Cunningham *et al.* (2013). [47] Fearon (2004).

TABLE 4.3 *Rebel groups and resource reliance*

Resource reliance		Number of rebel groups	Example
None	None	52 (24%)	Abu Sayyaf (Philippines)
One	Domestic support	98 (45%)	EPLF (Ethiopia)
	Foreign support	93 (43%)	KNU (Myanmar)
	Natural resources	90 (41%)	FARC (Colombia)
Two	Domestic and foreign	43 (20%)	SPLM (Sudan)
	Domestic and natural resources	25 (11%)	LTTE (Sri Lanka)
	Foreign and natural resources	35 (16%)	Hezb-i-Wahdat (Afghanistan)
Three	All three	10 (5%)	UNITA (Angola)
Total		251 (33 with missing records)	

Among 251 contemporary rebel groups operating between 1989 and 2009, thirty-three have missing records for their financing portfolio. These groups are mostly obscure groups for which reliable data do not exist. Among 218 groups that have records for their financing methods, 24 percent of them rely on none of the resources specified. This does not necessarily mean that these groups do not operate on any income, but that the listed three are not the dominant sources of their finance. These groups, for example, have low mobilization capacity, not necessarily relying heavily on domestic mobilization to support their rebellion. Some of this is due to rebel groups' operational methods of relying on a small number of devoted recruits, such as the case of certain terrorist groups, rather than needing mass mobilization of domestic civilians. We can see that roughly about 40 percent rebel groups rely on at least of one of the sources of funding: domestic support, foreign support, or natural resources. Looking at the combination of two funding sources, we see that the combination of domestic and foreign support is most popular, constituting 20 percent of rebel groups. The combination of domestic support and natural resources is less frequent, constituting about 10 percent of rebel groups. Groups that are able to use all three types of funding are rare. Only 5 percent groups are able to pull off managing domestic and foreign support as well as commanding natural resources.

The distribution of rebel financing reported here has implications for the strategic legitimacy theory. As assumed as part of the theory, resources are an important part of rebellion. Most of the rebel groups have at least one type of financing to sustain their rebel movements. Second, commanding all the supports or resources is a tall order for most rebel groups. The rarity of rebel groups that have all three financing methods indicates that rebel groups might want to have all three supports, but not many are able to do so. Third, and most importantly, the variations among these financing types indicate that these differences in financing methods might have consequences for how rebel groups manage their military wars and political battles. This will be more closely examined in the subsequent empirical chapters.

The above description of rebel group financing gleaned from the RGIL database provides a rough sketch of the nature of rebel support channels, but its limitations must be noted. Recent studies on rebel groups dig into their economic structure and market aspects,[48] but not much is known in terms of exact amounts. We do not know, for example, how much the Islamic State in Syria is supporting its rebellion through foreign support or through extraction from its rebel-held areas. This is largely due to the opaque nature of rebel financing. As such, the rebel groups' portfolio cannot be determined with absolute certainty.

For the purpose of this book, more important than these exact amounts are the sources and the implications of rebel financing. How rebels fund their activities will have a great impact on how they behave with respect to the laws of war. Depending on their political principals or audiences, or lack thereof, rebels may face constraints or run unimpeded. Exclusive dependence on natural resources may affect rebel compliance by putting no constraints on behaviors. Consider the case of the RUF in Sierra Leone. Relying on Charles Taylor's support from neighboring Liberia and the timber and drug trade, the group serves as a prime example of a rebel group facing few to no constraints in their maiming and killing of civilians.

Knowledge of rebel financing alone is not sufficient for understanding rebel groups' compliance behavior, but it is necessary. As the rest of this book will show, how rebel groups fund their movements will be conditioned by a number of other factors, such as their organizational structure or relationships with domestic and foreign constituencies. The key patterns of rebel financing spelled out here will help to illuminate the issue of rebel compliance as it is discussed in later sections.

LIMITATIONS AND DRAWBACKS OF THE RGIL DATABASE

Despite the potential benefits of the RGIL database, I want to caution the reader regarding some limitations and drawbacks of the data. Although I will be attentive to these data features and qualities when I later interpret the evidence of compliant rebels, I want to be upfront about what will be forthcoming. Readers who are interested in measurement and data issues beyond what is described in this section should refer to Appendix "Notes on Data."

[48] Byman *et al.* (2001); Zahar (2001); Ross (2004); Weinstein (2006); Keen (2012).

The first limitation is the paucity of information for some rebel groups. Prominent rebel groups that attracted international attention, such as the LRA in Uganda or the RUF in Sierra Leone, leave researchers ample secondary sources. Many of these are historical facts vetted by many researchers over time, and in many cases large parts of this knowledge have already been gleaned from primary sources and documents. This is not the case for more recent, small, and obscure rebel groups as information is scarce. The only available source for very recent rebel groups may be journalistic. Information can also come directly from the rebel groups themselves, but researchers have had problems in distinguishing propaganda from fact. The paucity of information and veracity of facts are primary challenges in researching contemporary rebel groups. One potential solution may be to focus on a small sample of rebel groups. But since the purpose of this book is to draw a general picture of contemporary rebellion across the globe, I acknowledge these limitations and continue my empirical inquiry.

Another limitation, for the purpose of my investigation of compliant rebels, is that some of the measures do not change much over time. This problem of static measure poses some problems in testing dynamic predictions. For example, this is the case for rebel use of child soldiers. It is often unclear when the use of child soldiers by rebel groups starts and ends, so we cannot track down the change with ease. Marking the ending may be easier than pinpointing the start because some of the groups disband or go through the demobilization process. Even then, however, the messy nature of rebellion might kick in. Some rebel factions may not participate in the demobilization and reintegration process and come back using child soldiers when the conflict breaks out again. For these reasons, identifying the exact period of child soldiering during rebellion is a tall order.

This measurement problem is similar to the case of the use of a rebel political wing. The presence of a rebel political wing cannot capture all the dynamics over the course of organizational evolution of a rebel group. The rebel political wing might be strong at times, but weak at others. The political wing might be involved in power struggles with military wing at some point, but not in others. Or some rebel political leaderships might launch new political programs, while other leaders at different periods might be more submissive to military decisions. These kind of details will not be profitably captured in quantitative measures of rebel political wing activity. In many cases on obscure groups, these kind of data are almost impossible to obtain, and in the case of rebel groups for which ample information is available, these graduated measurements may not be reliably comparable across groups. Recognizing these limitations, I also rely on qualitative case studies where I can be more flexible and nuanced in the discussion of measures. The process tracing of the wax and wane of the legitimacy-seeking characteristics of rebel groups will help overcome the limitations of quantitative analysis.

Despite these current limitations, we have to start somewhere. This starting point may not be sufficient, but I believe this is part of scientific progress and knowledge accumulation. Future studies will improve upon what went previously, and this rule, hopefully, will apply in our understanding of compliance. With these caveats about measurement qualities, the next three chapters will attempt to uncover the patterns of rebel compliance and the reasons behind compliance and non-compliance.

HYPOTHESES

Based on the theoretical discussion in the previous chapter and empirical measures presented in this chapter, I now present the empirically testable hypotheses. The key expectation of the legitimacy-based theory of compliance is that legitimacy-seeking rebel groups are more likely to comply with international law when pursuing legitimacy both at home and abroad. More specifically, three testable hypotheses are presented below.

Hypothesis 1: rebel groups with political wings are more likely to comply with international norms. Rebel groups with political wings advance their political agenda in the midst of their armed struggle. This expectation would be stronger especially when the political wing has a firm control over the group's military wing and particularly when the opposing government allows the rebel political party to operate in normal politics.

Hypothesis 2: rebel groups with secessionist aims are more likely to comply with international norms. Secessionist aims prime rebel groups to seek international legitimacy due to their desire to be a part of the international community. At the domestic level, they are likely to maintain governing functions in the form of providing healthcare, education, or even the provision of justice, which indicates a rebel group's social ambitions.[49] These secessionist rebel groups are more likely to aspire toward becoming a viable political entity in the future, and in order to achieve that aim, they are more likely to be attuned to the needs of civilians and local elites and less likely to mistreat them. These rebel groups can establish social relations with civilians even without social provisions because of family or ethnic ties. Thus, the expectation is that secessionist groups with social embeddedness are more likely to refrain from violence against civilians, relative to non-secessionist ones.[50]

Hypothesis 3: rebel groups that rely on foreign state sponsors with human rights organizations are more likely to comply with international norms. Rebel groups that accept international actors in their controlled zones are more likely to have aspirations for international legitimacy. As a result, these groups are more likely to abide by international rules. Those groups that open themselves to international humanitarian organizations, such as the ICRC, or NGOs, such as Geneva Call, are especially more likely to make commitment to international law and subsequently change their behaviors to conform with international standards. This may be a tactical concession or a

[49] Mampilly (2011). [50] Staniland (2012a).

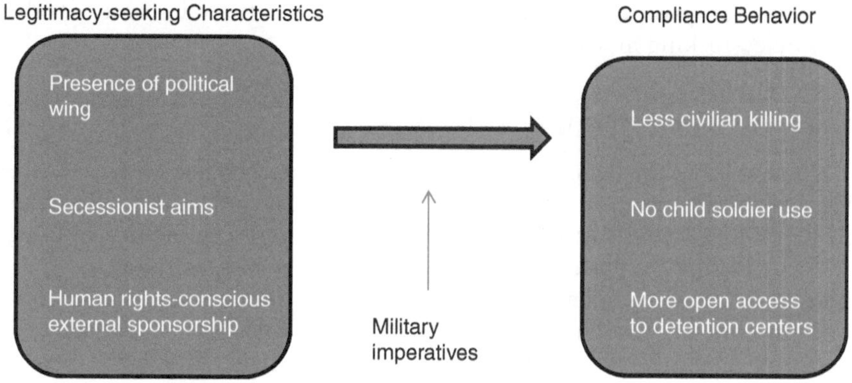

FIGURE 4.2 Legitimacy and compliance: summary of hypotheses

"commitment tactic"[51] on the part of rebel groups to gain a favorable bargaining position vis-à-vis government. Rebel leadership may assume that they have more bargaining power at the negotiation table with a government when they have the backing of international actors. Alternatively, the change in behavior may stem from the prospect of receiving material benefits from international actors, such as aid materials.[52]

The hypotheses are summarized in Figure 4.2 in the context of the three issues I will examine in the following empirical chapters: civilian killing, child soldiering, and access to detention centers. In summary, the theory of rebel compliance indicates that the reduction in violence is a political strategy for the rebel groups with long-term goals in mind. This theoretical framework can be used to explain non-compliance and persistent compliance, as well as the change from non-compliance to compliance. If a rebel group lacks legitimacy aims – with no political appetite for normal political processes, no established relationship with civilians, and little openness to outside actors – it is more likely to resort to unconstrained violence without ever attempting to restrain its violence. In contrast, some fully legitimacy-seeking groups will refrain from violence at the outset of the conflict because of their political experiences and social embeddedness. Other partially legitimacy-seeking groups may initially start as being violent, but may move on to

[51] Muthoo (2000).

[52] However, it is important to note that not all transnational supports are alike. For example, some diaspora populations will support the rebels' cause no matter what, see Collier and Hoeffler (2000). Other diaspora populations may organize HROs to keep rebels' violent behavior in check (Adamson 2013). Recognizing the role of transnational supporters seems to be consequential, but relative to other sources of rebel support (foreign state support or the role of resources) it is poorly understood. If a certain category of transnational support has a violence-reducing effect, we would like to leverage that knowledge for better policies.

non-violence positions or reduce violence over time because of their legitimacy-seeking motivations.

ROADMAP FOR EMPIRICAL EVIDENCE

In the next three chapters, readers will see the empirical evidence of my theory. The issue coverage will include the three humanitarian and human rights issues: civilian killing, child soldiering, and detention access. The inquiry will begin with uncovering the patterns of compliance. I will report temporal and spatial patterns of rebel compliance between 1989 and 2009. Some examples and vignettes will be introduced by way of presenting descriptive statistics. The statistical analyses will be then presented to assess the association between legitimacy-seeking motivations and compliance behaviors by rebel groups. Case studies will follow. That will enrich the discussion of causal pathways and causal links that connect rebels' legitimacy concerns to their compliance behaviors. I will provide a background for a particular rebel group, and discuss how the rebel group complied or changed its behavior from non-compliance to compliance in the course of building its political legitimacy. This process tracing will also involve discussion of similarities and differences to other groups operating within a similar region for comparative purposes. I will also consider the key alternative arguments for compliant rebels, weighing the importance of legitimacy as an explanatory factor. With this roadmap in mind, let us start with the examination of how contemporary rebel groups treated civilians under international law.

5

Civilian Killing

> Persons taking no active part in the hostilities ... shall in all circumstances be treated humanely.
>
> Common Article 3 of the Geneva Conventions

> We will do our utmost to guarantee the protection of civilian populations in accordance with the principles of human rights and international humanitarian law.
>
> Justice and Equality Movement (JEM) and Sudan Liberation Army (SLA)–Unity in 2008[1]

"When two elephants fight, it is the grass that suffers."[2] The African proverb captures the idea that the powerless suffer the most when the powerful fight. In the same vein, civilians often face much suffering during civil conflicts: disappearances, abductions, arbitrary arrests, rapes, beatings, extortions, and summary executions are the harsh reality of ordinary people in internal conflicts. Civilians are frequently caught in the crossfire, having to flee from their homes and become refugees, often times permanently. Many have perished in mass killings and atrocities.

Against this harsh reality, international humanitarian law provides an idea of legal protection for civilians. The "principle of distinction" is the idea of distinguishing civilians from combatants in order to shield civilians from the conduct of war. The norm has been shaped by historical experiences of brutal wars and has gained a firm ground with legal codifications.[3] For instance, the above quotation from the Geneva Convention embodies the principle that

1 JEM and SLM-Unity, "Statement by the Opposition Movements," 2008. Statement made during a meeting between the Geneva-based Centre for Humanitarian Dialogue (HD Centre) and the opposition movements in Darfur. The document is available at "Their Words: Directory of Armed Non-State Actor Humanitarian Commitments," at: theirwords.org/media/transfer/doc/1_sd_jem_slm_a_unity_2008_18-9786ecfeda2b4605ff60bcdc4aab48b2.pdf.

2 Healy and Sybertz (1996: 36–37).

3 See Kinsella (2011) for the development of these ideas and norms on civilians in the laws of war.

civilians should be treated humanely. However, accepting the idea is one thing, the practice of it is another. Despite the compelling nature of the normative force of the principle, its implementation has been full of non-compliance. Mass killing has plagued many modern wars in places such as Rwanda, Yugoslavia, and Sierra Leone.[4]

In general, war is a messy affair. Soldiers respond to psychological impulses. Even if a leadership wants to impose the norm of respecting civilian life, it may not be able to reach every foot-soldier and every battlefield. Civilian killings occur even within states with clear command-and-control structures. Imagine rebel groups that usually have less clear command-and-control structures than government armies.

Given these obstacles to the civilian protection during civil conflicts, how and when would compliant rebels emerge? This is the question this chapter attempts to tackle. Like the Darfur rebel groups quoted above, some rebel groups commit to the cause of protecting civilians. Certain rebel groups sometimes go beyond the commitment and actually comply with the norms of treating civilians humanely. In contrast, many rebel groups have perpetrated some of history's worst atrocities, flouting the principle of distinction. To untangle this variation in rebel behaviors, I examine the related international norms, explore the empirical patterns of rebel civilian killing, and trace the cause of compliant and non-compliant rebels in the issue of civilian killing.

THE NORM: PRINCIPLE OF DISTINCTION

The distinction between combatants and non-combatants is as old as the idea of war. However, distinguishing civilians from military objects is fairly a modern notion, although the concepts of honor, chivalry, and mercy have always existed and can be traced back as the roots of the principle of distinction.[5] Over time, the norm has progressed to the point where it has been legally codified and universally accepted. More recently, beyond the norm of distinction, some policymakers suggest that there should be a "responsibility to protect" (often dubbed as "R2P"), where civilians are actively protected from the harmful effects of war.[6] The idea goes beyond the passive admission of the need for distinction to acknowledge that there is an active need for protection.

The list of significant codified legal instruments affirms that the principle of distinction is a widely accepted norm. The idea of distinguishing civilians from combatants is codified in the Common Article 3 of the Geneva Conventions (1949) and subsequently in the Geneva Conventions Additional Protocol II (1977).[7] The Common Article stipulates that non-combatants (or civilians)

[4] The rough figure of people who have died in civil wars for various causes is 17 million. See Laitin (2007); Regan (2008).

[5] Kinsella (2011). [6] Thakur and Weiss (2009).

[7] See Mantilla (2015) for the negotiating history of Article 3.

that do not take part in hostilities should be treated humanely. That is, non-combatants should not be tortured, arbitrarily detained, or summarily executed. The Common Article 3 also holds that non-combatants should be distinguished from combatants and that they should be treated as such. To borrow the words of law professor, James E. Bond, "one must continue to distinguish between what a soldier can do to the enemy firing an AK-47 at him, and what he can do to an old man plowing a rice paddy."[8]

According to international law, not only government soldiers but also rebel groups have an obligation to follow this norm of distinction.[9] On the international legal scene, rebel groups are increasingly under pressure from international criminal law. In fact, they can be tried at the international level. While the Common Article 3 sets the tone of governing rules within civil conflicts, the Rome Statute to the ICC is the most recent international law that governs the treatment of civilians, along with other atrocity crimes. Abusive rebel groups can be prosecuted at the ICC if their country is not willing, or able, to try them at their national courts. Among the thirty-five persons indicted between 2002 and 2013 at the ICC, more than half are rebel group leaders.[10]

The norm of prohibition of civilian killing is global and widely accepted across cultures and ideologies. The principle of distinction mainly grew out of the Christian culture,[11] but the protection of the weak is also consistent with other religions such as Islam.[12] One of the first caliphs (rulers of the Muslim community), Caliph Abu Bakr told his warriors:

> When you meet your enemies in the fight, behave yourself as befits good Muslims ... If Allah gives you victory, do not abuse your advantages and beware not to stain your swords with the blood of one who yields, neither you touch the children, the women, nor the infirm, also men, whom you may find among your enemies.[13]

Despite its wide acceptance of the norm, the practice has proven to be problematic.[14] In civil conflict situations, distinguishing combatants from non-combatants is not easy. Sometimes clad in civilian clothes, rebel group members are often indistinguishable from civilians. Civilians often assist rebel movements or become government sympathizers, generating questions as to whether they should be regarded as "enemy combatants." Also, depending on the interpretations of who is a civilian and who is not, the norm is practiced differently by war participants. An expansive definition of civilians is to include anyone that is not partaking in the active war effort. Defined narrowly,

[8] Bond (1971: 793). [9] Clapham (2010). [10] See Chapter 2 on the related discussion.

[11] Kinsella (2011). [12] Bassiouni and Guellali (2010); Bassiouni (2013).

[13] Aly (2014). Despite the commonality in principle, however, the different factions of Islam can exhibit different interpretations of civilian targeting. For instance, the defensive jihad interprets the principle to mean that civilian targeting is not prohibited when it is necessary to protect Islam from destruction.

[14] Swiney (2005).

however, any civilians that provide food or logistical support will be classified as enemy combatants, thus leaving them as legitimate military targets.

The disconnection between the idea in principle and the norm in practice sets the background for rebel compliance. Some rebel groups will accept the norm in principle, but sometimes have difficulty in complying as a result of practical reasons. Other groups disregard the rules outright or interpret the norm in their own ideological light. The reasons why and the mechanisms by which these differences between compliant and non-compliant rebels are produced is the topic that I turn to next.

THEORETICAL EXPECTATIONS

Civilian abuse and political violence have puzzled many students of politics because of their deadliness and significance in modern life. Recent horrific experiences of the Rwandan genocide, the Srebrenica massacre in Bosnia, and the "Killing Fields" in Cambodia shocked the world and have demanded explanations. Many people have suggested different reasons for civilian abuse. Ethnic hatreds, discrimination, undemocratic governments, and dysfunctional societies are cited as the major causes. Other studies have shown that governments kill civilians when they expect future opposition groups in order to prevent defections.[15] As these multitudes of explanations show, state leaders' strategic incentives for mass killings are well studied.[16]

We know relatively less about why rebel groups kill. Recent studies on political violence show that a territorial contest is the prime condition for civilian killing,[17] and that rebel groups without internal discipline are more likely to commit violence against civilians than those under strong organizational control.[18] Little attention has been given to the political relations of rebel groups with their key constituencies at home and abroad.

Distinguishing my own from previous works, I focus on rebel political relations as the key determinants of compliance with international norms of civilian distinction. To be fair, the previous studies primarily look at the causes of "political violence," while I look at the causes of "compliance." The two topics overlap, but the important difference is my attention to how rebels view international norms and how they sometimes change their behaviors because of those considerations. In this respect, an international norm is an important intervening variable for me, whereas previous studies do not consider international law.

With the distinction from previous works in mind, this particular section provides theoretical expectations about rebel civilian killing in the light of the

[15] Kalyvas (2006); Downes (2008). [16] Valentino (2004). [17] Kalyvas (2006).
[18] Weinstein (2006).

strategic legitimacy theory posited in Chapter 3. These theoretical expectations also build on the empirical indicators of rebel legitimacy characteristics that I developed in Chapter 4.

My theory of rebel compliance suggests that legitimacy-seeking groups are more likely to refrain from civilian abuses compared with legitimacy-indifferent groups. In line with my legitimacy thesis, I expect that legitimacy-seeking rebel groups refrain from civilian abuses in internal conflicts because of strategic reasons to gain legitimacy. Specifically, I focus on three legitimacy-seeking traits of rebel groups to arrive at three empirically testable hypotheses.

The first expectation is that rebel groups with political wings are more likely to comply with international norms. Some political wings initiate political programs such as elections to attain domestic legitimacy. An organizational focus within a rebel group on political programs can also check military wings' unconstrained incentive to win. Additionally, the presence of a political wing will often help a rebel group to win international legitimacy through its conduct of foreign diplomacy or on the basis of its knowledge of international affairs. Therefore, the expectation is that rebel groups with political wings are likely to kill fewer civilians than rebel groups without this trait.

The second theoretical expectation is with regard to secessionism – the second indicator of legitimacy-seeking characteristics by rebel groups. The hypothesis is that secessionist rebels are associated with a smaller number of civilian killings than non-secessionist groups. Rebel groups with secessionist aims will strive to achieve support in their home base, while reaching out to external actors for international recognition. In this process, the secessionist groups might exercise restraint in order to not lose domestic legitimacy and to gain international legitimacy. It is no coincidence that secessionist rebel groups are the ones that actively conduct foreign diplomacy while developing governance functions in their control regions.[19] In contrast, legitimacy-seeking concerns are expected to be weak in the case of non-secessionist groups. If a non-secessionist rebel group wants to take over the central government, it does not establish a new statehood, but assumes power and continues the previous state. Therefore, non-secessionists' core constituencies are national, which reduces the incentive to appeal to a more focused ethnic or regional base. The expectation arising from this comparison of legitimacy concerns is that secessionist rebels are more likely to exercise restraints in killing civilians than non-secessionist groups.

The third expectation arising from the strategic legitimacy theory is as follows: rebel groups with outside supporters under human rights pressure will be less likely to kill civilians than those without such support. To the extent that contemporary rebel movements seek outside funding, this dependency will result in differing behaviors of rebel groups. Rebel groups

[19] See the recent research in Huang (2013).

relying on state sponsors under human rights pressure are more likely to pay heed to their behaviors than those with state sponsors that do not necessarily concern themselves with the group's behavior toward civilians.

These theoretical expectations about legitimacy-seeking rebel groups and compliance in the treatment of civilians will be examined more systematically in the next section. To do so, I first introduce general patterns of rebel compliance behaviors in the context of civilian killing, discuss brief examples, conduct statistical tests, and then move to a detailed case study to provide evidence for these theoretical expectations.

GENERAL PATTERNS

This section provides a general view of rebel civilian killing patterns. The discussion on data and measurement will serve as the basis of subsequent quantitative analysis. Specifically, I present the patterns of rebel civilian killing across space and time, as compared with the behavior of governments. The pattern reporting will also entail brief examples of specific rebel compliers and non-compliers to give readers a more detailed picture of the dataset.

Data on Civilian Killing

Rebel groups have committed extensive violence against civilians. Gauging violence against civilians in an accurate manner is extremely difficult. Among the many potential data sources that record the treatment of civilians, killing counts may be the best reported, compared with, say, sexual violence or torture. Pillage and destroying homes rarely get reported in the media, but killings do.[20]

Acknowledging the limitation on political violence data, the starting point of my empirical inquiry on civilian killing is the One-Sided Violence (OSV) dataset assembled by the UCDP.[21] The OSV dataset is a good place to start to examine the pattern of rebel treatment of civilians because of its focus on civilian killing counts at the level of rebel groups. The name "One-Sided" comes from the fact that the violence is either committed by a government actor or a rebel actor in civil conflicts. Since the OSV dataset reports how many civilians a particular rebel group killed, its unit of analysis is adequate for testing my theory that was particularly constructed at the rebel group-level. The temporal coverage I examine is between 1989 and 2009. The starting point marks the beginning of contemporary rebel groups. This leaves out the pro-independence and

[20] Weinstein (2006). See his data appendix on the limitations and biases of civilian treatment measures.

[21] For the description of data sources and construction of measures, see Eck and Hultman (2007, 2012).

anti-colonial rebels during the 1970s and the Cold War rebels with their leftist ideologies in the 1980s.[22]

The other reason the OSV data are specifically used for testing my theory is its measurement strategy. The OSV measures approximate the legal definition of compliance that I have for the theory. Some of the measurement definitions are consistent with the principle of distinction. First, the OSV dataset considers "deliberate" killings, related to superior responsibility, one of the legal requirements for it to be a violation of international humanitarian law. Second, the OSV dataset explicitly excludes cases of collateral damage or deaths from environmental hazards during civil conflicts, coding only civilian killings during the "direct military confrontations." This proximity between the legal concept and the measure helps to ensure that my analysis is actually measuring international law compliance. This does not mean that all the cases of civilian killing cases are unlawful. In some cases where military necessity can be justified, civilian killing may be lawful.[23] However, as I noted in the introduction, my goal, as a political scientist, is to uncover general patterns, not to determine whether each case is lawful or not.

OSV data are the best systematic data available to compare civilian killings across rebel groups. This does not mean that the OSV data are perfect. Given that the counts data are gathered using news sources, there could be media bias.[24] Incidents in rural areas or killings by minor insurgencies may not have been reported in news sources. This may have created a downward bias in civilian killing counts by rebel groups. Moreover, when the case is unclear about the attribution of killing to a specific rebel group or the circumstances are unclear as to the number of civilians killed, the OSV data do not count those cases. Consequently, some potential civilian killings by rebel groups are recorded as "no killings" in the data. Naxalites in India, for example, have been involved in alleged civilian abuses, but OSV data classify this as an unclear case.[25] This coding strategy is likely to lead to an underestimation of the number of civilians killed in civil wars. For the purpose of my analysis, this underestimation would not cause much problem since the records are systematically culled across all the civil conflicts, making it still suitable for cross-rebel comparison. However, readers should note that the civilian killing numbers I provide are likely to be lower than they are conventionally thought to be.

More critically, these figures omit several important details that could have been useful in analyzing rebel compliance behaviors. For one, we do not know which civilians were killed, in what area, or the exact circumstances of these killings. Those killed could be rebel sympathizers or government sympathizers. They could be people in rebel-controlled regions or people in government-controlled regions. This kind of information about

[22] See Reno (2011) for the development of rebellion across the timeline.

[23] See Schmitt (2010) on the balance between military necessity and civilian protection.

[24] Otto (2013). [25] See Chandra (2014) for a description of the Maoist movement in India.

civilian characteristics would be theoretically relevant because these measures would allow us to trace back the rebel motivation more clearly. For example, if in a year a rebel group kills 500 people that live in a government-controlled area, it could be out of vengeance or with the aim of curtailing government power and control. However, if a rebel group kills 100 civilians in its own controlled area, this means that the rebels are not interested in governing that particular area or they may be rooting out government sympathizers. These cases will be characteristically different if we want to trace the causes of compliance or non-compliance, but I leave these kinds of micro-level analyses for future research. The key intellectual endeavor in this book is to uncover the general patterns of rebel compliance across the world. Recognizing these limitations in measurement, I proceed to infer some patterns in civilian killing below.

Recording violence is extremely difficult,[26] and "who done it" is not always clear. We know better now with more informative records from international tribunals and truth commissions as cross-checks. However, our knowledge is constrained by what is reported. Non-governmental organizations reporting these figures may have an incentive to exaggerate the figures for the victims to highlight their significance. Or, sometimes, they might under-report because of organizational credibility.[27] Government leaders may also have incentives to rig the rebel killing figures up or down. This opens up the possibility of over-reporting or under-reporting in both major and minor cases of rebel violence. The incentives of reporters are being studied by many scholars, and until we have a clear idea of how to deal with such media bias in this kind of data I recognize the problem in this book and give my best efforts with the available estimates for civilian killing.

With these measurement details, the OSV data reveal some patterns of rebel civilian killing. During the period 1989–2009, roughly 143,000 civilians died at the hands of rebels.[28] On the opposing side, government soldiers killed approximately 578,000 civilians. Without the figure from Rwanda, which amounts to a staggering 500,000,[29] civilian killing counts by governments total 78,000. With the total killing count by rebels (143,000) compared with the government killing count (78,000, excluding the Rwandan figure), rebel killing is twice as much as government killing. Collectively, the numbers tell us that both governments and rebels are substantial perpetrators of violence toward civilians.

Spatial Patterns

Map 5.1 provides a world map of civilian killing by rebel groups.[30] The world map plots the average number of civilians killed by rebel groups in each country

[26] Peterman *et al.* (2011). [27] Hill *et al.* (2013).
[28] Author's calculation, based on the OSV data v.1.4–2012.
[29] See Davenport and Stam (2009) for the revision of this number.
[30] This map as well as two other maps in this book were produced by using smap package in STATA.

MAP 5.1 World map of civilian killing by rebel groups
Source: RGIL database

with four intervals: zero killings, low level killings (1–25), moderate level killings (26–50), and high level killings (51+). The darker shades indicate the countries where rebel groups kill civilians at a higher level; the lighter shades indicate the countries where rebel groups kill civilians at a lower level.

The geographical patterns show hot spots of rebel violence with a darker shade. These atrocious rebel groups reside in the territories of Angola, the DRC, the former Yugoslavia, Nepal, and Myanmar. We also spot the moderately shaded areas where relatively less-atrocious rebel groups existed, such as India and Algeria. The white parts of the world are the countries that did not experience any civil war during the period I examined, 1989–2009, and, consequently, faced no rebel groups.

These geographical patterns show that there is variation to be explained, ranging from a low to high level of civilian killing. Although this map does not tell us the figures about a particular rebel group in a country, it is informative to show these variations, which require some explanation and analysis.

Temporal Patterns

Temporal trends show the fluctuations in the level of violence against civilians in contemporary internal conflicts. I examine the civilian killing by government first and then move on to the discussion of rebel killing. As Figure 5.1 shows, governments' civilian killing reached its peak in the 1990s with the Rwandan genocide and the conflicts in Yugoslavia. After 2005, civilian killing by national governments seems to have stabilized, with the exception of the slight uptick due to civilian abuse in Syria in 2011. Governments, democratic governments in

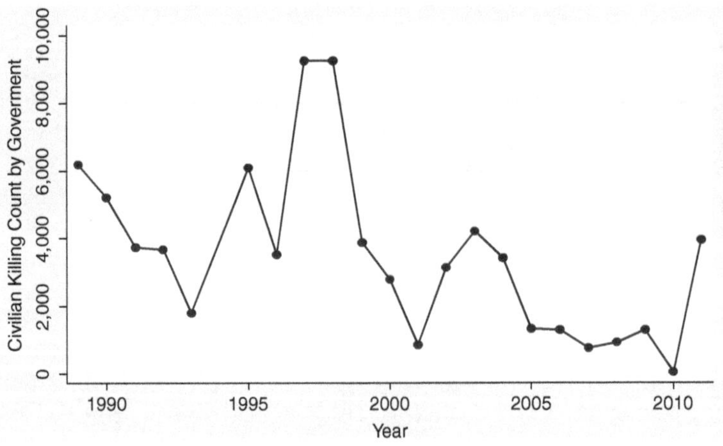

FIGURE 5.1 Governments' total civilian killing count by year (1989–2011)
NB: due to the scale of the *y*-axis, this graph excludes the Rwandan genocide, for which the estimated civilian killing figure is 500,000.

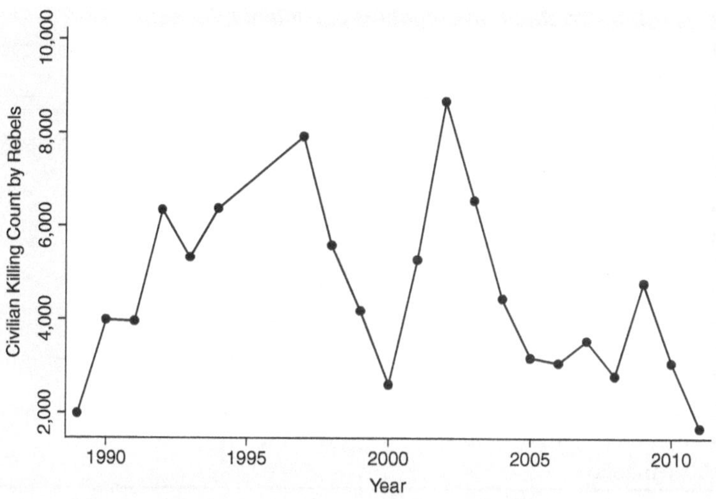

FIGURE 5.2 Rebels' total civilian killing count by year (1989–2011)
NB: due to the scale of the *y*-axis, the worst perpetrator, the Alliance of Democratic Forces for the Liberation of Congo, which killed about 27,000 in 1996, is excluded from the graph.

particular, are keen to avoid such violations. The NATO bombing in Kosovo generated intense debate as to how much caution governments have to exercise during their military offensives.[31] The principle of distinction is regarded as customary international law, exhibiting accumulated practice and *opinio juris* – a widely accepted norm throughout the majority of governments as states have developed national legislations and updated military manuals.[32] Although many criticize civilian casualties in Iraq, research shows that the practice of adhering to the principle of distinction has improved over time since the Vietnam War.[33]

Rebel group killing, as shown in Figure 5.2, reached its peak after 2000. This is around the time when Al-Qaeda, UNITA, and the LRA were actively operating. Although rebel civilian killing shows a declining trend after 2003, the human toll is still around 2,000. Noting that the OSV number is a conservative number with certain criteria based on media reports, the level of rebel violence is likely to be higher than reported here.

Examples of Rebel Compliance

In this section, I work with some examples to think through the plausibility of the legitimacy hypothesis in understanding rebel compliance. To aid the

[31] Whippman (2001); Murphy (2002: 402). [32] Henckaerts and Doswald-Beck (2005).
[33] Kahl (2007).

TABLE 5.1 *Compliers and non-compliers in civilian killing*

Compliant rebels	Non-compliant rebels
KDPI (Iran)	AFDL (DRC)
KNU (Myanmar)	ISI/Jama'at Al-Tawhid wa Al-Jihad (Iraq)
CPP (Philippines)	RCD (DRC)
RSO (Myanmar)	CNDD (Burundi)
URNG (Guatemala)	LRA (Uganda)
KDP/DPK (Iraq)	Renamo (Mozambique)
MDJT (Chad)	NPFL (Liberia)
SPLM (Sudan)	LTTE (Sri Lanka)
OLF (Ethiopia)	FPR (Rwanda)
Fretilin (Indonesia)	Al-Qaeda (Afghanistan)
MLC (DRC)	Shining Path (Peru)
MEK (Iran)	
FLEC-FAC (Angola)	

NB: compliers are rebels that kill fewer than 100 *and* refrain from killing for more than half of their operating years; non-compliers are rebels that kill more than 500 civilians for at least one year during their operating years.

discussion on rebel compliance in the issue area of civilian killing, I have classified rebel groups into compliers and non-compliers. Compliers are rebels that kill less than 100 *and* refrain from killing for more than half of their operating years.[34] Non-compliers are rebel groups that kill more than 500 civilians for least one year during their operating years. Table 5.1 contains the examples of rebel groups falling into each category.

Several observations follow. First, amid the brutal killings, there are many cases of persistent compliance among rebel groups. These are the rebel groups that do not kill civilians initially and continue not to do so. In some of these cases, strong governments seem to beget compliant rebels. In Myanmar, most rebel groups do not have civilian killing records, partly because of the heavy-handedness of the military government. The ethnic base of secessionist or autonomy-seeking rebel groups could play a big role as well, as the groups (Karen, Kayin, or Mon) rely on their domestic constituencies and seek out international support for their political movements.

The examination of rebel group attributes in Ethiopia lends some credence to the idea of strategic legitimacy. Ethiopia produced two relatively compliant

[34] Additionally, the following rebel groups are in this category of persistent compliers: ABSDF (Myanmar), KIO (Myanmar), ARIF (Myanmar), PUK (Iraq) 8 years, BRA (Papua New Guinea), ASG (Philippines), SSA–S (Myanmar), Naxalites/PWG (India), JEM (Sudan), SLM/A (Sudan), Hizb-I Islami-yi (Afghanistan), Jamiat-i-Islami (Afghanistan), Hezb-i-Wahdat (Afghanistan), and SCIRI (Iraq). See the abbreviations list for full rebel group names.

rebel groups: the Oromo Liberation Front (OLF) and the Ogaden National Liberation Front (ONLF). They were classified as compliant rebels since they did not kill civilians on a massive scale. The OLF announced that they would seek political solutions and the group now resorts to peaceful demonstrations in global locations, including Germany.[35] As a consequence, the group rarely killed civilians. The ONLF is a separatist rebel group aiming at the secession and autonomy of the Somali-dominated Ogaden territory in southeast Ethiopia. The group gained popular support in regional parliamentary elections, later forming the Somali People's Democratic Party.[36] The group has a record of civilian killings in some instances, but largely remains compliant.[37] These legitimacy-seeking characteristics and their need for domestic political support may have contributed to its behavior of no civilian killing within its politically controlled regions. These casual observations render some plausible evidence for my legitimacy-based theory of compliance.

The other pattern to note is that governmental reactions make some rebels look compliant. Relatively stronger governments might produce inoperable rebel groups. The cases of Myanmar and Ethiopia illustrate the importance of taking government responses into consideration when accounting for rebel compliance.

Weak groups comply, but some strong groups also exhibit compliance. Groups such as Rohingya and Arakan in Myanmar do not kill mainly because they do not have the capacity to kill. Others have the capacity to kill, but do not do so, as in the case of the Guatemalan National Revolutionary Unity (URNG). The group engaged in "sporadic but persistent acts of sabotage and terrorism in towns that do not have military detachments," as the Inter-American Commission on Human Rights (IACHR) found.[38] But there is no evidence of systematic and widespread killing of civilians by the group. Although the URNG did not control its own extensive territory, the group drew support from the rural poor and urban intellectuals and had domestic political bases, which later helped the group become a successful political party in Guatemalan politics.[39] The URNG provides a prime example for the power of legitimacy-seeking characteristics as explanatory factors for compliant rebels. The group could have killed civilians, but appears to have refrained from doing so.

Additional examples illustrate that the strategic legitimacy lens helps to explain rebel compliance in civilian killing. Many compliers assume legitimacy-seeking qualities. The Kurdistan Democratic Party in Iran (KDPI) is one such example. Within the KDPI's organization, the Political Bureau of the

[35] See Cheney (2012). The author also checked the OLF Facebook page.

[36] Markakis (1996); Bloom (2007).

[37] Eighty-two civilians were killed in 2007 by the ONLF during an attack on a Chinese-run oil field. See the other human rights abuses by the ONLF, including kidnapping of government officials and summary execution of government sympathizers, at Human Rights Watch (2008a).

[38] IACHR (1993). [39] Allison (2006).

Central Committee is the main decision-making body that denounces the use of violence against civilians. Having its own diplomatic machines in Europe and North America, the group has committed to the Geneva Convention Article 3, the Universal Declaration of Human Rights, and, as of 2007, is one of the signatories to Geneva Call's ban on anti-personnel mines.[40] The Revolutionary Front for an Independent East Timor (Fretilin) was a rebel movement in Indonesia that received support from Australia.[41] In its three-decade-long violent struggle against Portuguese colonialism and later Indonesian authorities, the group limited its attacks primarily to military personnel belonging to the opposition.[42] It is possible to think that the heavy-handed military approach of the Indonesian Government prompted Australian support, but it is equally plausible to think that Fretilin's conformity to international rules was motivated by a strategy to use humanitarian appeals as a means to garner international support for their independence. The examples of the KDPI and Fretilin hint that building domestic and international legitimacy may have shaped the behaviors of these two groups.

In contrast to the profiles of compliant rebels, non-compliers often lack legitimacy-seeking qualities. The LRA in Uganda and Al-Qaeda are prime examples. The groups did not forge deep social relations with civilians; their political activities in normal politics were limited at the outset; and there was no observed reach to human rights-conscious international actors for support. Rather, the LRA failed to garner support from the Acholi region from which it originated. Instead, the group relied on the Sudanese support that had intentions to use the LRA to disrupt southern Sudan's independence movement. Al-Qaeda, primarily because of its terrorist tactics, did not gain any territory to forge relations with local civilians. The group initially relied on a global financial network and radical Islamic supporters, although its support base is expanding to the disenfranchised Muslim locals and members of the Arab and Asian diaspora community.[43] These relatively legitimacy-deficient characteristics appear to be associated with a larger magnitude of civilian killing.

My theory of rebel compliance traces the cause of rebel compliance during wartime, but it is also instructive to examine the fates of non-legitimacy seeking groups after the conflict.[44] Among the list of non-compliers, some groups eventually became governments, usually after a decisive military victory. The list includes three rebel groups in Africa: the Alliance of Democratic Forces for

40 Geneva Call (2010a).

41 Australia did not initially support East Timor independence during the 1970s and early 1980s to maintain relations with the Indonesian Government, but gave support for the movement in the 1990s when the violence in East Timor was widely publicized. See Clark (1980); also Jardin (2010).

42 Capizzi *et al.* (1976). 43 Riedel (2007).

44 See Huang (2012) for the wartime origins of post-war politics.

the Liberation of Congo (AFDL) in the DRC, the National Patriotic Front of Liberia (NPFL) in Liberia, and the Rwandan Patriotic Front (FPR) in Rwanda. These groups were effective perpetrators against civilians that became future governments.

The three rebel-turned-government groups did not enjoy civilian support initially. The FPR started as a refugee organization in Uganda without substantial Tutsi backing from Rwanda and no previous political experience. Although the former leader of the FPR, now president of Rwanda, Kagame has attempted significant political maneuvering to appear legitimate in the face of international community, the FPR's initial legitimacy-seeking nature as a rebel group was weak. The same applies for NPFL and AFDL. They were successful in becoming governments, but they have struggled to become legitimate political entities. NPFL was Charles Taylor's party, whose decisions were dominated by its military wing. The AFDL, led by Laurent Kabila, was successful in ousting Mobutu, but his son, Joseph Kabila's regime is still struggling to obtain legitimacy to this day in the DRC, partly because the AFDL rebellion was backed by Rwanda, not by the Congolese civilians. These cases show the importance of looking at legitimacy-seeking characteristics to trace back the compliance behaviors of rebel groups.

STATISTICAL ANALYSIS

The statistical analysis gives us a more concrete sense of how compliance and non-compliance emerge. I first develop legitimacy-seeking indicators for each rebel group, browse the patterns between legitimacy-seeking indicators and compliance behaviors, and then perform statistical analyses to examine the association between legitimacy-seeking characteristics and restraint in civilian killing behavior.

Legitimacy-seeking indicators of rebel groups mainly come from the NSA dataset.[45] For more detailed information about each variable, readers should consult Chapter 4 as well as the Data Appendix, as these measures are common to all three empirical chapters. The first indicator is the presence of a rebel political wing. Rebel groups with a political wing will have more information about international affairs and international law than those without. In addition to political knowledge, if the political wing has control over the military wing, they are more likely to exercise restraint in their armed struggle for political reasons. The second legitimacy indicator is whether the rebel group has secessionist aim or looks for political autonomy. Secessionist rebels are more likely to be attuned to the needs of the civilian population than non-secessionist groups.[46] They are also likely to aspire to

[45] Cunningham *et al.* (2013).

[46] I would like to make a note here about the availability of the measure for voluntary civilian support. Ideally, I would like to measure the extent to which civilians willingly support rebel

have sovereignty vis-à-vis other international actors, designating them as natural candidates for international legitimacy.[47] The third indicator is the human rights influence in foreign state sponsorship. I measure this with the number of HRO secretariats active in rebel groups' foreign sponsor states.[48] The logic here is that if a rebel group has an international political audience that cares about human rights, it is more likely to exercise restraint in its armed struggle, in the expectation of either political or material support.

Legitimacy Indicators and Civilian Killing

As expected from the strategic legitimacy theory of rebel compliance, legitimacy indicators appear to be associated with civilian killing behavior by rebels in a reliable manner. We see some evidence from descriptive statistics produced by the RGIL database.

Rebels with a political wing are likely to kill fewer civilians than those without political arms within a rebel organization. Rebels with a political wing kill thirty-three people on average, while rebels without a political wing kill about ninety-six. Here, fitting examples include the Islamic Salvation Front (FIS; Algeria), Front for the Liberation of the Enclave of Cabinda (FLEC; Angola), Front for the Restoration of Unity and Democracy (FRUD; Djibouti), OLF (Ethiopia), and KDPI (Iran). The KDP in Iran is especially notable for its historical roots. The group had party activities in the core regions of its domestic constituencies. Also, the series of congresses from the political party leadership shaped its political goal of autonomy by continuously updating political platforms and unifying the opposition.[49] This case will be revisited again in Chapter 7 in comparison with other Kurdish groups in the region.

Secessionist groups kill fewer civilians than their non-secessionist counterparts. Secessionist groups kill thirty-one civilians on average, while non-secessionist groups kill about 118. The examples of compliant rebels with secessionist aims include FLEC in Angola, the EPLF against the Ethiopian Government, Fretilin against the Indonesian Government, and the KNU in Myanmar. We can note that all these rebel group names feature the geographical areas for which these groups seek autonomy:

groups. Such opinion data do not exist. Also, it is difficult to measure individuals' intention to support rebel groups. Forced support may be captured in the ordinary measure of civilian support (Valentino *et al.* 2006), which does not correspond to my theoretical conception of a domestic legitimacy measure. Mobilization capacity is another potential measure available at NSA data, but the variable captures the forceful nature of mobilization, so we do not have a good measure for domestic legitimacy for rebel groups. For want of good measure, then, my choice for the measurement was to assess rebel groups' objective characteristic to care about the population.

[47] Fazal (2013). [48] Salehyan *et al.* (2014). [49] Gunter (1996).

Cabinda, Eritrea, East Timor, and Karen state. The case of the Karen National Union (KNU) will be discussed later in the context of detention issues in Chapter 7, but it is useful to note at this point that the group aimed at the independence of or an autonomous region for the Karen people in eastern Myanmar, and had close a relationship with its own Karen ethnic people and had its own civil society organization.[50]

Additionally, if foreign state sponsors have a large number of human rights organizations, then those rebel groups are less likely to be associated with civilian killing compared with rebel groups with no such support. Rebel groups that rely on foreign sponsors with no HRO presence kill eighty-six civilians on average. This number compares with fifteen for those groups that rely on foreign sponsors with more than twenty human rights organizations. The groups demonstrating this possible relationship include FLEC (Angola), supported by France; the MEK of Iran, supported by the United States;[51] and the Liberians United for Reconciliation and Democracy (LURD), supported by Liberians in exile in the United States.[52] These examples show some association between rebel groups' compliance with international law and their legitimacy-seeking on the international stage.

The history of the MEK from Iran is particularly instructive on the usefulness of the legitimacy thesis as a theoretical lens. The MEK had been designated as a Foreign Terrorist Organization by the US State Department in 1997. It was delisted in 2012 partly due to its successful lobbying effort in Washington, DC, by its political wing, the National Council of Resistance of Iran (NCRI), a powerful lobbying machine.[53] The group primarily resorted to assassinations of key Iranian politicians and coordinated terrorist attacks that sometimes included civilian casualties.[54] But the group denounced violence as of 2001, and there is no evidence that they have committed any acts of terrorism since.[55] One plausible explanation of this transformation in strategy is the group's legitimacy-seeking needs. As one of the largest militant group opposing the Tehran government, MEK needed international recognition to keep its movement alive and make it legitimate. With the previous supporter, the Iraqi Government gone, the group perceived that Western interests met the group's interest in fighting against the authoritarian regime in Iran. The group did not enjoy civilian support as it was operating outside Iran. Such a lack of domestic legitimacy led the group to focus more on employing the strategy of relying on elite support from the United States and Europe. This

[50] South (2011). [51] After the end of terrorist designation in 2004. [52] Brabazon (2003).

[53] McGreal (2012).

[54] Global Terrorism Database (GTD) search of MEK activities returned a total of 112 of these incidents.

[55] Masters (2014).

allows the group to establish its own legitimacy by delegitimizing the Iranian regime,[56] which fits the bill of the strategic legitimacy story.

Statistical Results

The more comprehensive statistical analysis using regression provides a more rigorous test of the legitimacy-compliance hypothesis, taking into account alternative explanations. Table 5.2 reports the results of the statistical analysis of civilian killing counts. The model is negative binomial regression, a count model often used in civilian killing literature.[57] The unit of observation is the rebel-year where each rebel group's civilian killing is recorded during its armed struggle.

Model 1 estimates the strength of the strategic legitimacy variables. The presence of a political wing within the rebel organization seems to reduce the incentive to kill civilians intentionally. Likewise, rebel groups in secessionist conflicts tend to kill fewer civilians than their non-secessionist counterparts. The concern for international legitimacy also predicts civilian killing by rebels well. If a rebel group is sponsored by foreign states that are under the influence of human rights organizations, that particular rebel group is more likely to refrain from civilian killing.

The remaining models, Models 2–6, control for dominant existing explanations for civilian killing. Model 2 controls for the strategic imperatives and capabilities of rebel groups with the measure of the relative military strength of a rebel group vis-à-vis the government force. The results show that militarily strong rebels relative to government forces are more likely to kill than their militarily weak counterparts.[58]

Model 3 takes into account the aspect of military discipline within rebel groups, reflecting the organizational aspect of rebel groups.[59] The strength of central command and control has an ambiguous effect. The reason may be because internal discipline can be good or bad at the same time. Internal discipline may increase the group's ability to exercise restraint, as in the case of Renamo in Mozambique. However, internal discipline can also produce

[56] Bakke (2007).

[57] See Salehyan *et al.* (2014) for a recent example. The models presented here are robust standard errors, but the results do not change with clustered standard errors around rebel–government dyads.

[58] The interpretation of this result is confined to the measure of rebel strength. Wood (2010) finds that weak rebels are more likely to be engaged in civilian victimization using the measure of rebel estimates relative to the number of government soldiers, divided by the rebel group that the government faces. However, using the measure of fighting capacity, Salehyan *et al.* (2014) find that more fighting capacity by rebel groups is more likely to be associated with more civilian killing. My additional analysis with other measures of rebel strength from the NSA data, including the size of rebel group (in manpower) and the mobilization capacity, finds the positive relationship between rebel strength and civilian killing.

[59] Weinstein (2006).

TABLE 5.2 *Statistical analysis of civilian killing by rebel groups*

	Model 1 Legitimacy indicators	Model 2 Military strength	Model 3 Command structure	Model 4 Lootable resources	Model 5 Territorial control	Model 6 Reciprocity
Rebel political wing	−1.169*	−0.936*	−1.415**	−0.916*	−1.117*	−1.234*
	(0.429)	(0.286)	(0.558)	(0.280)	(0.351)	(0.424)
Secessionist aim	−1.195*	−0.386	−1.864*	−1.158*	−1.081*	−1.161*
	(0.404)	(0.268)	(0.422)	(0.330)	(0.303)	(0.402)
Human rights influence in	−0.120*	−0.092*	−0.086**	−0.133*	−0.120*	−0.119*
Foreign state sponsorship	(0.033)	(0.033)	(0.040)	(0.041)	(0.034)	(0.033)
Rebel strength		1.082*				
		(0.328)				
Strength of command and control			−0.082			
			(0.208)			
Lootable resources				0.658		
				(0.401)		
Territorial control					0.556	
					(0.437)	
Government civilian killing						0.000**
						(0.000)
Observations	836	836	743	835	835	836

The results are based on negative binomial regression analysis.
Robust standard errors in parentheses.
* $p < 0.01$; ** $p < 0.05$.
Constants suppressed to save space.

killing machines, as in the case of the RUF. The RUF Trial Chamber from the Special Court of Sierra Leone encapsulates this limited effect of discipline:

> The RUF's disciplinary system was critical to maintaining its operation as a cohesive military organization, particularly as the force grew with the addition of captured civilians trained as fighters. There is evidence of radio messages sent from Sankoh periodically to reiterate the importance of discipline, respect for the chain of command and of obeying RUF rules. Fighters who failed to obey orders were liable to be executed ... the RUF disciplinary system functioned essentially to allow the leadership to maintain control over all the RUF fighters and impose and maintain order in RUF-held territory. It failed to systematically deter or regularly and effectively punish crimes against civilians or persons hors de combat.[60]

It follows, then, that the nature of rebel leadership goals or intentions matters more than the internal discipline of rebel organizations. If internal discipline is for civilian protection, the organizational structure will lead to less civilian killing. If internal discipline is simply for maintaining the order within the rebel group, it cannot produce any effect on the treatment of civilians.

Model 4 looks at the effect of lootable resources – resources that can be easily looted such as diamonds or timber – on rebel groups' civilian killing behavior. Lootable resources have ambiguous effects. It is probably because for some groups, lootable resources may prompt rebels to engage in civilian killing, but in other cases, rebels with lootable resources can finance their rebellion without victimizing civilians.

Model 5 examines the role of territorial control by rebel groups on civilian killing. Territorial contestation between government and rebels has been suggested to be the source of civilian abuse.[61] If rebels have a firm grip on the territory, then civilian killing is less likely to occur. In the case of rebels having a weak grip on the territory, we would expect more contestation and therefore more instances of civilian killing. Although I cannot measure directly the level of contestation, the results seem to suggest that rebels who control territory have more opportunities for civilian abuse than rebel groups without such a control, but this relationship is not statistically significant.[62] The result thus renders some support for the contestation hypothesis.

Finally, in Model 6, I control for government killing behavior to see whether reciprocal killing is happening. Reciprocal civilian killing seems to be at work in internal armed conflicts. When governments kill more civilians, rebels kill

[60] Re-quoted from Sivakumaran (2013: 140). [61] Kalyvas (2008).

[62] In the multivariate regression setting, the relationship between territorial control and civilian killing is not significant. However, the relationship is significant in a bivariate model. I suspect this occurs because in multivariate regression, secessionist conflict variable takes away some of the explanatory power of territorial control. The correlation between secessionist conflict and territorial control is statistically significant with a Spearman rank statistic of 0.116 ($p = 0.000$), which indicates that secessionist groups are more likely to hold territories under its influence.

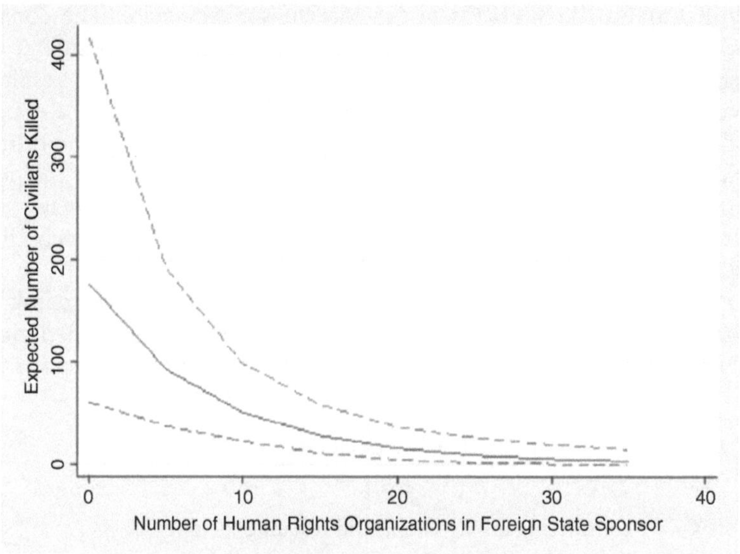

FIGURE 5.3 Expected number of civilians killed according to the number of human rights organizations in foreign state sponsor

more, too. This supports the notion that the contestation produces civilian victimization.[63]

Overall, this examination of alternative explanations strengthens the explanatory power of legitimacy-seeking characteristics influencing civilian killing behavior. The connection between legitimacy-seeking indicators and rebels' restraint in civilian killing holds up even after taking into account other dominant alternative explanations for rebel violence.

Since the coefficients from the negative binomial analysis are not directly interpretable, except the sign and the significance of them, I calculate substantive effects of key variables. According to the estimates reported in Model 1, rebel groups kill almost zero civilians with all the legitimacy-seeking indicators at the maximum (with rebel political wing, with secessionist aims, with foreign state sponsor with seventy HROs), the estimate being 0.08 [0.00, 0.42]. Without any legitimacy-seeking characteristic (without rebel political wing, without secessionist aims, with foreign state sponsor with zero HROs), rebel groups kill about 176 people (176.37 with confidence intervals of [60.80, 415.63]).[64] The effect of HRO presence in a foreign sponsor is substantial as Figure 5.3 shows. With other variables fixed at their means, the expected killing count with no HRO presence is about 200, while the expected killing count diminishes to almost

[63] Kalyvas (2006).

[64] These substantive effects were calculated using Clarify, an add-on program in STATA.

zero with around thirty HROs in the foreign sponsor state. The confidence interval is large when the HRO presence is small, but it gets tighter as the number of HROs grow, giving us more confidence about the results. For instance, when the number of human rights organizations is at the maximum in the data, the range of expected civilian killings is between ten and thirty.

Now that we have examined the general patterns of compliance and how the restraint in civilian killing behavior is connected to legitimacy-seeking characteristics of rebel groups, we are left to wonder how rebels actually seek legitimacy and how they exercise restraint in their armed struggle. The case of the M23 rebellion will illustrate a story of a legitimacy-compliance link – why other groups in the DRC seemed to have engaged in unconstrained violence, while M23 attempted to exercise restraint in their pursuit of legitimacy.

M23 REBELLION: JOCKEYING FOR LEGITIMACY, PRETENSE FOR COMPLIANCE

> ... We are considering taking Goma and rescuing the population ...
> we are going to protect them.
> We are going to prevent those crimes against civilians.
>
> Vianney Kazarama, spokesperson for M23, October 1, 2012[65]

The above quote is rather unexpected from a rebel group in the DRC, a country ridden with civil wars for over two decades. The spokesman for M23 in the DRC was using the so-called "language of protection of civilians," which is unusual for a rebel group to acknowledge in a sincere fashion. The message can be interpreted simply as justification for placing a territory under rebel control, but it is notable in that such protection language is unprecedented for conflict environments as violent as the one in the DRC.

Similarly, on July 8, 2012, Colonel Sultani Makenga, the leader of M23, publicly announced that the rebels would leave major towns in North Kivu to "let MONUSCO [United Nations Organization Stabilization Mission in the Democratic Republic of the Congo] and the national police secure the civilian population."[66] This announcement represents a surprising volte-face in M23's policy toward the protection of civilians. What explains its conciliatory move and what is the implication for the peace in eastern DRC?

The announcement came when MONUSCO was poised to attack rebel elements. Regional meetings on potential actions against the movement were already under way. An African Union summit meeting was being held that week, and the International Conference of the Great Lakes Region (ICGLR) was scheduled to meet on July 11, 2102. Despite this motivation of deterring potential international and regional responses to their movements, there was still a surprising element in the announcement. It came at the start of the rebellion, distinguishing the rebel group from the rest of the pack – the

[65] Re-quoted from Gorur (2012a). [66] Boutellis (2012).

myriad of rebel groups roaming in the cauldron of violence that is eastern Congo. The audience of the announcement was not just MONUSCO and regional security organizations. It was also civilians in eastern Congo and the military of the DRC (FARDC), the national army. By 2012, the MONUSCO's image of "impartiality" had been tarred by human rights violations committed by the FARDC, sometimes at an even greater level than the rebels. So, it was a message to civilians that it was M23, not the national army, that would protect them. It was also a message to FARDC to debase their legitimacy as a viable political authority in the region.

M23 mutinied from the national army and formed a new rebellion in April 2012. Its name, M23, came from the peace accord concluded with its predecessor, the CNDP, on "March 23," 2009, the terms of which, claim the rebel group, the Congolese Government reneged on. The CNDP forces were integrated into the national army, but turned against it, citing poor conditions in the army and opposing the relocation of troops out of North Kivu, the group's traditional home base in eastern Congo.

The previous sections of this chapter examined the patterns in civilian killing and established correlations between legitimacy-seeking characteristics and compliance behaviors toward civilian killing. The present section presents the story of M23 in the DRC to illustrate how manifested legitimacy-seeking characteristics can generate compliance behaviors by closely following the history of a rebellion.

I chose M23 as a case study for three reasons. First, the security situation in the DRC does not provide a favorable environment for compliant rebels to emerge. The country has one of the worst security situations in Africa. The DRC is often called "the heart of darkness" for its continuing conflicts in the North Kivu area. It is estimated that more than 5 million people have died as a result of violence in the DRC.[67] North Kivu has become a prime example for when peace-keeping efforts and state-building efforts have not borne fruit.[68] I wanted to see whether it is *at all* possible to observe any compliant rebels in that harsh environment. Second, my initial conjecture was that M23 was a slightly legitimacy-seeking group. Instead of utilizing examples of fully legitimacy-seeking or legitimacy-indifferent rebel groups, I thought it would be empirically important to examine a group that lies in between the extreme scales. Third, from a policy point of view, M23 is relevant to the current security policy of the DRC and the Greater Lakes region. This allows me to examine the possibility that my theory of rebel compliance sheds light on a policy solution.

[67] Hogg and Charbonneau (2013). [68] Autesserre (2010).

Background

M23 embodies the troubled and complicated history of rebellion in the region. The lineage of rebellion goes back to the Rally for Congolese Democracy (RCD), which led the Second Congo War (1998–2003). The National Congress for the Defense of People (CNDP, 2005–2009), the successor of the RCD, made a pact with the government on the condition that its soldiers would be incorporated into the national army. The ex-CNDP soldiers broke out to form M23 in April 2012 and took control of Goma, the capital of North Kivu province, for a short period in November 2012. However, by October 2013, the group was nearing the end of its eighteen-month uprising as the government forces had retaken Kiwanja and Bunagana, the group's strongholds in eastern Congo, with assistance from MONUSCO.

The security situation involving M23 was further complicated because of the involvement of the Tutsi-based Rwandan Government, which shares the same ethnicity with M23. Further complicating the conflict is the fact that Hutu militias in eastern Congo, such as Interwhame (hardline Hutus) and the Democratic Forces for the Liberation of Rwanda (FDLR), are partly backed by the DRC Government. The United Nations peacekeeping force had been in the region since 1999, but had not been able to contain all the violence by various armed groups and militias.

The ending of the M23 rebellion involved many regional and international efforts with multiple pressure points. M23 forces withdrew from Goma in November 2012 after a one-week occupation under international and regional pressure. The ICGLR mediated between Kinshasa and M23, and urged M23 to leave Goma.[69] Also, a UN sanction was imposed on the group's leaders in November 2012, followed by US sanctions.[70] Subsequently, in June 2013, the UN Security Council sent a 2,500-strong peacekeeping force in addition to the effort by MONUSCO, totaling 17,000, with a budget of US $1.4 billion per annum. At that time, in October 2013, M23 was operating in the North Kivu region with 6,000 men.[71] Outnumbered and significantly weakened, the group later signed a peace agreement with the DRC Government in December 2013. Box 5.1 summarizes this complex history of internal conflict and the rebel lineage of the M23 rebellion in DRC.

Role of Legitimacy-Seeking Characteristics

Under my strategic legitimacy theory, M23 will be an example of a "partially" legitimacy-seeking rebel. I say "partially" because the group does not have all the requisite characteristics to be classified as fully legitimacy-seeking, but we

[69] Kok (2013). [70] BBC (2012). Also see US Department of Treasury (2012).

[71] This compares with the 20,000 troops of the RCD and about 6,000 of the CNDP (Stearns *et al.* 2012).

Box 5.1 Timeline and key events of M23 movement

March 23, 2009	M23's predecessor, CNDP signed peace accord, integrated into FARDC
April 4, 2012	Start revolt, formation of M23
November 20, 2012	Control of Goma, capital of North Kivu province
December 1, 2012	Withdrawal from Goma
January 2013	UN voted on sanctions (asset freeze and travel ban) of two M23 leaders, Eric Badege and Jean-Marie Lugerero Runiga
February 28, 2013	Sultani Makenga took the leadership, removing Rugerero (former CNDP member)
December 2013	Peace Agreement with the DRC Government

cannot dismiss the group as not legitimacy-seeking.[72] Among the characteristics for fully legitimacy-seeking rebels – influential political wing, secessionism, and foreign sponsor with human rights concerns – M23 has the first, but not quite the last two.

The group had an organized and influential political wing and attempted to reach out to external actors to build legitimacy. However, the group did not fully develop domestic legitimacy. They collected taxes in some pockets of the land near Goma that they controlled, but failed to garner full domestic support as some secessionist groups would have done. The goal of M23 is ambiguous and difficult to pinpoint. However, we know that M23 did not actively demand the political autonomy of eastern Congo or territorial independence. The group, sharing ethnic similarity with the Tutsi government in Rwanda, was allegedly supported by the Rwandan Government.[73] Rwanda does not score high in terms of human rights movements, and its history of interference in eastern Congo suggests that it would not care much about the humanitarian consequences for the region.

As Table 5.3 shows, M23 has a political wing that is politically active, and that they seek out international legitimacy for their movement. The leadership has a public relations spokesman, Rene Abandi, who has appeared in major newspapers and broadcasting systems. The group also followed the Twitter pages of many influential politicians around the world and ran a Facebook web campaign. Although the genesis of the movement originated from the breaking of the promises outlined in the 2004 peace agreement (for which reason the rebellion was punished by international society), the leadership

[72] Also see a separate evaluation by Van Den Bosch (2013) on the legitimacy-seeking characteristics of M23.

[73] Trefon (2013).

TABLE 5.3 *Anatomy of M23*

Characteristics	Evaluation	Note
Political wing	Influential but dominated by armed wing	In February 2013, M23's political leader Lugerero was ousted by its military leader Makenga.
Autonomy aim	Unclear	Its political demands include decentralization. Took control over Goma in November 2012 for ten days, but its control was short-lived. The group also suffers from lack of manpower (peak 2,500, but 500 in general.
Foreign support	Weak	The major funder of M23 rebellion was Rwanda. The Tutsi-based Rwandan Government backed the Tutsi-based M23 to fight against Hutu rebels in the DRC.
Territorial control	None	The group operated in North Kivu province in the DRC. Although M23 took over Goma, capital of North Kivu, the takeover lasted only about two weeks.
Governing function	None	Like its predecessor, the CNDP, M23 did not have governing functions, partly because of its lack of territorial control, partly because of rebel rivalry in North Kivu region.
Internal discipline	Moderately strong	CNDP had internal discipline. Soldiers were beaten harshly when they mistreated civilians. A well-coordinated pullout from Goma in November 2012 after a one-week capture indicates a moderate level of discipline among its soldiers.

Sources: Lidow (2008); Gorur (2012b); Stearns (2011); Stearns et al. (2012).

was keen to portray an image of political involvement to the international community.

The key legitimization strategy of M23 is to convey the message of "we are better than the government." M23 uses its communications strategy primarily to delegitimize Kabila's regime and highlights human rights violations by the national army, FARDC. For instance, the group's military spokesperson, Vianney Kazarama, has emphasized that M23 used light weapons to lessen the risk of civilian casualties, whereas FARDC uses tanks, helicopters, and mortars.[74]

In terms of pursuing domestic legitimacy, M23 attempted some tactics of rebel governance, including collecting taxes and providing some services. In several towns under M23 control, including Kiwanja and Rutshuru,[75] M23 collects taxes under the assertion that they maintain security and provide public services, such as road repairs in the areas.[76] M23 does not yet have serious governing functions or long-held territory given its short history of existence.

M23 has demonstrated discipline amongst its soldiers, as a consequence of its rising out of the government army, as shown in its well-coordinated pullout from Goma. However, instead of foreign backers under human rights influence, M23 was mainly supported by Rwanda in their initial phase of rebellion. Previously, the Rwandan Government did not seem to mind the violence in eastern Congo as it served their aim to preserve its Tutsi-based interests. As Rwandan support dwindled because of international accusations, M23 appears to have shifted its financing method. The group said it relied on taxation of truck transportations, but it is highly likely that they may have been relying on the illegal trade in gold and ivory, sold to Uganda.[77] This shift in support base seems to provide a more favorable condition for diplomatic engagement. If the Rwandan Government was the sole benefactor of the M23 movement, the group would have less incentive to care about international legitimacy. The new financing method, to rely on the local population as well as vying for international legitimacy, may have provided the conditions conducive to the peace agreement in December 2013.

According to the theory of legitimacy and compliance, the partially legitimacy-seeking characteristics of M23 lead us to expect that this rebel group will exhibit a moderate level of compliant behavior. We will examine this expectation by following the sequence of events concerning M23's movements. Additionally, we will compare M23's legitimacy-seeking characteristics with those of other rebel groups within the same region (the eastern part of the DRC). Far from the capital Kinsasha, at any point of time, dozens of rebel groups and militias have been roaming the eastern region of the DRC for the past two decades. The rest of the rebel groups will provide a point of comparison as to the degree of legitimacy

[74] Boutellis (2012).
[75] Other areas under M23 control include Kibumba, Bunagana, and Rumangabo.
[76] Kay (2013). [77] BBC (2013a).

that M23 seeks and its associated compliance behavior, particularly the group's treatment of civilians.

The case of the M23 rebellion shows how rebel groups can pretend to comply and engage in a "war of words." M23 emerged in April 2012 out of former CNDP soldiers that made a peace pact with the government in 2009. M23 claimed that the government violated the terms of the 2009 peace deal and revolted over unpaid wages and poor living conditions. The group later distanced itself from Bosco Ntaganda, the former CNDP leader who eventually surrendered himself to the ICC in May 2013 after being indicted. This may have been due to internal fighting within M23, particularly between Ntaganda and Makenga (a new leader who ousted Ntaganda). The internal rivalry was revealed to the public around February 2013, but the announcement of their severing came well before then, in late 2012. When M23 announced that it would abide by humanitarian rules,[78] it is also quite plausible to think that the M23 leadership would have been conscious of the mounting international pressure. In March 2012, a month before M23's rebellion, Thomas Lubanga, leader of another former DRC rebel group (the UCP), was found guilty of humanitarian and human rights violations by the ICC, the court's first ever decision.

Contrary to its rhetoric, M23 has committed human rights abuses for their cause of "improving living conditions of the people in the eastern Congo."[79] The rebellion generated 800,000 displaced people.[80] The weakened support from Rwanda also drove the group to conduct recruitments that involved child soldiers in their ranks. The reported incidents of child soldering show that when push came to shove, M23 started breaking its promises to supplement its troop shortage.[81] Lastly, M23's takeover of Goma was not a peaceful affair; many human rights violations were documented during its ten-day capture of the city, including an August 2013 UN report that accused M23 of shelling and bombing the local population.

Comparison with Other Rebel Groups

Despite all the discouraging signs from M23's violence, my theory of rebel compliance suggests that the "partially" legitimacy-seeking M23 will be more likely to follow international norms than groups with no legitimacy-seeking motivations. The behavior of M23 is in contrast to other armed groups currently operating in the DRC, such as Mai Mai or the FDLR, which frequently resort to rape and civilian killing. These other groups lack legitimacy-seeking characteristics almost completely compared with M23, which possesses some of these legitimacy-seeking characteristics. The series of

[78] Boutellis (2012).

[79] For a comprehensive report on M23 human rights violations, see UN Joint Human Rights Office (2014a).

[80] Plett (2013). [81] See Smith (2013) for reported incidents of use of child soldiers by M23.

actions by M23 – the use of protection language, its willingness to engage outside peace actors, the well-organized withdrawal from Goma, the initiative for peace talks, and the relatively lower level of violence compared with its predecessors the RCD and CNDP – is the key difference between M23 and other groups in the DRC.

Although the DRC has a complicated rebel history, it provides a good test for my theory by providing multiple groups operating in a similar environment, and thus more direct comparison points. Depending on how we count various rebel factions, at any point in time about twenty armed groups operate in the DRC. The main groups include two rebel groups (RCD-Goma and CNDP) and four local defense militias.[82] The list of groups in Table 5.4 reveals the ethnic tensions in the region. The tension between Tutsi and Hutu groups is one of the remnants of the Rwandan genocide. The Tutsi-based rebel lineage runs from the RCD, CNDP and then to M23. In opposition, the Hutu-based groups include the FDLR and Interahamwe.

Almost all the groups lacked experience in normal political processes, did not have governance functions, or failed to reach out to international communities with a clear political platform. Instead, most groups relied on Uganda, Rwanda, or illicit trade to support their rebellion. Almost all the groups are engaged in targeted civilian killings, summary executions, sexual violence against women and girls, and abductions. Although civilian violence is prevalent across groups, there is some variation in the extent and level of violence. From the table, one can easily see that the scale and frequency of civilian abuse approximately correlates with rebel group strength, where the FDLR and the RCD factions are the two groups that top the list. The correlation indicates that strong rebel groups are more likely to have the capacity to inflict pain on civilian populations. Almost all the groups engage in the illicit mineral trade. When M23 had to survive after the waning of Rwandan support, the group also engaged in illicit trade supplemented by taxing commercial trucks.

The Movement for the Liberation of Congo (MLC) (1997–present) was the most disciplined among the bunch. Emerging from a political party, the group had its own trial for internal discipline (rape was disciplined, for example) in 2003.[83] However, there is a view that such discipline was exhibited to cover up the accusations of cannibalism reported to the UN Organization Mission to the Democratic Republic of Congo (MONUC).[84] The group was led by Jean-Pierre Bemba, who was the vice president of the DRC and had national political ambitions. Bemba was later charged by the ICC, but the charges only covered the crimes committed in the CAR during the coup d'état attempt of the Patassé government in 2002. Bozizé succeed in the coup attempt, and later he indicted Bemba for helping Patassé. Although

[82] These are the Coalition of Congolese Patriotic Resistance (PARECO), Alliance of Patriots for a Free and Sovereign Congo (APCLS), Mai Mai Kifuafua and Mai Mai Simba. See Spittaels and Hilgert (2008).

[83] Immigration and Refugee Board of Canada (2012). [84] Willms (2012).

TABLE 5.4 *Rebel groups in the DRC and violence against civilians*

	Number of incidences (ACLED)	Yearly average number of civilian fatalities (ACLED)	Total number of civilians killed (OSV)	Rebel strength	Aims	Funding sources
FDLR (2001–present)	365	30	1,786	15,000–20,000	Hutu ethnicity, greater control over mineral trade	Mineral trade, DRC Government
M23 (2009–present)	59	59	NA	Over 2,000	Secure conditions of 2009 peace agreement, greater government representation for Tutsi minorities	Rwandan Government, illicit mineral trade, taxes on commercial trucks
Mai Mai (1993–present)	125	6.97	487	8,000–12,000	Removal of foreign influence from eastern Congo	Local business support, illicit mineral trade
MLC (1997–present)	NA	NA	NA	Around 15,000	Fall of Kabila Government	Ugandan Government, illicit mineral trade
RCD (1998–2003)	68	4.27	6,739	Over 10,000	Greater Tutsi representation in Congolese Government, stability in Ituri region	Rwandan and Ugandan Governments, illicit mineral trade
UPC (1998–2006)	21	7	2,368	Around 15,000	Greater Hema political control over Ituri region	Ugandan Government, illicit mineral trade
CNDP (2006–2012)	16	2.29	115	Over 10,000	Protection of Tutsi communities in the DRC	Taxes on border crossings and Tutsi-held businesses
AFDL (1995–1997)	NA	NA	29,593	Around 60,000	Dissolution of Seko Government	Uganda, illicit mineral trade

FRPI (2002–2006)	NA	NA	293	Around 9,000	Lendu ethnicity, fight UPC (Hema)	Uganda, illicit mineral trade
FNI 2003	NA	NA	2,335	NA	Lendu ethnicity, fight UPC (Hema)	Uganda, illicit mineral trade

Sources: NSA dataset, OSV dataset, Armed Conflict Location and Event dataset (ACLED).

Notes: (1) NA = "not available"; (2) OSV data cover up till 2009 in the RGIL database, so the figures are missing for the very recent rebellions such as M23; (3) Mai-Mai figures are the total for the numbers for different factions of Mai-Mai (PARECO, Raia Mutombo, Yakutumba). Similarly, the figure for the RCD is a total of various factions' figures (RCD-Goma, RCD-K, RCD-N, and RCD-K-ML); (4) some armed groups listed in the ACLED are not listed here. Those are ADF-NALU, FPJC, FRPI, HEMA, Interahamwe, Rastas and LRA; (5) civilian abuse from FRPI, FNI, RCD-K-ML joint operations were not counted; (6) full group names can be found in the List of Abbreviations.

the MLC may have exercised restraint in terms of civilian abuses in the DRC (except in some cases),[85] the group committed major atrocities in the CAR, including murders, rapes, and pillaging. Bemba was a prosperous businessman in the cell-phone industry, the vice president in the DRC, and pursued the presidency in the 2006 election. He has a lot of reasons to refrain from violence in the DRC. However, MLC had little reason to refrain from violence in the CAR, where his political constituencies do not exist and where he does not have to establish legitimacy.

With their diffused and prevalent violence, the case of DRC rebels shows little evidence of compliant, legitimacy-seeking rebels. Without many rebel groups that truly seek legitimacy and are interested in governance, the much suggested solution seems to be strengthening state institutions. The theory and empirical story of rebel compliance tell us that compliant rebels are going to be rare in the DRC as rebels seek resources from illegal trade and easy foreign support with little regard for human rights standards. With diminishing and hindered support from Rwanda, M23 sought outside actors to engage for its survival and tried to weather the short-term temptation to harm the population; however, its legitimacy-seeking activities and short-lived rebellion once again proved the difficulty of compliant rebels emerging from one of the world's most violent places.

CONCLUDING REMARKS

The norms of distinguishing civilians from combatants are engrained in international law. Yet it is so violable in the face of rebel groups' military and strategic incentives in civil conflicts. Indeed, we find evidence that many rebel groups do not care about international norms and rules and continue to kill civilians. Militarily strong groups in particular kill many civilians when waging their wars. However, we also find that some legitimacy-seeking rebel groups are abiding by the rules and are refraining from killing civilians. Rebels with secessionist aims are one of the best candidates for compliant rebels. Groups that rely on international supporters and care about their human rights records also abide by humanitarian rules and refrain from civilian abuse.

The results do not necessarily mean that all of those rebel groups consciously follow international rules. Some rebels might not kill civilians out of their own conviction or because of local norms, which are consistent with international norms. But as the M23 case illustrates, some rebel groups consciously care about international law and conduct diplomacy about their human rights records. Notably, rebel groups with a political wing seem to be aware of the changing legal environment in international criminal law and the likelihood of

[85] One instance to note is the campaign known as Operation Erase the Blackboard in November 2002, which generated potential human rights violations. The campaign was originally named "*effacer le tableau*," translated as "wipe the slate." See Human Rights Watch (2010).

prosecution. These groups are more likely to adjust their tactics accordingly, ultimately reducing their incentive to commit violence against civilians. These compliant rebels will build practices of no civilian abuse over time, and eventually, and hopefully, will contribute to the production of international customary law and practice.

In essence, international law, particularly the norm of distinction between combatants and non-combatants, matters to rebel groups when the adherence to legal norms has consequences for their political survival. In the case of M23, acquiring international support was particularly crucial when it did not rely on minerals (copper, gold, and diamonds) and when civilian support alone could not sustain its movement. Outside engagement meant that they also had to play by outside rules and follow dominant norms. Rebel groups' openness to agents of international law also has consequences for their violent action against civilians. Overall the findings show that in contemporary rebellion strategic factors loom large in the case of civilian killing, with international law having some conditional effects on legitimacy-seeking rebels. The evidence in this chapter lends the theory of rebel compliance some empirical support in the issue area of civilian killing. Does the theory travel to other issues of international law? Chapter 6 puts the theory of rebel compliance to the test with a different set of issues: violence against children.

6

Child Soldiering

> Armed groups that are distinct from the armed forces of a State should not, under any circumstances, recruit or use in hostilities persons under the age of 18 years.
>
> Article 4(1), Optional Protocol on the Rights of the Child on the Involvement in Armed Conflict

> We need to respect children's rights and the right to childhood. Children are sacred to us – bodily, mentally, spiritually.
>
> Interview with Dr. Samir al-Qadi, Hamas MP, Hebron, February 2006[1]

> My husband was in al-Shabaab. He came and said to my eldest son [who was 10 years old], "You must also join." He overpowered me and took my son. Later I heard my son died in the war. I went to where my husband was, Horera mosque, and I said, "I heard my son died." He said, "I am pleased to inform you that our son died a martyr. He went straight to paradise." He showed me footage he took of my son being killed in the war. His blood. His body. I cried.
>
> Human Rights Watch interview with Nadifa K (not her real name), mother, Kenya, June 1, 2011[2]

In Somalia, as the above passage conveys, a woman's husband sent their son to be a child soldier for Al-Shabaab, an Islamic rebel group. In Liberia, a girl was abducted from school to serve rebel commanders in the NPFL.[3] In Algeria, a family handed over their sons and daughters to Al-Qaeda in Islamic Maghreb (AQIM) for US$600.[4] In Colombia, FARC kidnapped a child to become a drug mule.[5] In India, a boy joined a rebel group in Manipur to earn some money so that he could help his family out of poverty.[6] This is a montage of child soldier recruitment practices around the world. Rebel groups' abuses and violence are common parts of all these stories. Child soldiers join rebel ranks for a variety of reasons, but in many cases they are forced to join. Forced recruitment fundamentally violates the rights of children, depriving them of their will to decide their own future.

[1] Child Soldiers International (2008a). [2] Human Rights Watch (2012).
[3] Advocates for Human Rights (2009). [4] *The Guardian* (2012).
[5] Child Soldiers International (2001). [6] Devi (2008).

In 1990s, about sixty armed opposition groups in sixteen countries used children in their ranks.[7] Around the world, as many as 250,000–300,000 children are used as human shields, soldiers, porters, cooks, messengers, and spies.[8] Some girl soldiers are abducted to live as sex slaves or to serve as "wives" for rebel commanders. More than a dozen government forces have used child soldiers over the course of modern history, including the DRC, Myanmar, Nepal, Sudan, and Yemen. Now the number is down to five: the DRC, Myanmar, Nepal, Sudan, and Yemen. However, the practice of child soldiering persists in those conflict zones. Among child soldiers, about 70 percent are found in the ranks of rebel groups, with 40 percent of those child soldiers being girls.[9] The practice of child soldering is not just a contemporary phenomenon. Modern wars are populated with stories of children in warfare, such as Hitler's *Jugend* during the Second World War and the employment of children during the Iran–Iraq War.[10] Even during the US Civil War, drummer boys were not uncommon.[11]

Conflict takes a toll on children. Children can become malnourished, spend their childhood in refugee camps, or worse yet, they can be killed or raped. In contemporary world politics, the child soldier issue has taken a particular prominence. Child soldiering goes against the central tenant of human rights – the dignity and freedom of individuals – earning it a place in the discussion of human rights and humanitarian rules. Forcefully recruited children in rebel ranks are too young and too weak to resist. Further, child soldiers often take the brunt of suffering in some conflict zones even beyond the war's end, as they must go through a long and arduous healing process.

Broadly speaking, child soldiering is not just a conflict issue, but ultimately a development issue. These children lose the opportunities to garner a formal education and participate in the labor force outside war. Although some rebels claim that they educate children and feed them in their ranks, we cannot reliably measure the opportunity costs of those children, and we can never know what alternative lives they could have pursued. The psychological impact on these children's lives, not to mention the associated economic costs of losing the youth population for some years, is a critical detriment to these war-stricken societies. In this chapter, I examine the patterns of child soldiering, the role of rebel groups in committing violence against children, and, most importantly, the reasons why some rebel groups stop the use of child soldiers.

[7] RGIL database.

[8] See McHugh (2009). The estimates vary: War Child, a charity organization, estimates 250,000; 75,000 in Myanmar (Singer 2006); and 3,000 in India according to the Asian Center for Human Rights (2013).

[9] Gazagne (2009); also see Patel (2013). [10] Kaplan (2005). [11] Murphy (1993).

NORMS: "STRAIGHT-18" PRINCIPLE?

International norms have progressed to ban the use of child soldiers, but its history is short. The growing norm of prohibiting child soldiering is embodied in the Convention on the Rights of the Child – Optional Protocol on the Involvement of Children in Armed Conflict (CRC-OP), adopted in 2000 and entered into force in 2002.[12] The Optional Protocol stipulates the right of children not to be used as soldiers. It is this legal instrument that formally recognizes that children have the right to education and growth instead of spending their childhood as soldiers. CRC-OP has been ratified by 100 countries, which signifies the reach of the law at the international level.

Soft law (principles and declarations) has also been developed in lock-step with the hard law (agreements and conventions). The coordination of soft legal instruments such as the Paris Commitments to Protect Children from Unlawful Recruitment or Use by Armed Forces or Armed Groups (1990) and the Cape Town principles (1997) spurred the movement by NGOs and international organizations to focus on the issues of children in armed conflicts. Some even claim that this standard of banning child soldiers has achieved the status of customary international law.[13] Such customary status gives the norm more serious weight, leading to its acknowledgment as being an established practice with broad acceptance.

Public awareness of child soldiering has also increased over time. The world was shocked to see to images of Johnny and Luther Htoo, the twin brothers leading a brigade of the God's Army in Myanmar, smoking cigarettes, and leading other children in uniform. The viral Kony 2012 video was released by Invisible Children, an NGO that advocated for a ban on the use of child soldiers and the capture of Joseph Kony, the leader of the LRA. These images helped to usher the issue more deeply into the public domain. Despite the motivations provided by these disturbing images and news, devising a strategy to solve the problem of child soldiers is not so simple. Understanding the causes and finding ways to make a change is the first step in such an effort.

With the growing norm, institutional reach has also been widening. The United Nations has also established the Office of the Special Representative of the Secretary-General for Children and Armed Conflict, a special office to deal

[12] It was adopted along with the Optional Protocol on the sale of children, child prostitution, and child pornography. This reflects the growing standards on the protection of children. Other relevant legal instruments include earlier legal documents, such as the Geneva Conventions Additional Protocols I and II, which specify the warring parties' obligations to refrain from using children in hostilities. The norm also is written into the Rome Statute, and the ICC handed down its first decision on a child soldier perpetrator, Thomas Lubanga, the rebel group leader of the UPC in DRC. In this normative development, abduction and forced disappearance have become war crimes in and of themselves.

[13] The ICRC lists the ban on child soldiering as customary international law (Rule 136). See Henckaerts and Doswald-Beck (2005). Also see at: www.icrc.org/customary-ihl/eng/docs/v2_rul_rule136.

with child soldier issues. The Office has worked with many rebel groups around the world, urging them to stop the practice, including the recent use by Al Houthi in Yemen and Ansar Al Shari'a, an organization affiliated with Al-Qaeda in the Arabian Peninsula. A total of nine rebel groups have signed an Action Plan with the United Nations to stop the use of child soldiers.[14] This institutional reach indicates that rebel groups are now exposed to the norm of prohibiting the use of child soldiers.

Despite the international efforts and increasing public awareness, the implementation of the legal norms has not been easy. For one, cultural differences have been obstacles to ending the violence against children. In some cultures, particularly in Muslim countries, children over the age 15 (or as early as 13) are considered adults. In these societies, with different beliefs about the role of children, the norm prohibiting anyone under the age of 18 from serving as a soldier is not well accepted. The unclear normative status gives rebel groups ample opportunities to justify their use of child soldiers, thus dodging international obligations. For example, Abu Musab, the military spokesman of Al-Shabaab in Somalia, issued a statement saying: "The allegations from Human Rights Watch say that Al-Shabaab recruits young children at the age of 14, 15 and 17 as soldiers. In Islam, a person becomes adult at the age of 15 so he or she must do what all other adults have to do."[15] Even within developed countries, the "Straight-18" principle, which prohibits children under the age of 18 from joining armed forces, is debated. In the United States, Germany, and Italy, children under 17 can join the army, although they are not deployed in combat zones. The Straight-18 principle is heralded by human rights organizations, but the acceptance of the norm varies across societies.

The matter is further complicated when we consider cases where children "voluntarily" become soldiers.[16] Out of the sixty-nine children surveyed from various countries in East Asia and the Pacific, including Cambodia and East Timor, UNICEF reported that 57 percent voluntarily joined the military service.[17] This statistic is based on a small sample, but goes against our conventional thinking that child soldiering is based on forcible recruitment. The Survey of War Affected Youth (SWAY) project has also found many cases of voluntary recruitment.[18] In poor regions of India, some children may recognize that being a child soldier provides them with a better economic future and a higher social status than having no job at all. Children may be unemployed, orphaned, or cannot support their families by other means. "We are helping children economically when economic alternatives are not good." This is the argument often invoked in India, where economic development is at the heart of the issue and minor conflicts are not expected to go away any time soon.[19] In Chattisgarh, one of the poorest states in India where the Naxalites

[14] Jo and Barrett (2014). [15] Tancos and Adow (2012). [16] Drumbl (2012).
[17] United Nations Children's Fund (UNICEF) (2002). [18] Blattman and Annan (2010).
[19] See Patel (2013).

roam, economic necessity is the primary reason child soldiers are used. Put simply, the economic roles of children are different for developing and developed nations, creating a divergence of views on the issue of child soldiers.

In addition to the problem of disputed norms, international enforcement mechanisms are also weak. In 2012, the ICC obtained its first conviction for the conscription of child soldiers: Thomas Lubanga, the leader of the UPC, a rebel group in the DRC. However, many other rebel group leaders, such as Joseph Kony of the LRA in Uganda, are at large, having escaped the reach of international justice thus far. Countries rarely punish each other for using child soldiers. The United States announced waivers to its Child Soldiers Prevention Act, allowing military assistance to Chad, the DRC, and Yemen – the countries that used child soldiers in the governments' military ranks.[20] Economic sanctions placed on rebel group leaders, such as travel bans and asset freezes, are rarely applied on the sole grounds of using child soldiers, but as a result of larger geopolitical considerations.[21]

Legal uncertainty and cultural differences make it difficult to enforce the norm in a meaningful way.[22] International law cannot say to rebels in a definite fashion: "Do not use children under the age 18. It is the law." Such a statement does not hold the same weight as a domestic traffic law telling citizens: "Buckle up. It is the law." Yet, despite their weak enforcement, some rebel groups willingly choose to relinquish their practice of using child soldiers to conform with these international norms. Various groups have signed Action Plans with the United Nations, making commitments to stop the use of child soldiers.[23] In spite of the weak enforcement, unclear normative status, and cultural differences, other groups have committed to accepting the norm prohibiting the use of child soldiers. What explains this variation? What is the motivation of rebel groups to employ children in their ranks and when would they want to stop the practice? These are the core questions I will explore next.

THEORETICAL EXPECTATIONS

As demonstrated in the previous chapters, the theory of rebel compliance identifies the key mechanisms that explain why rebel groups comply with international norms. The case of child soldiers is no different. In the theoretical framework, rebel groups choose to recruit child soldiers into their ranks based on a cost calculation, weighing the benefits versus the cost of using

[20] Becker (2011). [21] Charron (2013).

[22] See Drumbl (2012) on the legal, social, and political complexities of child soldier issue.

[23] The list of rebel groups that committed to the United Nations Action Plans include the People's Army for the Restoration of Democracy (CAR), Convention of Patriots for Justice and Peace (CPJP), CPN-M (Nepal), MILF (Philippines), Sudan People's Liberation Army/Movement (Sudan), and Sudan Liberation Army (various factions: Minni Minnawi, Free Will, and Abu Gasim). See United Nations Office of the Special Representative for Children and Armed Conflict (2014).

child soldiers. Also, in this calculation, rebel groups' legitimacy-seeking characteristics will be key determinants of their compliance behaviors. Three legitimacy-seeking indicators, namely, secessionist tendencies, legal political parties, and interaction with human rights-conscious external actors, will alter the cost calculations of rebel groups.

In the following discussion, I am going to lay out the costs and benefits associated with complying with the no child soldiers norm. Then, I am going to explain how legitimacy-seeking behaviors factor into the child soldiering decisions of rebel groups. These considerations will lead me to propose concrete theoretical expectations about rebel group behavior with respect to the use and the restraint in child soldiering.

In deciding whether to comply with the international norm of having a child soldier ban, rebel group leadership has to weigh the benefits of compliance against the cost of compliance. Although children may be easier to indoctrinate, they are difficult to train as soldiers. Against this potential cost, some rebel groups may nonetheless be compelled to use child soldiers to fill the void in their recruitment. Increase in manpower is one of the strongest motivations for using child soldiers.[24] Children can be used as an easy mechanism to fill the ranks and boost combat manpower. This is particularly true for militarily weak rebels that do not have the money to pay adult soldiers. Children can be used to transport weapons, spy, or even lead small and adaptive brigades when rebel groups lack adult soldiers for the same tasks. Not using child soldiers may disadvantage some groups militarily vis-à-vis the opposing government's military might. An anonymous rebel leader's remark to Olivier Bangerter, the ICRC's delegate, is particularly instructive: "You know, Mister Delegate, in my country, we have this saying: if you want to make a large fire, you need lots of wood."[25] Having children in the rebel ranks helps rebel groups to overcome their asymmetric power vis-à-vis the government's military power by increasing manpower. In these cases, the cost of compliance is usually high. Non-compliance easily compensates military advantage, leaving many rebel groups to have child soldiers in their ranks.

However, when rebels recognize the benefits of compliance, adherence to the child soldier norm becomes more plausible. It is the legitimacy-seeking rebels that are likely to see those benefits of not using child soldiers. For example, if there is a promise of associated aid or the prospect of increasing their international standing and legitimacy, rebel leadership may recognize the benefits of changing alignment from child soldiering to no child soldiering. Now, recall that one of the key facets of legitimacy-seeking behavior is the regard for constituency preferences. If the core domestic supporters do not strictly prefer abandoning child soldiers because of economic or cultural reasons, even legitimacy-seeking rebel groups may not go against those social relations and may not see the benefits of complying.

[24] Singer (2006). [25] Bangerter (2011: 354).

With these rebel–constituency relationships in mind, the theory of rebel compliance leads to three major expectations. First, the presence of a rebel political wing, particularly legally allowed ones, is likely to engender more compliant behavior from the rebel group. In the context of violence against children, rebel political wings are likely to discourage the practice of child soldiering. Political wings care more about domestic and international legitimacy due to their electoral ties or relations with civilians in local politics. They are also likely to consider international legitimacy important for the purpose of furthering their political goals vis-à-vis the opposing government. If the rebel political wing has influence and control over the military wing, a rebel group would be more likely to influence the military wing to prioritize military incentives and subsequently to curb their use of child soldiers.

The second expectation is that secessionist goals will increase the likelihood that those rebel groups would use child soldiers. To the extent the key domestic audience cares and has leverage over rebel groups, rebel groups will respect social ties with the domestic population and might violate international rules. With frequent ethnic ties and civilian volunteers, secessionism makes it easy for rebels to adopt child soldiering strategies. Secessionist groups usually draw on local popular support and thus are more likely to use children in their ranks than those groups without such voluntary civilian support. In the case of secessionist groups, families sympathetic to the group's ideals provide a strong recruiting pool of children.

The social relations between rebels and civilians will matter in terms of how secessionist rebels recruit and use children in rebel ranks. My theory expects that secessionists will use child soldiers in a manner that is less abusive than non-secessionist groups. Among the rebel groups that use child soldiers, secessionists grounded in social relations will recruit from their ethnic or family pool, and then use them more in non-combat roles. Non-secessionists, on the other hand, do not have local constituencies to hold them accountable, which gives them more incentives to abuse child soldiers during their use. Those non-secessionists without a social base are more likely to recruit children in a forceful manner through kidnapping or abduction.

International legitimacy also matters for rebel groups' choice of child soldiering. When a rebel group cares about how outside supporters view their rebellion, they are more likely to comply with international rules. In general, rebel groups with foreign state supporters where human rights movements are vibrant, are more likely to abide by international rules than groups without such support due to financial incentives. However, this effect is conditioned by the magnitude of *interests* and political *leverage* of foreign sponsors. The interests will be curtailed by several factors. For one, not all human rights organizations care about child soldier use, although they would care about general human rights and humanitarian issues. The norm of humanitarian intervention has taken root to some extent, but no intervention has ever occurred solely because of child soldiering.

It is also important to note that the status of the norm on the prohibition of child soldiering is neither as prevalent nor as salient as that of civilian protection, given that the norm is contested due to cultural and religious reasons. Recall that the norm has only recently been established with the CRC-OP in 2000, with an institutional mechanism in place with the United Nations Action Plans after 2005. Coupled with this lack of urgent interests, the leverage of human rights-conscious foreign sponsors is often limited. Naming or shaming from human rights organizations is not going to be as effective as desired. Material support that is attached to child soldiering will be too scarce to alter the incentives of rebel groups. All these factors indicate that the interests and leverage from external sponsors rallying on this issue will be weak, and, therefore, we cannot expect a strong relationship between external sponsorship and child soldiering.

One additional expectation from the strategic legitimacy theory is the differences between legitimacy-seeking and legitimacy-indifferent rebels regarding how they recruit and treat child soldiers. Child soldiers in legitimacy-indifferent rebel groups are more likely to participate in violence such as mutilation and the killing of civilians. Legitimacy-seeking groups are more likely to use children in non-combative roles such as porters and cooks. Some legitimacy-seeking groups may use child soldiers when they are outnumbered by government forces, but the theory expects that the use of child soldiers would be less violent in nature. The theory would also expect that legitimacy-seeking rebel groups resort to voluntary recruitment, whereas legitimacy-indifferent groups rely on forcible recruitment.

GENERAL PATTERNS OF REBEL CHILD SOLDIERING

This section has two aims: one is to uncover the general patterns of child soldiering, and the other is to explore the empirical support for my legitimacy-based theory of rebel compliance. To that end, the following discussions will include brief reports on the data-collection efforts, as well as on the key spatial and temporal patterns identified by the database regarding rebel groups' child soldier use. I will additionally provide some examples that link rebel groups' legitimacy-seeking characteristics and their compliance behaviors. Once these building blocks for empirical inquiry are introduced, we will examine the statistical evidence for the theory in the next section.

Data Collection and Sources

I assembled the database for child soldiering by rebel groups between 1989 and 2009. The RGIL database includes qualitative reports as well as the quantitative dataset. The qualitative reports include relevant information such as the recruitment methods, the manner in which children were used (either in combat or non-combat roles), and estimates on the number of children in rebel ranks. A dataset for child soldiering is in its infancy, reflecting the fact of the norm being little more than a decade old with the passing of the CRC-OP. This leads to a difficulty in quantification as much of the relevant information is found in qualitative reports. Therefore, in this section, I report rough patterns found in quantitative data, but augment the story with the information found in qualitative reports.

The quantitative dataset I utilize here records only whether a rebel group used child soldiers or not. I note the risk of using this binary measure, lumping together the egregious violations and infrequent uses. However, the threshold to distinguish the frequency or magnitude of use is often unavailable or unreliable. The estimated numbers of children in rebel ranks are rarely reported and, even if reported, they are rough estimates. This problem gets worse for obscure rebel groups where limited information is available. If the sources say that child soldiering is not documented or if there is no source that mentions child soldiering for a particular group, we coded them as non-use cases. To reflect this measurement uncertainty and to account for the lack of information in some cases, I opt for the binary measure in the statistical analysis.

I well recognize that the details, of course, matter beyond the binary distinction between use and non-use. Information such as how children were used, if they were directly involved in war efforts or not, how many were involved, and whether there were girl soldiers, helps tell a richer story of rebel groups' child soldier use. The wax and wane of the use, battlefield events, and rebel financing will also be relevant to our inquiry of compliant rebels. I first present general patterns in the dataset with the dichotomy of use and non-use, but then dive into more detail in the interpretation of the data.

The primary sources I relied on are the documents from the United Nations Children and Armed Conflict Office, which detail and list the names of rebel perpetrators, and from various NGO sources, such as the reports produced by Child Soldiers International, Human Rights Watch, and Amnesty International. My research team also cross-checked our coding with existing studies on rebel child soldiering. Simmons (2010) studied the use of child soldiers by national governments between 1967 and 2008, with some additional coding on non-state actor use. Lasley (2012) studied about 100 rebel groups between 1998 and 2008. Beber's and Blattman's (2013) data cover about forty African rebel groups.

Spatial Pattern

Map 6.1 presents the geographical pattern for the use of child soldiers by rebel groups in civil wars between 1989 and 2009. The numbers reflect the maximum value for child soldier use within each country. So, if a country is marked as "Presence of Child Soldiers," it means that at least one rebel group in that country is using child soldiers. We can see that the use of child soldiers is clustered in Africa's Great Lakes region, but its practice is also observed in

MAP 6.1 World map of child soldiering by rebel groups
Source: RGIL database

Asia (India, Myanmar, and Indonesia) as well as some parts of Latin America (Colombia, in particular).

One notable feature in this world map is the connection between government use and rebel use of children in the military ranks. The use of child soldiers by rebel groups closely tracks the use of child soldiers by governments. About fifteen governments have a record of using child soldiers at one point in time between 1989 and 2014. These are, in alphabetical order, Afghanistan (Afghan National Police, Afghan National Security Forces, ANSF), Burma (Tatmadaw Kyi, Burma's National Army), Chad (Armée nationale tchadienne, ANT), Colombia (mostly via paramilitaries), the DRC (Forces armées de la République démocratique du Congo, FARDC), India, Iraq, Somalia (Transitional Federal Government, TFG), Sri Lanka (paramilitary group, Tamil Makkal Viduthalai Pulikal (TMVP), otherwise known as the Karuna faction), South Sudan (Sudan People's Liberation Army, SPLA, following independence in 2011), Sudan (pro-government militias), Uganda (Uganda People's Defence Force, UPDF), and Yemen (Yemeni Government Forces, YGF).[26]

Note that some national governments, such as Colombia and Sudan, do not directly use children in the national army, but do so through the use of paramilitaries and pro-government militias. These non-state armed groups fight rebel groups on behalf of governments.[27] This makes it harder for the international community to stop those violations as these irregular forces are often not under a centralized command-and-control structure, but are often fragmented and divisive organizations. There are some places where rebel groups use child soldiers, but governments do not, such as Algeria, Thailand, Philippines, and Senegal. Although there are many rebel groups that use child soldiers despite the governments' non-use, child soldiering is definitely one of the weapons that rebel groups utilize more than governments across the world. Also, in many governments, the employment of child soldiers comes in a milder form than the use by rebels.

Temporal Pattern

Figure 6.1 plots the macro-trend of the use of child soldiers around the world over time. The solid line plots the total number of rebel groups each year and the dashed line plots the number of rebel groups that used child soldiers for each year. Out of roughly 300 rebel groups operating in civil wars between 1989 and 2009, approximately sixty have used child soldiers in one form or another since the early 1990s. The practice of child soldiering is phasing out slowly. About forty groups used child soldiers in 2000, but, as of 2010, the number has reduced to about twenty. The practice, however, seems to be entrenched in

[26] Asian Center for Human Rights (2013); Human Rights Watch (2014a); United Nations (2014c).

[27] See Bapat (2012) for an analysis of the use of paramilitaries by governments.

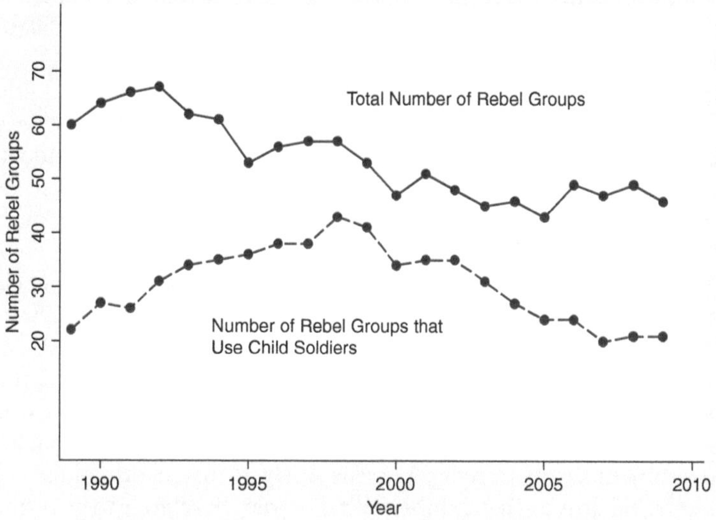

FIGURE 6.1 Yearly trend of child soldier use by rebel groups
Source: RGIL database

the places that have long-running civil wars where multiple rebel groups are present. Almost all the rebel groups in Myanmar, Afghanistan, Colombia, India, and the DRC have a history of using child soldiers, and most of them continue to do so. In cases where multiple rebel groups are vying for influence in one country, once the practice of child soldiering is established, other groups use child soldiers in order to compete in the recruitment drive.

Groups that use child soldiers are usually longer lived. Among the 241 rebel groups in the RGIL database for which records of child soldering exist, the average duration for the seventy-seven groups that resort to child soldering is eight years, whereas the average for the 164 non-users is three years. This difference in duration is statistically significant. Likely reasons for this observed difference include the time required for rebels to recruit child soldiers, as well as the notion that children are drawn into a conflict when adult males become scarce.[28]

The practice of child soldiering is most prevalent in poor and war-stricken societies. In fact, many countries experiencing civil wars are poor by world standards. However, poverty does not seem to be a sufficient condition for child soldiering. There are many countries that have poverty, but manage to get out of the conflict trap of child soldiering. In the RGIL database, rebel groups that use child soldiers live in slightly poorer countries (with an average GDP of US$286 billion) than those groups that do not use child soldiers (with an average GDP of

[28] Singer (2006).

US$318 billion). Moreover, the relationship between GDP and child soldiering is not statistically significant within the sample of civil wars, indicating that poverty does not carry a significant explanatory power.

Another contributing factor may be the groups' military strength. Child soldiering is usually considered a weapon of the weak. Militarily weak rebel groups use children to fill up their ranks because children can be indoctrinated and trained more easily. This strategic incentive is very strong. Even regularly compliant rebels recruit child soldiers when they are short on manpower. However, the weakness of the group does not always lead to child soldier use. Path dependency seems to matter more. When the practice is entrenched in a society, such as in Myanmar or Colombia, militarily strong warring parties (e.g., the Myanmar Government, Colombian paramilitaries, or FARC at times) have been known to use child soldiers. Among rebel groups in the RGIL database, weak groups are no less likely than stronger groups to resort to child soldiering.[29] Rebel groups that are relatively weaker or much weaker than government groups are 15 percent likely to use child soldiers. It is 16 percent for rebel groups that exhibit military strength relative to governments at parity, stronger, or much stronger. Note that this is cross-rebel comparison and not a comparison across time within a rebel group. Given the limitation of the data, we cannot assess the fluctuations over time, but it is likely rebels that become weaker can resort to children as a source of recruitment.

Legitimacy Indicators and Child Soldier Use

The RGIL database helps us to connect the dots between rebel groups' legitimacy-seeking characteristics and child soldiering by rebels. I report some descriptive statistics with some examples.

The first legitimacy-seeking indicator – the presence of a legally allowed political wing – is associated with less frequent use of child soldiers. Among seventy-seven rebel groups that used child soldiers between 1989 and 2009, twelve groups (15 percent) have legally allowed political wings. In contrast, among 165 rebel groups that do not use child soldiers, thirty-four (20 percent) have legally allowed political wings. This difference is statistically different and tells us that the presence of a legal political wing is associated with restraint in child soldering among contemporary rebel groups. The examples of rebels with legally allowed political wings that did not use child soldiers include ONLF in Ethiopia, MEK in Iran, and KDP in Iraq. It is notable that the ONLF in Ethiopia has told Child Soldiers International, a human rights organization, that the group "fully recognizes and has adopted all articles enshrined in the Convention on the Rights of the Child and in particular the Optional Protocol to the Convention."[30] It is not 100 percent certain that the group had no child

[29] This is cross-group comparison. When we consider a group using child soldiers for a long period of time, weaker rebel groups are more likely to use child soldiers.

[30] Child Soldiers International (2008b).

soldiers, but there has been no verification of child soldiers within the ONLF by any independent source.

The second legitimacy-seeking indicator – secessionism – is also related to the use of child soldiers. Among the 165 rebel groups that did not use child soldiers, thirty-four (21 percent) are secessionist. Among seventy-seven rebel groups with a record of child soldiering, twenty (26 percent) are secessionist. Secessionist rebel groups that used child soldiers include the Front for the Liberation of the Cabinda Enclave–Cabinda Armed Forces (FLEC-FAC) in Angola, the KNU in Myanmar, the PKK in Turkey, the LTTE in Sri Lanka, and ETA in Spain. Note that the names include either the region for which they are claiming independence (e.g., Cabinda, Basque) or the ethnicity associated with the group (Karen ethnicity, Kurds, Tamil population). For these groups, I would expect that the rebel–civilian relations were tight as rebels may have provided social services or were able to foster some voluntary support from the civilian population. Secessionist rebels that did not use child soldiers include the MFDC in Senegal and the KDPI in Iran. For these secessionist types, I would expect low levels of rebel–civilian interactions. In fact, the KDPI mainly operated from Iraq and the highly fractured MFDC is known to have alienated the local population in Casamance.[31]

One example that captures the connection between secessionism and rebel child soldiering is the case of FLEC-FAC in Angola. The group fought for the independence of the Cabinda region in Angola, and children were often employed to ambush the enemy to procure weapons. One child soldier in the FLEC-FAC remarked: "My parents are poor. I had no choice but to take up arms for my country. In the army I am looked after and I am useful to the community."[32] These children become soldiers because they believe they are "useful" to their own "community" in achieving the aim of political independence. In this way, the use of child soldiers is likely to be a strategic choice by the secessionist rebel group to take advantage of the child's willingness shaped by social ties and economic circumstances.

The third legitimacy-seeking indicator is the number of human rights organizations (HROs) in foreign state sponsors. The measure partly captures rebel groups' openness to an outside constituency that cares about human rights records. The number of rebel groups that have foreign support with no HRO secretariat is 142. Among them, forty-five do use child soldiers, approximately 30 percent. Foreign states with HRO secretariats rarely support rebel groups in civil wars, but there are few cases where they do. In the few cases where these foreign states supported rebel groups with child soldiers, this assistance was motivated by Cold War politics: UNITA was supported by the United States and South Africa; Jamiat-i-Islami and Hezb-i-Islami in Afghanistan were supported by the United States. The data indicate that foreign governments under HRO influence choose to support rebels less frequently than their

[31] Jahate (2013). [32] Okamba (1996).

counterparts without strong HRO influence. This pattern further suggests that rebel groups may be conditioned to refrain from child soldiering if they were ever to be supported by foreign governments under HRO influence.

Persistent and Switchover Compliers

Although the quantitative data measure the rebel child soldiering as a binary one, the qualitative reports in the RGIL database provide examples of persistent and switchover compliers. FMLN in El Salvador is an example of a persistent complier for the issue of child soldiers. The group did not use child soldiers and its legitimacy-seeking profiles fit the example for rebel compliance: (1) the group was a non-secessionist movement seeking broader appeal nationally, particularly drawing support from rural areas; (2) the group had a clear political agenda and programs emanating from its political party, the National Opposition Union; and (3) the group waged war largely autonomously, but was able to garner support from foreign states such as Vietnam and East Germany.[33] Though some rebel groups may appear compliant, this can often be the result of the tactics adopted by these non-state actors. For example, groups such as the Eritrean Islamic Jihad Movement (EJIM) in Eritrea or Devrimci Sol in Turkey did not use child soldiers partly because they engaged in terrorist tactics that were not adequate jobs for children. As they did not confront the government with conventional warfare, waging their rebellion using terrorist tactics, their non-use of child soldiers cannot be interpreted as true compliance.

The RGIL database also gives us some idea about changed behaviors of rebels' use of child soldiers. It is difficult to ascertain when rebel groups start or end child soldiering, so I mainly look at the rebel groups that have signed the United Nations Action Plans to stop the use of child soldiers. Among fourteen groups that have signed the Action Plans with the United Nations, many of them exhibit legitimacy-seeking characteristics. The FAFN in the Côte d'Ivoire was the coalition of three political parties; the Unified Communist Party of Nepal-Maoist (UCPN-M) had governance functions in their controlled area; MILF is a separatist group with a secessionist agenda in the Philippines; and the SPLM agreed to abide by the CRC by signing the OLS ground rules,[34] and the group's reach to outside supporters, including Christians in the United States, is well known.[35] I do not want to read too much into the list of rebel groups that have signed United Nations Action Plans because the signing also involves the willingness of the United Nations and governmental approval to allow such agreements with the rebels. Nonetheless, the list is suggestive of the fact that those who made the commitment to comply in the issue of child soldiers are the rebel groups that exhibited some legitimacy-seeking characteristics.

[33] Alavrez (2010). [34] Child Soldiers International (2004). [35] Hamberg (2013).

In the case of KNU, MILF, and SPLM/A, the motivation of all three rebel groups to comply and change their behavior was not entirely benign, but the moves rather appear to have been politically motivated to ensure their survival. In the case of KNU, the group attempted to sign the Action Plan with the United Nations to stop child soldiering in both 2004 and 2005.[36] Although the conclusion of the Action Plan was thwarted by the Myanmar junta, the attempts came during the peace talks between 2004 and 2005 where the KNU sought a similar level of governmental recognition that had previously been given to another ethnic group, the Kachin Independence Organization (KIO).[37] In the case of MILF, the 2009 Action Plan came almost as a prelude to the peace agreement it signed with the government in 2012.[38] Around 2009, domestic support for MILF was waning and the group was experiencing potential defection by extremist factions such as the Bangsamoro Islamic Freedom Fighters (BIFF).[39] These political circumstances persuaded the group to negotiate the terms of agreement with the United Nations to end child soldiering, to gain international legitimacy, and to have more leverage in their negotiations with the government. In the case of SPLM/A in Sudan, the Action Plan was signed in 2009 and the independence of South Sudan came in 2011. Upon signing the Action Plan, the group issued an executive directive ordering all units to release children by January 2010, and revised their internal code of conduct with the help of international actors including UNMIS, UNICEF, and Save the Children.[40] However, its promise was short-lived as there was an increase in the recruitment of some 300 children by the SPLA, although the number was smaller than number of children released under the Action Plan.[41] At the time of writing, in the wake of instability in South Sudan, the rebel groups, including the SPLM/A, are reverting to child soldiering.[42] All three rebel episodes indicate that compliance came as conciliatory moves coinciding with political compromises.

STATISTICAL ANALYSIS

The preceding section reported general patterns and some associations between legitimacy-seeking characteristics and rebel compliance. The statistical analysis in this section will allow us to gauge the importance of legitimacy-based explanations pitted against other alternative explanations. While presenting the results from the statistical analysis, I will also bring in some additional and qualitative evidence from the RGIL database, as the interpretations are often subtle because of the limitations of the data or the roughness of measurements.

Table 6.1 presents the results of the statistical analysis on the determinants of child soldiering by rebel groups. The dependent variable, as before, is the binary

[36] United Nations (2013b). [37] Keenan (2012a). [38] United Nations News Center (2009).
[39] Podder (2013). [40] United Nations (2011b). [41] *Ibid.* [42] United Nations (2014c).

TABLE 6.1 *Statistical analysis of child soldiering by rebel groups*

	Model 1 Legitimacy-seeking indicators (1)	Model 2 Legitimacy-seeking indicators (2)	Model 3 Legitimacy-seeking indicators (3)	Model 4 Rebel strength	Model 5 Command and control	Model 6 Lootable resources	Model 7 Territorial control	Model 8 Reciprocity and duration
Rebel political wing	0.379** (0.154)							
Rebel political wing legally allowed		−0.720** (0.328)	−0.215 (0.255)	−0.804*** (0.287)	−0.910*** (0.283)	−0.602* (0.309)	−0.687** (0.321)	−1.159*** (0.384)
Secessionist conflict	0.360** (0.152)	0.532** (0.244)	0.971*** (0.255)	0.799*** (0.267)	0.177 (0.258)	0.711*** (0.251)	0.652** (0.256)	0.790** (0.360)
Number of HROs in foreign state sponsor	−0.002 (0.013)	0.754 (0.750)		0.579 (0.545)	0.599 (0.382)	0.599 (0.669)	0.623 (0.714)	0.226 (1.014)
Transnational constituency			−0.730*** (0.152)					
Rebel strength				0.594** (0.285)				
Strength of central command and control					−0.780*** (0.223)			
Lootable resources						0.635** (0.309)		
Territorial control							0.726*** (0.250)	
Child soldiering by opposing government								0.192 (0.304)
Conflict duration								0.123*** (0.035)
Observations	828	353	380	353	330	353	352	207

The estimates are based on logit analysis. Robust standard errors in parentheses.
*** $p<0.01$; ** $p<0.05$; * $p<0.1$.
Constants suppressed to save space.

indicator of rebel use of child soldiers. The unit of observation is rebel-year. The record of child soldiering does not vary over the years because of the difficulty of determining when child soldiering starts and ends. However, independent variables vary over time, so instead of discarding the variation in the independent variables, I chose to present analysis with the rebel-year unit of observation, assuming each year of rebel child soldiering matters. Surely, the records of child soldiering within one rebel group will not be strictly independent, so I try to take the interdependence into account by adjusting standard errors using clusters by dyads and using robust standard errors. Since the dependent variable is a binary variable, I employ logit analysis to get at the significance of the correlates of child soldiering by rebel groups.

The effects of legitimacy-seeking indicators are broadly consistent with the theoretical expectations but with some twists. According to Models 1 and 2, the presence of a rebel political wing seems to dampen the use of child soldiers, if it is legally allowed, with clear political activities like electoral participation. However, the presence of rebel political wing itself might increase child soldiering. Again, I attribute this to the imperfect measure of rebel political wing, not incorporating the *de facto* influence of rebel political wing, where, for instance, it does not account for how much control a rebel political wing has over its military wing. A weak political wing may not be able to control a military wing's child soldier recruitment practices. We cannot also exclude another possibility, that a strong political wing may operate as useful political machine to recruit child soldiers. The sudden drop in observation numbers from Model 1 to 2 is due to the restrictive observations of the legally allowed political wing variable. Therefore, from Model 2 and on, we see the results from a restricted sample of rebel groups that have some level of political wing, where the link between the rebel group and its political wing is alleged or explicit.

The second legitimacy-seeking indicator, secessionism, is shown to fuel the use of child soldiers in all specifications but one.[43] Again, my theory suggests that this result may be driven by the cases where voluntary recruitment in some secessionist movements in which domestic legitimacy may be strongly perceived among sympathizers within the domestic populace in the separatist territory. This relationship between secessionism and child soldiering seems to support the notion that secessionism with support from a domestic populace may receive volunteers, which makes child soldiering an easy option to rely on as a recruitment strategy. However, this result does not preclude the possibility that secessionist rebels can be switchover compliers. Indeed, looking at the cases of the United Nations Action Plans, I find that the switchover compliers are

[43] This result is different from Lasley's (2012) finding that secessionism is associated with less use of child soldiering. The difference comes from the use of the sample. He analyzed 103 cross-rebel cases, while I analyzed rebel samples that have some level of political wing with their rebel-year as the unit of observation. However, his finding is not inconsistent with mine. I also find that secessionist rebels are the best candidates for switchover compliance.

usually secessionist rebel groups seeking political autonomy domestically and internationally. Take the examples of MILF in the Philippines, the SPLM in Sudan, and the KNU in Myanmar.[44] The process of change from non-compliance to compliance is similar to all three groups. They struggled to stop filling their ranks with children at the outset of their rebellion, but as the movement got older all three groups openly engaged transnational actors, NGOs, religious organizations, and humanitarian groups to commit to change. It took each of them almost ten to fifteen years to take the first steps to commit to the Action Plans, but these steps seem to be fruitful ones to date. In all three groups, many children were demobilized after the implementation of the Action Plan, and the respective rebel leadership made conscious efforts to adopt the new codes of conduct. Of course, compliance is not perfect in all these cases. Low-ranking commanders occasionally do not follow orders, especially in rural areas, as in the case of the KNU. Sudden eruptions of conflict often puts them back on the track of child soldiering when they are in desperate need of recruits, as in the case of the SPLM, a rebel group turned political party in South Sudan. Nevertheless, the example of these groups suggest potential pathways of switchover-compliant rebels, who started as secessionist rebels with a practice of child soldiering, but went through transformations to become compliers after external involvement.

In all models, the dependency on foreign support under the influence of human rights organizations does not seem to have an effect on whether rebels use child soldiers or not. However, non-military transnational support in Model 3 seems to reduce the incentive to use child soldiers. This ordinal measure ranging from no, tacit, and explicit support is from the NSA dataset, which counts the financing by sympathizers abroad such as charities, help by ethnic kin across the border, or diaspora support.[45] This result prompts us to think more carefully about different kinds of external supporters and their preferences, as well as the consequences on rebel behavior.

Other potential explanations for child soldiering carry some explanatory power. The positive coefficient of rebel strength variable in Model 4 indicates that militarily strong rebels are more likely to use child soldiers. Child soldiering, then, is not necessarily the weapon of the weak. The interpretation should be subtle, however. Since I do not have fine-grained measures of the ups and downs of the military strength of a group, it may be true that rebel groups might resort to child soldiers when they become weak over the course of their armed struggle. This result is for cross-rebel comparison only. The result simply suggests that strong rebels use child soldiers, perhaps because of their capability for recruitment. The relationship between military strength and child

[44] See the discussion of the MILF (in this chapter) and the KNU (in Chapter 7) for related references. For the SPLM case, see Hamberg (2013).

[45] This measure excludes help from INGOs or NGOs, so transnational constituency measure is not similar to the number of HROs in foreign state sponsor.

soldiering also implies that weak rebels may be excluded from using child soldiers in the first place.

The result from Model 5 indicates that the stronger a command-and-control structure that a rebel group has, the less likely it is that they will use child soldiers. This may be due to the fact that those groups may have good internal monitoring and discipline within the ranks, or because those groups with strong command structures are likely to have effective adult fighters who do not need child soldiers in their ranks. Turning to Models 6–8, the presence of lootable resources, rebel's territorial control, and conflict duration, all increase the use of child soldiers by rebel groups. Lootable resources seem to make it more profitable for rebel groups to employ child labor to collect and sell their products. Territorial control is also associated with secessionism, which may give rebels more opportunity to recruit from their own population in their controlled territory. Longer conflict is definitely related to the use of child soldiers. As manpower is depleted over time because of the protracted conflict, rebels search for children in to fill military ranks.

Lastly, as Model 8 suggests, reciprocity is not operating in a statistically significant way. While rebel use follows the opposing government's use of child soldiers, only a small number of governments (about twenty) use child soldiers, while many rebel groups (over seventy) across the world have resorted to child soldiering for the past two decades. As the phenomenon of child soldiering is not exactly stemming from reciprocal interactions between governments and rebels, we do not find much systematic evidence of reciprocity in child soldiering. The result is also reflected in the general geographical pattern. Whereas six or seven governments currently use child soldiers actively, rebel use is more widespread even in regions where governments do not use child soldiers. Consider the cases where both governments and rebels use child soldiers. Both Guatemala and the URNG recruited children into their ranks during Guatemala's thirty-six-year civil conflict, which ended in 1996. Additionally, the Myanmar Government and various ethnic rebel groups continue to use child soldiers to this day. The same is true of the DRC. In contrast, in many countries such as India, Pakistan, Algeria, Senegal, Philippines, Turkey, Indonesia, and Thailand, governments rarely use child soldiers while rebels actively use them. These patterns are collectively borne out by the statistical results of the reciprocity effect on child soldiering.

The substantive effects were calculated based on Model 4. When a rebel group does not have a legally allowed political wing, the probability of using child soldiers is 0.931 [0.761, 0.990]. With a legally allowed political wing, rebel groups are likely to resort to child soldiering with the probability of 0.866 [0.618, 0.979]. The difference between 0.93 and 0.86 is not large, and although the presence of a political wing may explain the variation in child soldiering, the variable does not do the heavy lifting in explanation. The probability of child soldiering for secessionist groups is 0.641 [0.464, 0.787]. For groups without secessionist aim, the probability of child soldiering is 0.451

[0.252, 0.654]. Some overlap in confidence intervals is consistent with the observation that some secessionist groups do refrain from using child soldiers. The probability of weak rebels using child soldiers is 0.591 [0.484, 0.693]. The probability for strong groups is 0.873 [0.649, 0.971]. The difference of 0.28 appears to be large, indicating that militarily strong rebel groups vis-à-vis governments are more likely to use child soldiers.

Overall, the results are supportive of the legitimacy-seeking hypothesis. Some of the takeaway points are the following. Legally allowed political wings seems to matter, but do not have huge effect in explaining the difference between groups that use child soldiers and groups that do not. Secessionist rebel groups do use more child soldiers than their non-secessionist counterparts, although the nature of the treatment by secessionists is a lot milder than non-secessionists. Also, the results around foreign support – number of human rights organizations in foreign state sponsors, as well as the non-military transnational support from abroad – seem to suggest that the measure for international legitimacy should be carefully calibrated in the child soldier issue.

In sum, the statistical test gives some empirical support for the strategic legitimacy theory by taking into account alternative explanations of child soldiering. Given the preliminary stage of the data-building in rebel child soldiering, the results should be taken with some caveats that the comparisons were mainly cross-rebel and that the dynamics within groups should wait for further analysis in the future. With the broad statistical patterns in mind, the next section tells the tale of one rebel group that changed behaviors from non-compliance to compliance, tracing the history of its ups and downs.

MORO ISLAMIC LIBERATION FRONT (MILF): A TALE OF SWITCHOVER COMPLIER

> We are fighting for the cause of self-determination ... you have to conform to international standards.
>
> MILF chairman Al Haj Murad Ebrahim (April 2013)[46]

MILF is an Islamic group that seeks a separatist state called Bangsamoro ("Muslim homeland") in the southern Philippine region of Mindanao.[47] The group began its struggle in 1980s to fight for the political fate of the Muslim region in a largely Catholic/Christian dominated Philippine state. MILF originated in 1978 as a breakaway faction of the secularist Moro National Liberation Front (MNLF). After the MNLF signed a peace agreement with the government of the Philippines in 1987, MILF continued its armed struggle,

[46] Integrated Regional Information Networks (2013).

[47] In the peace talks in 2014, MILF's goal was expanded autonomy rather than independence in a separatist state. Espejo (2014).

criticizing the MNLF's record. The main criticism was that the MNLF had compromised the autonomy aim by accepting a small pocket of land in the Autonomous Region of Muslim Mindanao (ARMM).[48] Taking into account the lineage of the forty-year Islamist armed struggle from MNLF to MILF, the associated conflict in the region killed 120,000 people.

The case of MILF will show the working of legitimacy-seeking motivation in inducing compliance behavior. Specifically, the case will illustrate that a secessionist group started using child soldiers with civilian support, but then switched its behavior over time, influenced by the interaction with external sponsors who cared about children's rights. In this transition period, the role of MILF's political wing was crucial in a concerted effort with its military wing. Gathering these facts, the case will show how MILF attempted to build its legitimacy over time, at both the domestic and international level, and how compliance emerged out of this legitimacy-building processes. The case will also show that the transformation of MILF from non-complier to complier was not driven by factors other than legitimacy-building motivations. The discussions will show that the behavioral change occurred *not because* the group sought a military advantage, *not because* the group changed its ideology, *not because* the group had the capacity to comply, but because the group had to struggle to gain domestic and international legitimacy to achieve its political goal of autonomy for its desired Bangsamoro region.

The case of MILF was chosen for several reasons. As an example of relatively compliant rebels, MILF is a good illustrative case to link the legitimacy-seeking characteristic of rebel groups to compliance behavior. The other is more comparative. The Philippines has a multiple number of rebel groups that provide points of comparison. The MNLF was the mother organization of MILF; and MILF itself was the mother organization of another breakaway faction of a more extremist nature, the Abu Sayyaf Group (ASG), translated as "Bearer of the Sword." The New People's Army is another group that operates in the Philippines, although the group's geographical coverage is not Bangsamoro and its ambition is to overthrow the government. The rationale here is that it is analytically better to compare MILF with other Philippines groups rather than to, say, an African rebel group that might be operating in a substantially different political and cultural context.

Background

After a decade of armed struggle, MILF made several commitments to abide by international law. First, it committed itself to human rights and international humanitarian law in the 2001 Tripoli agreement with the government. More recently, in 2008, MILF decided to drop the practice of child soldiering by

[48] McKenna (1998).

TABLE 6.2 *Child soldiering by MILF*

	Features
Estimates	13% of 12,000 as of 2005; thousands, 15% as of 2008.
Recruitment method	Minimal forceful recruitment, many cases of voluntary joining based on religious and ethnic reasons.
Tasks and roles	Fetching water, cleaning, providing support for troops, manning the checkpoints.

Sources: Makinano (2001); Özerdem *et al.* (2010).

signing an Action Plan with the United Nations.[49] The Action Plan contained MILF's pledge to stop the use of child soldiers and to allow a UN monitoring body to check the progress. The Action Plan also included restructured internal codes.[50] Recent reports note that MILF is still using child soldiers, but its use is declining.[51]

Was it a cheap commitment? Not a big deal for MILF? At its height, child soldiers accounted for approximately 15 percent of MILF's forces. Giving up about one-seventh of their forces may not have been an attractive option for the organization.[52] As Table 6.2 indicates, thousands of children were in MILF's ranks. MILF was giving up 15 percent of its total strength at its peak, which is not easy task for any militarized force. MILF could instead have responded with forcible recruitment, but the group did not seem to revert to a widespread forcible recruitment policy. Also, the policy change ran counter to local societal norms, which indicated that youth involvement in the jihad was a collective obligation or duty.[53]

The recruitment pattern reveals the preferences of the civilian population in the Mindanao region. Many of them were not forcibly recruited as the

[49] United Nations (2009). The full name of the Action Plan is "Action Plan between MILF and the United Nations in the Philippines regarding the Issue of Recruitment and Use of Child Soldiers in the Armed Conflict in Mindanao." The document is available at Geneva Call's "Their Words" database at: theirwords.org. The Action Plan was subsequently renewed in 2013 (Interview with Alec Wargo, the Program Officer at the United Nations Office of Children and Armed Conflict, August 7, 2014).

[50] MILF and United Nations (2008). [51] Özerdem *et al.* 2010; and Watchlist 2013.

[52] The UN figure estimated the number of MILF child soldiers to be about the low thousands (out of a 12,000-strong total MILF strength/manpower), or roughly 15 percent of all MILF soldiers as of 2008. MILF's child soldiering pales compared with that of rebel groups in the DRC or LRA. But it may not be easy to give up 15 percent of soldiers. Although many child soldiers seem to have been used for mainly non-combat roles, any reduction in productivity has to be addressed by other rebel group members, thus making the commitment to reduce child soldiers a costly activity. See Integrated Regional Information Networks (2011).

[53] Fajardo (2003).

recruitment was community-based. Some joined under the approval of family members, especially if any relatives were in MILF's ranks already.[54] The use of child soldiers by MILF was extensive but relatively mild in form, as expected from the legitimacy-based theory of rebel compliance outlined previously. MILF primarily used children as porters and for manning checkpoints, while the other breakaway faction, the ASG, used children as human shields.[55]

The gradual move from non-compliance to compliance is all the more surprising considering that two other groups in the region, the MNLF and ASG, continued their practice of child soldiering. Why did MILF commit itself to international rules and take a step toward initial compliance, while other groups did not alter their behavior?

The sequence of events in Box 6.1 details the events related to MILF's changed behavior toward compliance. MILF split from the MNLF in 1978 when the moderate faction of the MNLF made an agreement with the Philippines Government to establish the ARMM. MILF was dissatisfied

Box 6.1 Timeline and key events related to MILF

1960s	MNLF emerged.
1976	Tripoli Agreement between MNLF and the Government of the Republic of the Philippines (GRP).
1978	MILF Split from MNLF.
1987	Establishment of the Autonomous Region of Muslim Mindanao (ARMM) by MNLF.
1996	Seven-point agreement between the government and MILF to halt hostilities.
2000	"All-out-war" policy by the Estrada administration.
2001	Tripoli Agreement between MILF and GRP.
2005	Issuance of General Order No. 1, internal code of conduct.
2006	General Order No. 2.
2007	MILF–UNICEF joint communiqué on child soldiering.
2008	Signing of United Nations Action Plan to ban child soldiering.
2012	Framework Agreement on the Bangsamoro (October 15, 2012) signed with GRP.
2013	GRP and MILF sign the wealth-sharing agreement for Bangsamoro (July 13, 2013).

Sources: Schiavo-Campo and Judd (2005); MILF-UN (2010); Podder and Özerdem (2012)

[54] Özerdem *et al.* (2010). [55] Makinano (2001).

with the arrangement, which limited the political autonomy of the Mindanao region. The government reacted with the "all-out-war" policy, which curtailed the military capacity of MILF at the surface. However, MILF sustained its rebellion in a more decentralized fashion, hiding in remote areas.[56]

In the course of reaching out to external actors, the group signed an Action Plan to ban child soldiering with the United Nations in 2008. The Action Plan consisted of five articles detailing: the scope covering both the political and military wings of MILF (Article 1); commitments to prevent the recruitment of children via internal policies and external support for registration (Article 2); processes of cooperation with international organizations, providing access for monitoring and prevention, release and reintegration as well as awareness raising and capacity building procedures (Article 3); applicable principles of rights of children (Article 4); and the timeframe of a year and then a review by the UN Country Team (Article 5).[57] These detailed commitment schedules and coordinated plans were backed up by the General Orders released by the armed wing with the support of the political wing of MILF. In 2013, MILF signed an agreement with the government. The sequence of events signals that MILF's compliance came partly as a conciliatory move and an overture for moderation. One interpretation for those compliant moves was the group's strategic positioning to obtain its preferred power-sharing and wealth-sharing in the Mindanao region. However, the fundamental question is why the group made those kind of compliant moves; the analysis I take up in the next section.

Role of Legitimacy Motivations

The theory of strategic legitimacy helps to explain the change in MILF's behavior. Three legitimacy-seeking characteristics appear to be the main contributors to the change. MILF's political wing provided a favorable environment for compliance as it controlled the military wing in order to implement an internal code of conduct in 2005 and 2006 that is consistent with international humanitarian standards. Second, the group's secessionist aim to gain autonomy in the Mindanao region initially provided some voluntary support from civilians who sent their children to join MILF's ranks, but the civilians' preferences seemed to have changed over time as the group lost domestic support.[58] This increased the incentive for MILF to reduce its reliance on child soldiering for their survival. Third, MILF gradually reached out to outside actors to gain international legitimacy. The indicators of domestic and international

[56] Schiavo-Campo and Judd (2005).

[57] Moro Islamic Liberation Front/Bangsamoro Islamic Armed Forces (MILF/BIAF) 2009, "Action Plan between MILF and the United Nations in the Philippines Regarding the Issue of Recruitment and Use of Child Soldiers in the Armed Conflict in Mindanao," accessed at "Their Words: Directory of Armed Non-State Actor Humanitarian Commitments," at: theirwords.org.

[58] Podder (2012a).

legitimacy-seeking characteristics seem to have contributed to MILF's change over time to join the ranks of compliant rebels.

The objective of the following discussion is to trace down how changes in these legitimacy indicators brought about the changes in MILF's behavior toward child soldiering. The discussion will specifically show this: the confluence of *change* in organizational focus on political programs; the *change* in the nature of secessionist aims; and the *change* in external sponsorship catalyzed the shift in MILF's behavior. Table 6.3 presents

TABLE 6.3 *Anatomy of MILF*

Characteristics	Evaluation
Political experience	No election experience; significant role by the political wing, Executive Council in the Central Committee.
Autonomy aim	Territorial aim in Mindanao for the "Bangsamoro people" of thirteen Sunni Islam ethno-linguistic groups.
Communal support	Moderate support initially; waned over time.
Local rebel governance (quasi-governance functions)	Grass-roots structures at *barangay* (village)-level: "Political Committee Setups"; Islamic courts for dispute settlement based on Sharia law; provision of healthcare, education, and other social services; Bangsamoro Development Agency (BDA) (MILF's own development agency); agricultural production.
External non-military support	Malaysia, Egypt, Saudi Arabia, and Pakistan in the 1990s.
Terrorist network	Training from Al-Qaeda, tie with the Jemaah Islamiya (JI), Indonesia-based terrorist group in the 1990s.
International involvement	ICG with four third-party governments (UK, Turkey, Japan, and Saudi Arabia) and four international NGOs (Asia Foundation, Centre for Humanitarian Dialogue, Conciliation Resources. and Muhammadiyah) in the 2000s.
Command-and-control structure	Military discipline within ranks (with regard to ammunitions and defections) with BIAF serving as its military wing.

Sources: Fajardo (2003); Rogers (2004); Chaulia (2011); Podder (2012a); Podder and Özerdem (2012).

relevant information to this discussion in terms of MILF's organizational structure, political aims, community relations, and external sponsorships.

The first legitimacy indicator – the rebel political wing–played a significant role in devising military strategies for MILF. The political wing, MILF Central Committee, appears to have had strong control over its military wing, the Bangsamoro Islamic Armed Forces (BIAF).[59] One of the significant milestones that indicated the strength of the political wing vis-à-vis the military wing is the issuance of an internal code of conduct in 2005 and 2006. The General Order No.1, "An order promulgating a code of conduct regulating the affairs of the Bangsamoro Islamic Armed Forces prescribing its powers, duties and functions, and other related purposes," was issued in 2005, paving the way to a general commitment to international law. The subsequent General Order No. 2, "An order amending Articles 34 and 36 of the Code of Conduct of the Bangsamoro Islamic Armed Forces and for other purposes," was issued in 2006, detailing the commitments with an eye toward reducing child soldiering, suggesting the internal sanctioning policy for violations.[60] The UN Action Plan followed with the supplemental general order, which included an educational program for soldiers and modified their recruitment policy. These were works of MILF's political wing, which presided over the behavior of the military wing and its entire command-and-control structure.

The political wing did not participate in regional elections with its own candidates and thus was not legally allowed. This was mainly because MILF's leadership, run by Salamat Hashim, believed that running for political office would result in recognition of the ARMM governing structure, the initial reason why MILF split from MNLF.[61] However, the group was a "quasi-political party" in the sense that it developed social and economic programs as part of a transition plan to become a successful political party in the future.[62] The Central Committee also imposed political structures at the village level for community policing, with representatives that implemented cultural and political tasks.[63] The group also collected taxes based on community loyalty and donations, provided social services, and performed judicial functions based on Sharia law.[64]

The second legitimacy indicator – secessionist aims – also significantly featured in MILF's initial use of child soldiering and its eventual move to compliance. Here, understanding how the group constructed its domestic legitimacy is the key. The group had substantial support at the start of the movement from a population that did not agree with the MNLF's compromise with the government. MILF regarded the MNLF as a corrupt leadership, which used private benefits from the agreement to establish a small pocket for the autonomous region in Mindanao. In MILF's thinking, MNLF's compromise was not the comprehensive political autonomy Mindanao's Muslim population

[59] See Podder (2012a) for the discussion of MILF's organizational structure.

[60] MILF/BIAF 2010, "Supplemental General Order for General Order Nos. 1 & 2," accessed at theirwords.org.

[61] Rudolph (2013: 160). [62] *Ibid.*, 161. [63] Podder (2012a: 502). [64] *Ibid.*, 503.

had desired. MILF enjoyed voluntary support from youth in their strongholds,[65] which made it easy for the group to use child soldiers in their ranks at the start of their rebellion. As the rebellion went on for over two decades, MILF gradually lost support from the domestic population, perhaps due to dissatisfaction over the group's performance after many displacements or evacuations, or because of the growing social distance between the group and civilians.[66] This loss of support meant that the group could no longer rely on some voluntary support from citizens to supply child soldiers in their ranks that they had previously enjoyed.[67] This change in civilian support catalyzed by social change also altered the group's goal. The traditional community–recruitment nexus was breaking over time, and MILF might have been more accepting of the need to reduce the use of child soldiers.

The influence of secessionism on compliance behavior was thus conditioned by rebel–civilian relations. When domestic constituencies for rebels were willing to sacrifice for the military cause of the rebellion, the secessionist rebel group violated international standards. In contrast, when the population no longer contributed to the wartime effort, the gains from violating international law waned and the secessionist rebel group gave more weight to international legitimacy. It was MILF's autonomy struggle and its relationships with domestic constituencies that contributed to its initial use of child soldiers, as well as to its latest decision to ban the policy of child soldiering. Since MILF was community-based, domestic legitimacy had a complex role to contribute to non-compliance in the first place, and was later a major obstacle in moving toward perfect compliance.

The fact that MILF had a greater incentive to use child soldiers when civilian support waned and that they chose not to use child soldiers demonstrates the robustness of the theory of rebel compliance. The secessionist goal of MILF made them seek the support of the population, thus increasing the costs that they would face if they forcefully recruited children against the wishes of civilians. When taking into account the robust political structure of the organization and level of HRO involvement, MILF chose to comply, even when the circumstances of being a weakened rebel group would propel them to use child soldiers.

The third legitimacy indicator – openness to outside actors that care about human rights behavior – appears to have also contributed to MILF's changed behavior. The group's ambition and effort toward internationalization is well documented.[68] At the early stage of rebellion in the 1990s, the group was initially supported by Malaysia, Saudi Arabia, Egypt, and Pakistan.[69] The financial support network was based on the sympathetic view of the "Islamic" movement in the Philippines. Those countries forced the government into the 1997 ceasefire agreement.[70] Note

[65] *Ibid.* [66] *Ibid.* [67] Özerdem *et al.* (2010). [68] Chaulia (2011). [69] Abuza (2003a).
[70] Rudolph (2013).

that these early sponsors did not pressure MILF on human rights as the financial support hinged on ideological similarity.

MILF gradually opened itself to international organizations starting in the early 2000s. Partly affected by the anti-terrorism efforts in the Philippines by the United States after September 11, MILF started to cut its previous association with Al-Qaeda and interacted with outside actors more. Outside influence by the United Nations and Geneva Call also played a role in the background. MILF signed an Action Plan to stop the use of child soldiers with the United Nations in 2008. With Geneva Call, the group engaged in the fact-finding mission to investigate allegations of anti-personnel landmine use.[71] Also, MILF participated in mediation efforts by the International Contact Group (ICG), which led to the conclusion of a peace agreement in 2012. The ICG was the partnership between four states (the United Kingdom, Japan, Turkey, and Saudi Arabia) and four international NGOs (Conciliation Resources, Muhammadiyah, the Asia Foundation (TAF), and the Centre for Humanitarian Dialogue (HD)). Such was the extent of international involvement with MILF. Both domestic and international legitimacy were important to MILF, but gradually more weight was given to international legitimacy. When MILF's civilian support waned in the late 1990s, the group looked for international legitimacy, which led to the development of an internal code of conduct in 2005–2006 and its subsequent commitment to the Action Plan with the United Nations to ban child soldiering in 2009.

Legitimization Process

As many other compliant rebels, MILF engaged in a legitimacy battle by delegitimizing its key opponent and rivals. It is interesting to see that MILF engaged in a legitimation strategy of highlighting the violations of others. The group stated:

> the office of the UN Secretary-General reported sometime in 2008 regarding alleged violations on child soldiers in the Philippines that of the more than one hundred violations committed against children, 50 percent were committed by the Armed Forces of the Philippines (AFP). Another 15 percent were committed by the NPA-CPP, while the rest were committed by the ASG and other groups. Only one percent of the violations were attributed to the MILF-BIAF, the report concluded.[72]

The reaction of the Philippines Government is also interesting. The Arroyo Government blocked the United States' efforts to list MILF as a terrorist group as it wanted to engage the group in peace negotiations, recognizing

[71] Geneva Call (2010b).

[72] MILF/BIAF (2010), "Submission of the MILF to Geneva Call," "In Their Words: Perspectives of Armed Non-State Actors on the Protection of Children from the Effects of Armed Conflict," p. 3, accessed at: theirwords.org.

that it had "legitimate grievances and considerable popular support and legitimacy."[73]

At a minimum, MILF's compliant move defended the organization from government accusations. The Philippine Government intended to arrest some rebel leaders for child soldiering, and MILF's commitment provided a cover from this strategy. Since the Philippine Government was not using child soldiers, the rebels had to follow some conciliatory steps to avoid criminal prosecutions.[74]

Alternative Arguments

Three key alternative arguments to compliant rebels focus on military advantage, ideology, and capacity. Specifically, I am going to examine the following three arguments: (1) MILF might have complied to gain a military advantage; (2) MILF complied because of an ideological change; and (3) MILF complied because the group had the capacity to do so.

The first argument focusing on a military advantage does not seem to explain MILF's switchover behavior. Some may suggest that MILF's compliance move came as the group became militarily weak and as peace negotiations drew near. It is true that the military operation by the Estrada administration's "All-out-War" that started in 2000 weakened the rebels. Operation Enduring Freedom in 2002, after September 11 and the US counterinsurgency support to the Philippines Government also contributed to MILF's weakening.[75] This military weakening may have contributed to MILF's thinking that political solutions should be sought. Also, significant weakening contributed to the war-weariness of MILF's civilian supporters. However, MILF did not seek a military advantage in agreeing to stop the use of child soldiers. The group could have pursued a strategy that employed forceful recruitment tactics similar to those that rebel groups in other parts of the world have done. However, MILF did not do that, primarily because it was bound by its social relations with the Mindanao population, and also because its external support was helping its cause to gain political autonomy. Since MILF was bound by its secessionist aims, it could not adopt a forceful recruitment strategy.

The second alternative argument posits that ideology played a role in inducing compliance in MILF's case. MILF's ideology did not change much over time. Its ideology is based on Islam, radical Islamic revivalism, or radical political Islamism, but it never amounted to jihadi Islamism due to

[73] Abuza (2003b: 99).

[74] The Philippines case is in stark contrast to rebels in Myanmar in this aspect. The Myanmar Government has used child soldiers, so Myanmar rebels' compliance looked better compared with the government's wrong-doing. Myanmar rebel groups used their compliance as propaganda for debasing the legitimacy of a government. KNU's news outfit, for example, frequently denounced the government's use of child soldiers.

[75] Maxwell (2004).

secular and moderating influences.[76] Its political programs and views on Moro nationalism changed over time, but those changes were prompted by political relationships with the local population and international actors engaged in the Mindanao conflict. Due to its stagnant nature, ideology does not seem to offer much in terms of explaining the change in MILF's behavior.

The third alternative argument may be simply that MILF was able to comply because it had the organizational capacity to do so. It is true that MILF was not a fractured organization when compared with other rebel groups that often splinter due to organizational infighting, but an explanation hinging on organizational capacity does not provide a mechanism by which the political impetus would trigger compliance. In fact, organizational capacity was a contributing factor in the implementation of the Action Plan with the United Nations to stop the use of child soldiers. Although organizational capacity can serve as an instrument to enforce compliance, it is not sufficient to be the cause. The main driver and initiator was the coordination between the political wing (Central Committee) and military wing (BIAF) in forging their relations with the Mindanao populations and outside supporters.

Comparison with Other Rebel Groups

Comparison with other groups in Table 6.4 helps us to understand MILF's position better and offers insight into the role of legitimacy-seeking in ushering in compliance. Scholars also note that MILF's targets were limited specifically to government and military.[77] It seems that its autonomy-seeking goal in combination with the involvement of transnational actors led to the commitment. The autonomy aim alone was not sufficient given that the MNLF, despite its autonomous goal, did not give up the practice of child soldiering. MILF's outside involvement with international human rights and humanitarian actors stands out, compared with the MNLF's continued use of child soldiering. The comparison also allows us to evaluate the role of peace agreements in the picture of compliance. NPA also committed to banning the practice of child soldiering,[78] but peace talks are not in the offing. So, the explanation that legal commitment is to position for peace talks is not that applicable in the case of the NPA. Other groups in the Philippines also conducted peace negotiations. The MNLF did not change their behavior at the time of the ARMM agreement in 1996, which signifies the role of international organizations in prompting compliance.

The role of ideology stands out in this cross-rebel comparison within the Philippines. The wide spectrum of ideology from moderate to extremist appears across the Philippine rebels. The MNLF was a secularist, MILF was moderate Islamist, and ASG was the most extremist with jihadist connections. MILF initially had some alleged connections with Al-Qaeda, but

[76] Santos and Santos (2010). [77] Rudolph (2013).
[78] Integrated Regional Information Networks (2011).

TABLE 6.4 *Rebel groups in the Philippines and child soldiering*

	Use	Behavioral change in child soldiering	Percent of child soldiers	Use of child soldiers	Goal, ideology, religion	Political experience	Funding structure	Rebel strength	Agreement with the government
MNLF (1969–2001)	Yes	No	N/A	Auxiliary positions including porters, messengers, assistants, etc.	Independence, autonomy, Muslim.	Observing member of the Organization of Islamic Cooperation (OIC), involved in negotiations since 1976 working toward independence.	External sources, extortion, kidnappings.	17,000 (in 1996).	Yes (Tripoli Agreement 1976; 1996 official peace agreement).
MILF (since 1978)	Yes	Yes – 2009 UN Action Plan	13% (2005 estimate)	Manning check-points, auxiliary roles.	Independence, religious, Muslim.	Organizing political wing for 2016 elections, provides schools and 'self-defense' training camps.	External support, kidnappings, extortion, and drug trafficking.	10,000 members.	Yes (cease-fires on and off since 1997).
Abu Sayyaff Group (ASG) (since 1990)	Yes	No	15–30% (2004 estimate)	Combatants, human shields, hostages.	Religious state, Muslim.	No party, but has political aims of an Islamic state.	External support, drug trafficking, marijuana cultivation, kidnappings, and extortion.	Estimated 500 armed members.	No

TABLE 6.4 (*continued*)

	Use	Behavioral change in child soldiering	Percent of child soldiers	Use of child soldiers	Goal, ideology, religion	Political experience	Funding structure	Rebel strength	Agreement with the government
New People's Army (NPA) Since 1969	Yes	Yes	3–14% of the regular fighters; 20–25% of new recruits (2002 estimate).	Officers, combatants, auxiliary roles, human shields.	Overthrowing government, Communist.	National Democratic Front (NDF)/ Communist Party of the Philippines (CPP); the NDF is the overt wing of the CPP, who traditionally operate clandestinely; has a national publication as well as a news source.	External support, taxes extorted from businesses.	9,000–10,000 regular fighters.	Yes (peace talks from 1995, halted in 2001)

Sources: Child Soldiers International, various years; Podder (2012); Podder and Özerdem (2012a); Rudolph (2013); Santos and Santos (2010) abandoned the networks in the early 2000s in the wake of terrorist branding. As hypothesized with regard to the connection between ideology and legitimacy, it is usually the moderate faction that seeks legitimacy. While ASG relied on training of extremists and the MNLF made early conciliatory gestures to the government to reach a bargain, it was MILF that continued to seek out legitimacy both domestically and internationally.

Overall Evaluation

As MILF's evolution as a rebel organization demonstrates, the legitimacy-based theory of compliance is informative in predicting MILF's eventual compliance move. MILF gradually opened itself to outside humanitarian actors over the decade. Also, as a rebellion that sought autonomy in the Mindanao region, MILF started with communal support and relied on voluntary troop contributions. But over time, the civilian support waned and its international engagement grew. This shift in support types from civilian support to international support came in tandem with its decision to ban its child soldiering policy.

Other legitimacy-related factors seem to have played less influential but beneficial roles in inducing its compliance behavior. MILF did not have substantial political experience, although its political wing, the Executive Council in the Central Committee, was influential in its policy decisions. MILF's moderate level of control structure, in concert with its political wing, allowed the group to exercise control and implement internal codes of conduct, General Order Nos. 1 and 2. As Table 6.3 sums up, pillars of MILF's legitimacy included the organizational structure of its political wing, its autonomy aim, its association with civilian support, and its openness to international humanitarian actors.

MILF's journey from non-compliance to compliance involved the active role of international human rights organizations and humanitarian actors as well as MILF's willingness to engage them. The government of the Philippines was also amenable to such an engagement approach and did not play a gatekeeper role to block access to MILF by outside actors. This provided favorable conditions for compliant rebels to arise. The political vision and programs of MILF political committee (over the military wing, BIAF) played a large role in this process, prompting the military to put orders and internal discipline in place. Those legitimacy-seeking tendencies of MILF led the organization to attempt to abide by international law.

The compliance has never been perfect. There are still reports that lower ranking soldiers use children in their ranks. Here, ethnic and religious factors appear to play a role in explaining the slow change. MILF's spokesman Eid Kabalu said that "boys older than 13 are normally considered adults in local Islamic law, and if born into families involved in the fight for independence, are duty-bound to help in the struggle."[79] Also, there is always a danger that the extremist elements may not comply with the general policy of rebel leadership.

Conventional wisdom has it that Asia is less accepting of international law in general. The case of MILF shows that Asian rebel groups on the world stage may abide by international law and change their behaviors. The case also shows that non-extremist Islamist groups can be engaged and induced to compliance. Although the rebel movement experienced a split and the ASG took a more extreme route, the moderate faction was able to be engaged diplomatically.

The recent fate of MILF is notable. It signed a wealth-sharing agreement in 2013 with the government of the Philippines. The main terms of the agreement included 75 percent of taxation to local government and 75 percent of resource revenues going to the Bangsamoro Government (except in the case of oil, where there is a 50:50 split). I think MILF's case shows the successful engagement of a non-compliant rebel group by the international community. The timing was such that it coincided with peace talks, and the legitimacy-seeking characteristics and command structure of MILF indicated that it was the right group to target. At the present time, the group is moving toward being active in normal politics.

The peace in Mindanao is not certain given the presence of other factions. In 2010, the BIFF splintered from MILF in opposition to MILF's conciliatory moves.[80] But compliance by MILF at least saved some children from having to serve in a rebel military, giving them a chance to have a childhood.

CONCLUDING REMARKS

The practice of child soldiering is a complicated issue laden with different cultural practices and entangled with development and economic issues. The enforcement is not strict and the norm is contested. This is the normative and institutional environment where rebels may face a difficult path to compliance. However, we do observe them emerging in certain contexts. I want to conclude with some thoughts about policy implications based on what we have learned in this chapter on rebel groups' practices of child soldiering.

The effect of international law on the issue of child soldiers is felt by rebels in their interaction with international or NGOs that push for humanitarian diplomacy with the groups. External involvement with an eye toward engagement served as an important conduit for rebels accepting international norms. Not every transnational engagement succeeds.[81] Intransigent non-compliers still exist in such places as the DRC, India, and

[79] Integrated Regional Information Networks (2011). [80] Chalk (2013).

[81] The LTTE in Sri Lanka was not easily engaged until the Action Plan with UNICEF in 2003. However, the breakaway Karuna faction continued to use child soldiers and the LTTE itself recruited more than it released. See Human Rights Watch (2004).

Chad, and the impact of prosecution based on international law has yet to be seen. Only time will tell what the long-term reverberating effects will be of the verdict from the Charles Taylor trial at the Special Court for Sierra Leone in May 2012[82] for using child soldiers, as well as the Lubanga decision by the ICC in March 2012. However, the complexity of an issue involving cultural, social, and economic dimensions tells us that no simple solution would eliminate persistent non-compliers on the issue of child soldiering.[83]

Unlike civilian killing, this chapter finds that civilian support sometimes encourages the practice of child soldiering by rebels.[84] This tells us that in these cases, naming and shaming of rebel groups would not work to discourage their practice of child soldiering. It will not be enough to break the deep social ties between civilians and rebels. Civilians will keep supporting rebel groups and the rebel leadership will keep making justifications that recruitment is totally voluntary. Although voluntary recruitment of children is also a violation of international law, rebel groups will politically justify their use. In these situations, it is doubtful that prosecution would be an effective method of inducing compliance. If most of child soldiers are volunteers, it would be difficult to attribute responsibility to rebel commanders.

The best way to stop child soldiering in the case of potentially compliant rebels would be to engage the communities and rebel groups directly. This would then have to be followed by improvement of the alternatives for the children and families by assisting the demobilization, demilitarization, and reintegration of child soldiers. For rebels with voluntary recruits, such internal capacity-building in steps toward compliance can be an effective compliance-inducer.[85] I turn to this policy issue again in the concluding chapter of this book.

[82] With appeals on the decision issued in September 2013.

[83] For a policy discussion in a similar tone, see Drumbl (2012).

[84] For instance, according to a UNICEF survey, within the ranks of the FMLN in El Salvador, 91.7 percent were said to be volunteers: Verhey (2001).

[85] This policy conclusion is similar to the one in Beber and Blattman (2013).

7

Access to Detention Centers

> In the case of armed conflict not of an international character ... an impartial humanitarian body, such as the International Committee of the Red Cross, may offer services to the Parties to the conflict.
>
> Common Article 3 of the Geneva Convention 1949

The capture and detention of enemy soldiers, civilian sympathizers, or international military personnel is a common phenomenon in civil conflicts. Warring parties use detainees as bargaining chips or as sources of intelligence. In some cases, captured civilians or enemy soldiers do not face detainment, but are instead killed or summarily executed on the spot. Diplomatic attention and international efforts have led to thorough documentation of the fate of some captives, particularly in cases involving high-level politicians, peacekeepers, journalists, or aid workers.[1] In contrast, many civilian detainees caught between governments and rebels perish without ever having their fates publicly exposed.

As in the case of civilian killing, detention may function as part of a rebel group's reprisal strategy. Rebel members often detain civilians on suspicion of aiding governments or rival rebel factions. Civilian detentions are often conducted arbitrarily, depriving those detained of their right to due process. Rebel groups usually lack a justice system and it is extremely unlikely that detainees will face a fair trial, virtually guaranteeing a fate of indefinite detention.[2]

Human rights violations surrounding detention methods and conditions play an important role in the understanding of rebel groups' compliance behavior. Detainees are another type of conflict victims, along with civilians and children. How rebels treat enemy soldiers or civilian detainees as a matter of strategy provides a good indication of the group's wartime political violence. Also, the

[1] Fast (2013). [2] Sivakumaran (2012).

detention issue broadly relates to the question of humanitarian access – aiding conflict victims for humanitarian purposes.

In civil wars between governments and armed opposition groups, the nature of asymmetric conflict dictates the circumstances of detention. Detention in civil conflicts differs from those occurring in interstate wars. In the fighting between or among countries, soldiers are able to identify enemies easily by national army uniforms. This is not the case in civil wars, where soldiers are often indistinguishable from civilians. In these instances, civilians are often subject to similar treatment as enemy soldiers, making monitoring detention conditions a particularly difficult and tricky task.

Little information is known concerning the treatment of prisoners detained by rebel groups. We do not have much knowledge about whether detainees are held arbitrarily, whether they face humane treatment, or whether they are provided due process in some formalized standard of justice. As such, systematic patterns of detention treatment are difficult to identify. The most knowledgeable organization, the ICRC, whose access to detention centers is unparalleled, maintains a strict confidentiality policy. Local NGOs in countries may help to bring to light some information on detainment practices. For instance, in the DRC, local groups like the Centre for Research and Investigation into the Environment, Democracy and Human Rights (CREDDHO), in concerted efforts with the international organization Human Rights Watch, ultimately revealed the brutal detention practices of the RCD.[3] However, these revelations may just be the tip of the iceberg.

This lack of knowledge on rebel groups' detention centers and detainee treatment is in stark contrast to our substantial knowledge on governments' detainment practices. We now know a lot about how countries treat enemy soldiers based on the experiences of two world wars and other international wars.[4] Unlike these events, however, the treatment of prisoners in conflicts taking place within a country's borders rarely becomes international news unless they are recent or maintain high profiles, like the recent conflict in Syria. Additionally, access to reliable data concerning the treatment of detainees is extremely restricted. Few detention centers are open to the public, and those that are inaccessible will almost certainly include centers where abuse and torture normally take place. As such, outside actors have little means of providing consistent, systematic monitoring. Even if the ICRC does its best to monitor prison conditions, the organization is not always guaranteed access, and every new civil war will present varying difficulties and challenges.

In the absence of reliable measures of detainee treatment in the world's detention centers, I have chosen to examine the issue of *access* rather than

[3] Integrated Regional Information Networks (2002). [4] See Morrow (2014) and Wallace (2012).

treatment in this chapter.[5] According to international law, rebel groups are encouraged to open their doors to the ICRC. The Common Article 3 quoted at the head of this chapter lays out the minimum standards for warring parties in civil conflicts, and, historically, the ICRC has been trusted with the function of providing humanitarian assistance in conflict zones, including detention centers. The ICRC is present in almost all the conflicts around the world with the help of the national Red Cross societies. In principle, the organization makes an effort to reach out to all the warring parties, except for some cases of difficult security situations.[6] The organization has visited armed opposition groups in such places as Djibouti (1992), Mali (2008), Somalia (1992), and Sudan (1992).[7]

Granting access to the ICRC does not entail full compliance by rebels, but rather it *signals* a commitment by rebel groups to abide by the procedural aspect of compliance. If a rebel group grants visits to the ICRC, the permission may be an indication that rebels are at least committed to the spirit of the Geneva Conventions. Because of the ICRC's confidentiality policy, we cannot discard the possibility that rebel groups invite the ICRC while still retaining poor conditions in detention centers.[8] However, in extreme cases of non-compliance, the ICRC speaks out about the violations, so groups playing a game of cat and mouse may exist, but not to the extent that it may compromise the link between granting access and weak to moderately humane detainee treatment. Also, if a rebel group grants access to the ICRC, the access itself does not prevent ill-treatment or torture. However, the rebel group will have the opportunity to improve their prison conditions and correct for the ill-treatment alongside ICRC consultation.[9]

This chapter attempts to address several issues related to detention access. Why would rebels give access to the ICRC? Despite the strategic advantage of mistreating detainees for interrogation purposes, some rebels permit ICRC access to their detention centers. Sudanese and Myanmar rebel groups, for instance, opened their rebel-held territories and allowed international monitors such as the ICRC into their detention centers. What are their exact motives behind these engagements in relation to international humanitarian law? Why did rebel groups not show flagrant violations of the norms?

In line with the central thesis of this book, the evidence will show that these compliant rebels tend to be legitimacy-seeking. Rebel groups with influential political wings, civilian support in secessionist regions, and human rights-based

[5] One can alternatively look at the justice system of each rebel group based on the most comprehensive study by Sivakumaran (2009, 2012). For the purpose of present study, I think access provides a better measure because having a justice system does not necessarily mean that rebel groups will conduct fair trials. It may be better than summary executions, but it is unclear whether having a justice system itself falls under compliance behavior.

[6] International Institute of Humanitarian Law (2010); Gillioz (2012); Tuck (2011).

[7] Casalin (2011); and see ICRC annual reports.

[8] For example, governments with bad human rights behavior *do* accept ICRC visits.

[9] Aeschlimann (2005).

outside support are more likely to reveal detention information and allow outsiders to visit their detention facilities than those without. As shown below, the command-and-control structure of a rebel group also factors into the issue of access. More specifically, the group's centralized organizational structure is conducive to interaction with outside actors. If an interlocutor is easily accessible, this can ease the implementation of new compliant detention access policies. In what follows, I examine the norms related to detention, analyze the patterns of rebel groups' access-granting behavior, and narrate the behavior of some compliant and non-compliant rebel groups.

NORMS RELATED TO DETENTION ACCESS

An understanding of the detainee issue begins by answering the following questions: who is being detained?; who does the detaining?; where are detainees held?; and how are these detainees treated during detention? Who is detained presents one of the thorniest legal questions related to civil conflicts. How should the term "enemy combatant" be defined? What about those cases that involve civilians detained and facing criminal charges in the name of "providing assistance to the enemy"? When a person provides the adversary with logistics and information, does that make an individual an "enemy combatant"? These difficult questions of contemporary security have especially developed over the course of the war on terror. In this period, the international community re-interpreted the Geneva Conventions and the national application of terrorism laws has varied widely over time and across regions.

Amid some legal uncertainties about the definition of detainees and enemy combatants, one legal principle that has withstood the test of time pertains to the humane treatment of detainees. This principle was codified in the Geneva Conventions, and the Common Article 3 bestows the ICRC with the authority to monitor and facilitate international humanitarian law, ensuring detainees are provided with their right to a fair trial and the right to dignity. The International Covenant on Civil and Political Rights also rebukes any justification for indefinite detention except in the case of public emergency.[10]

Norms related to detention conditions include several other dimensions of human rights and humanitarian issues. The first is the issue of torture. Detainees are often ill-treated for the purpose of interrogation. The detaining authorities often want useful intelligence or information about their opponents. The second is the issue of due process. In the context of civil wars, all kinds of people are detained by rebel groups ranging from political prisoners to suspected government supporters. These civilians often do not fit the status of enemy combatants and are often denied access to justice. Indefinite detention often

[10] De Zayas (2005).

characterizes the life of these civilian detainees. Among these twin human rights issues surrounding detention conditions, some issues receive more attention than others: human rights organizations have put a lot of effort into identifying cruel, inhumane, or degrading treatment, while the right to a fair trial is given less attention.[11] In some cases, the fact that rebels keep detainees at the very least suggests that those groups did not execute their enemies outright. But still, even in those cases, the adherence to the norm of humane treatment of detainees is not at all guaranteed in the hands of rebel groups in civil conflicts.

EXPECTATIONS FROM THE STRATEGIC LEGITIMACY THEORY

The central argument of this book is that rebel groups that seek legitimacy are likely to adhere to international standards on the conduct of warfare. This argument was developed in Chapter 3, and this section applies the theory in the issue area of detention access. Despite the military imperatives to get information and to conduct reprisals, legitimacy-seeking rebels are more likely to allow the visitation of international monitors to their detention centers, sometimes to their benefit in receiving humanitarian assistance in prison centers or to the political benefit of engaging international actors.

Before I state my expectations about rebel groups granting access to their detention centers, I want to point out a somewhat peculiar aspect of this topic when compared with the previous topics of civilian killing and child soldiering. The issue concerns the amount of control that the opposing government exercises over the rebels' compliance behavior. Civilian killing involves action–reaction processes where rebels make their own decision, and child soldiering is also a group-level decision within rebel organizations. However, the issue of detention access is different. Access must be granted by the government first to international organizations before international organizations can reach rebel groups. Therefore, the amount of control by the opposing government should be directly factored into the calculus of rebels in the issue of detention access. This special aspect of detention visits will be featured in the following theoretical discussion as well as in subsequent discussion of empirical cases.

The first expectation arising from the strategic legitimacy theory proposed is that rebel groups with political wings are more likely to grant access to the ICRC. Political wings within rebel organizations supposedly have more information about international affairs and larger political programs involving international actors in their controlled region, relative to rebel organizations with military wings that primarily focus on military

[11] In line with this observation, Cole and Ramirez (2013) find, in the context of states' adherence to human rights, that physical integrity norms (the issue of torture in the case of detention issues) have made progress while civil and political rights (the issue of fair trial in the case of detention issues) have not improved.

campaigns. In particular, if those political wings are legally allowed by the government, those will receive a wider opportunity to provide unfettered access to the ICRC than rebel counterparts without legally allowed political wings.

Legal allowance of a rebel group operating as a political force in a nation means that the opposing government may be open to political interactions of rebel groups with outside actors. If the opposing government does not allow rebel parties to operate legally, it is highly likely that the government itself will play the gatekeeper's role and will not allow the ICRC into their territories, let alone give the organization access to rebel-held areas. Also, the motivation of the political wing of a rebel group matters as well. The political wing will be more likely to engage international actors for the purpose of painting a positive public image that the military wing is mainly concerned about military wins. These checks and balances within rebel organizations will be conducive to compliance in the issue of detention visits.

The second theoretical expectation is with regard to the role of the secessionist aims of rebel groups and their compliance behavior. My initial expectation is that secessionist rebels would be more motivated to engage international actors than their non-secessionist counterparts. The reason is that secessionists want to further their cause of territorial gain or political autonomy from the central government, as highlighted in previous chapters.

However, in terms of detention access, the key question is whether the government would be willing to allow such interaction between secessionist rebels and international actors. Governments may prevent access to rebel groups, particularly rebel groups that pursue autonomy with territorial controls. Non-secessionists would not have territorial controls or would not run detention centers as a result. This legitimacy-seeking aspect of secessionist movements through domestic territorial control and international recognition would make governments wary of allowing access by international organizations to rebel-held areas. Recent studies on civil war also show that governments in civil wars are likely to care about their reputations and will attempt to deter future secessionist movements.[12] In line with this reasoning, I conjecture that we are not likely to see secessionist rebels granting frequent access to the ICRC.

An additional international legitimacy aspect of rebel groups that factors into the calculus of detention access is external sponsors. Rebels who rely on foreign state support and who engage in a human rights agenda are more likely to allow visits to the ICRC. They might play in a cat-and-mouse game to cover up their bad detention practices, but the access is at least granted in accordance

[12] Walter (2009).

to the Common Article 3 of the Geneva Conventions. This compliant conduct may not necessarily be the product of rebels' conscious effort to abide by the Common Article 3. Rather, rebels may see some advantage of allowing international actors into their controlled zones, be it to gain increasing aid or a perceived increase in legitimacy. This does not mean that the ICRC increases rebel groups' legitimacy. It is well known that the organization strives to maintain its impartiality and neutrality. But on the part of the rebel group, the legitimacy-seeking characteristic may guide their behavior of granting access to their detention centers and allow the ICRC to operate in their prisons and monitor detention conditions.

GENERAL PATTERNS OF DETENTION ACCESS

Several difficulties complicate accurate observation and measurement of detainee treatment. Some rebel groups rarely detain, opting instead to kill or conduct hit-and-run operations; others detain, but do so in remote places. Only the ICRC has had consistent access to the rebel groups' detention centers, but it keeps its information confidential. So, while the organization has knowledge of detention conditions and treatment situations, its working method prefers consultation with a rebel detaining authority for improvement without providing public record of it.[13]

Given these difficulties in directly observing detention records, I present an alternative measure of detention treatment. The measure will determine whether or not a rebel group grants a visit to the ICRC. To reflect the degree of compliance, the measure will range from no visit (measured as 0), partial visit (measured as 1), and full visit (measured as 2). Full visits are where rebel groups granted unimpeded visits to the ICRC; partial visits are where the ICRC may inspect only designated areas or conduct visits on all prisoners except for security detainees; no visits are where rebel groups did not allow the ICRC to visit.

The biggest complication facing this measure is that data remain missing for roughly 78 percent of total observations. The data are missing when the ICRC did not mention that they visited the detention centers of the opposition groups in a certain conflict. We do not know whether the ICRC failed to visit a certain rebel group because of the security situation, or whether a rebel group was contacted but denied access, or whether the government blocked the access by the ICRC to rebel groups up front. These are the possible scenarios. The missing data are not taken lightly but rather will be rigorously analyzed given our knowledge about the ICRC operations, governments' behaviors in civil conflicts, and rebel group attributes.

The statistical analysis of missing data in the subsequent sections will reveal important patterns about missing visitation records. Strong rebels are less likely to be omitted from detention records than weak counterparts; rebel groups with

[13] Aeschlimann (2005).

terrorist labels are more likely to be missing;[14] rebels with strong command structures are more likely to appear in detention records; and secessionist rebels are more likely to be omitted from detention records. This analysis will show that there are systematic patterns in the missing-ness. Weak rebel groups are difficult for the ICRC to identify or they might not hold detainees at all; governments might be blocking the access to secessionist groups or those that are labeled as terrorists.

Given these data features and limitations, this section provides geographical and temporal patterns of detention records, notes some relevant examples, and attempts to link legitimacy-seeking characteristics of rebel groups to their detention access behavior. After this preliminary look at the data, the following section will present the full statistical analysis of missing data, as well as the analysis of rebel groups' decision to grant the ICRC access to visit their detention centers.

Spatial Patterns

Map 7.1 plots the broad geographical patterns of detention visits granted by rebel groups to the ICRC. According to the coding scheme, no visit, partial visit, and full visits are noted. Missing or no visit cases are in lighter shades, while partial and full visit cases are in darker shades.

The map is a much reduced version of the data. The map records maximum values spanning all the periods for a particular country. This means two things. One, the amount of missing data is substantially reduced because of this aggregation and averaging. For instance, even if the detention record for a rebel group was missing for three years out of four years of its operation, that one year's existing record was plotted in the map. Also, for the multiple rebel group cases within one country, the maximum value of visitation record was plotted. This means that even if one rebel group granted full visits while other groups granted no visits, readers will see full visits in the map. Therefore, this map should not be taken as the detailed record of each rebel group's visitation record.

Rather, what is important is to see the prevalence of no visits or missing detention records, despite the efforts of the ICRC to visit warring parties in every conflict. Also, we can note the variation among no visit, partial visit, and full visit cases. The cases of full visits indicate that there *are* compliant rebels in the issue of detention visits.

Temporal Patterns

Figure 7.1 plots average visitation records over time among no visit, partial visit, and full visit, contrasting the access records of national governments during the period 1991–2009. Figure 7.2 plots those of rebel groups.

[14] This does not mean terrorist rebels do not detain. For example, LTTE, PKK, and Taliban had terrorist designations, but they granted access to the ICRC at one point during their armed struggle.

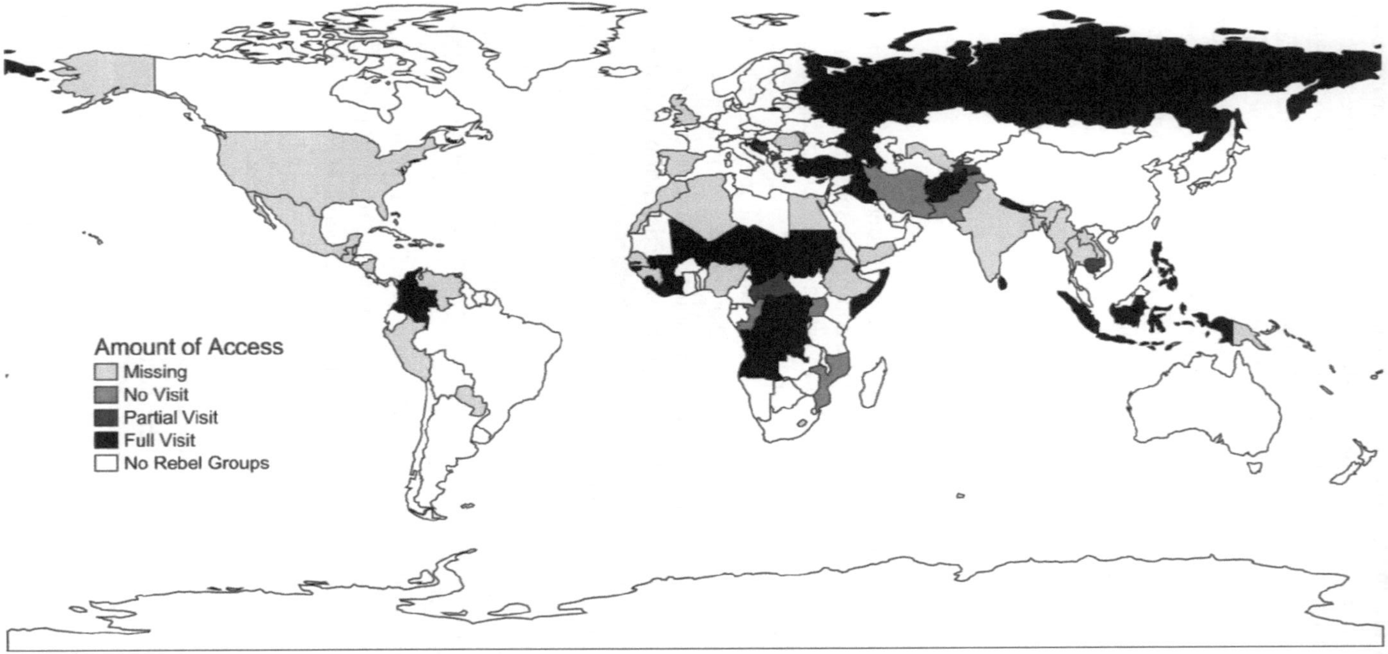

MAP 7.1 World map of detention visits granted by rebel groups to the ICRC
Source: RGIL database

At first glance, the comparison of the two graphs in Figures 7.1 and 7.2 reveals that access granted by governments is higher on average than that of rebel groups. In other words, the compliance record is better for national governments than for rebel groups. The second trend is that the norm of detention access took a stable course of improvement for states until 2002, whereas the norm in the case of rebel groups remained low.[15] The trend indicates that, as with other international standards, the development and establishment of norms related to detention access is slower to take root for rebel groups than state actors. States have established institutional mechanisms, such as ratification procedures, in addition to judicial and enforcement bodies to implement international agreements. In contrast, rebel groups lack such institutions to help foster norm development within the group. For these reasons, the norm of detainee access appears to have been more entrenched over time among the state actors when compared with rebel groups.

Examples

Figure 7.3 shows the variation across groups and across time. The LTTE in Sri Lanka admitted the ICRC in most of the years, excluding times where the group restricted access to security detainees. The SPLM also complied with the spirit of the Geneva Convention and respected the ICRC's access in most of their operating years. In contrast, the PKK in Turkey and UNITA in Angola were far less compliant and restricted the ICRC's access for the majority of the time. What explains this variation in behavior lies at the core of the investigation which I address below.

In the RGIL database, armed opposition groups that consistently granted full visitation rights to the ICRC include the Military Junta for the Consolidation of Democracy, Peace and Justice in Guinea-Bissau, the NPFL in Liberia, and the KLA in Yugoslavia. Rebel groups that consistently granted partial visits include the United Tajik Opposition (UTO) (although a couple of data points are unfortunately missing for this particular rebel group). Rebel groups that varied their access behavior include UNITA in Angola, the SPLM in Sudan, and the LTTE in Sri Lanka, as graphed in Figure 7.3. Note that all the groups in the latter category experienced dramatic fluctuations in their military and security situations over periods of conflict, which might have caused variation in their access granting behavior.

Transition rates in Table 7.1 show how visitation records by rebels changed from one category to another over time, indicating the degree of oscillation with regard to compliance behavior. Rebel groups granting no visits continued to do so for 66 percent of the time (cases of persistent non-compliers); groups granting partial visits continued to do so for 38 percent of the time; and groups granting

[15] A regression analysis that estimates the previous year's behavior guiding the subsequent access behavior also shows that norm diffusion seems to occur among the governments, but not among the rebels. See more in Jo and Thomson (2013: app.).

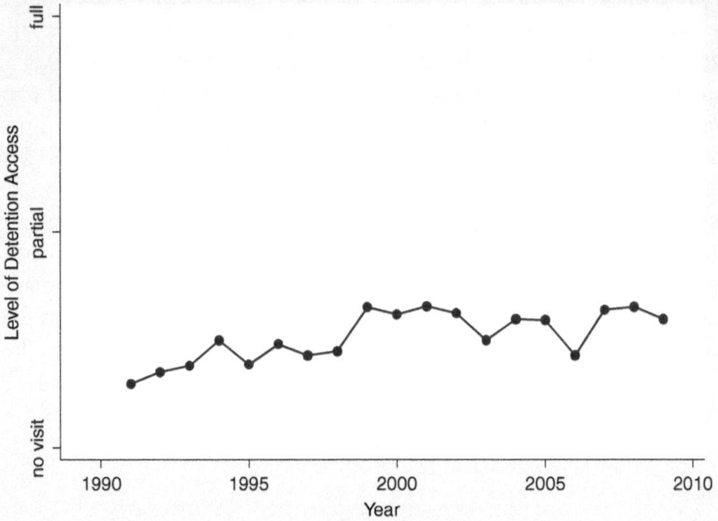

FIGURE 7.1 Evolution of detention norm: average government visitation records by year

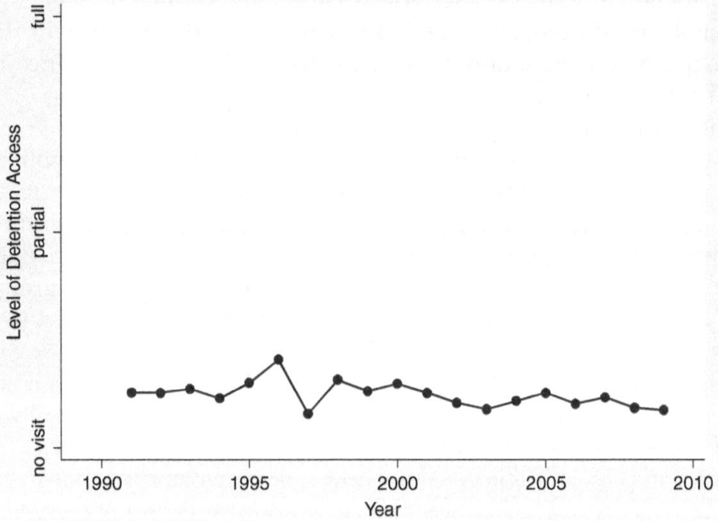

FIGURE 7.2 Evolution of detention norm: average rebel group visitation records by year

full access continued to do so for 69 percent of the time (cases of persistent compliers). Not all cases are stable and switchovers do occur. In 25 percent of the cases, groups granting no access the previous year then granted full access,

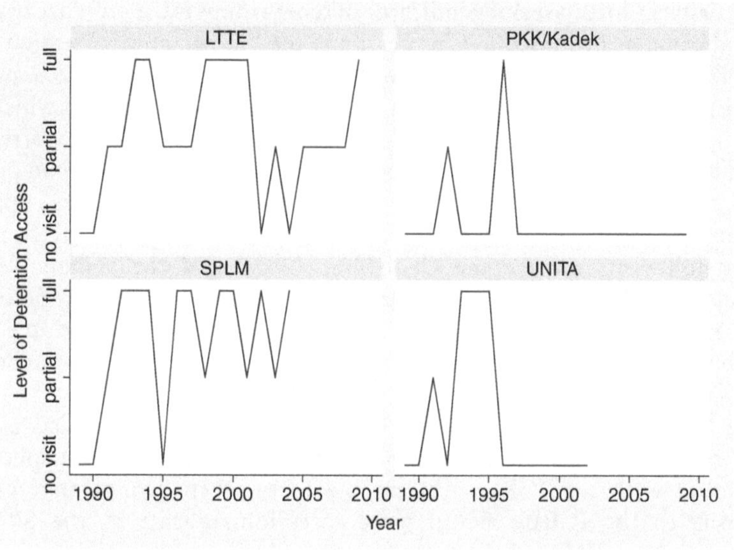

FIGURE 7.3 Examples of rebel groups' detention visitation records

TABLE 7.1 *Transition rates of detention access granted by rebel groups to the ICRC*

		Following year			
		No visits	Partial visits	Full visits	Total
	No visits	66.67%	8.33%	25.00%	100%
Current year	Partial visits	5.56%	38.89%	55.56%	100%
	Full visits	7.14%	23.81%	69.05%	100%
	Total	16.67%	25.00%	58.33%	100%

and groups granting only partial access gave full access the next year 55 percent of the time. These are the cases of switchover compliers. However, 7 percent of rebel groups granting full access restricted access completely the next year, and granted only partial access 23 percent of the time. These are the cases of switchover non-compliers. These transition rates show that transitions from non-compliance to compliance occur as well as transitions from compliance to non-compliance.

Legitimacy Indicators and Detention Access

The RGIL database helps us uncover the connection between legitimacy-seeking characteristics and access to rebel groups' detention centers. As an initial exploration of the connection, some descriptive patterns show the association between legitimacy indicators and detention access.

The first legitimacy-seeking indicator of rebel groups is the presence of a rebel political wing, as proposed in Chapter 4 and the "Expectations" section in this chapter. Among 172 groups that granted no visit to the ICRC at one point in their armed struggle, fifty-seven had a political wing, twenty-nine of which were legally allowed, while 103 did not have a political wing.[16] Among forty-seven rebel groups that granted full visits to the ICRC, fourteen of them had political wings, six of which were legally allowed by the respective opposing government. Examples of rebels with a legally allowed political wing that granted full visits include the CPN-M in Nepal and the Somali National Movement (SNM) in Somalia. The later fates of these rebels are notable: the CPN-M established its own party in post-conflict Nepal; and the SNM contributed to the construction of the non-recognized *de facto* statehood of Somaliland.[17]

The list of secessionist and non-secessionist rebel groups also gives us some sense of how legitimacy-seeking characteristics influenced the interaction with the ICRC. Among the forty-seven groups that granted full visits to the ICRC, eleven were secessionist, such as the SPLM in Sudan and the LTTE in Sri Lanka for some, but not all, years during their armed struggle. Thirty-five non-secessionist groups such as the JEM or SLM granted full visits to the ICRC, which is consistent with the legitimacy-based story of compliance when we think about those Darfuri groups that waged war against the central Sudanese Government. Darfur was a place where international engagement was high when compared with other places because the atrocity level was labeled as genocide. Among 172 rebel groups that did not grant visits to the ICRC, forty-three were secessionists and 121 were non-secessionists. Secessionist conflicts such as those waged by Kashmiri or Patani insurgents were prominent ones where both the governments of India and Thailand used a heavy-handed approach to limit rebel interactions with international organizations.

As the third indicator of legitimacy-seeking attributes of rebel groups, the relationship to the foreign state sponsors under HRO influence seems to matter as well. Among 172 groups that did not grant visit to the ICRC, 115 had no connection to human rights-friendly foreign state sponsors, while forty-three had such connections. Among forty-seven rebel groups that granted full visits at one point during their armed struggle, twelve received foreign support from states under HRO influence. The other twenty-four groups were not under the influence of HRO-friendly support, but nonetheless granted full visits. Some secessionists, such as the Patriotic Union of Kurdistan (PUK), a Kurdish group in Iraq, show up on this list, as does the MLC in the DRC, which had a fairly

[16] The remaining twelve groups have missing records for the presence of a political wing.
[17] Renders and Terlinden (2010).

organized political wing led by Jean-Pierre Bemba, one of the indictees by the ICC. It appears that the combination of various legitimacy-seeking indicators from a political wing to HRO connections is associated with rebel groups' behavior in granting detention access to the ICRC.

STATISTICAL ANALYSIS

This section is composed of three parts. The first part is the analysis of missing data, given that many detention visit records are missing. The analysis will give readers ideas about the extent and cause of missing data. The second part is the comprehensive statistical analysis that takes into account alternative arguments to legitimacy theory. The results will compare the empirical support for the strategic legitimacy theory relative to existing arguments about rebel behavior. The third part is devoted to an in-depth examination of the government–rebel interplay. As the government takes center stage on the issue of detention access, the discussion will give readers a detailed sense of the politics of detention access in relation to rebel compliance.

Analysis of Missing Detention Access Records

Due to the large amount of missing data in the visitation records of above 70 percent, I first attempt to fill in the gaps by doing a little bit of detective work to uncover the cause of no-record in the ICRC's annual reports with respect to detention visits. The procedure will involve statistical analysis of missing data identifying the cause for missing-ness. I substantiate my analysis through conversations with humanitarian workers[18] and through a close examination of my data on missing patterns. Surprisingly, the fact that the ICRC did not mention anything about detention visits can in fact tell us a lot about detention situations in civil conflicts.

The dependent variable to be analyzed is the record of whether a rebel group granted a visit (partial or full) to the ICRC to monitor its detention centers. The codes are based on the ICRC annual reports. The detailed coding procedures are described in Jo and Thomson (2013).

If a rebel group does not grant visits to the ICRC, it may be because of the group's poor detention conditions. The groups that block ICRC visits might be hiding these conditions up-front. Unfortunately, I cannot subject this conjecture into an empirical test due to the lack of systematic data on the treatment of detainees. The second possibility may be that the rebel group chooses not to detain at all. Groups that employ guerrilla tactics will not detain due to their mobility; groups with weak militaries are unlikely to detain due to the fact that they rarely capture government soldiers. I test this second possibility by looking

[18] I am especially thankful for the inputs from David Tuck (ICRC's Legal Advisor) and Olivier Bangerter (formerly at the ICRC, now at the Swiss Government).

at the relationship between terrorist labels and missing-ness as well as the relationship between rebel groups' military strength and missing-ness. The expectation here would be that militarily weak rebel groups and groups that use terrorist tactics are more likely to be in missing categories than militarily stronger groups or groups that do not employ terrorist tactics.

The third possibility lies in the accessibility to rebel groups due to their command-and-control structures. Difficulty in locating the appropriate interlocutors decreases the likelihood that the ICRC reaches out to a given rebel group or that the rebels conduct any kind of diplomacy with outside actors. I examine this third possibility by looking at the relationship between rebel groups' command structure and missing data. In a fourth scenario, the government, fearing that it may confer legitimacy on the opposition group, may assume the role of gatekeeper and block access. I can test this third possibility by looking at the relationship between secessionist conflicts and missing data. The rationale here is that governments in secessionist conflicts are more likely to block access up-front.[19]

As reported in Table 7.2, statistical analysis supports these conjectures on the omissions in detention access records in the ICRC's annual reports. Strong rebels are less likely to be omitted from detention records than weak counterparts; rebel groups with terrorist labels are more likely to be missing;[20] rebels with a strong command are more likely to appear in detention records; and secessionist rebels are more likely to be omitted from detention records. This missing-ness could also result in an underestimate of the groups' willingness, as several groups ask for ICRC monitoring but those requests are prevented by the opposing governments. This possibility of governments serving as gatekeepers should also be taken into account in understanding the process of missing data generation. Recognizing the problem and patterns of missing data, I assume that none of the relevant cases of no access involve rebel groups failing to grant access or lacking the capacity to do so. For this reason, I control for these factors throughout this chapter by analyzing the frequency of occurrence between instances of no access, partial access, and full access.

Results from Statistical Models

The results of more detailed statistical analysis in Table 7.3 reveal additional patterns of rebel behavior related to detention visits. Since the dependent variable is an ordinal measure of no visit, partial visit, and full visit, I employ an ordered probit analysis. The unit of observation is again rebel-year. In the reported results, we are left with only about 300 observations because the records for legally allowed political wings in the NSA dataset have about 60 percent missing data. The number of total observations in the RGIL database is

[19] Classification as a terrorist rebel comes from the START database.

[20] This does not mean terrorist rebels do not detain. For example, LTTE, PKK, and Taliban had terrorist designations, but they granted access to the ICRC at one point during their armed struggle.

TABLE 7.2 *Analysis of missing data in detention records*

	Model 1 Weak rebels	Model 2 Terrorist rebels	Model 3 Rebels with strong command	Model 4 Secessionist rebels
Rebel strength	−1.325* (0.154)			
Terrorist rebels		0.860* (0.186)		
Strength of command and control			−0.428* (0.162)	
Secessionist conflict				0.620* (0.201)
Observations	763	742	684	751

Dependent variable is whether the visit record is missing or not from the ICRC annual reports. The results are based on logit models. Robust standard errors in parentheses.
* p <0.01.
Constant suppressed.

1,128. Among those, 20 percent of total observations in rebel-years have "yes" records for a legally allowed political wing; 17 percent have "no" records, and the rest of the records, 63 percent, are missing. We also lose some observation by the virtue of the fact that we use a lagged value of the number of human rights organizations in the foreign sponsor state. A lagged value was used in this case to stave off potential endogeneity concerns where detention visits may influence the decision of foreign sponsor states in selecting their potential supporting rebels. Although it seems unlikely that the detention records would change the number of HRO secretariats, I report the result with a lagged value of it. Also, readers may be interested to know that I report robust standard errors here, but that standard errors clustered by each rebel group yield similar results.

These results are generally in support of the legitimacy thesis and its explanation of compliance behavior. Rebels that exhibit some legitimacy-seeking characteristics, such as the presence of a legally allowed political wing and foreign support under the influence of human rights, are more likely to grant visits than those lacking such characteristics. Secessionist rebels seem to be affected by the role of government as gatekeeper as they are less likely to accept full visits from the ICRC.[21]

[21] An additional finding that was not reported here is the effect of ethnic conflict on the probability of granting access. Traditionally, in-group and out-group distinction would tell us that rebel groups would treat out-group (i.e., different ethnicities) worse than their in-group detainees. My analysis finds that rebels in ethnic conflicts are less likely to grant access. This means that either governments block the access because of legitimacy concerns (as the Turkish Government did for some periods), or rebel groups blocked the access because of the potential maltreatment of detainees. Unfortunately, the data cannot tell us which is the primary cause.

TABLE 7.3 *Statistical analysis of detention access granted by rebel groups*

	Model 1 Legitimacy indicators	Model 2 Military strength	Model 3 Command and control	Model 4 Lootable resources	Model 5 Territorial control	Model 6 Reciprocity
Legal political wing	1.045***	0.849***	1.002***	0.925***	0.920***	0.668**
	(0.269)	(0.262)	(0.272)	(0.248)	(0.254)	(0.270)
Political regime of opposing government	−0.066***					
	(0.019)					
Secessionist aim	−1.045***	−0.976***	−1.238***	−1.314***	−0.890***	−0.949***
	(0.321)	(0.357)	(0.397)	(0.324)	(0.300)	(0.310)
Human rights influence in foreign state sponsorship	0.061**	0.075***	0.074**	0.097***	0.059*	0.071**
	(0.030)	(0.029)	(0.030)	(0.026)	(0.032)	(0.029)
Rebel strength		0.547**				
		(0.263)				
Strength of central command and control			0.848***			
			(0.208)			
Lootable resources				−0.355		
				(0.259)		
Territorial control					0.806***	
					(0.213)	
Government access						0.015
						(0.309)
Observations	255	261	244	261	260	181

The dependent variable is whether a rebel group granted a full, partial, or no access to the ICRC. The results are based on the ordered probit analysis.
Robust standard errors in parentheses.
*** p <0.01; ** p <0.05; * p <0.1.
Constants suppressed to save space.

Since the coefficients of ordered probit are not directly interpretable, I calculated substantive effects. When a rebel group has a legally allowed political wing, does not have a secessionist aim, and has sponsorship from a foreign state under the influence of civil society, then the likelihood of that group granting visits to the ICRC is 78 percent, with the estimated probability of 0.78 [0.18, 0.99].[22] In contrast, for a rebel group without a legally allowed political wing, having secessionist aims, and a foreign sponsor with no HRO connection, the likelihood of that group granting access drops to almost 0 percent, with the estimated probability of 0.003 [0.0001, 0.016]. The difference of 78 percent is largely due to the differences in legitimacy-seeking indicators.

Note that in reference to the detention issue, unlike other issues, rebel group capacity – military strength and command structure – work favorably to induce compliance. Rebels with strong militaries and highly centralized command-and-control structures *can* ensure that they are accessible because their strength and structures allow them to be an interlocutor to open up to international organizations like the ICRC.

Lootable resources do not have significant effect on rebel groups' detention access. Unlike other issues of civilian killing or child soldiering, lootable resources may not have an impact on whether and how rebels run detention centers, so we do not have much of a baseline expectation here. Lastly, there does not seem to be reciprocity occurring in the issue of detention access. It may be because governments have a lot of control over rebel access in the issue of detention, so reciprocity may not occur in this asymmetric power setting.

In sum, the results of statistical analysis reveal additional patterns of behavior related to detention visits. These results are in support of the legitimacy thesis and its explanation of compliance behavior. Rebels that exhibit some legitimacy-seeking characteristics, such as the presence of a political wing and foreign support associated with human rights, are more likely to grant visits than those lacking such characteristics. Unlike other issues of civilian killing and child soldiering examined in previous chapters, rebel group capacity – military strength and command structure – work favorably to induce compliance in the detention issue. It appears that rebels with strong militaries and highly centralized command-and-control structures *can* ensure that they are accessible because their strength and structures allow them to be an interlocutor to open up to international organizations.

Compliant Rebels and Government Regime Types

One of the interesting results relates to the role of legal political wings. Here, state behavior figures importantly into whether a group complies with regard to detention, as governments solely determine the legality of a rebel political wing.

[22] These probabilities were calculated using Clarify. In the parentheses, 95 percent confidence intervals are reported.

TABLE 7.4 *Rebel groups' legal political wings and opposing governments' political regimes*

	No legal political wing	Legal political wing	Total
Autocracy	121	22	143
Democracy	43	12	55
Total	164	34	198

Source: RGIL dataset. NB: the number of rebel groups is in each cell.

As such, state authorities decide whether rebels can exercise legitimate political action, such as forming a party or holding an election. Further examination of government regime types and rebels with legal political wings presents interesting observations concerning the government–rebel interplay.

Table 7.4 summarizes the comparison across regime types. As would commonly be expected, rebel groups with legal political wings are more common in democratic states than in authoritarian states.[23] The proportion of rebel organizations that have legal political wings in democratic states is about 20 percent. The proportion of autocracies with rebel organizations that have legal political wings is about 15 percent. However, there are some democracies that do not legally permit political wings to operate, and some autocracies that do. The evidence is in line with the literature on terrorism, which suggests that some democracies do not permit insurgent groups to operate legal political entities due to the security risk involved.[24] This supports the reasoning behind why some democracies may ban legal operations by rebel groups in their territories. The implication of this in connection with rebel compliance suggests that rebels in authoritarian states also have incentives to comply, and that there is no guarantee that rebels in democracies will comply with international law. Regime type matters in inducing compliance, but in more complex ways than traditionally thought in the context of rebel compliance.

Table 7.5 lists the rebel groups in authoritarian states with legal political wings in the RGIL database. Surprisingly, authoritarian regimes do allow rebel groups to legally operate in their political environment. Rebels in authoritarian regimes seem to fall into two camps in terms of compliance with humanitarian law. Members of one camp of compliant rebels in authoritarian states attempt to display compliance behavior while actively striving to "debase" the legitimacy of the opposing government. From the perspective of the MEK of

[23] Following convention, we considered governments as democratic if their polity scores were equal to or greater than 6, and as autocratic if the scores were equal to or lower than −6. The original code for the NSA dataset for legal political wing variable was 1 = no, 2 = does not apply, 3 = unclear, 4 = yes. We conservatively consider only 4 to be "yes," and 1–3 to be "no" in Table 7.4.

[24] See Bale (2007) on this debate.

TABLE 7.5 *Rebel groups with legal political wings in authoritarian regimes*

Rebel group	Opposing government	Year
GIA, MIA/FIS/AIS	Algeria	1993, 1994
OPON forces	Azerbaijan	1995
MEK	Iran	1991, 1992, 1993
KDP, PUK	Iraq	1991, 1992, 1993
RUF	Sierra Leone	1991, 1992, 1993, 1994, 1995
UTO	Tajikistan	1992, 1993, 1994, 1995, 1996

Iran, for example, it was relatively easy to garner international support by highlighting the blight of the Iranian regime. With regard to detention visits, it is likely that the MEK did not hold detainees when operating outside Iran as the group was constantly on the move.

The other camp of non-compliant rebels in authoritarian regime reacts in kind. The RUF in Sierra Leone became notorious for their amputations, rape, and killing, the cause of which has been attributed to the group's organizational culture and brutality incited by Charles Taylor.[25] There is no mention in the ICRC annual reports of a visit to the RUF's detention centers by the organization. RUF leaders were subsequently tried in 2009 for their war crimes in the Special Court for Sierra Leone. The opposing Kabbah government, ruling under the corrupt All People's Congress Party in a one-party system, displayed a similar level of brutality in its treatment of civilians.

In 1992, the Armed Islamic Group of Algeria (GIA) reacted with a similar amount of violence when the Algerian Government voided the election victory of the group's political arm, the Islamic Salvation Front (FIS). A 1988 constitutional amendment legally permitted FIS operations, but the Algerian Government never agreed to allow for FIS political representation, later banning the group and sparking GIA violence following the 1992 elections. According to the RGIL database, the GIA did not permit ICRC access during its rebellion. This bifurcation of rebel strategies in authoritarian regimes presents an interesting pattern worthy of further exploration. Nonetheless, these cases illustrate that government regime type itself is not a decisive factor in inducing compliance. The presence of a rebel political wing and its interactions with the opposing government, however, are critical.

The case involving Kurdistan rebels nicely illustrates the importance of a legal political wing in determining access behavior. The experiences of the PKK are worthy of examination because the group operated in three states: Iraq, Iran, and Turkey – producing variation to exploit in terms of political regimes and the legality of rebel political wings. The group legally operated a political

[25] Humphreys and Weinstein (2008).

TABLE 7.6 *One rebel, three states: comparison of Kurdistan rebels*

State	Political regime	Name of political party	Legally allowed?	Did the rebel group allow access to ICRC?
Turkey	Democratic (polity score of 7, 8, or 9, depending on years).	Democratic Society Party (DSP)	Yes	Yes
Iraq	Authoritarian (polity score of −9 throughout the years).	Kurdistan Democratic Party (KDP) and the Patriotic Union of Kurdistan (PUK)	Yes	Yes
Iran	Authoritarian (polity score of −6 throughout the years).	Kurdistan Democratic Party in Iran (KDPI)	No	Missing

wing both in Iraq (classified as autocracy) and Turkey (classified as democracy), but not in Iran (classified as autocracy).

The Kurdish parties in Iraq were the KDP and the PUK. These political-cum-armed movements benefited from the Kurdish Autonomous Zone in Iraq, which was established in 1980s, and by achieving the autonomous Iraqi Kurdistan in 1991, which allowed these two major nationalist ruling Kurdish parties to participate in elections and establish their support bases.[26] The party in Turkey was named the Democratic Society Party (DSP). The party in Iran was the Kurdish Democratic Party in Iran (KDPI). The KDP and PUK in Iraq held local elections and had a tax base, and the DSP in Turkey maintained a geographical constituency base in southern and eastern Turkey.[27] According to our dataset, the PKK admitted access to their detention centers in Turkey and Iraq (where it operated a legal political wing), but not in Iran (where it was banned from political activities). Table 7.6 summarizes these similarities and differences across the three Kurdish groups.

The PKK's relation with the state, and the state's response to the group, differed across the three states. Iraq, as an authoritarian state, allowed the KDP

[26] This does not mean that Saddam Hussein fully supported the Kurdish movement. Saddam attempted to undercut Kurdish nationalists by supporting nascent Islamists. See Romano (2006).

[27] Yildiz and Breau (2010).

to flourish.[28] The Baath Party, the majority party of Saddam Hussein, initially took an amenable approach to the Kurdish question, perhaps to reduce the risk of violent resistance from the Kurdish population, and the KDP largely cooperated with Iraq's ruling regime. Later, when Saddam Hussein strengthened his position by isolating the Kurds after the first Gulf War, ironically enough, KDP and PUK held their own elections. In contrast, the Iranian regime repressed the KDPI, killing its leadership and inciting further conflict. In the 1990s, armed clashes continued between KDPI and government forces, including bombing raids on Iranian Kurds in western Iran.[29] The experiences in Iraq and Iran tell us that authoritarian states may react differently to the actions by a rebel group's political party. The ruling government in Iraq was relatively lenient, while that of the Iranian Government was much less so. The Turkish Government, while considered a democracy, employed repressive policies and repeatedly closed down political parties with pro-Kurdish platforms to limit DSP authority.[30]

The comparative case of the PKK in three states with different regimes reveals the consistent pattern with the recent findings that authoritarian states do allow multiparty systems to flourish.[31] This evidence is in line with the statistical results indicating that the role of the state or political regime does not necessarily determine a rebel group's decision to grant access to detention centers; rather, at least in the case of the PKK, it is group characteristics that drive this decision. Having a legal political wing, be it in an authoritarian or democratic state, appears to have influenced the PKK's decision to grant access. As Table 7.6 shows, the explanatory power for access lies more in having a "legally permissible political wing," than in "political regime."

Now that we have an overview of detention access patterns and have found some support for the strategic legitimacy theory, I want to tell a story of a rebel group to see whether the theoretical mechanisms are at play. Specifically, to examine the effects of this government–rebel interplay and how rebel group characteristics affect compliant behavior, I present a case study of the KNU in the next section.

KAREN NATIONAL UNION (KNU): REBEL COMPLIER IN AN AUTHORITARIAN STATE

The KNU has waged the longest running rebellion in Myanmar among dozens of other ethnic groups. Those groups often include ethnic-based ones such as the Wa and Kachin, or religious-based ones such as the Muslim Royinga in a dominantly Buddhist society.[32] These rebel groups reside mostly on the peripheries of the Myanmar state. Wa and Royinga are in the western part of

[28] McDowall (2004). [29] Minorities at Risk (2015).
[30] Yildiz and Breau (2010); Sànchez-Cuencaa (2007). [31] Gandhi and Lust-Okar (2009).
[32] Steinberg (2011).

the territory near the Bangladesh border; Kachin are in the neighboring areas of China and India. The Myanmar Government has been an authoritarian government characterized by the junta regime with the strong military presence of its Myanmar Armed Forces, officially known as *tatmadaw*. For the last two decades, the regime has faced no shortage of rebellion on its peripheries, and has consequently employed various tactics of co-opting some of the groups, containing them, or fighting them militarily.[33] The thus-far closed junta recently began to open up politically and economically.

In this authoritarian state with many ethnic groups and rebellion, the KNU is one of the rebel groups with a long history of governance in its own Karen state, and has maintained a long-running relationship with the Myanmar Government and with external political actors. The many historical points of this group's ups and downs are one of the reasons why the KNU was chosen for the case study in this chapter. The second reason is to explain and illustrate the phenomenon of compliant rebels emerging from an authoritarian state, given that the group battled against the junta for more than two decades. In the following, the rebel group's motivations and legitimacy battles are highlighted for this reason. The third reason for the case selection of a rebel group in Myanmar is for the purpose of comparison with other rebel groups in a similar environment. Within Myanmar, dozens of rebel groups have waged rebellion against the junta, but with variations in terms of funding and rebel capacity. This heterogeneity in one political regime provides a quasi-controlled experiment in the context of case studies, to illuminate the role of legitimacy and international law in fostering compliance by rebels.

Background

The Karen ethnic population lives in the Karen state of southeast Myanmar. The opposing government, the State Peace and Development Council (SPDC), had been the military government notorious for its repressive policies against its population before the country's eventual democratic transition in 2010. The rebellion has waged wars on both political and military fronts. Its political wing, as a representative of its rebel movement is, the KNU and its armed wing is the Karen National Liberation Army (KNLA).

The group can be classified as a "complier" in terms of international law compliance for the issue of detention access. The ICRC began its operation in Myanmar in 1986.[34] Its work focused on disaster relief in cooperation with the national Red Cross, prison visits to improve water and sanitation conditions, and humanitarian relief at refugee camps. Over the years, the organization worked in rebel-held areas.

[33] Staniland (2012a). [34] International Committee of the Red Cross (2013).

The KNU admitted the ICRC into their controlled zones regularly following the opening of the Myanmar Government. However, due to government restrictions that blocked ICRC access to the group, visits did not occur throughout the 1990s and 2000s. Since the KNU's military was weak relative to government forces, it is unlikely that the group took many SPDC detainees. Nor would it have been likely to have taken a large number of civilian detainees as the Karen state was not a contested territorial zone, but rather under KNU control. The junta tried to implement development projects to relocate the population in KNU-held territory, but other than that the KNU and the SPDC did not engage in many overt, violent battles.

The group seems to have refrained from civilian killing. The records of civilian killing in the one-side violence dataset used in Chapter 5 identified that the group engaged in deliberate civilian killing in the early 1990s, which led to about thirty civilian deaths, but during the late 1990s and 2000s, there are no recorded incidents of civilian killing. This could have been due to the tight military grip of the junta, but in some of those years where direct military confrontations were observed, there were no civilians killed by this group.

As any other rebel group around the world, the record of the KNU is not clean in terms of human rights or humanitarian violations. The group has used anti-personnel mines, although the KNLA forces have reportedly informed villagers in the areas where the mines were placed by issuing a verbal warning.[35]

Coming back to the issue of detention visits and the KNU's compliance behavior, one of the motivations behind KNU admission of the ICRC into their controlled area appears to be that access could legitimize its own struggle. In explaining the reason for the acceptance of access, the KNU Chairman, Padoe Saw Ba Thin Sein, said in 2000: "If the SPDC can give them [i.e., the ICRC] permission why can't the KNU because the KNU are the ones suffering the oppression from the SPDC troops. So I would like them to see for themselves, with their own eyes what is happening in the KNU area. That's why we agree."[36] This story highlights one of the theoretical mechanisms of legitimacy-seeking groups: compliant rebels become compliant so that they may contrast their behavior to that of a brutal government, thereby lessening the legitimacy of the government. The KNU example illustrates the legitimizing reason why compliant rebels sometimes emerge from authoritarian states. The next section goes deeper into the legitimacy-seeking behavior of the KNU to trace the cause of the group's moderate level of compliance behavior.

Role of Legitimacy

The three legitimacy-seeking characteristics, based on the theory of strategic legitimacy, are the presence of a rebel political wing, secessionist aims, and

[35] Landmine and Cluster Munition Monitor (2013). [36] Irrawaddy (2000).

having a human rights-based external sponsorship. The examination of these three factors leads us to expect that the KNU would be a complier on the spectrum of international law compliance.

The first legitimacy-seeking characteristic is the nature of the rebel political wing and how it controlled its political programs. In the case of KNU, the armed wing of the rebel movement, the KNLA, controlled around 4,000–6,000 active troops and was generally in command of the group's political wing, the KNU. The group's official political positions, however, were presented by the KNU rather than the KNLA.

The second is secessionist aim. The link between secessionism and international law compliance critically hinges on a rebel group's close social ties with its home base. The group's political and social relations with the civilian population within the Karen state were in line with the rebel goal of secessionism, or at least having political autonomy short of full secession. The KNU has forged deep social ties over the years within its controlled territory. As we will see in the comparison with other rebel groups in Myanmar, the KNU is the only rebel group, with the exception of the Chins, that relied on civilian taxation. Some of the taxation may have been forced, but its funding structure distinguishes itself from the other Myanmar groups, which mostly relied on heroin and the logging trade.[37] In addition to this reliance on taxation, the relationship between the KNU and the civilian population in the region also reflects the Karen ethnic group's moderately strong civilian support base. Support has waxed and waned, of course. As the rebellion drew out and the KNU concentrated on appeasing the Karen's Christian population, isolating the Buddhist population, Buddhist supporters broke away to form the Democratic Karen Buddhist Army (DKBA).[38]

The third is HRO-based sponsorship that the KNU actively sought out. The KNU is one of the most open rebel groups in Myanmar, and it successfully connected with foreign religious organizations. Its separate foreign affairs division also conducted frequent diplomatic operations within the United Nations. The group was also open for engagement with Geneva Call to stop the use of anti-personnel mines, although the full agreement with the organization to sign the Deed of Commitment was blocked by the Myanmar Government. Also, the Christian section of the KNU reached out to the Christians abroad to appeal to their cause, forming a transnational religious network.[39] It is in this context that the KNU showed its international law compliance.[40]

[37] Booth (1996). [38] South (2011). [39] Horstmann (2011).

[40] Engagement with the KNU by the international community did not come without a cost. As the KNU sought political solutions and engaged the outside world, some factions of the Karen population became dissatisfied and established the separate extremist DKBA organization. DKBA backtracked many of the compliant policies formerly enacted by the KNU, including the ban on child soldiers and engagement with the international community. The DKBA was later bought off by the SPDC to fight against the KNU and engaged in factional fighting.

Comparison with Other Rebel Groups

The comparison of Myanmar groups lends some extra support to the connection between rebels' legitimacy-seeking characteristics and their compliance behavior. Table 7.7 summarizes various rebel groups in Myanmar with relevant information for predicting compliance behaviors: their political wings, funding structures, and military capacity. In terms of links to a political party, the Karenni Army (KA) was the other rebel group

TABLE 7.7 *Rebel groups in Myanmar*

	Detention visit	Links to political party	Funding structure	Rebel strength
United Wa State Army (UWSA)	Unclear	No (broke away from the Communist Party of Burma (CPB)	Drug production and trafficking	15,000–20,000 members
Democratic Karen Buddhist Army (DKBA)	Unclear	Democratic Karen Buddhist Organization (DBKO)	Extortion, logging, mining, drug trafficking	2,000–3,000 armed members
Mong Tai Army (MTA)	No	No	Opium cultivation and trafficking	3,000 members
Kachin Independence Army (KIA)	Yes	Kachin Independence (KIO)	Exploitation of timber and resources in region	At its height, 7,000–10,000; since 5,000 members
Shan State Army South (SSA-S)	No	Progressive Party (since 1971)	Heroin production and trade	4,000–6,000 members
Karenni Army (KA)	Yes	Karenni National Progressive Party (KNPP)	Black market trade, local taxation	1,500 combatants
Chin National Army (CNA)	No	Chin National Front (CNF)	Taxation of villagers and cross-border traders	200 troops

(*continued*)

TABLE 7.7 (*continued*)

	Detention visit	Links to political party	Funding structure	Rebel strength
Karen National Liberation Army (KNLA)	Yes	Karen National Union (KNU)	Black market trade, local taxation	4,000–6,000 soldiers
Arakan Liberation Army (ALA)	No	Arakan Liberation Party	NA	100 troops
Myanmar National Democratic Alliance Army (MNDAA)	No	Split from CPB	Drug trafficking	1,000–2,000 armed members
Mon National Liberation Army (MNLA)	No	New Mon State Party (NMSP)	External sources (diaspora)	1,000 members
Rohingya National Army (RNA)	No	Arakan Rohingya National Organization (ARNO)	NA	1,000 members
All Burma Students' Democratic Front (ABSDF)	No	Political Movement for Democracy	Support from KNU	At height 2,000; mid-1990s 500 members

Source: South (2011); Steinberg (2011)

that was politically active with its Karenni National Progressive Party (KNPP). It should be noted that historically, the Karenni shared similar political visions with the Karen, residing in a similar area in Myanmar.[41] In terms of funding structure, the Wa and Kachin rebel groups, represented by the United Wa State Army (UWSA) and Kachin Independence Army (KSA), relied heavily on drug trafficking and the exploitation of natural resources. This means that the groups were rather detached from forging social ties with civilians in their home base. In fact, many of these rebel soldiers have become border guard forces, co-opting with the government, which has diluted the rebel goals of autonomy.

41 Keenan (2012b).

Among these differences, one stark similarity is observed. Most of the visits by the ICRC were not to these Myanmar rebel groups. The case of non-compliant rebels in Myanmar's rebel detention access provides some lessons about the causes of rebel non-compliance. Actions by non-compliant rebels in Myanmar show that the groups' non-compliance behavior is often the function of the state's unwillingness to permit compliance. These groups failed to comply simply because ICRC access was blocked by the state, not because of purposeful defiance. Myanmar's military government severely restricted ICRC access in 2005, tailing the ICRC delegations by a government-backed civil organization. In order to avoid sacrificing its independence and objectiveness, the ICRC discontinued the visitation. Visits resumed in 2012 after the opening up of the Myanmar Government.

The cases involving Myanmar rebel groups also show that the capacity of rebel groups is an important factor in the issue of detention visits. Weak groups, such as the Royinga organization, are almost irrelevant to the issue of detention visits because they do not have the capacity to detain in the first place. The implication of this for the study of compliance entails that we must distinguish between irrelevant and relevant populations in a meaningful way depending on the issue at hand. In the civilian killing issue, almost all the groups are relevant, while in the issue of detentions, only some groups are relevant either because of the government's gatekeeping role or the baseline capacity of rebel groups. Understanding what rebels can do in their interactions with national governments is important in explaining their compliance behavior.

Overall Evaluation

The Myanmar case draws an interesting parallel with the Sudanese case. In both Myanmar and Sudan, rebels challenged authoritarian governments with poor human rights records. Both states housed multiple rebel groups, including some with autonomy goals (SPLM in Sudan; KNU in Myanmar) and others with ethnic-based aims (Darfur groups in Sudan; Royingya in Myanmar). Both states experienced what I refer to as "compliance cascades" among rebel groups; groups in both countries based their claims for international legitimacy on the ruthlessness of the ruling regime. The initial rebel group, SPLM in Sudan's case and KNU in Myanmar's, successfully engaged outside actors. Rebel groups that followed adopted their practices. Darfur groups, for instance, signed the Action Plan to stop child soldiers in 2009 with the United Nations after the SPLM signed the OLS in 1998, which entailed a similar commitment to ban child soldiering. Other Myanmar groups, the KNPP and the Mon National Liberation Army (MNLA), signed an Action Plan in 2012 with Geneva Call called the "Deed of Commitment for the Protection of Children from the Effects of Armed Conflict," following suit after the KNU signed on to a similar commitment in

2009.[42] In these various ways, the SPLM and KNU were norm-leaders as well as norm-followers. The emergence of compliant rebels in authoritarian states does not tell us that these groups are, at their core, necessarily good, but rather that these groups take steps toward compliance as part of calculations related to survival and changes in their security and political environments.

CONCLUDING REMARKS

The case of KNU in Myanmar illustrated that many of the legitimacy-seeking characteristics of the organization explained their willingness to allow the ICRC to visit. What rebels want, especially their legitimacy aims, matters in explaining compliance patterns in the issue of humanitarian access to detention centers. Rebels with a legal political wing are more likely to grant access. The legal status of a political wing is important in relation to the detention issue. Governments can play a gatekeeper role to block access and, therefore, the initial legal allowance determined by a government can sometimes provide an easy pass for rebels to ignore international organizations. Permits are issued under governmental authority, and this determines whether an international organization, such as the ICRC, receives access to visit rural and conflict areas. For example, when the Sudanese Government did not permit visits by international organizations in 2009, those organizations had to suspend their operations in all regions of the country, including Darfur.

Rebel capability also factors prominently in any understanding of compliance behavior with regard to detention visits. Weak rebel groups lack the capacity to significantly detain any government soldiers or civilians, making them ineligible to comply at the outset. Tactical concerns, like terrorist methods, will also lead some rebel groups not to detain in the first place. Rebel groups that control territory, are led under centralized command and control, and have strong militaries are more likely to grant access than those that do not.

Research on detention visits shows the patterns of commitment and compliance by rebel groups in relation to international norms. As the media becomes more global, we might receive better information about people detained. Still, some cases of detention are featured prominently in the media. The experience of the American soldier Private Bowe Bergdahl, who was detained by the Taliban in Afghanistan in 2009, was broadcast on YouTube and by numerous media outlets. Also, consider the case of the Colombian politician Ingrid Betancourt. She was detained by FARC in Colombia for six years and released in 2008. During her capture, a lot of media attention was given to the case because of her high-profile status.

[42] Geneva Call (2012b).

Many cases of detention will remain anonymous and we will never have complete and perfect information on detention practices. The organization with access to the best information keeps its records confidential and rebel groups can play cat-and-mouse games with the potential inspector. These difficulties aside, my analysis shows that legitimacy-seeking rebel groups are more likely to seek out engagement with an agent of international law, such as the ICRC. From the rebel groups' perspective, such outreach is part of their broader political strategy to signal their commitment to international standards.

PART III

IMPLICATIONS OF COMPLIANT REBELS

8

Repertoires of Rebel Compliance

The preceding three chapters have attempted to unwind the political complexities of rebel compliance in three compliance issue areas: civilian killing (Chapter 5), child soldiering (Chapter 6), and granting visits to rebel detention centers (Chapter 7). The three issues are also crucially interrelated in practice. The detention issue and violence against children are linked: some child soldiers are detained and used as sexual slaves. The issues of the treatment of civilians and violence against children are also interconnected: civilian casualties often include children and women. These overlaps across different forms of violence are prevalent in most protracted conflicts, as in the case of the DRC.

The empirical examination of the three chapters reveals commonalities and differences in rebel compliance across the three issues. Building on the findings, this chapter compares and contrasts the three issues of rebel compliance. The key common finding is that achieving strategic legitimacy influenced rebel groups' decision to comply with international rules in concrete ways. All three cases show that rebel compliance or non-compliance occurs in a larger strategic setting. Compliance decisions were made in the course of rebel groups' domestic political activities to consolidate their home base, in their pursuit of goals of rebellion, and during the formation of external networks for sponsorship.

Along with these commonalities, the empirical records also reveal important differences. Depending on the strength of norms in question and depending on the role of rebel capacity in implementing compliance decisions, legitimacy-seeking motivations appear to be translated in a variety of ways across the three issue areas. Therefore, it is important to take stock of these findings to compare and contrast the lessons we have gained in the previous three chapters.

The second objective of this chapter is to go beyond these three issues. I explore additional issues of rebel compliance, particularly the issues of anti-personnel mines and sexual violence. Along with the three issues I have examined, brief discussions on those two additional issues will constitute the "repertories" of rebel violence where I fruitfully engage discussions on my findings in this book.[1] What emerges by the end this chapter is a more nuanced view of rebel compliance. This nuanced view, in turn, will provide a foundation for Chapter 9, which delves into policy implications for possible ways forward.

SIMILARITIES IN THE THREE ISSUES

The analysis of the three issues shows similarities in terms of factors that lead to rebel compliance (or non-compliance). I discuss several common findings below. The topics include the evidence of strategic legitimacy, the role of opposing government, rebel military strength, rebel financing structure, rebel organizational capacity, and, lastly, the role of rebel groups' life cycles. In discussing these findings, I mainly rely on the cross-rebel findings from my statistical analysis, essentially comparing one rebel group with the other, as well as the findings from my qualitative case studies.

Evidence of Strategic Legitimacy

Overall, the empirical evidence from the three previous chapters gives support for the strategic legitimacy theory espoused in Chapter 3. In all three issues of rebel civilian killing, child soldiering, and detention visits we have seen the crucial role of strategic legitimacy in the calculus of rebel compliance. In pursuit of political and military survival, rebel groups seek domestic and international legitimacy, and their decision to comply or not to comply occurs in this political environment.

At times, caught up in asymmetric warfare against a usually much better equipped opponent, with ongoing pressure to procure weapons and secure recruits, rebels' short-term tactical behaviors may dominate their long-term strategic incentives. In this context, rebels might commit atrocities to discourage civilians from siding with the government; they might use child soldiers to fill their ranks in an easy and fast way; and they might block international access to the territory they control.

However, for rebels who take a longer view of their struggle, who see the value of strong relations with their local civilian population, who see the positive value of political programs, and/or who recognize a need to achieve international legitimacy, those are the ones to which compliance with international law becomes important.

The three legitimacy-seeking characteristics introduced in this book generally received empirical support in their association with compliant rebels. First, having a rebel political wing generally curbed the unconstrained violence in the issues of civilian killing, child soldiering, and detention visits.

[1] The title of this chapter is an adaptation from Wood (2008).

Second, secessionism was often an efficient checker of non-compliant behaviors. Except when civilians support non-compliant rebel behaviors as in the case of child soldiers, secessionist rebels exhibited compliant behaviors. Third, human rights-based rebel external sponsorship discouraged rebel civilian killing and encouraged rebel groups to open their detention centers to outside monitors. This association between legitimacy-seeking behaviors and rebel compliance is the central finding that cuts across the three issues.

Role of Opposing Governments

Opposing governments play important roles in inducing or hindering rebel compliance. This is because rebel compliance emerges from an action–reaction dynamic between the opposing government and the rebel group in question. When the government is militarily dominant, rebel groups usually comply primarily due to their military weakness. Their capacity will limit them in causing violence on a massive scale. Also, if the government fails to provide basic services, legitimacy-seeking rebels will be able to fill the void in governance functions, and therefore prime themselves to less violence against civilians in those rebel-held areas. It is in this military-cum-legitimacy battle where rebel groups determine their behaviors in response to government actions.

Take the example of the long-running civil wars in the DRC. The role of states partly explains why rebels in the DRC are so egregiously non-compliant. One of the rebel leaders, Bosco Ntaganda, is even being dubbed "The Terminator" due to his willingness to kill civilians. The DRC also has the largest rebel-controlled area, earning it the title of "rape capital of the world." Indeed, the DRC's central government itself is frequently accused of gross humanitarian violations carried out by government soldiers, and the government itself is engaged in recruiting child soldiers. Most of the rebels in the DRC survive without relying on political principals that care about human rights and are incapable of providing governance functions to domestic citizens in eastern Congo. The M23 was the recent example where a rebel group tried to pretend to abide by humanitarian law, but its practice fell short of the international standards, as discussed in Chapter 5. In the case of the DRC, rebel compliance is trapped in a bad cycle where neither the government nor the rebels seek viability as a political authority.

The DRC example is in contrast to the political environment in the Philippines, where some rebel groups, such as MILF, have taken some concrete steps toward compliance with international law. Civilian killings have declined over time, and people in Mindanao are now turning to the government for basic services while retaining their political ambitions for autonomy. The Philippines Government also took steps to clean up its own house by signing various human rights agreements. The government also refrained from using child soldiers, despite reports that some rebel groups did. Because the Philippines Government attempted to buy the allegiance and loyalty of citizens through various political programs, even secessionist groups such as MILF that traditionally enjoyed voluntary civilian support and relied on child soldiering were no longer able to afford to continue the path of non-compliance.

Given this important conditioning effect of the opposing government rebel compliance, it is interesting to see the relationship between the regime type of the national government and rebel compliance. In general, rebels fighting democratic governments kill fewer civilians than their counterparts in autocratic regimes. However, democracies are not immune to rebel non-compliance. For instance, Chapter 6 found that within the sample of countries having civil conflicts, rebels in democracies are more likely to use child soldiers than their counterparts in autocracies. This effect was due to the fact that, in some middling democracies, such as Colombia, India, the Philippines, and Turkey, conditions are especially susceptible to child soldiering by rebel groups. This may also be due to the fact that those conflicts are long running and so demand manpower extraction from children by creating a war economy, and not necessarily to do with democracy. Despite the confluence of other factors, these cases nonetheless remind us that democracies do not necessarily produce compliant rebels. Rebels in autocracies such as the Sudan, Myanmar, Uganda, and the DRC also exploit children for their war efforts, and the evidence shows that democracies are just as susceptible to violence against children once an internal conflict has become protracted.

Another finding to note is the legitimacy-seeking behavior of rebel groups in autocracies. The theory of rebel compliance generates an expectation that rebel restraint will produce a contrast to an autocratic government in a legitimacy battle. Consistent with this logic, the RGIL data analysis shows that rebels in autocracies are more likely to grant detention visits to the ICRC than their rebel counterparts in democracies. The governments in middling democratic regimes, such as in Colombia, India, and Turkey, tend to have a big advantage in the public-relations fight over perceptions of legitimacy as well as a certain level of control over access to rebel groups by humanitarian actors like the ICRC. These advantages enjoyed by some democratic governments may lower rebel compliance on the issue of detention visits. Rebels in autocracies, by contrast, often allow visits because they perceive visits as a way of boosting their chances of winning the war of legitimacy. Examples of this pattern include the SPLM in Sudan, the LTTE in Sri Lanka, and the RCD in the DRC.[2]

Surprisingly, compliant rebels sometimes *do* emerge from struggles with non-compliant or imperfectly compliant authoritarian regimes. This is because of the legitimacy battles that rebels wage on the sidelines of military confrontations. For example, rebel group leaders in Darfur voluntarily appeared at the ICC to advance their fight against the Al Bashir government.

[2] It should also be noted that detention access is never complete or straightforward; it will typically fluctuate based on security situations. For example, the LTTE allowed the ICRC to visit between 1993 and 2001, but as security conditions worsened in subsequent years, it granted only partial visits or no visits at all.

The voluntary appearance of Abu Garda, formerly the Vice President of the JEM in Darfur, at the ICC in 2010 was in stark contrast to the evasive Al Bashir, who was also indicted by the ICC for atrocity crimes but did not appear at the Court. The real reasons behind the voluntary appearance are difficult to verify, but subsequent international engagement with various Darfuri groups and the JEM's commitment to ban child soldiering is telling.[3] Such rebel commitments will not be enough to end all the atrocities in Darfur, but still, those are positive indications toward international law compliance in terms of increasing awareness of the rebels about international standards, at the very least.

The rebellion by the KNU in Myanmar provides another story of a rebel group in an authoritarian regime, as detailed in Chapter 7. The group conducted active diplomacy at the United Nations and signed several agreements committing to international humanitarian standards in order to prove to the world that the Myanmar Government, for its part, was not abiding by international rules. This is evidence of strategic legitimacy in action, with rebels becoming compliant in order to impugn their opponents' legitimacy and achieve a win on the political battlefield in the eyes of its outside supporters.

Role of Military Strength

In the RGIL database, about 90 percent of contemporary rebel groups are militarily weaker, or much weaker, than the opposing government. But some rebel groups exhibit at-parity or stronger military power in terms of mobilization capacity or arms procurement vis-à-vis the government. The examples include the RCD in the DRC, UNITA in Angola, the Bougainville Revolutionary Army (BRA) in Papua New Guinea, and Hezb-i-Islami in Afghanistan. The commonality of these relatively strong groups is that they grew in failed states with a weak military force. This pattern of weak versus strong rebel groups once again reminds us of the nature of military and political competition in civil conflicts.

In accordance with conventional wisdom, I find that that militarily strong rebel groups are rarely compliant across the three issue areas I examined. "The strong do what they can," in the Melian dialogue of Thucydides' *History of the Peloponnesian War*, still rings true in the case of contemporary rebel group behaviors. In the dialogue, militarily strong Athenians emphasize the reality of military strength before writing-off the weak Melians. Likewise, contemporary rebel groups privilege military capacity over exercising restraint.

Strong rebels often show no regard for the consequences of their violations. Generally, strong groups are capable of inflicting pain with relative impunity and thus regularly generate human rights abuses. Curbing their incentives for non-compliance is difficult as military incentives for disregarding humanitarian

[3] Watchlist (2013).

rules for tactical purposes are large. More often than not, militarily strong rebel groups do not need to attract further support to be viable as they try to impose their authority by force. Strong groups are rare among persistent compliers for this reason.

This connection between military strength and non-compliance is generally shown in the case of civilian killing and child soldiering. Strong rebels are more likely to kill civilians deliberately than weaker ones; strong rebels are more likely to exploit children in their ranks than their weaker counterparts. This strength–non-compliance connection was absent in the detention issue. When it came to the issue of allowing external monitors in to rebel detention centers, rebel strength was positively correlated with compliance behavior. This pattern indicates that military strength might play a positive role in inducing compliance in the issue areas that feature the importance of "capacity to comply." In this particular case, strong rebels were able to be contacted by outsiders and were more likely to run detention centers, which gave them more opportunity to comply.

In contrast to strong groups, militarily weak groups rarely violate international rules. Such groups often do not have the capacity, such as the manpower or the deadly weapons, to commit massive or systematic humanitarian violations. This point is crucial for understanding the mechanism of rebel compliance with international law and the probable effect of international pressure to comply. For example, if the international community uses aversive pressure to influence rebel groups, this approach is likely to have limited success vis-à-vis militarily incapable rebel groups. A more fruitful approach would involve augmenting the capacity to comply. In militarily weak rebel groups, the military incentive and capability to violate is not as large as in the case of militarily strong groups. Therefore, measures such as assisting them with the development of internal codes of conduct or providing hygiene for detention centers may improve compliance.

From the perspective of rebel compliance, the most interesting category is the rebel groups that are slightly weaker than the opposing government. Many compliers seem to reside in this category, including the FMLN in El Salvador and MILF in the Philippines – two rebel groups that were frequently mentioned as rebel compliers in this book. Consistent with the theory of strategic legitimacy, these rebel groups appear to be the ones that seek out legitimacy to compensate for their weaker military strength vis-à-vis the opposing government in order to survive as a viable rebel movement and to win the civil conflict.

Role of Resources

Students of civil conflicts often turn to the role of resources for the explanation of many social and political behaviors. Especially, the presence or exploitation of lootable resources (i.e., materials that are easily subject to looting) has been pointed out as one explanatory factor for rebel behaviors. The role of lootable resources seems to be more complicated than simple suggestions of either increasing or decreasing rebel compliance. The statistical results show that the existence of lootable resources affected the rebel groups' decision to use child soldiers, but did not change rebel behaviors in civilian killing and detention visits in a systematic fashion. This quantitative result, however, does not take into account the variety of rebel resources and how they can affect rebel behavior.

Groups that depend on oil, for example, choose strategy to seek international legitimacy as they look for international markets to sell their good. This was true in the case of the NTC in Libya, for example, which entered into agreements with France and Qatar. Although the NTC's human rights record was not clean, at least its leadership is committed to cooperation with the international community.[4] Rebel groups can rely on black markets to sell oil, as Islamic State is currently doing in Syria without seeking international legitimacy necessarily. However, this strategy is risky since refineries are easily exposed to air attacks and less refined oils sell much cheaper than highly refined ones.

Rebel groups that rely on illicit trade care less about international legitimacy. They can sell their "stuff" in the black market and still finance their rebellion in a profitable way. This was the case for many DRC rebel groups as well as for Al-Shabaab in Somalia. The group sold charcoal to the international market, mostly to the Middle East countries via the ports of Dubai, earning the equivalent of US$25 million in 2011 alone.[5] The profit from the charcoal trade financed their war against the weak Somali Government. In a very adaptive Hydra-like fashion, Al-Shabaab flouted the UN charcoal ban by selling charcoal illicitly to the Middle Eastern countries where the price of charcoal was three times higher than the local market.[6] The group also launched a terrorist attack on the Westgate Mall in Kenya in 2013, further flouting international rules. For their part, groups that rely on drug trafficking usually witness the degeneration of rebels into criminals, such that the humanitarian violations being committed are no longer massive civilian killings, but rather criminal actions such as abductions and extortion, dipping into child soldiering. All these examples show how rebel groups' use of resources may affect their compliance behavior, but not in a simple and straightforward fashion.

Rebel Organizational Structure

The analysis in Chapters 5, 6, and 7 finds that the organizational structure of rebel groups provides an important context for rebel compliance. On the issue of civilian killing, the command-and-control structure of rebel groups was not statistically significant. One explanation for this non-finding is that strong command can produce both more civilian killing and less civilian killing at the

[4] Amnesty International (2011). [5] Auber (2013).
[6] Voice of America (2013). Also see Radtke and Jo (2013).

same time, depending on their directives. If the directive is in conformity with international rules, strong control within rebel ranks will guarantee easy implementation. But if the directive is to kill civilians indiscriminately, strong control can generate massive and systematic civilian abuses. In the other two issues of child soldiering and detention visits, rebel command-and-control structure provides a favorable condition for compliance. The evidence shows that strong command and control discouraged child soldiering, while it encouraged detention visits. The interpretation for this pattern may be subtle: strong command might allow strict admission of adult soldiers on the issue of child soldiering; on the issue of detention visits, strong command and control is related to the identification of a relevant interlocutor to contact to authorize detention visits for external monitors.

After all, rebel compliance is a group-level behavior. The finding indicates that a certain minimum level of command and control is beneficial for compliance in the case of legitimacy-seeking rebels. As the detention issue shows, command and control is necessary to establish access and strengthen rebels' commitment to international law. Strong command and control, however, is not a perfect guarantor of compliance. When tactical motivations dominate, strong command and control can actually fuel or intensify violence. In the case of enrichment-seeking rebels with a focus on profit-seeking, strong command and control also often results in more concentrated violence. This is especially so if rebels rely on foreign support or illicit trade rather than on civilian support. One such example is the atrocities committed by the RUF in Sierra Leone with support from Liberia's Charles Taylor.

Life Cycle of Rebellion

The three empirical issue areas show how compliance unfolds as the rebellion matures. Recall the life cycle of rebellion in the context of theory of strategic legitimacy in Chapter 3. The stages introduced were incubation, strategic violence, political violence, and political transformation.[7] In empirical investigations in Chapters 5, 6, and 7, I considered these stages primarily in the case studies, as the statistical analysis was primarily cross-rebel comparisons, not necessarily tracking the ups and downs of each rebel movement.

My theory of strategic legitimacy would predict that rebel groups are more likely to develop the urgency of pursuing legitimacy in the latter part of the life cycle. This is because the key audience plays a critical role in the success and failure of rebellion as the movement matures and as the outcome of rebellion is in sight. The records from the cases in three issue areas – the stories of M23, MILF, and KNU – lend preliminary support for this idea.

In the case of M23, the group's legitimacy-seeking behavior came at a later stage when it was pressured by the African Union as well as by the United

[7] Adapted from Donohue and Cristal (2012).

Nations to withdraw from Goma. This I would classify as the M23's "political transformation" period in their short-lived rebellion, after their "political violence" was waged in Goma and neighboring areas in eastern DRC. In the case of MILF, many of the compliant moves came when the group engaged in peace talks with the government, again at the "political transformation" stage. In the case of the KNU, we again find the common pattern that this thirty-year rebel struggle was ripe for political engagement after all the phases of incubation, strategic violence, and political violence passed. Currently, the KNU appears to face its "political transformation" stage. The group contacted the United Nations to commit to the UN Action Plan to stop the use of child soldiers in the late 2000s. The group is also in peace talks with the government at time of the junta's political opening. Its Christian leaning is increasingly engaged with outside sponsors that are human rights-conscious.

The consideration of rebel life cycle also leads us to connect the empirical findings to different sets of rebel compliers. The available evidence suggests that compliant rebels are not a rare phenomenon. Persistent compliers are numerous among legitimacy-seeking rebels in a domestic environment with clearly articulated norms and insurgents with ties to the domestic population, well past the political transformation stage. Switchover compliers are less frequently observed, but, surprisingly, they emerge especially when they come to recognize the value of international legitimacy as their rebellion matures. These different incentives for compliance, non-compliance, and for making the move from non-compliance to compliance, or vice versa, are keys to a nuanced understanding of the emergence and evolution of rebel compliance.

The coming of age for switchover complier rebels carries policy implications. Compliance sometimes occurs when rebels open up to external relations. This was the case for the KNU in Myanmar featured in Chapter 7, or as in the case of MILF in the Philippines featured in Chapter 6. Some rebel groups comply not at the initial stage, but in a later phase as rebellion matures. At the initial stage of rebellion, the commitment to humanitarian norms is little more than propaganda, as was the case for the M23 rebel group discussed in Chapter 5. Compliance becomes a more concrete and real option when a rebel movement recognizes the value and potential benefits of its options for exercising restraints, especially when the organization contemplates peace negotiations. When a movement realizes that it could some day become a political authority, it will be more likely to comply with existing norms of restraint. Long-running rebellions give rebel groups time to weigh various options and, depending on their strength and support levels, rebel groups may "realize" that armed struggle with restraint pays and unchecked violence does not pay.[8] These

[8] Chenoweth and Stephan (2012) find that violent terrorist groups rarely win.

various cases illustrate that there might be "opportune times" or strategic opportunities for policymakers to engage rebel groups.

DIFFERENCES ACROSS THE THREE ISSUES

The three issues I have examined in this book – civilian killing, child soldiering, and detention access – share important commonalities in that they are all related to human rights and humanitarian rules. However, there are also important differences across the three issue areas that have consequences for rebel compliance. This section dissects the differences in several dimensions: in legitimacy indicators; in other dimensions besides legitimacy indicators; in distribution of compliers and non-compliers; and, lastly, in compliance behaviors. These discussions will help readers synthesize the findings further, building on our previous understanding of the similarities among the three issues.

Differences in Legitimacy Indicators

The explanatory power of strategic legitimacy also differs across the three issue areas. The presence of a rebel political wing generally helped rebel groups to curb their violence, but in some cases it also contributed to rebel groups developing more effective political propaganda machines for recruiting children into their ranks.

The rebel aim of attaining political autonomy generally kept rebel groups in check in terms of civilian killing, but the goal of political secession also often increased popular support and increased the likelihood of child soldiers being recruited into rebel ranks.

Foreign sponsors also have considerable influence over rebel compliance. The strength of human rights movements in foreign sponsor states is associated with improved compliance behavior among rebels. Rebel groups dependent on such human rights-driven foreign support are more likely to refrain from killing civilians and more likely to allow ICRC detention visits. This is partly due to the selection on the side of foreign sponsors, but also due to the fact that the rebel groups actively engage foreign sponsors in conducting their own diplomacy. The evidence attests to the influence of foreign sponsorship in contemporary rebellions and suggests that international legitimacy is a crucial factor shaping the behavior of some rebel groups.

Overall, the evidence suggests that looking at only one issue may be misleading in assessing rebel groups' compliance behavior, as groups may make different choices – and exhibit different behaviors – in different issue areas that present sometimes unique opportunities and constraints. Despite these potential differences across issue areas, however, what hangs those issues together is the recurrent finding that legitimacy-seeking rebels are more likely to conform to international rules and exercise restraints in their otherwise unconstrained violent struggle.

TABLE 8.1 *Comparison of the three compliance issues*

	Civilian killing	Child soldiering	Detention
Level of violations committed	Systematic killing at the leadership level; spontaneous killing at the individual soldier level	Mostly at the leadership level, although sub-commanders reject central policy because of a need to fill the ranks	Mostly at the leadership level
Clarity regarding international norms	Clear in principle; messy in practice	Moderate clarity (over the definition of *children*); religious differences exist (e.g., in some Islamic cultures, 15-year-olds are considered adults)	Moderate (over the definition of *enemy combatants*)
Reasons for non-compliance	To maintain control over civilians or to obtain intelligence information	Immediate need to fill the ranks	Use of guerrilla tactics; incapacity to run prisons

Differences in Additional Dimensions

Differences across issues occur along several dimensions, as indicated in Table 8.1. One difference is in terms of the level of violations. Some humanitarian violations are spontaneous, while others are entrenched over time. The killing of civilians can be systematic and widespread, but the act of killing itself can be spontaneous, committed by rebel rank-and-file soldiers without orders to kill. In contrast, the child soldier issue is more entrenched over time. Child soldiering is usually a practice of long-lived rebel groups that try to fill their ranks with children. The rebel organizational capacity to institute and implement the measures also varies. In the case of granting access to outside monitors, the role of capacity and interlocutors seems to matter more than in the issue of civilian killing, where organizational structure plays a lesser role in controlling the individual soldiers' behaviors.

Certainty and clarity regarding norms is another dimension of difference. The degree of norm contestation varies depending on the clarity and acceptance of the issue, with consequences on rebel compliance. Since norm clarity affects the shared understanding, unclear and disputed norms are less likely to be complied with for that reason. Some norms, such as the prohibition on child soldiering, are more contested and newer than others, such as the prohibition on

TABLE 8.2 *Distribution of compliers and non-compliers in the three compliance issues*

	Civilian killing	Child soldiering	Detention
Number of compliant rebels	181	165	54
Number of non-compliant rebels	74	85	143

civilian killing. The principle of distinguishing between combatants and non-combatants centrally undergirds norms for the treatment of civilians, being an important pillar of international humanitarian law. The prohibition on civilian killing is undisputed and uncontested in principle. With respect to the issue of child soldiers, however, the status of the norms is less clear, with different parties disagreeing over the economic role and cultural standing of children. In some Islamic cultures, for instance, children over 15 are viewed as adults, but this view conflicts with the Western notion of adulthood beginning at age 18. These conflicting norms can sometimes become a hindrance to compliance.

The third difference is in the reasons for non-compliance. The capacity issue is large in the case of rebel groups granting visits to external monitors such as the ICRC. As Chapter 7 finds, the norm regarding access to detainees is less established among rebel groups than among national governments. Due to the nature of asymmetric conflicts, many rebel groups do not have the means or the desire to hold detainees; violations against detainees are therefore mostly committed by state authorities. Weak groups generally do not have the capacity to detain people; other rebel groups that use terror tactics rarely establish and maintain permanent or semi-permanent detention facilities, but instead run temporary "makeshift" prisons. Non-compliance in these cases may occur because of the volatile nature of armed struggle, not necessarily because rebel groups intend to defy established norms.

Differences in Distribution of Compliers and Non-compliers

The make-up of compliant and non-compliant rebels in Table 8.2 tells another interesting story with regard to rebel compliance. The number of compliant rebel groups (181) in the area of civilian killing is higher than that of non-compliant rebels (74). The ratio between compliant rebels and non-compliant ones is approximately 2.5:1. In the context of civilian killing, compliant rebels are those that do not kill civilians intentionally, so the ratio tells us that there are many rebel groups that do not deliberately target civilians. Some of these groups may have been deterred at the outset for reasons of local norms, entrenched civilian support, or fear of international support being cut. One-third of the rebel groups, seventy-four out of a total of 255 groups, are non-compliant with respect to the norm of protecting civilians. This is bad news for humanitarianism. These are the rebels that kill civilians directly and intentionally. Among these groups, we see two major types: (1) those that have articulated, systematic policies for using violence against civilians to achieve military objectives and win the fight against the national government; and (2) those with undisciplined rebel soldiers who commit violence against civilians without (apparently) any direct instructions to do so.

In the area of child soldiering we see more compliant rebels (165) than non-compliers (85). The ratio between compliant and non-compliant rebels is approximately 2:1. This number and ratio, however, should not give us much comfort, as the groups that use child soldiers often persist in doing so over the long term. Non-compliers tend to be long-established rebel groups that have used child soldiers to their benefit. The violations often persist because they perceive child soldiers as a military necessity and/or because the practice of recruiting child soldiers is such a well-established tradition. Still, there are examples of groups changing their ways. MILF, a Philippines rebel group discussed in Chapter 6, for example, changed its behavior under the influence of international law. MILF's compliance was the product of favorable conditions that all aligned at the same time: the international effort, increased sensitivity of MILF to international norms, and the timing of MILF making conciliatory moves to negotiate peace with the government.

Finally, with regard to the issue of detention access, the ratio of compliant rebels to non-compliant rebels is relatively low, with fifty-four compliers and 143 non-compliers. Only 25 percent of rebel groups granted partial or full access to the ICRC for detention visits. This low rate of compliance is due, first, to the fact that norms regarding detention access are, in general, less well known and less well established among rebel groups. Second, many non-compliance cases are due to the weak capacity of rebels to run prison facilities in an organized manner or due to the use of guerrilla tactics that do not allow rebel groups to accept and organize ICRC visits in their operating areas. Overall, the distribution of compliers and non-compliers across the three issue areas tells us that reasons for compliance and non-compliance are more nuanced than traditionally conceived, going beyond factors such as rebels' military strength and organizational structures.

Differences in Compliance Behaviors

At this point, readers might ask: does a group that violates one rule violate other rules as well? For instance, are civilian-abusing rebel groups more likely to use child soldiers and more likely to deny visits to detention centers? To examine this pattern, Table 8.3 reports correlation and statistical significance. The Spearman rank test is often used to test the correlations among ordinal data and count measures. The numbers show overall support for the correlated behaviors across three issue areas. Groups that exercise violence

TABLE 8.3 *Spearman correlation among the three compliance issues*

	Civilian killing	Child soldier use	Detention visit
Civilian killing	–	–	–
Child soldier use	0.150*	–	–
Detention visit	−0.257*	0.030	–

* Significance test at 0.1 level.

against civilians are also likely to use child soldiers and less likely to grant visits to detention centers. This pattern is not surprising when we think about child soldering as part of the treatment of civilians and that those non-compliant groups in the treatment of civilians are more likely to disregard the recommendations in the Geneva Conventions to accept external monitors in their detention centers. Overall, non-compliance patterns go together, as expected.

Note, however, that the coefficient is not tremendously high. This conveys an important lesson that we should be careful about dissecting the unique characteristics of issue areas, as the low correlation indicates that rebel groups that comply in one issue area may not do so in other areas. One example I can bring in is the case of the PKK in Turkey. The PKK gradually reduced the number of civilians killed between 1989 and 1999, demonstrating its increasing compliance over time. However, the group continued to use child soldiers, which indicates that abandoning this long-term practice is difficult and that child soldering practice may not be directly connected to civilian killing behavior. The PKK also frequently denied access to international organizations, as they primarily relied on extortion from the local population as well as diaspora support from Europe. The case of the PKK illustrates that not all compliance behaviors go hand in hand.

At face value, this low correlation may look like a challenge to the strategic legitimacy theory I propose in this book. This pattern across three issue areas shows that rebel compliers with legitimacy-seeking characteristics do not always comply across the board. With a closer look, however, this pattern does not provide a challenge to the theory, but rather urges us to pay closer attention to the differences across issue areas. For instance, one legitimacy-seeking characteristic that performed well in one issue area might not work so well in other issue areas. Recall that the human rights-based sponsorship was significant in the issue of civilian killing, but not in the issue of child soldiering. This difference can be attributed to the saliency and longevity of norms to the external human rights sponsors, the divider that wedges humanitarian issues, as discussed above. In general, large numbers of civilians killed abroad attracts news and generates humanitarian need and response, but the protracted issues like child soldiers receive relatively less attention. These relative weights of legitimacy-seeking characteristics might have produced the low correlation among these three issues. What the theory proposes is a general pattern that links between legitimacy-seeking characteristics and compliant behaviors. The statistical significance of correlations shows that the general pattern stands, but the low level of correlation coefficients shows that more a nuanced understanding of each issue area is needed to complete the picture of rebel compliance. In particular, if we were to predict specific behaviors in a certain issue area, the relative weight of legitimacy-seeking characteristics as well as additional factors, such as the status of the norm and the dynamics the issue generates within rebel organizations, or the reactions from the opposing governments, should be taken into account as well.

The companion database to this book, the RGIL database, provides a classification of rebel groups in terms of their compliance behaviors across issues. The RGIL database identifies what I would call all-compliers, partial-compliers, and non-compliers, depending on their compliance records across the three issue areas examined in Chapters 5, 6, and 7. There are about a dozen rebel groups that can be classified as "all-compliers," that is, groups that killed no civilians, did not use child soldiers, and granted detention visits. The list of all-compliers includes the New Forces (FN) in Côte d'Ivoire, the Supreme Council for the Islamic Revolution in Iraq (SCRI) in Iraq, the PUK in Iraq, the SPLM in Sudan (at least for a couple of years), the SNM in Somalia, and the FRUD in Djibouti. It is notable, within the framework of my legitimacy theory of rebel compliance, that the PUK, SPLM, and SNM are secessionist movements, and that the FN and FRUD are rebel forces forming a political party against the Côte d'Ivoire and the Djibouti governments, respectively.

The majority of rebel groups are "partial-compliers," guilty of committing violations in at least one area. For example, the KNU in Myanmar did not systematically kill civilians, but has been a long-time user of child soldiers. Again, the explanation for these partially compliant behaviors hinges on the relative strength of legitimacy characteristics, normative structure of the issue, and additional factors that can affect the opportunity structure of rebels. To analyze using the lens of strategic legitimacy theory, in the case of KNU, child soldier use was sustained by its home base and its cause in fighting for its own ethnicity and region. Also, secessionism gave the group the motivation not to resort to civilian killing in its own region, although operations beyond its regions were checked by the much stronger military government in Myanmar. The group sought legitimacy and reached out to external actors such as the United Nations. However, the junta government struck down the group's legitimacy-seeking motivation. This combination of legitimacy-related factors prompted the group to be compliant in one area but not in others, in response to the government actions.

Among contemporary rebel groups, outright "non-compliers" – groups committing violations in all three issue areas – are numerous. The FARC in Colombia, the Khmer Rouge in Cambodia, the LRA in Uganda, and the PKK in Turkey are examples of groups that killed at least one civilian, used child soldiers, and did not permit detention access. It is interesting to note that the two Kurdistan groups – the PKK in Turkey and PUK in Iraq – are classified differently in the compliance bin. Note that the PKK in Turkey is classified as a non-complier, whereas the PUK in Iraq is classified as an all-complier. Both the PKK and the PUK fight for an independent Kurdish region. But the differences may have resulted from the differing responses of the two involved governments, in Turkey and Iraq. Turkey tried to repress the PKK, whereas Iraq allowed the PUK to have a legal political party, as discussed in Chapter 7.

BEYOND THE THREE ISSUES

> God Almighty teaches us in the holy Quran: "Whosoever killeth a human being for other than man-slaughter or corruption in the earth, it shall be as if he had killed all mankind" ...
>
> At national level, the Islamic Emirate of Afghanistan (IEA) announces a total ban on the production, trade, stockpiling and use of landmines, and makes a commitment to the suffering people of Afghanistan and the international community that IEA would never make any use of any type of landmines.
>
> Taliban declaration, October 6, 1998[9]

The declaration made above by Taliban will come as a surprise to many readers. We have known the Taliban as the armed group in Afghanistan that has committed numerous human rights violations. The declaration states, however, that the Taliban would stop using landmines as a matter of policy. It issued a ban on anti-personnel landmines through a decree in 1998. What are the circumstances under which the Taliban issued such a decree consistent with international humanitarian law? And was the intent genuine?

With the engagement of the UK-led Provincial Reconstruction Team, the United Nations' Mine Clearance Program for Afghanistan, and mine clearance NGOs, the Taliban pledged to give up the practice of planting mines.[10] Words and deeds were not aligned, however. Despite the decree in 1998, the Taliban started using anti-personnel mines again in 2001,[11] and continued to use them and improvised explosive devices to attack NATO forces.[12] The Taliban was not a complier on the issue of child soldiers or on the issue of civilian killing. It used child soldiers throughout its rebellion against the Afghan Government in 1990s, as well in its fighting against the foreign forces in 2000s. The group killed more than 100 civilians on a yearly basis. The declaration came against this backdrop where Taliban committed humanitarian violations, but at the same time made moves to comply. The case motivates us to further examine the fleeting nature of compliance and differences of rebel compliance behavior across issue areas.

[9] Re-quoted from Reusse-Decrey (2000). [10] Maslen (2001).
[11] Landmine and Cluster Munition Monitor (2004). [12] Farmer (2011).

The empirical core of this book has examined three issues of violence: violence against civilians, against children, and against detainees. The issues I examined in this book do not constitute an exhaustive list of human rights abuses. Sexual violence and the use of anti-personnel mines stand out among a list of other issues of human rights abuses and humanitarian violations.[13] This section will expand the scope of research into the other issues of humanitarian and human rights issues and lightly test the generalizability of the theoretical approach I outlined in the strategic legitimacy view of rebel compliance.

Anti-Personnel Landmines

The issue of anti-personnel mines gained its prominence due to the large number of civilian injuries resulting from their use. Anti-personnel mines are landmines designed for use against humans with their primary aim being not to kill, but to injure. The detonation usually results in blowing off limbs and amputations. International law bans the use of anti-personnel mines because of the unnecessary suffering caused and the indiscriminate nature of killing both soldiers and civilians. The International Campaign to Ban Landmines, a coalition effort of six NGOs,[14] produced the 1997 Ottawa Treaty, the Anti-Personnel Mine Ban Convention (often called the Mine Ban Treaty).[15] About 160 states have signed up to the treaty, affirming the universality of the norm.

In asymmetric conflicts, rebels are especially incentivized to use anti-personnel mines to inflict damage on better armed and organized government soldiers. In combating the use of landmines, the work of many international organizations such as Geneva Call and the Landmine Monitoring Group was instrumental. The organizations engaged rebel groups in Colombia, Sudan, and Sri Lanka to persuade them to stop using landmines as weapons of choice and assisted them with clearing landmines. This concrete help, together with the realization that their civilian supporters were also suffering harm while the tactical advantage of deploying landmines against government soldiers was decreasing, prompted many rebel groups to renounce their long practice of using anti-personnel mines. International groups first encouraged rebel groups to sign up to a commitment to end the use of landmines, believing that concrete steps would then be easier with a signed commitment on the table. These commitments were titled the Deed of Commitment (shortened as "the Deed"

[13] The exhaustive list is in the Rome Statute and the Geneva Conventions. Morrow (2007) examined this comprehensive list of compliance areas in his study of laws of war adopted by states. Some categories are not applicable to the armed non-state actor setting. For example, the matter of formally declaring war would not apply because armed rebellions are normally surreptitiously planned.

[14] These are Human Rights Watch, Medico International, Handicap International, Physicians for Human Rights, Vietnam Veterans of America Foundation, and the Mines Advisory Group. See Anderson (2000).

[15] The treaty's official name is the Convention on the Prohibition of the Use, Stockpiling, Production and Transfer of Anti-Personnel Mines and on their Destruction.

from here). The Deed was followed by assistance with the de-mining process as well as verification missions. Recent research finds that the groups that signed the Deed also complied by refraining from using explosive devices.[16] Among the groups that have signed the Deed, few were accused of being in violation.[17] These successes appear to be due in part to the focus in a number of countries and to the concrete assistance the organization provided to rebel groups for clearing mines.

The forty plus groups that to date have signed the Deed of Commitment include rebel groups in Burma, Burundi, India, Indonesia, Iran, Iraq, Morocco, Nepal, Philippines, Somalia, Sri Lanka, Sudan, and Turkey.[18] Browsing the list of groups that signed the Deed, we see many rebel groups that were in the process of seeking legitimacy at home and abroad. In Burundi, the National Council for the Defense of Democracy (CNDD-FDD) signed the Deed, while the Palipehutu-FNL did not. It is worth noting that the CNDD-FDD's wartime political activities led it to become a ruling party in current Burundi politics, while the Palipehutu is still dominated by a military wing centered on its ethnic Hutu fighting against "Tutsi domination."[19] In the Philippines, MILF signed the Deed, while the Communist Party of the Philippines (CPP) and the MNLF did not. As Chapter 6 noted, MILF's legitimacy-seeking characteristics compared with the MNLF and CPP lead us to expect that MILF is the prime candidate for such humanitarian commitment.

The list of rebel groups that have signed the Deed also includes groups that are not likely candidates for applying for compliance – the Taliban in Afghanistan, for example. Geneva Call is also engaging FARC in Colombia, the group that is known for its recent criminal activities. However, at some level, these commitment moves came when the circumstances were ripe for those groups to seek legitimacy. The Taliban signed the Deed in 1998 when it assumed government functions as the Islamic Emirate of Afghanistan between 1996 and 2001. The group did not forget to mention that their audience was both the "people of Afghanistan" and the "international community" (see above quote). FARC is being engaged when it started peace talks with the Colombian Government, trying to gain leverage in the negotiations. With the objectives being to receive amnesty and to sustain its organizational power in some fashion, this international engagement came when FARC needed to gain some legitimacy. This observation is consistent with the strategic legitimacy theory that compliance moves often come when armed groups seek political legitimacy.

The theory of strategic legitimacy and rebel compliance appears to travel well to other cases of anti-personnel mines. The MFDC had been fighting for

[16] See Gleditsch *et al.* (2011). [17] Roberts and Sivakumaran (2012).

[18] The full list of rebel groups that signed can be found at: www.genevacall.org/how-we-work/armed-non-state-actors.

[19] Nindorera (2012).

independence in southern Senegal since 1982. The group used mines at the height of its movement, and one faction near the border of Guinea-Bassau was heavily using mines.[20] By 2004, 652 people had been killed as a result of landmines.[21] The group did not know much about the Ottawa Convention, but it was open to talks in response to Geneva Call. When Geneva Call and other NGOs (e.g., Senegal's Association of Mine Victims (ASVM) and the International Campaign to Ban Landmines (ICBL)) alerted the group that the mines were killing more civilians on their side than government soldiers, the MFDC decided to cease using anti-personnel mines.[22] This example nicely illustrates the pattern we saw with regard to the previous three issue areas: a rebel group that is open to outside actors and deeply rooted in local society is likely to abide by humanitarian rules. In short, compliance made strategic sense for the MFDC.

In the case of the MFDC, the defining characteristic that convinced the group to abandon the use of mines was its territorial control and strong relations with civilians. Other characteristics seem to have mattered less. Although it had a political wing, which had some limited control over its military wing, both political and armed wings were somewhat internally fractured. Consequently, Geneva Call targeted those factions that used anti-personnel mines the most. The MFDC's autonomy-seeking characteristics also helped in converting their behavior from non-compliance to compliance. The MFDC had enjoyed political autonomy during colonial times, and its strong autonomy goal prompted the group to embrace anti-personnel mines (for the lack of other stronger weaponry) to pursue a vigorous military strategy. From the long-term perspective of governing the territory, however, the same political autonomy goal appears to have given the group an impetus to switch to compliance. All these observations are aligned with the expectations of the strategic legitimacy theory, with different weights applied to different kinds of legitimacy-seeking characteristics of rebel groups.

Anti-personnel mines are not the only weapon of choice used by rebel groups. The flow of small arms, especially AK-47s, has been pointed out as an important factor contributing to the increase in child soldiering among rebel groups.[23] In many conflict zones, light weapons are often very easy to procure. Children can carry these lightweight guns and actively participate in combat. Other weapons, including chemical and biological weapons, are prohibited by international law as well. Guided light weapons, including portable, shoulder-fired air defense systems or anti-tank guided weapons, can be illegal when used indiscriminately

[20] Geneva Call (2012a).

[21] Evans (2004). According to the government anti-mines action center (CNAMS), the figure for mine accident victims is 748, 586 surviving since 1990s; 52 since 2005. However, the figure is likely to be higher because of unreported incidents and the MFDC's practice of never leaving the dead on the ground.

[22] Email correspondence with Carole Frampton, Geneva Call, April 19, 2013. [23] Singer (2006).

to kill civilians.[24] Fifty-nine armed groups from thirty-seven countries are known to have used such weapons since 1998.[25] The list includes Al-Qaeda in Afghanistan, the CNDP in the DRC, the Omoro Liberation Front (OLF) in Ethiopia, Boko Haram in Nigeria, Al-Shabaab in Somalia, and the Free Syrian Army (FSA) in Syria. The list also includes some rebel groups who are compliant in the areas of child soldiering and detention visits, such as MILF in the Philippines and the SPLM/A. This variability and inconsistency in compliance behaviors across issue areas suggests the need for more research on why some groups are compliant in one area, but non-compliant in other areas.

Sexual Violence

Sexual violence is another hidden story of rebel violence. Only recently have scholars started uncovering the causes and consequences of sexual violence during wartime.[26] Macro-conditions, such as respect for women's rights, are one important factor in explaining patterns of sexual violence.[27] Among the micro-causes of rebels' sexual violence, research suggests that rapes are often committed during the socialization of new recruits. The consequences are devastating for the lives of many women in conflict zones. Adding to the suffering of civilians, women take the brunt of the burden of being abducted and held as sex slaves. Some female children are recruited as soldiers and then additionally subjected to sexual violence and kept as sex slaves. The psychological and physical impacts of such experiences strain comprehension. The extent to which rebel groups commit sexual violence in comparison with government soldiers is not known, but the undisciplined nature of many rebel groups means that much sexual violence is probably frequent and also underreported or entirely unreported.

My analysis of the Armed Conflicts Location and Event Data (ACLED) in the region of the DRC shows that the governments and rebel groups engage in sexual violence at a roughly similar level. The DRC is often called the "rape capital of the world," with multiple rebel groups committing sexual violence at different levels and to different degrees.[28] Between 1996 and 2012, almost all rebel groups were associated with incidents of rape, including the FDLR, the Mai Mai, the LRA, the RCD, the Nationalist and Integration Front (FNI), M23, and the CNDP. The violations during 2007–2012 seem infrequent rather than systematic or common, relative to the period of 1996–2004 with reports of 36,000 rapes. Among the approximately 140 cases reported by news media, more than fifteen were committed by the FDLR, more than ten attributed to Mai Mai, about ten to the LRA, and about five each to the other rebel groups.

[24] I thank Olivier Bangerter and Nicolas Forquin at Small Arms Survey on this point.

[25] Rigual (2013). The list of armed groups can be found at: www.smallarmssurvey.org/fileadmin/docs/M-files/Armed%20groups%27%20guided%20missiles%20-%20March%20update.pdf. The facts reported in this book are based on the records as of March 2013.

[26] Wood (2009); Cohen (2013). [27] Hudson *et al.* (2012). [28] Baaz and Stern (2009).

The FARDC, the DRC's national army, accounts for about fifty incidents of rape. The rest are alleged cases or cases committed by unidentified groups.

Given the reality of underreporting and media bias against coverage of remote rural areas, it is difficult to draw firm conclusions about these patterns.[29] However, the fact that the FDLR lacked legitimacy-seeking characteristics compared with, say, the CNDP, may partially explain the different patterns of sexual violence between the FDLR and the CNDP. The FDLR's political wing was weak relative to its military wing. The group relied on support from ethnic Hutus who fled Rwanda after the Rwandan genocide. In contrast, the CNDP had national political aims and, in an agreement with the government, it affirmed its commitment to the "strict respect of the fundamental standards and principles of international humanitarian law."[30] When one of the CDNP's factions, M23, later resorted to some humanitarian violations (thereby breaking the 2009 peace agreement), the CNDP was concerned that allegations of violence were "tarnishing their image."[31] Strategic legitimacy theory would have predicted that the CNDP would commit less sexual violence (relative to the FDLR) due to its legitimacy concerns. This appears to be the case. The theory of strategic legitimacy thus seems applicable to patterns of sexual violence, at least among rebel groups in the DRC.

Further broadening the scope, I have analyzed rebel groups' sexual violence and examined whether legitimacy-seeking characteristics are associated with less sexual violence using the Sexual Violence in Armed Conflict (SVAC) data.[32] The data include various types of sexual violence: rape, sexual slavery, forced prostitution, forced pregnancy, forced sterilization/abortion, sexual mutilation, and sexual torture.[33] SVAC data also have the measure of prevalence of sexual violence at the rebel group level, which is perfect for testing rebel compliance behavior for this book's purpose. The ordinal measure of prevalence records whether the violence was massive (3), common (2), some (1), or no recorded sexual violence (0). The preliminary statistical test supports the strategic legitimacy theory. The three indicators I proposed – rebel political wing, secessionism, and human rights-based external sponsorship – are each associated with lower levels of sexual violence.[34]

The examination of macro-data using SVAC and micro-data of DRC rebel groups gives some preliminary support for the strategic legitimacy theory. The statistical association, however, will not tell the whole story. In future study, we have to further inquire whether a rebel group's decision toward sexual violence was actually driven by its concern for legitimacy in various circumstances and

[29] Peterman *et al.* (2011).
[30] Peace Agreement between the Government and the CNDP, 2009, available at: www.iccwomen.org/publications/Peace_Agreement_between_the_Government_and_the_CNDP.pdf.
[31] Human Rights Watch (2008b). [32] Cohen and Nordås (2014).
[33] For the definitions of each act, see Cohen and Nordås (2013).
[34] These results are on file with the author.

political contexts. Scholars are just beginning to understand sexual violence committed by rebel groups, and this section is part of such initial efforts connecting the dots between rebel motivation and sexual violence.

CONCLUDING REMARKS

The comparison of the three issues of rebel compliance as well as the additional inquiry into two other issues leaves us with several lessons. Most importantly, the recipe for rebel compliance will not be simple. It first requires a desire and a willingness on the part of rebel groups to seek international legitimacy. In some cases, the pursuit of legitimacy at the domestic level may be enough to ensure the good behavior of persistent compliers that have an inherent propensity to comply with humanitarian rules from the start; but the pursuit of domestic legitimacy is rarely enough to ensure the good behavior of switchover compliers – rebel groups that at some point change their behaviors from non-compliance to compliance. In these cases, the role of international humanitarian organizations in engaging rebel groups becomes crucial.

The recipe for compliance also requires that rebel group leadership's central command and control take charge of the humanitarian issue, usually by enforcing an adopted code of conduct. However, this strong internal control should be preconditioned by the "right" initiatives of the central command that seeks legitimacy in some fashion. With strong directives to violate international rules, strength of command can generate rebel groups that are non-compliantly obedient.

In producing persistent compliers, militarily strong national governments are also essential ingredients. Militarily strong governments can deter rebels and make them refrain from using violence in the first place.[35] Gleaned from the five issues of rebel compliance, the reality is that law-abiding rebels are not born that way; nor are their law-abiding choices driven by some sort of natural respect for international law. Rebel compliance evolves through the strategic decisions made by rebel leadership during the political process of securing political support for sustaining their rebel movements and for winning their war.

With this brief note on the recipe of compliant rebels in this penultimate chapter, the concluding chapter broadens the temporal scope, looking past and present, with closer examination of historical and current rebel groups. The goal again will be to test the strategic legitimacy theory informally and assess its portability. Once I examine the theoretical scope of issue coverage and temporal coverage in various empirical realms, I will then be ready to explore the policy implications of this endeavor. All this is the topic of this book's concluding chapter.

[35] This is the basis for Walter's (2011) claim, and also the basis for Lake's (2007) argument regarding the importance of state monopoly of power.

9

Conclusion

> Armed groups are not just problems. They are part of solutions.
>
> Jonathan Somer[1]

Jonathan Somer works at Geneva Call, an organization that engages armed groups in conflict zones with the aim of securing their adherence to fundamental humanitarian rules. He arrived at the insight that serves as the epigraph to this chapter while working with his colleagues on the daunting task of convincing rebel groups to seek compliance with international law and submit to monitoring and verification missions.

My research sends a message similar to Somer's in that I, too, argue that some rebel groups are part of the solution, and that in many cases, if not all, windows for meaningful engagement with armed groups can be found. Moreover, there are particular conditions under which the likelihood of finding such windows of opportunity is greatly increased. This chapter therefore delves into the question of how and when such conditions may arise, connecting my research to specific policy applications. I review selected findings from the preceding chapters in order to make recommendations for diplomacy with rebel groups and determine under what conditions such engagement can serve as a sensible policy option. My goal in this chapter is to inform policymakers and practitioners about the policy options, advantages, trade-offs, and challenges related to bringing about rebel group compliance.

I begin this concluding chapter with a summary of my key findings, and in particular what my research has discovered concerning compliant and non-compliant rebels. Then I provide a space for readers to explore legitimacy theory and related evidence through a number of historical examples from different decades. It is my hope that an up-close examination of the similarities and differences between old and new rebels will illuminate the

[1] Somer (2012).

portability of my strategic legitimacy theory of rebel compliance. The examples will also show how legitimacy considerations may have shaped rebel groups' decisions to exercise restraint in what otherwise would likely have turned into bloody and treacherous conflicts. The penultimate section of this chapter is devoted to policy aspects of this book's findings. I will conclude by discussing implications for research and practice surrounding the issue of rebel groups and international law.

MAIN FINDINGS

The central finding of this book is that rebels in contemporary civil wars can be compliant. Contrary to conventional thinking that rebel groups are violent whenever it suits them and flout international law, my research shows that some rebel groups are aware of international law, sometimes commit to adhere to international law, and often try to advance their rebellion by exploiting the normative structure of international law. Some of these rebel groups are the ones that refrained from deliberately killing civilians, did not use child soldiers, and opened their detention centers to outside monitors such as the ICRC.

The emergence of compliant rebels has occurred amid ongoing violence and brutality perpetrated by large numbers of rebel groups. Over the years, rebel violence has resulted in the death and suffering of millions of people. Conservative estimates put the cumulative count of rebel killings between 1989 and 2009 at approximately 97,000 deaths. This figure includes only those civilians who were intentionally killed by rebel groups, and excludes civilians classified as "collateral damage." The actual number of civilians killed is likely to be much higher than has been previously reported. When we include rape, pillaging, and other forms of brutality committed against civilians, the amount of suffering caused by rebels may be inestimable, as detailed in Chapter 5. Furthermore, rebels have targeted not only ordinary civilians, but children as well. As mentioned in Chapter 6, 77 out of the 250 contemporary rebel groups operating between 1989 and 2009 used child soldiers at one point or other in their armed struggle. Detainees may also become victims of rebel violence, as discussed in Chapter 7. Only 30 percent of rebels have some record of interacting with the ICRC. The other 70 percent remain in the dark – sometimes because they lack visitable detention centers, sometimes because they operate in a region governed by an authority that has decided to block access to rebels in an attempt to deny them potential legitimacy.

In addition to presenting evidence of compliant rebels, this book has delved into the question of *why* compliant rebels exist and emerge. I started this book with a puzzle: why would a rebel group that did not negotiate the terms of international rules decide to abide by those international rules? Through an examination of rebel groups' political and economic environments and their key constituencies, I arrived at the conclusion that it is in the interests of legitimacy-seeking rebel groups to comply with international standards. In general, interest in compliance is shaped by interactions with potential rebel supporters, conditioned by the institutional structure of rebel groups. These compliant rebels often have strategic motives – to gain more political support, recognition, or material resources to sustain their movement and ultimately achieve the goals of their rebellion. Other groups may start with a military-dominated organizational structure, without any governance aims that benefit civilians, or they may try to appease political supporters that do not consider human rights consequences.

The commonality among compliant rebels is that they seek legitimacy in one way or another in the eyes of political constituencies that influence their decision to comply. Compliant rebels arise in the context of the political and social relations that rebel groups forge during their lifespan. These compliant rebel groups often interact with what I call agents of international law – the actors who promote the norms related to humanitarian rules and human rights. They usually have external sponsors who care about human rights to a certain degree. Also, at the domestic level, compliant rebels usually build political experiences and deep social ties that connect them to a civilian population that makes them aware of the social consequences of their unrestrained violence.

The empirical records of contemporary rebel groups between 1989 and 2009 lend strong support to the strategic legitimacy theory of rebel compliance. With regard to civilian killing, child soldiering, and detention access, legitimacy-seeking rebel groups were more likely to comply with international standards of behavior than legitimacy-indifferent groups. Evidence showed that rebel groups with a political wing, secessionist agenda, and foreign support influenced by civil society are more likely to comply with international humanitarian and human rights standards than those without.

The degree to which each legitimacy-seeking characteristic matters differs across issue areas. Rebel political wings appear to matter more when they are legalized in their domestic political sphere, backed by political experiences in deep social relations with the civilian population that rebels aim to govern. Secessionist groups sometimes do not comply when the civilian population supports their non-compliant behaviors. As well, external support based on human rights concerns did not matter much for such issues as child soldiering, where norms are still nascent and contested.

The book also uncovered a typology of rebel compliance, identifying two main types of rebel compliers: persistent compliers and switchover compliers. Persistent compliers usually have inherent motivations to comply at the outset. In these cases, legitimacy-seeking motivations will lock a group into a compliant mode from the start. And this initial compliance does not usually produce much deviation over the course of the ensuing rebellion. In many cases of persistent compliers, rebel ideology and associated political platforms are often congruent with the norms of international law, so compliance emerges as a natural progression of rebel behavior. By contrast, switchover compliers may be observed oscillating between compliance and non-compliance. Rebel groups in this category shift from non-compliance to compliance in their pursuit of legitimacy. Seeking greater international legitimacy, these rebels change their behavior to be consistent with international norms in order to gain recognition or material support. Also, on the domestic front, these rebels might form a political party and respect civilian life in accordance with humanitarian and human rights norms in order to garner more domestic support.

The book also finds that rebel compliance is never perfect. It is neither easy nor stable. The legitimacy-seeking incentive of compliant rebels is sharply conditioned by strong motivation to win the civil war, so that when the military and tactical advantages of non-compliance become too great, international law may no longer factor into the rebel decision-making calculus. Indeed, many of the instances of rebel violence presented in this book in Chapters 5, 6, and 7 displayed an oscillation between compliance and non-compliance, with compliance reversing into non-compliance just as often as the opposite.

REBELS, OLD AND NEW

This book primarily focuses on contemporary rebellion, but my theory of strategic legitimacy and compliance can help to explain rebel group behavior from the more distant past, as well as recent examples.[2] This section will explore the more general applicability of the book's theory through several historical examples of older rebel groups as well as recent ones. By "old" I mean groups that were active before 1989, which is the starting point of this book's empirical inquiry. By "new" I mean rebel groups that became active after 2009, the end point of this book's empirical inquiry.

Broadly construed, the core issue this book addresses is how new political organizations like rebel groups attempt to generate legitimacy and build authority over time, when doing so conflicts with their military imperatives. Putting the issue of rebel compliance in this broad historical and recent context may allow us to tell a larger story about the dynamics involved when existing structures of authority are challenged and the attempt is made to construct new ones.

Historical Examples of Compliant Rebels

Anti-colonial movements and the Cold War heavily influenced the design of most contemporary rebel groups, specifically those occurring between 1945 and 1990. Wars of independence against colonial rule produced many rebel groups seeking international legitimacy, while the Cold War generated many rebel groups on both sides of the great East–West ideological divide. Many of these

[2] I thank Professor Robert Keohane for suggesting the creation of the historical section.

newly established groups displayed legitimacy-seeking behavior and made initial steps toward compliance by committing themselves to international law.

The list of rebel groups that complied with international law is not short. The ANC of South Africa, for instance, made their "Freedom Charter" declaration to commit to the Geneva Conventions in 1980.[3] From the mid-1960s to the late 1970s, during its struggle against Ian Smith's Rhodesia, the Zimbabwe Patriotic Front made a pledge to adhere to the Geneva Conventions when dealing with victims of war.[4] Other groups making similar commitments included the EPLF in Eritrea, 1977, UNITA in Angola, 1980, the South West Africa People's Organization (SWAPO) in 1981, the Afghan National Liberation Front (ANLF) in 1981, the Islamic Society of Afghanistan (ISA) in 1982, the Palestine Liberation Organization (PLO) in 1982, and the MNLF of the Philippines in 1981.

Each of these groups made explicit verbal or written commitments to adhere to international standards. At the very least, these cases illustrate that, in the wake of the Geneva Conventions' Common Article that covered civil wars and national liberation movements, many rebel groups had knowledge of international law as well as the will to commit to international law. And in most cases, the commitment translated into meaningful action. The compliance records of these legitimacy-seeking groups appear more positive than those of the legitimacy-indifferent rebel groups, like the RUF in Liberia and the LRA in Uganda. As well, the overall level of civilian suffering inflicted during conflicts involving groups such as the ANC, SWAPO, and the MNLF compares favorably with the level of suffering inflicted during other roughly similar conflicts. The ANC, SWAPO, and the MNLF all made peace after an armed struggle involving fewer than 1,000 civilians killed per conflict. Further, while the ANC and SWAPO were both accused of torture, the alleged violations were neither widespread nor systematic.[5] For the MNLF, the records from the ACLED show that they committed fewer than twenty civilian killings per year. By comparison, other groups were responsible for fifty or more killings annually. And groups like the RUF and the LRA – groups indifferent to international opinion – committed heinous atrocities involving maiming, mutilations, and massacres.

Although many of these compliant groups made commitments to human rights causes, public commitments are not always a perfect guarantor of compliance. In the case of UNITA and the PLO, for example, records of human rights abuses indicate that verbal commitments did not result in actual compliance. UNITA, for its part, made a unilateral declaration during its war of independence (1961–1975) against Portugal that it would abide by the Geneva

[3] The ANC notified the ICRC that the group was acceding to the Geneva Conventions and Additional Protocol I. See Veuthey (2002: 143–144).

[4] Soames (1980).

[5] Regarding the ANC, see the Truth and Reconciliation Commission Report (1998), implicating the ANC in the torture of its own members. On SWAPO, see Wallace and Kinahan (2011).

Conventions and the fundamental rules of international law applicable in armed conflicts.[6] However, its multi-headed nature with diversified funding sources did not bode well. The group famously relied on revenue from the diamond trade and on aid from multiple sponsors including South Africa, Zaire, and Zambia, and later the United States as well.[7] The group's commitment to comply with international law came to an end when the group failed to honor the results of the 2002 election and engaged in massive violence against civilians.[8]

The history of the PLO tells a similar story with regard to commitment and compliance. Although the PLO signaled its commitment to international law in 1982, the commitment was quickly shown to be little more than cheap talk. In its quest for self-determination and international legitimacy, the PLO chiefly relied on support from the Arab states that cared more about defeating Israel than about human rights. In its legitimation process, "terrorism [as a means of insurgency] has had a beneficial rather than a deleterious effect on PLO's legitimacy."[9] Relying on external sponsors who do not have human rights concerns and adopting terrorism as a key legitimization process, the PLO's commitment did not lead to compliance. These two examples (UNITA and the PLO) illustrate the importance of looking at "in whose eyes rebel groups seek legitimacy." As well, these examples underscore the importance of distinguishing between rebels' strategic signals of commitment and genuine commitment, together with the difficulty of sustaining rebel compliance over time.

Going further back in time, I note that some of history's most notable rebellions and civil wars (e.g., the American Revolution (1775–1783), the American Civil War (1861–1865), the Russian Revolution and Civil War (1917–1920), the anti-apartheid struggle of the 1980s in South Africa, the extensive civil war in Colombia in the 1950s ("La Violencia")) also lend support to the plausibility of the legitimacy thesis. The revolutionaries in these conflicts attempted to displace the authority of ruling regimes, often through violent means. Yet the amount and type of violence used varied significantly from one conflict to the next.

The American and Russian revolutions illustrate this variability. They diverged with respect to their bloodiness due to the contrasting nature of the regimes they opposed, specifically the type of government led by King George III as compared with that led by Tsar Nicholas II. At the same time, both movements faced burdensome uphill battles for legitimacy. Leading the American Revolutionary Army, General Washington received the directive to obey "the rules and discipline of war" from a Continental Congress aiming to portray the British as barbarians. Thomas Jefferson struck a similar tone when he accused the British of violating the laws of war in the Declaration of Independence. John Fabian Witt, professor at Yale Law School, writes in his book *Lincoln's Code* that "the aim of the Revolution was to establish the membership of the United States in the club of civilized nations. The Congress

[6] Sivakumaran (2013). [7] Dietrich (2000). [8] Bøås and Dunn (2007). [9] Merari (1993).

and General Washington . . . understood that by displaying respect for the club's bylaws, Americans [would] move that much closer to an independent seat at the table of nations."[10] External support was also crucial as the American-Franco alliance generated much fear among the British about how to deal with pressure points globally.[11] We see in this example the importance of legitimacy and external sponsorship.

In the case of the Russian Revolution, the Bolsheviks enjoyed strong domestic support for their revolutionary cause under the oppressive tsarist regime. International powers – both the Allies and the Central Powers – did not actively support the revolution, but implicitly welcomed the movement.[12] In fighting the tsarist regime, the Bolsheviks relied on terrorist tactics to enhance their chances of winning, as exemplified in the Red Terror period between 1918 and 1922, which involved mass killings of tsarist supporters as retribution for government violence.[13] Without any international checks, the Bolsheviks did not have to care much about international standards of warfare. Nor did they start caring about international standards once the revolution was won. In the aftermath of the revolution, the terror was exported to Europe and around the globe, as Russia "attempted to promote civil war abroad which internationalized the Russian Revolution."[14] This example illustrates that rebels and revolutionaries do attempt to establish political authority by terror, not necessarily by abiding by the rule of law, if unchecked by countering international efforts.

Other historical instances, such as the American Civil War, go a step further, revealing the connection between obtaining political legitimacy and complying with international standards. The Confederate rebels appear to have not sought legitimacy as systematically and persistently as the Northerners did vis-à-vis the general public. In 1863, President Abraham Lincoln aimed to restrain the behavior of Union soldiers, believing that their conduct was negatively affecting public perception of the Union, and, more importantly, eroding public support. To this end he established the Lieber Code, which instructed the Union Army to provide humane treatment to prisoners of war as well as to the civilian population of occupied areas. The Code significantly impacted the behavior of soldiers, increasing compliance with laws of war, providing a legal framework for military commissions that operated in the last two years of the war, and later providing the blueprint for the Hague Convention of 1899.[15] Prior to the Geneva Conventions of 1949, international humanitarian and human rights norms were infrequently affirmed. Lincoln's substantial initiative in this area therefore stands out as an early example of political legitimacy concerns translating directly into improvement in soldiers' behavior in the field.

Returning to more recent history, consider the case of FARC in Colombia during La Violencia. The case illustrates the complex interactions between legitimacy and compliance characterizing the post-Second World War period in

[10] Witt (2012: 27). [11] Rakove (2010). [12] Pipes (2011: 607). [13] Werth *et al.* (1999).
[14] Pipes (2011: 608). [15] Witt (2012).

South America. Before degenerating into an enrichment-seeking rebel group in the 2000s, FARC emerged in the 1950s as an organization aimed at providing a viable political alternative for the local population. However, over the course of its rebellion, the group's leadership gradually stopped caring about domestic and international legitimacy, which paved the way for the human rights violations that accompanied this loss of concern. FARC's heavy reliance on drug trafficking justified the use of children as drug "mules," and the group's relationship with civilians soured over time as social connections frayed and then disintegrated.

On the other side of the South Atlantic, the anti-apartheid struggle waged by the ANC in South Africa reveals a similar picture of the evolving role of political legitimacy. After starting its armed struggle in the 1960s, the ANC struck an aggressive political tone during the late 1980s when it mobilized a centralized organizational structure that distributed its clear anti-apartheid political agenda both locally and internationally.[16] According to the Truth and Reconciliation Commission Report published in 1998, the ANC's human rights record during these decades was relatively good, with violations mostly restricted to the maltreatment of detainees.[17] Although these violations tainted the ANC's record, the relatively low number of violations is consistent with the idea that the ANC's legitimacy-seeking political programs led them to exercise restraint in other areas of humanitarian violations.

A quick tour of these historical episodes thus suggests that the pursuit of legitimacy by revolutionary and rebel groups is not a new phenomenon. Some period differences are, however, worth noting. Today's rebels, for instance, are much more keenly attuned to the optics of international legitimacy than were their counterparts in the past. Relative to their predecessors, contemporary compliant rebels tend to tap into the new technologies of globalization. Given the proliferation of potential international supporters, ranging from state supporters to international organizations, to diaspora populations, and even to casual sympathizers abroad, contemporary rebels typically possess a strong understanding of the most current state of international affairs, sometimes dipping into social media to propagate their goals, influence public opinion, and recruit supporters.

It is also important to note that old revolutionaries before 1945 did not operate within an environment dominated by a complex network of human rights organizations. With the influx of international aid, contemporary rebels know how to benefit from the efforts of outside groups. They tax international aid groups that want to operate in their territory of control and sometimes even pit organizations against each other to negotiate better terms.[18] Because of these differences in political environments, at the present

[16] Van Kessel (2001); Graver (2005).

[17] See Truth and Reconciliation Commission (1998); also see the ANC's response at African National Congress (1998).

[18] Magone *et al.* (2011); and the author's interview with Gerald McHugh, former UNOCHA official, May 2012.

time I cannot determine exactly how well the theory of rebel compliance travels back in history. However, it is safe to say that a concern for political legitimacy seems to have exerted some degree of influence on the compliant behavior of older revolutionary and rebel groups. Despite the differences in political environments, the pursuit of political legitimacy appears to be a primary goal for rebels, both old and new, shaping their behavior with regard to the laws of war.

Recent Rebels in Syria: Free Syrian Army (FSA) and Islamic State of Iraq and the Levant (ISIL)

The rebel group scene in Syria, with numerous rebel groups fighting the Assad regime, provides an example of "new" and contemporary rebellion. And the behavior of these Syrian groups nicely illustrates many of the key points made in this book about the dynamics of rebel compliance with international law. To underscore these key points, and to provide another example of the relevance of my theory and evidence, this section discusses two major rebel groups in Syria: the FSA and ISIL.[19] These examples will complement evidence in preceding chapters that focused primarily on the period up to 2010. Although some evidence and facts will no doubt be subject to further historical scrutiny in the light of events unfolding even as I write these lines, the discussion presented here will be of interest to readers seeking a highly relevant contemporary example.

The Syrian conflict started with non-violent demonstrations in March 2011 against the Assad regime. The rebellion was the outgrowth of the Arab Spring that affected many Arab nations, including Egypt, Libya, Tunisia, and Algeria. Compared with other Arab Spring cases, the Syrian conflict has now lasted longer and been bloodier than any other, with dire human security consequences. As of August 2014, the human death toll is estimated to be more than 190,000, and the number of refugees in Turkey, Lebanon, Iraq, and Jordan reached more than 3 million as of September 2014.[20]

[19] The name of this group has undergone several changes, including ISIL and the Islamic State of Iraq and al-Sham (ISIS). Levant refers to an area encompassing Syria, Lebanon, and Jordan. Al-Sham refers to Damascus and its environs. As of August 2014, the group named itself "the Islamic State" to emphasize its legitimacy as a caliphate, but many governments, including the US Government, still refer to the group as ISIL or ISIS. Since ISIS is also the name of an ancient Egyptian goddess, experts prefer the name ISIL, as I do in this book. See Public Radio International's interview with Tarek Masoud, a professor at Harvard's Kennedy School of Government. Public Radio International (2014).

[20] The number of conflict-related deaths is from Price *et al.* (2014), who report the estimate from the Human Rights Data Analysis Group, commissioned by the Office of the UN High Commissioner for Human Rights. The report identified 191,369 unique killings. The figures do not distinguish combatants and non-combatants. The refugee figure is from the Syria Regional Refugee Response run by the UN High Commissioner for Refugees (http://data.unhcr.org/syrianrefugees/regional.php) reported on September 24, 2014. The exact figure reported was 3,005,283.

Along with this tremendous toll in human suffering, the conflict has also inflamed existing geopolitical tensions and caused new ones. Syria's neighbor Iraq is struggling to develop as a unified country and the fighting in Syria has put pressure on Iraqi sectarian divides. Meanwhile, Kurds in Syria, Iraq, and Turkey have their eyes on gaining their own independence in their respective zones, and the fighting in Syria has presented them with new threats as well as new opportunities. Against this backdrop, the ongoing Syrian conflagration – now in its fourth year – shows no signs of abating. Box 9.1 outlines the major milestones related to rebel movements in Syria.

The total number of rebel groups in Syria is difficult to ascertain due to the fragmented nature of the opposition.[21] Fighters typically identify themselves with

Box 9.1 Chronology of the FSA and ISIL

March 2011	Start of Syrian Arab Spring with protests calling for release of political prisoners.
December 2011	Formation of the FSA.
July 2012	FSA captures Aleppo in northern Syria.
November 2012	National Coalition for Syrian Revolutionary and Opposition Forces (also called the Syrian Coalition) unites several major opposition groups.
December 2012	Formation of the Supreme Military Command (SMC) and unification of armed opposition; the United States and other world powers recognize the National Coalition as the Syrian population's "legitimate representative."
March 2013	Capture of al-Raqqa by the FSA (central Syria).
November 2013	The Islamic Front breaks away from the FSA.
May 2014	Rise of ISIL and capture of Mosul.
	Weakening of the FSA as rebels withdraw from Homs (central Syria).
June 2014	US aerial bombing of Iraq to stave off ISIL threat.
August 2014	ISIL responds to bombing by executing American journalist James Foley.
	UN cites "mass atrocities" committed by ISIL in Syria.
September 2014	US President Barack Obama announces intention to combat ISIL.

Sources: O'Bagy (2013); Reuters (2013); Sinjab (2013); BBC (2014).

[21] Slim (2011); Lund (2013); O'Bagy (2013); IHS Jane's Terrorism & Insurgency Center (2013).

an individual commander rather than with a larger movement. Consequently, there are estimated to be as many as 1,000 armed groups under the umbrella of the Syrian opposition.[22] The FSA and ISIL have been the biggest groups in the pack for some time. The FSA is the most moderate group and comprises a number of affiliated "brigades."[23] ISIL grew out of Iraq, and in early 2014 demonstrated its military prowess by capturing several Syrian cities. Other major groups include the Islamic Front and Jabhat al-Nusra. The Islamic Front is the merger of seven regional forces in Damascus, Aleppo, and Homs, formed in November 2013, and following a Salafist Islamic ideology.[24] For its part, al-Nusra may be characterized as the alliance of Al-Qaeda with jihadist ideology. It is in this kaleidoscopic rebel landscape that the FSA and ISIL are operating.

A comparison of the FSA and ISIL will show the general applicability of strategic legitimacy theory. In particular, the FSA's legitimacy-seeking motivations can be linked to their compliant behaviors. In contrast, ISIL's extreme ideology and indifference to public opinion can be connected to their numerous violations of international law.

The legitimacy-seeking characteristics of the FSA have been apparent in many instances. Its leadership, run by General Idris, is in exile in Turkey, trying to exert operational control over the forces on the ground in Syria on various fronts. The group wants to be seen as the moderate alternative to the many jihadist groups that are operating in the region. At the core of the FSA's organizational structure is the Supreme Military Council (SMC), which brings together several affiliates including the Martyrs of Syria Brigades, Northern Storm Brigade, and Ahrar Souriya Brigade.[25] The SMC has coordinated its actions with the Syrian National Coalition, the political wing of the opposition, although the coordination has not been strong.[26]

As the primary representative of the Syrian opposition, the FSA participated in humanitarian training and committed to follow humanitarian principles. Geneva Call, an NGO specializing in humanitarian affairs, engaged FSA-affiliated groups in 2012, including the FSA. One key commitment made by the FSA in this context was a promise not to use child soldiers, as noted in a statement sent to Human Rights Watch in June 2014 – a statement signed by the Chief of Staff of the Supreme Military Council, Abdulellah Al Basheer:

> The General Staff of the Free Syrian Army emphasizes its active role in combating this despicable practice. We work with all affiliated military units via a mechanism for monitoring and reporting to ensure non-recruitment of fighters or under any title who are under the age of eighteen. This approach complies with all international conventions regarding the rights of children, in particular the Optional Protocol to the Convention on

[22] Sinjab (2013). [23] O'Bagy (2013).

[24] BBC (2013b). The predecessor of the Islamic Front was the Syrian Islamic Liberation Front (SILF), a group affiliated with the FSA since September 2012. The break up in November 2013 undermined the supremacy of the FSA. Salafi means "predecessor" or "ancient," emphasizing the importance of earlier thought in Islam.

[25] Sinjab (2013). [26] O'Bagy (2013).

the Rights of the Child of 2003. We, in the FSA General Staff, refer to the recruitment of children, by the Assad regime, for the so-called People's Committees and National Protection Forces. The Assad allies, including Hezbollah and Iraqi battalions fighting in Syria, also work in a systematic manner on the recruitment of children.[27]

Two things are notable in this statement. One is that the FSA rejected child soldiering as a matter of policy. Although human rights groups noted some use of children in the FSA's ranks as a matter of practice, the recruitment of children does not seem to be widespread, and when children were recruited, they were generally confined to non-combat roles. The second notable point pertains to the latter part of the statement, which criticizes the actions of the Assad regime. One interpretation of this accusation is that it is part of an ongoing battle for legitimacy: by delegitimizing the Assad regime, the statement attempts to increase the international standing and legitimacy of the FSA vis-à-vis the regime forces.

In terms of its relationships with civilians, the FSA has sought legitimacy, but has so far failed to establish so-called "transactional legitimacy": legitimacy bought by distributing resources to civilians in rebel-held areas to secure their loyalty.[28] In general, close rebel–community relations have not been a hallmark of the FSA's activities. By contrast, it is notable that the People's Protection Units (YPG),[29] the Kurdish element in Syria, have made close relations with their civilian supporters a top priority. One indication of this is the fact that they signed the Deed of Commitment covering the areas of sexual violence and anti-personnel mines with Geneva Call.[30] Given its secessionist aims in Kurdish areas, and its dependence on local support, it makes sense that the YPG is highly motivated to adhere to international law.

Foreign patronage appears to have been a significant influence on the FSA. The reliance of the group on international support has prompted the group to be keen on complying with international law. One example of this involved the capture of international peacekeepers in March 2013 by the Martyrs of Yarmouk Brigades, a group linked to the SMC, the military wing of the FSA. The brigade captured twenty-one peacekeepers from the United Nations Disengagement Observer Force (UNDOF), accusing the UN troops of assisting regime forces. The SMC pressured the brigade to release the peacekeepers, and the release occurred.[31]

Despite its high level of motivation to seek international legitimacy, and despite its willingness to follow through with concrete actions, the FSA has

[27] Quoted from Free Syrian Army, June 26, 2014, "Supreme Military Council: A Statement About the Recruitment of Child Soldiers," Syrian Arab Republic Supreme Military Council Military and Revolutionary Forces. The link to the document is included in Human Rights Watch (2014c).

[28] O'Bagy (2013).

[29] Geneva Call, see country page "Syria," available at: www.genevacall.org/country-page/syria, accessed November 10, 2014.

[30] *Ibid.* [31] O'Bagy (2013: 20).

lacked organizational capacity. Its command structure appears weak and exerts only very loose control over different brigades – a situation that costs the group internal legitimacy within and among its membership. The break up of the Islamic Front in November 2013 was detrimental to the already loose coalition of brigades within the FSA. By early 2014, the FSA was losing influence in Syria to the newly risen ISIL. A spokesman for an FSA-affiliated brigade captured the essence of this decline in August 2014 when he lamented: "We don't have central command, whereas they [the ISIL] have central command and an ideology."[32]

Human rights records regarding children's rights tell a similar story about the lack of FSA's organizational capacity. Since 2011, almost all the rebel groups in Syria have used child soldiers, including the FSA, although as a matter of policy the FSA had pledged not to use child soldiers. However, the FSA did not refrain from using them when they volunteered.[33] An interview with an FSA brigade commander by Human Rights Watch is telling:

> If a boy is hardheaded or stubborn, if he lost someone, we'll keep them in the camp. But 16, 17 is not young. [If we don't take him,] he'll go fight on his own. In clashes they'll be in the second or third row, or doing first aid, driving, loading ammunition for people who attack.[34]

Three things are notable in this FSA commander's comments. First, he does not exclude the possibility that children under 18 can join the rebel ranks. Second, he thinks 16 or 17 is not young, which is a viewpoint at odds with the "no children under 18" rule enshrined in international law. Third, he also mentions that children are used in support roles rather than in combat roles. This comment illustrates the difficulty of imposing international rules in a situation that some actors perceive to have cultural and operational gray areas. The FSA needed manpower, and despite its policy commitment to not use child soldiers, it rationalized using children to fill its ranks.

The rise of ISIL is an important milestone in the chronology of the FSA. From the start, ISIL, with its aim of establishing a caliphate (an umbrella state under Islamic rule), was a rival to the FSA and over time it weakened the moderate faction. Armed with cash, and making deft use of social media, ISIL was able to "oust" the FSA.[35] ISIL rose as a major rebel group in March 2014, fighting its rival al-Nusra on many fronts. In June 2014, the FSA lost Raqqa, a central Syrian city of utmost strategic importance (which had been under FSA control for over a year), to ISIL.

[32] *New York Times* interview with Abu al-Hassan, a long-time spokesman for a rebel brigade in Marea, north of Aleppo. See Barnard (2014).

[33] Human Rights Watch (2014b).

[34] The interview by Human Rights Watch with Abu Rida, leader of the Saif Allah al-Maslool brigade, an FSA group, in Daraa, conducted in Irbid, Jordan on December 17, 2013. See Human Rights Watch (2014b: 18).

[35] Shane and Hubbard (2014).

ISIL also asserted its legitimacy, but the source of this legitimacy lay in religious doctrines and governance practices that were exclusive rather than inclusive. For example, the group's "takfiri" doctrine legitimizes attacks on other Muslims. The key source of ISIL's supposed legitimacy is religious. In its digital magazine, *Dábiq*, ISIL claims that "ISIL is 'unquestionable' because 'Allah has blessed it with victory, consolidation and establishing the religion'."[36] Besides this religious legitimacy, on the political front, ISIL has tried to garner local support through tribal outreach, providing aid to civilians in the areas they control. The group's governance functions include the provision of services in several areas: education, justice, security, humanitarian aid, and infrastructure projects.[37] Rudimentary court systems, bakeries, water supply systems, and electricity lines were some of the governance programs that ISIL conducted in the Raqqa region.[38] Despite these efforts, ISIL's institutions and processes do not appear to be well established, and the results and longevity of these governance efforts are yet to be seen.[39]

The foreign sponsorship of ISIL is also notable and includes alleged support from Saudi Arabia's Sunni population.[40] Although today ISIL earns cash income locally – in the areas it controls – from extortion and selling oil, the forerunner of ISIL benefited from support from Saudi Arabia.[41] The kingdom suspended support when ISIL suddenly became a regional power – a power that might even pose a threat to Saudi Arabia.[42] With its local sources of income and its historical reliance on foreign support from countries that do not weigh its human rights records, ISIL has had little reason to seek international legitimacy.

The restraint exercised by the FSA is in stark contrast to the unrestrained brutality exhibited by ISIL. Indeed, ISIL has made no secret of its brutality and has broadcast beheadings and other executions over social media. ISIL's capture and maltreatment of detainees is well known to human rights groups.[43] Its practices included detaining women, children, and enemy soldiers of the Syrian army, and many arbitrary detentions have involved inhumane treatment such as flogging and summary killings in public.[44] ISIL is also responsible for ethnic cleansing actions against the Yazidi ethnic minority in northern Iraq. The Yazidi practice a religion that is close to Christianity, and ISIL therefore classifies them as infidels (Islamic non-believers). Numerous human rights violations by ISIL against the Yazidi have been documented.[45]

The Syria case illustrates the importance of legitimacy-seeking characteristics as well as the interplay of other factors, including ideology, rebel organizational

[36] Gambhir (2014: 6). [37] Caris and Reynolds (2014). [38] *Ibid.*

[39] In his analysis of the governance approach of the Lebanese branch of Hamas, Cammett (2014) writes that, when governance is divisive and when services are restricted to supporters and withheld from non-supporters, adverse effects are likely in the long run.

[40] Boghardt (2014). [41] Clemons (2014). [42] *Ibid.*

[43] Caris and Reynolds (2014: 19–23); also see Amnesty International (2013a).

[44] Amnesty International (2013b). [45] Jalabi (2014).

capacity, and military prowess in explaining rebel compliance. Ideology looms large in the Syrian context, as it dictates the military strategies of ISIL and at the same time causes ISIL to see legitimacy as stemming from religious principles – which fundamentally clashes with the order of international law and with political notions of legitimacy. And the consequences of ISIL's religiously-based conception of legitimacy have been plain to see: civilians who do not support ISIL are labeled as enemies to their jihad rule and as justified targets of ISIL violence – in stark contrast to the generally accepted view that civilians must be protected as long as they do not actively participate in war efforts.

The case study of Syrian rebel groups leaves us with several policy lessons. The FSA's military wing made a humanitarian commitment and trained its soldiers in accordance with international humanitarian law. And its human rights record has indeed been relatively less abusive than that of other Syrian jihadist groups. But the case illustrates that a moderate faction committed to building support and legitimacy may not be able to compete against a well-organized extremist group. In the Syrian context, the FSA's command and control was simply too weak and dysfunctional to enable it to succeed against ISIL. The case illustrates the crucial importance of rebel organizational capacity when it comes to delivering on principled humanitarian commitments.

The case of the FSA also raises questions about the short- and long-term benefits of compliance. In some cases, compliant rebels succeed in achieving their goals. For instance, MILF in the Philippines successfully negotiated a peace agreement with the government after going through a compliance phase, as discussed in Chapter 6. However, in the case of the FSA, which found itself fighting wars on two fronts – against the Assad regime as well as against enemy extremist groups – compliance did not lead to a favorable outcome. The conflict drained the group of its resources and its military struggle failed to produce the result the group envisioned. Whether in general compliant rebels are more likely than non-compliant rebels to prevail in armed conflict and ultimately achieve their goals is a question that deserves further inquiry.

REBEL ENGAGEMENT AS A POLICY

Rebel violence is one of the security challenges of our time, and increasing rebel compliance with international law is one approach to alleviating the suffering of civilians in conflict zones. This part of the book explores the policy implications of the main findings presented earlier, and in particular the topic of *rebel engagement*. In the following pages, I will define what *rebel engagement* is and what methods it entails, weigh its benefits and challenges, discuss which rebel groups to engage, and explain the requirements for successful engagement. I will end with practical recommendations for policymakers and practitioners.

The choice of methods for engaging rebel groups discussed here will be constrained by what is known about the political incentives of relevant actors, including the opposing governments, foreign governments, international organizations, and NGOs. Further, the aim of the discussion will be to distill specific recommendations for each policymaking party that may potentially be involved in rebel engagement. That said, I also want to acknowledge right away that I am not the first to discuss methods for engaging rebel groups.[46] What will be new in this section is how I integrate my findings from this book and link those findings to specific policy recommendations.

The findings on compliant legitimacy-seeking rebels should be interpreted cautiously, especially with regard to drawing policy implications. Based on the connection we have shown between legitimacy and compliance, some readers might reason that rebels should be given legitimacy in order to make them more compliant. This would *not* be a sound interpretation of the book's findings. The book's analyses uncovered the general pattern that legitimacy-seeking rebels are more likely than other groups to be compliant. Yet this does not mean that we should attempt to persuade all rebel groups to seek legitimacy. This approach would not be realistically feasible. Nor do the book's findings suggest that we should encourage all rebel groups to form political wings or seek out foreign sponsors with a concern for human rights. Rebel groups' incentives have their history and cannot be changed overnight so that all groups may suddenly become legitimacy-seeking.

The desirable legitimacy-seeking characteristics that may in some cases be instilled grow out of a unique set of political and economic environments, the conditions for which cannot easily be contrived. Also, from a practical standpoint, the very idea of encouraging rebel groups to adopt compliance-directed behaviors – such as establishing a political wing – is likely to face strong opposition from national governments fighting to retain their political authority. Instead, what the theory and evidence of rebel compliance *do* suggest is that we can engage a certain class of rebel groups with an eye to making their behavior in war more humane. The common feature of compliant rebels, as we discovered in this book, is that they all were determined to seek out domestic and/or international legitimacy. So while we cannot turn legitimacy-indifferent rebel groups into legitimacy-seeking rebel groups, the motivations of legitimacy-seeking rebel groups provide an opportunity for external actors to influence their behavior in a meaningful fashion.

The short-term and immediate policy goal is to make civil wars more humane. It may seem counterintuitive to say that wars should be conducted humanely when wars are almost by definition violent and destructive. The findings in this book nonetheless imply that there is such a thing as humane warfare, and that it is possible to draw some lessons from the histories of compliant rebels and how their compliance comes about. Improving compliance means altering rebels'

[46] See, for example, the 2012 TED talk by Jonas Gahr Støre, former Norwegian Foreign Minister (Gahr Støre 2012), as well as a 2005 interview with Jimmy Carter, former US President (Carter 2005). Also see policy-oriented research by Ricigliano (2005); McHugh and Bessler (2006); Hofmann and Schneckener (2011); Bellal and Casey-Maslen (2011); Podder (2012b); Somer (2012); Krieger (forthcoming).

incentives in a way that directs them to fight a more humane war. The long-term policy goal is peace-making. Improving compliance is not equivalent to renouncing violence, but many cases show that rebel groups make commitments to international rules in the expectation of peace negotiations with the government they are fighting, and these compliant rebels are more likely than their non-compliant peers to enter into peace talks.[47]

Rebel Engagement Methods

There are many ways to deal with rebel groups. The options include hard and soft methods. "Hard" methods include military action, peacekeeping, economic sanctions, and legal punishments. "Soft" methods include rebel engagement. This could be either political engagement or humanitarian engagement.[48] Political engagement usually happens in order to achieve the goals of peace negotiations or ceasefires. Humanitarian engagement generally happens during a conflict and involves directly contacting and interacting with rebel groups diplomatically to achieve humanitarian policy goals. It can also occur in the aftermath of conflict, when it may take the form of demobilization, measures to prevent humanitarian violations, and so on. Political engagement can occur simultaneously with humanitarian engagement, with political engagement at Track I (official diplomacy) and humanitarian engagement at Track II (unofficial diplomacy) levels.

Although various forms of engagement have been studied one at a time, much less is known about their relative merits in context and about how and when to choose among different options. Depending on one's objective in a particular situation – be it ending a civil war, deterring humanitarian violations, or protecting civilians – the choice or the set of choices might differ, yet this choice calculus has not been dealt with in a thorough fashion in any academic literature.[49] And the largest lacuna in the literature pertains to the study of humanitarian rebel engagement.[50]

Given this gap in our knowledge base, the focus in this section will therefore be primarily on discussing alternative methods of humanitarian rebel engagement. However, I will also devote some attention to political engagement, because political engagement can entail humanitarian goals, and humanitarian engagement can lead to political engagement.

A first method of humanitarian rebel engagement focuses on education and training. The aim here is to promote rebel awareness of international law and

47 In the RGIL database, forty-four rebel groups that did not kill civilians terminated their conflicts with peace talks, while only fourteen that killed civilians reached peace talks.

48 Petrasek (2005). 49 One proximate effort is by Regan and Aydin (2006).

50 Notable exceptions include Ricigliano (2005) and Zartman and Faure (2011), but both focus on political engagement rather than on humanitarian engagement. Roberts and Sivakumaran (2012) also discuss various humanitarian methods of engagement, but mainly from legal perspectives.

discourage illegal behavior. This may be done by providing training regarding international humanitarian rules or by assisting rebel groups in drafting a new code of conduct. This kind of work has been done by the ICRC[51] and other NGOs in various places worldwide as part of promoting humanitarian norms.[52] For its part, Geneva Call, with the help of a network of mine-clearing NGOs, successfully engaged rebel groups in a mine education campaign and significantly reduced their use of anti-personnel mines.

"Education" in cases like these does not mean didactic preaching to rebel groups about things they should do or not do. Rather, this method of engagement crucially entails tailoring the chosen means of communication and persuasion to the particular audience being addressed during the education or training sessions.[53] Communication should, of course, always be as clear and effective as possible. That said, education at the commander level is important – because sub-commanders will subsequently follow their orders – and education to an audience of commanders will likely address issues that are not included in a training session for rank-and-file rebels. Indeed, targeted training of commanders – thoughtfully addressing their particular concerns – is likely to be an especially effective way of conveying information and improving compliance within rebel ranks.[54] Also, persuasion should include acknowledgment of the rebel perspective and of rebel constraints and concerns.[55] Training will be of no value if the rebels receiving the training feel like those rules have no connection to what they actually encounter on the battlefield. It is crucial that the audience should see compliance with humanitarian norms as both feasible and beneficial. Otherwise the training is unlikely to be implemented.

The second method of humanitarian engagement is to encourage adherence to already existing or new legal commitments. The United Nations is already doing this in the context of its United Nations Action Plans to stop the use of child soldiers with a dozen rebel groups around the world.[56] Some rebel groups have proactively signed on to various commitments, including their promise to abide by the Geneva Conventions.[57] Governments, home and foreign, have also engaged in committing rebel groups to humanitarian rules and human rights in the context of peace agreement negotiations. Including rebel groups in this legal process of law-making can be controversial, as it can mean acknowledging rebel groups as equal partners. When these political difficulties can be overcome, however, rebel commitments have sometimes borne fruit, not least because

[51] Gillioz (2012).
[52] See this book's cover image showing an ICRC dissemination session with the Sudanese Liberation Army combatants in 2006.
[53] Ratner (2011).
[54] I owe this observation to Chris Tomlinson at Associated Press from his many years of observing ICRC training.
[55] Bangerter (2011). [56] See Chapter 6 on the detailed discussion of United Nations Action Plans.
[57] These commitment patterns are noted in Chapters 2 and 4. The Appendix also provides a list of rebel group commitments.

engaging rebel groups in this manner often goes hand in hand with increasing their capacity to implement rules. For example, if a rebel group lacks capacity to verify the age of child soldiers or lacks resources to demobilize child soldiers (as is often the case), a commitment that is accompanied by managerial support may greatly increase the likelihood of compliance. That said, the danger also exists that rebel groups may try to leverage the engagement process to obtain material benefits only to then back out of a commitment they have made.[58] For the most part, though, encouraging rebel groups to adhere to their legal commitments has by and large been effective as a signal to comply and as a vehicle to increased compliance, especially when combined with critical managerial and organizational support.

Potential Benefits of Rebel Engagement

The above-mentioned humanitarian rebel engagement methods are classified as "prevention" methods because both are aimed at preventing acts of non-compliance from occurring. At the same time, both these methods – education and participation in rule-making – may sound like very weak methods of intervention. However, they do possess a number of advantages over other methods.

One of these advantages is that prevention methods allow rebel groups to take ownership of the rules. A sense of ownership increases the likelihood that rules will take root within a rebel movement and be perceived as meaningful and worthwhile. When rules are internalized in this way, compliant behavior may eventually become a matter of habit. Indeed, the hope is that, over time, rebel groups will develop attitudes that are shaped by humanitarian norms and rules. When this happens, self-implementation and self-policing replace outside supervision. Genuine home-grown compliance will always be more durable than imposed compliance.

With a view to fostering this kind of home-grown compliance, less may be more when it comes to outside intervention and involvement. Too much outside intervention may engender push-back from rebel groups. Also, in the long run, for rebel groups to implement a newly developed code of conduct, they themselves should be motivated to implement the policy, with internal monitoring and discipline mechanisms. It is important to remember that as international law goes global, international law cannot work without home-grown, grassroots efforts at the rebel group level.

Another advantage of prevention methods is that they encourage the development of shared understandings. One of the critical elements in advancing norms is to create a common understanding of basic principles.[59]

58 McHugh and Singh (2013).

59 This is a point of consensus across constructivist and rationalist schools in international relations. See Morrow (2014).

Before norms can become internalized, they must be both acknowledged and also well understood. Not all rebel groups have any basic knowledge of humanitarian norms, as many practitioners have observed.[60] Over the past two decades, awareness of norms has improved with the evolution of technology and new methods of communication, specifically social networking platforms such as Facebook and Twitter. Many rebel groups use these platforms to tout their battle successes, announce new policies, and recruit members. For example, an M23 representative in the DRC has followed the tweets of every important politician and media leader involved in the group's conflict, including the UN Human Rights Committee.[61] Although the extensive integration of social networks into rebel movements and increased rebel awareness of international standards do not guarantee compliance, they do provide an important first step toward rule compliance, especially for groups transitioning from non-compliance to compliance.

With regard to engaging rebel groups in honoring their commitments, an important benefit lies in rebel group participation in the drafting of rules and laws. From the rebel perspective, an opportunity to participate in this drafting process may also serve as a powerful incentive and rationale to change behavior. The basic idea is that rights and obligations under the law must be balanced: if armed groups are to be subjected to certain obligations and responsibilities under international humanitarian law, then they should have rights to participate in law-making too. To date, rebel groups have mostly been barred from participating in international law-making, whereas states have enjoyed an undisputed prerogative to do so. However, imposing obligations without giving any rights may hamper both the development and the implementation of sound laws. Also, there is now some evidence – at least with regard to the issue of anti-personnel mines – indicating that when armed groups make a commitment to abide by an international law that they have had a hand in drafting, this commitment is more likely to lead to compliance than when they have had no role in the drafting process.[62] Scholars studying norm development have also pointed out this link between participation and compliance, indicating that it promotes a process of internalization similar to that described above.[63]

Potential Challenges of Rebel Engagement

The potential benefits of humanitarian engagement with legitimacy-seeking rebel groups notwithstanding, any effort to induce compliance must take into account potential political obstacles. The biggest risk is that engagement will debase the legitimacy of the government being challenged. If this happens, or if it appears

60 Interview with Carole Frampton, June 2013.

61 The author personally followed the tweets of the M23 leadership. Some screenshots are on file with the author.

62 International Council on Human Rights Policy (2000).

63 See Roberts and Sivakumaran (2012); also see Franck (1990) for the case of state actors.

likely to happen, governments will typically respond by blocking access to rebels, through either military or diplomatic means. While humanitarian actors will hardly ever confer explicit legitimacy to rebel groups, governments may nonetheless view political engagement with rebels critically.

Governments are sensitive to the dangers of undermining their own legitimacy. In Sudan, for example, in 2009, the Al-Bashir government expelled major humanitarian organizations as a response to an indictment from the ICC.[64] When governments feel that their legitimacy is fragile and threatened, and that an increase in rebel legitimacy will inevitably mean a reduction in their legitimacy, a legitimacy war may arise. The likelihood of this happening is greatly increased when governments in civil conflicts fail to govern at the outset, producing ungovernable rebels determined to undermine the government's legitimacy.[65]

The second method of prevention, namely, letting rebel groups play a role in the international law-making process, tends to be especially controversial. Some states argue that allowing rebel groups any type of involvement grants them unwarranted legitimacy. Israeli resistance to the PLO's UN observer status in 2012 clearly illustrates this point. These kinds of political objections from state actors can sometimes be overcome by designating rebel groups as "observers" rather than as "signatories" in the law-making process.[66]

Engagement with rebel groups is also unpopular among many governments when counterterrorism policies are in effect. Also, anti-terrorism laws tend to present NGOs and international organizations with formidable legal and logistical obstacles that discourage engagement. For instance, the US Material Support Law instituted after September 11, 2001 prevented many humanitarian groups from engaging rebels abroad.[67] As a policy matter as well, US government agencies are generally very reluctant to embrace any approach involving direct rebel engagement.[68] USAID has painful memories of what can go wrong with this approach given the failures of the OLS. The mandate of the 1989 OLS was to save lives. An agreement was signed with the SPLM/A that specified the obligations of the SPLM/A with regard to guaranteeing the safe passage of humanitarian aid.[69] As well, the agreement included "ground rules" to ensure the protection of civilians and respect for children's rights.[70] Although the United Nations led the effort, the United States was the major funder. In this episode, the SPLM/A in Sudan continued committing human rights violations even after it started receiving USAID-supported aid within the framework of OLS.[71] In the face of such episodes, and in the context of heightened national security concerns following 9/11, state agencies

[64] Rice and Branigan (2009). [65] Bates (2008).
[66] Proponents of this approach include Zegveld (2002); Clapham (2010); Sassoli (2010).
[67] 18 USC § 2339A: Providing material support to terrorists. See more on this topic in Modirzadeh *et al.* (2011).
[68] Interview with an anonymous USAID official, April 20, 2013. [69] Akol (2005).
[70] Bradbury *et al.* (2000). [71] Harmer (2004).

worldwide have generally become increasingly unwilling to engage directly with rebel groups.

The United Nations is a bit more open than national governments to the idea of rebel engagement. Also, the UN does not face the same constraints that national governments do with regard to domestic politics. Consequently, the UN has had some success with persuading rebel groups to commit to specific Action Plans, and has assisted rebel groups with – among other efforts – the demobilization of child soldiers. The UN retains some agency autonomy, yet even its approaches to engaging with rebel groups have faced restrictions, depending as they do to a large extent on state cooperation. It also remains true that, even in the presence of state cooperation, a UN-led approach still relies on the commitment and implementation capacity of rebel groups. A limitation, in this regard, is that developing a sense of ownership of international rules among rebels may take a long time. Months, and perhaps years, may pass before this approach brings about rebel compliance.

Another reason why policies of direct rebel engagement are often avoided pertains to the fear that they will alter the military balance in a civil conflict. Some cynical critics argue that any humanitarian support to rebel groups will only add fuel to a violent conflict.[72] They cite incidents where humanitarian aid was snatched by rebels or where aid distributed in refugee camps was used for rebel recruitment efforts. While such accusations are not entirely without factual basis, instances where humanitarian aid actually tilted the military balance of a civil war are few and far between, as such assistance is almost never substantial enough to have any meaningful impact on the outcome of an ongoing conflict. Rather than abandon policies of rebel engagement on the basis of such fears, a more effective approach may therefore be to conduct humanitarian engagement in such a way that aid cannot easily be channeled to military purposes.

Humanitarian engagement may also carry the risk of causing divisions among rebel elements or exacerbating existing ones, thereby providing an environment conducive to the formation of extremist factions. Often, engagement with moderate rebel factions will be a high-profile affair mired in controversy. These cases may polarize rebel groups by widening the divides between extreme and moderate elements. However, the likelihood of humanitarian engagement provoking these kinds of schisms seems generally low. Divisions among rebel groups are more likely to develop during peace negotiations in situations where a coalition of moderates appears ready to sign an agreement with the government, but more extremist elements insist on having additional demands met. Divisions are less likely to arise during the earlier stages of humanitarian engagement.[73]

Take the case of MILF in the Philippines, for example, the rebel group discussed at some length in Chapter 6. This separatist group split from its

[72] Goodhand (2006). [73] See Potz-Nielsen (2013).

mother organization, the MNLF, in 1978 following the MNLF's decision to sign the Tripoli Agreement. MILF was dissatisfied with the agreement because the government granted only limited rather than complete autonomy to the Bangsamoro people. Following the group's own negotiations with the government in 1990, MILF itself experienced an internal split that led to the formation of the ASG. However, again, the timeline suggests that it was not humanitarian engagement that fueled this division, but rather deep-seated policy differences. The timing was such that the ASG split from MILF in 1990 around the time that MILF started to negotiate with the Philippines Government and also created the ARMM, a small pocket of land on the island of Mindanao.[74] This example illustrates that humanitarian engagement may not be a significant contributor to splits. Divisions and schisms tend to be the result of more fundamental disagreements about rebel goals.

Yet another challenge associated with humanitarian engagement may be the possibility of a political backlash among rebels themselves. Targeted humanitarian engagement can sometimes disrupt support at the local level. A survey of Taliban documents, for example, revealed that, with the possibility of humanitarian engagement on the horizon, individual Taliban leaders expressed concern about how such engagement could affect domestic perceptions of the Taliban. Specifically, they feared that accepting overtures from humanitarian groups might lead to blowback by the local population on several fronts, such as igniting tensions over women's rights, complicating military operations, and creating new security headaches.[75] This example illustrates that there will be cases when rebels themselves resist or refuse humanitarian engagement. (Chapter 7 provided another example of this kind of resistance in the case of rebels refusing to grant access to their detention centers.)

From the perspective of international organizations, rebel engagement is likely to face a number of practical difficulties. Armed groups may be unwilling to participate in training and educational programs. Or security policies may forbid human rights or humanitarian organizations from entering conflict zones. Also, any form of engagement beyond humanitarian assistance may be unpopular among national governments. In fact, some national governments may even block the efforts of international disaster relief agencies if it means that aid workers will operate in rebel-held areas. This is what happened in Syria in 2011, when the Syrian Government blocked humanitarian access by aid agencies during the early stages of its internal conflict.[76] In practice, it is often difficult to clearly demarcate the line separating humanitarian engagement from rebel support. Helping rebels build detention centers, for instance, may be initiated strictly as a matter of humanitarian engagement, but may later serve to strengthen the rebel cause.

[74] Memorial Institute for the Prevention of Terrorism (2013). [75] Jackson and Giustozzi (2012).
[76] See Hersh (2013). The Assad government was especially eager to block access to the Deraa region where rebel activity was most intense.

Cultural differences also sometimes hamper engagement efforts. For example, governments may have varying definitions of who counts as a civilian. In certain interpretations of the Koran, for instance, civilians may conduct "jihad of the sword" and still remain civilians, even if they take part in armed combat. In Western Judeo-Christian cultures, by contrast, there is a much clearer distinction between combatants and non-combatants, and as soon as a civilian picks up a weapon, he or she is counted as a combatant. Also, in some cultures, children become adults when they are 13 or 15, instead of 18, the international norm. In these societies, children may assume adult roles and status at this younger age, and may even participate in rebellion and armed conflict with their community's full approval. These cultural differences can discourage the adoption of international norms. Worse, they can create tension and political contestation, with the result that rebel groups may resist the imposition of particular humanitarian norms – or completely reject all engagement efforts.

At the end of the day, the discouraging reality is that, despite thoughtful and persistent efforts, some rebel groups remain non-compliant. In some of these cases, there are simply irreconcilable differences at the level of political, moral, and religious values. Al-Qaeda groups, for example, such as Al-Shabaab in Somalia, Lashkar-e-Taiba in Pakistan, Jabhat al-Nusra in Syria, and Al-Qaeda in the Islamic Maghreb (AQIM) in Algeria, show little interest in reconsidering their long-standing rejection of the international legal order. For their part, jihadist groups renounce central tenets of international law, such as its distinction between combatants and non-combatants. In pursuit of their ideology, and to support their broader cause, many of these groups believe that sacrificing civilian lives may be appropriate in certain instances. And rebel groups employing terrorist tactics often seek legitimacy through much more extreme and brutal means than rebel groups engaged in long-running secessionist civil wars. Unfortunately, the policy suggestions proposed in this chapter are unlikely to find success among these groups.

Choosing Rebel Groups to Engage

A central finding of my research on compliant rebels is that some rebel groups – though not all – are potentially engage-able. It therefore makes sense to consider a "targeted humanitarian engagement" approach aimed at engaging a particular set of rebel groups with particular characteristics. In this section, drawing on my empirical findings, I want to suggest three indicators of engage-ability. These indicators fall into three areas: political experiences of rebel groups, rebel aims, and interactions with external actors.

First, the past political experiences of rebel groups show that they have some knowledge about engaging with their domestic electoral population. This knowledge may derive from participating in national or regional elections. It may or may not signal that a group has an organized political wing, yet it generally indicates some level of organizational capacity and ambition.

For outside actors seeking to engage a rebel group, this history of organizational capacity and ambition is important. Finding interlocutors to talk to is the first step of engagement, and if a rebel group has past political experience, it is much more likely that interlocutors will be found. Further, if a rebel group has a political wing that communicates with, and perhaps exerts control over, its military wing, engagement is much more likely to result in actual implementation of new rules of conduct.

A second indicator of engage-ability pertains to rebel aims. In general, rebel groups with more ambitious aims – aims whose achievement requires gaining support and/or recognition – are more engage-able than groups with less ambitious aims. For example, my research findings indicate that, on average, secessionist rebels have a higher propensity to be switchover compliers than non-secessionist rebel groups. Secessionists want to gain recognition from the international community as sovereign states and therefore tend to care deeply about legitimacy and finding ways to earn it. Along the same lines, rebels who rely heavily on regional support tend to be more easily persuaded to the humanitarian cause to strengthen their home base with core supporters. The LTTE's responsiveness to the preferences of its diaspora supporters is an example of this phenomenon.

Third, the composition of external sponsorship matters. My analyses showed that when rebel groups seek legitimacy in the eyes of political audiences that care about humanitarian values and human rights norms, they are more likely to be amenable to engagement. This happens when external sponsors have clear goals in terms of humanitarian and human rights policies and these norms provide bright lines for rebel groups to follow.

Other basic facts such as rebel military and organizational capacity and rebel ideology should be part of the picture, too. Rebel military capacity signals the viability of a rebel group to win. If a rebel group is militarily weak or is perceived as weak, its chances of attracting support and surviving are diminished. On the other hand, if a rebel group is militarily dominant, some external sponsors may worry that the group no longer needs them and may no longer listen to them – causing them to pull back on their sponsorship (as was the case when Saudi Arabia suspended its support for ISIL). Ideology is important to the extent that it is consistent with international rules. If a group's ideology is diametrically opposed to the basic principles of humanitarian law, the group may well be beyond the reach of any engagement effort.

Any engagement effort centered around prevention may find success only among a limited number of rebel groups. These groups are those most vulnerable to humanitarian pressure and who most urgently want to gain legitimacy. To determine a group's likely response to engagement, policymakers must observe and analyze the group's legitimacy-seeking indicators to estimate how receptive its leadership will be to engaging with outside actors. Ironically, rebels facing authoritarian governments may have a higher than average likelihood of changing their behavior in response to engagement, given the urgent desire of these groups to boost their legitimacy by debasing that of the government.

Recall that I have distinguished two kinds of compliance: persistent compliance and switchover compliance. Among persistent compliers, some may consciously follow the international norms, but others might comply without actively considering the consequences of complying. Switchover compliance may occur when rebel groups respond to the views and preferences of their supporters – supporters who care about human rights or humanitarian issues. Policy prescriptions should be tailored to each type of compliance as the nature of the compliance, the existing reasons for non-compliance, and the processes toward compliance may differ.

Some rebels will not need to be informed of international law to reach compliance. In these cases, the role of international law will be minimal. The FMLN in El Salvador, for instance, received support from the Catholic Church, at home and abroad, and drew its membership from a domestic population that embraced Christian values of compassion and respect for human life.[77] The Catholic Church did not teach rebels international law; rather, rebels' local standards aligned perfectly with international standards. In these cases of happy coincidence between local and international norms, a group may reach compliance through social support and does not have to actively search for international legitimacy. In these cases, international law does not have any substantial impact as it is already embedded in an internal code of conduct, as was the case with the FMLN.[78] The behavior of these rebels is inherently consistent with international norms at the outset and no engagement is necessary to induce compliance.

The prevention method, therefore, will have the highest chance of success when applied to rebel groups that are inadvertently non-compliant due to a lack of awareness of the potential benefit of adhering to international norms.[79] These groups will have strong potential to transition from non-compliance to compliance. Assisting rebels of this kind in reaching an understanding and sense of ownership for international standards can sometimes be effective in inducing compliance. For instance, in the case of MILF in the Philippines and the MFDC in Senegal, many international organizations – including Geneva Call, Oxfam-GB, and the ICRC – provided the resources necessary for destroying stockpiles of anti-personnel mines.

Policymakers, especially foreign interveners, tend to select "moderate factions" of rebel groups when choosing which rebels to sponsor, as the

77 See Wood (2003) and Stanton (2013) for thick descriptions of the FMLN movement. For FMLN's religious ties, also see Central Intelligence Agency (1993).

78 See Bangerter (2012) on the internal code of conduct that exists for some armed opposition groups.

79 Capacity-building has long been suggested as one of the solutions to enhance compliance, especially with regard to international environmental agreements. See Weiss and Jacobson (2000).

recent case of Syria shows. The criteria invoked in these situations are often vague. The McKeon Amendment, proposed by the House Armed Services Committee Chairman, Buck McKeon, in September 2014, does not specify which rebel groups among the hundreds of groups and factions active in Syria should receive support; the Amendment stipulates only that groups should be "appropriately vetted," meaning that it must be determined whether they have connections to terrorist groups or receive support from the Assad regime in Syria or from Iran.[80]

In this context, the analytical criteria provided in this book could be a useful tool for policymakers in deciding whether rebel groups deserve outside support or not, with an eye toward the likely humanitarian consequences of attempting engagement and providing support. Further, these analytical criteria could help policymakers to see beyond the crude categorization of rebel groups as either "moderate" or "extremist." This classification scheme may lead policymakers to miss important opportunities to engage extremist groups that would actually be responsive to engagement efforts. Recall that MILF was at first branded as an extremist group in the early 2000s, but that the group changed course and joined the ranks of compliant rebels a few years later.

Humanitarian aid practitioners also have to choose which groups to engage. For example, humanitarian workers have to make decisions about which groups to engage in negotiations to obtain humanitarian access. To date, these decisions tend to be made in the absence of any kind of overarching, research-based framework. More developed guidance from my analytical framework could helpfully inform the decisions of people on the ground.[81]

Criteria for Successful Rebel Engagement

Regardless of the type of method being employed, any successful engagement must take rebel group interests into consideration. A key lesson of my study is that compliant rebels will reach compliance simply out of goodwill. As a matter of strategy, rebel groups seek legitimacy in order to survive and grow. Policy initiatives, if they are to succeed in their goal of fostering compliance, must strike a chord with the strategic objectives of the rebels that they are targeting. My investigation of rebel groups' compliance behaviors suggests a series of filtering questions policymakers can ask in order to identify rebels' interests and motivations for compliance. For example: in whose eyes exactly are rebel groups seeking legitimacy? Has the rebel group engaged with local civilians politically, perhaps through the electoral process? Is the rebel group open to international actors, and has it already taken steps to gain international legitimacy?

80 Blanchard and Belasco (2014).

81 I appreciate that Jonathan Somer used some of my book's draft material in the International Humanitarian Law workshop he taught for field staff working in the Syrian conflict.

Once legitimacy-seeking characteristics are identified, the next step of engagement often involves finding creative ways to alter rebel group interests. One way to proceed is to pick rebel groups for whom gaining legitimacy is already an active concern, and then to engage them by further persuading them of the upsides of compliance. In this scenario, the job of outside groups is mostly to help legitimacy-oriented groups commit to desired changes in their behavior. With rebel groups that are already aware of international rules or standards, and aware of the benefits of compliance, a method of engagement that places emphasis on the strategic benefits of compliance has a good chance of working.

Consider, for example, the case of the MFDC in Senegal. Geneva Call's efforts to provide the MFDC with new evidence and facts about the potential benefits of complying with international law had a clear and positive impact. Under the guidance of Geneva Call, the MFDC determined that compliance would likely help its constituents in a number of ways, which would in turn help to build the group's political base. Prevention methods centered on engaging entire local communities may sometimes prove to be even more fruitful than those focused on engaging rebels only. Such efforts could be conducted, for example, by informing civilians of the long-term negative effects of sending their children to join armed groups and the benefits of actively supporting local leaders.[82] As this example illustrates, the reach and value of prevention methods will depend on a number of factors, including the characteristics of the particular rebel group, the availability of international support, and the potential for meaningful engagement with local communities.

The success of any engagement method will also likely depend on a concerted effort being made by the national government, rebel group leadership, and the international community, as well as affected local communities.[83] The government must be willing to allow humanitarian organizations to operate in their jurisdiction. Rebel group leadership must be willing and able to adopt the prevention methods. International groups – such as diaspora populations – must be engaged to exert political influence based on their existing networks. Finally, people in affected communities must know their rights and pressure established authorities to influence the behavior of rebel soldiers and leaders.

RECOMMENDATIONS FOR POLICYMAKERS

This book will be helpful to policymakers and practitioners devising foreign policies. My findings about the link between legitimacy concerns and

[82] See Carole Frampton, "Improving the Protection of Civilians in Eastern Democratic Republic of Congo through Dialogue with Armed Non-State Actors: Concept Note," Geneva Call, 2012. The document is on file with the author.

[83] In spirit, this policy idea is akin to the stewardship strategy proposed in Hafner-Burton (2013), where leading human rights-minded countries operate as stewards to vulnerable populations.

compliance can be utilized in predicting whether rebel groups are likely to comply with humanitarian law in general. It is not easy to predict with 100 percent accuracy which rebel groups are likely to comply and which are not. That said, the checklist provided in this book – rebel political activities, rebel objectives, and rebel external engagement with potential human rights sponsors – may serve to identify rebel groups that are likely to be engaged by outside actors.[84]

Despite this general guideline, efforts to induce rebel compliance with international law can take many different forms, and different sets of policymakers and practitioners favor different methods. State governments fighting rebel groups will obviously favor different methods than will foreign governments, or international organizations, or NGOs. Given that the political constraints and the key objectives are different for each of these policy stakeholders, I discuss what rebel engagement may mean for each.[85]

For State Governments Fighting Rebels

For governments that have rebel groups as political opponents, it is recommended to be more open to rebel engagement methods. Governments choose how to deal with their insurgencies based on their threat perception – how detrimental they estimate a rebellion is or will become to their authority and legitimacy.[86] They have the right to decide whether to take a more military approach or a more political one. Whatever the basic approach a government chooses in terms of counterinsurgency, however, there should be some room for allowing rebel engagement for humanitarian purposes. Colombia in the early 2000s provides an example of this approach. Concurrent with military counterinsurgency efforts, humanitarian workers were allowed to operate for humanitarian reasons, unhindered by political interference.[87]

Governments fighting a rebel insurgency do not usually partake in rebel engagement for humanitarian purposes, but there are several ways that governments can nonetheless promote such activities. One is through peace negotiations with the involvement of external expertise. Peace talks are a forum for rebels and governments to discuss sharing power and resources, but they also provide a space to discuss the humanitarian implications of conflict and the sharing of rights and responsibilities. Governments can be open to the participation of mediators focusing on such humanitarian issues, such as the Humanitarian Dialogue Centre.

Another approach is to allow humanitarian workers to operate during conflict. As exemplified in many cases, governments generally do not want to acknowledge the reality of conflict and civilian suffering within their borders.

84 These indicators were introduced in Chapter 4.

85 See Petrasek (2005) for the differences between humanitarian and political engagement.

86 Staniland (2012b). 87 Reusse-Decrey (2005).

Nor do they want outside actors to engage rebel groups for fear of giving them legitimacy or aiding them materially. Turkey, India, Colombia, Sudan – all these countries at some point constricted what humanitarian workers call "humanitarian space." Government fears are not unfounded, but if an engagement strategy can separate out political goals from humanitarian ones, some governments may allow rebel engagement. Again, the Colombian Government's interaction with Geneva Call illustrates this approach,[88] showing that governments can be persuaded to endorse rebel engagement efforts – even in the context of ongoing violence.

For Foreign Governments as Interveners

Like state governments fighting a rebel insurgency, foreign governments rarely attempt rebel engagement due to political considerations. Stepping into the middle of a civil conflict in another country is likely to be controversial domestically and internationally – though much depends on the existing relationship between the foreign intervener and the government of the target country. If the intervener has a commitment to aiding rebels, and believes it is strong enough to withstand the push-back that it likely to come, it may choose to actively engage with rebel groups politically, militarily, and diplomatically. In other cases where a foreign intervener has a stake in reducing tensions between a government and rebel groups, it may choose to engage both warring parties. Normally, in these cases, foreign interveners interact with the target government based on established diplomatic relations and through political communication channels.

For International Organizations

International organizations such as the United Nations or the ICRC come into contact with rebel groups in various ways. When they deliver humanitarian aid to conflict zones, or in the midst of peacekeeping efforts, international organizations meet and interact with rebel groups. International organizations are politically constrained by their mandate – defined by their member states – but they are generally less constrained than are national governments with regard to rebel engagement. As independent decision-makers, international organizations can often initiate engagement efforts that states would never be able to undertake. The ICRC's educational training of rebel groups, and the United Nations Action Plans are examples of this phenomenon.

Given that the history of such engagement efforts is short, there seems, as yet, to be no systematic effort to assess the success or failure of the programs that

[88] *Ibid.*

have been implemented thus far.[89] For their part, the ICRC's training efforts have been preventive in nature, and it is thus especially difficult to measure their impact. Still, researchers could investigate how the training catalyzed changes in rebel groups' internal codes of conduct – and how these changes in turn trickled down to rebels in the field and affected their compliance behavior. The United Nations Action Plans also deserve closer study. The UN has been selective in its choice of rebel groups, and its efforts have met with some success. Yet we know little about how exactly its monitoring and reporting mechanisms have enhanced compliance of rebel groups. The program's impact should be further researched using social science methods along with policy impact evaluations. There is an urgent need for effective approaches to be identified and shared with other organizations.

For Non-Governmental Organizations

Non-governmental organizations are the most active actors that engage rebel groups. While international organizations often have to adjust their mandates in consideration of member states' preferences, NGOs have generally enjoyed greater latitude in deciding how and when to engage with rebel groups. Examples of NGOs in this category include Geneva Call, Médecins sans Frontières, and the Humanitarian Dialogue Centre. Geneva Call has been very active in the area of anti-personnel mines and has successfully garnered commitments from about forty rebel groups around the world to end their use of mines. Médecins sans Frontières has been upfront about its commitment to working in conflict areas where humanitarian needs are great and where other organizations will not go. Because of their special role in treating the wounded and the sick, they come into contact with rebel groups and rebel elements. Médecins sans Frontières recently published an honest and open account of its operations that specifically discussed the reality of having to negotiate with rebel groups in order to remain operational in given region.[90] The Humanitarian Dialogue Centre, for its part, works as a mediator focusing on orchestrating peace negotiations.

The diverse roles NGOs may play are curtailed, however, when a host government or other foreign government puts restrictions on NGOs' funding, level of access, and/or logistics. The US Material Support Law, for example, imposed restrictions on funding for humanitarian workers and their activities. The law also prohibited interactions between humanitarian actors and rebel groups deemed to be terrorists, specifying that such interactions may be unlawful.[91] In response to these developments, greater coordination among related NGOs appears to be necessary to reduce misunderstandings.

89 Email interview with Audrey Pamala, Advisor in Dialogue with Non-State Armed Actors at the ICRC (February 2014); phone interview with Alec Wargo, Program Officer at the Special Office in Children and Armed Conflict at the United Nations (August 7, 2014).

90 Magone *et al.* (2011). 91 Charity and Security Network (2012).

Specifically, new forms of communication and coordination may be necessary to avoid a situation where NGOs are accused of unlawfully aiding terrorist groups. Otherwise, there is a good chance that much humanitarian engagement will start occurring in the dark, as the Médecins sans Frontières case illustrates, which would seriously hamper our ability to learn collectively from past experience and identify best practices for successful engagement.[92]

INTERPLAY WITH OTHER POLICY INTERVENTIONS

It should be noted that efforts to engage rebels are rarely, if ever, conducted in isolation. Typically, their outcome is affected by multiple factors related to international policy. The child soldier issue, for example, will never be solved through rebel engagement during wartime alone. Efforts to end child soldiering must be made in concert with a disarmament, demobilization, and reintegration program lasting well into the post-conflict period, potentially in coordination with other peacekeeping efforts, in order to reduce the trauma of wartime violence, and to provide needed assistance for children to be reintegrated into their society by means of training and education.

Intervention efforts other than engagement – such as protecting civilians by deploying peacekeeping forces or arresting rebel leaders for trial by the ICC – have the potential to influence rebels to fight a more humane war. Research finds that the efforts by United Nations peacekeeping forces to create buffer zones between government and rebel forces generally help to reduce the number of civilians killed during hostilities.[93] Research also finds that the ICC can deter violations of international law by rebel groups, although the magnitude of this deterrence effect cannot be accurately determined given the court's young age.[94] Recently, the United Nations imposed so-called "smart sanctions" on rebel leaders in an effort to curtail rebels' capacity for violence. However, these "smart sanctions" have so far amounted to only a limited number of travel bans and asset freezes on a small number of rebel leaders. It is also the case that rebel leaders can often bypass such sanctions using black market channels that morph and regenerate like Hydra heads whenever one channel is disrupted.[95] Other policy options to deal with rebel groups such as amnesty or fully fledged military intervention are also available – controversial but. Blanket amnesty may lead some rebel soldiers to give up rebellion, but usually at the price of holding these rebels accountable for their past atrocities.[96] Also, military interventions on humanitarian grounds are still unpopular in most parts of the world due to

[92] I thank Simar Singh for this point on collective understanding. [93] Hultman *et al.* (2013).

[94] For the impact of the ICC, see the recent research in Jo and Simmons (2014). For the published works, see Akhavan (2009), and Song (2013) for the ICC's deterrence potential; and for critical views, see Branch (2011) and Clark (2011).

[95] For the analysis of economic sanctions on rebel groups, see Radtke and Jo (2013).

[96] Lessa and Payne (2013).

the norm of respecting the sovereignty of nations, although the norm of a "responsibility to protect" (R2P) is slowly gaining traction.[97]

What my findings suggest with regard to all these other policy mechanisms is that the characteristics of rebels must be thoroughly understood before intervention strategies can be wisely devised or evaluated. For legitimacy-seeking rebels, persuasion through humanitarian engagement should be tried first before considering punishment methods, such as economic sanctions or ICC indictment. Also, the findings in this book imply that peacekeeping forces may bring prompt resolution to conflicts that involve legitimacy-seeking groups (but not legitimacy-indifferent groups). In these cases involving legitimacy-seeking groups, observer missions may be enough to curb the rebels' violence against civilians.[98] My findings also suggest that cooperation with humanitarian agencies, such as the ICRC, can help to extend the outreach of international judicial institutions such as the ICC vis-à-vis legitimacy-seeking rebels. The ICRC, an organization privileging confidentiality, will generally decline to give testimony at ICC trials. However, the ICRC may be able to help the ICC at the prevention stage by pressuring legitimacy-seeking rebel groups to respect humanitarian rules and international standards.

One thing is certain: changing the beliefs and incentive structures of rebel groups will never be easy. It will be up to the efforts of future studies to figure out the right mix of policy interventions to induce these groups to exercise restraint in their armed struggle, and ultimately to reduce the level of violence and human suffering.

LESSONS AND THE WAY FORWARD

This book was not written to celebrate the existence of compliant rebels. Rather, this book was intended as an attempt to understand how and why they become compliant – or remain compliant. My research on rebel compliance can be summed up in one sentence: "Compliance makes strategic sense to some rebels – to gain support at home and abroad, and to gain bargaining leverage vis-à-vis the government." To arrive at this answer, I examined the logic of political survival of rebel groups and investigated the influence of the normative and institutional environment.

We have learned that some rebel groups are not impervious to developments in international norms and rules.[99] These compliant rebels are part of an

[97] Stewart and Knaus (2012); Weiss (2012). However, see Kuperman (2008) for the risks associated with humanitarian intervention.

[98] During these stages, coordination and cooperation among different UN agencies are crucial. The relevant UN bodies – UNICEF, UNOCHA, and the Special Office for Children and Armed Conflict – should together determine what would be the best sequence of policy steps to engage rebel groups.

[99] States, of course, are not impervious to the development of international norms and associated pressures, either. For example, the Rwandan Government stopped supporting Congolese rebels

international ecosystem and realize that, in order to survive, they cannot ignore the contextual environment from where most of their support originates. This is the logic that led M23 in the DRC to make conciliatory moves (Chapter 5), that motivated MILF in the Philippines to respond to diplomatic outreach efforts by the UN and Geneva Call (Chapter 6), and that guided the KNU in Myanmar to fight a "legitimacy battle" against the military junta with the help of international actors (Chapter 7). The available data suggest that, by itself, international law is not likely to have much impact on rebel groups' behavior. Unfortunately, as we have seen, there are many legitimacy-indifferent and extremist rebel groups that are impervious to the reach of international law. However, my research also shows that conventional thinking about rebel groups – which views them as being in general impervious to engagement and outreach – is incorrect. Rebel groups *can, and must* , be engaged – in targeted ways.

My findings about compliant rebels have a number of implications for international law. International law does not, by itself, have the power to directly mold rebel behavior, yet it can help to produce compliant rebels through the efforts of diverse agents of international law. To rebel groups with political wings and a knowledge of international law, and to groups seeking out territorial and political autonomy, outreach efforts focused on international law will not fall on deaf ears. Hundreds of cases of rebel compliance and non-compliance show that international law does not operate in a vacuum. There are agents that believe in international law, like human rights organizations in democratic countries or humanitarian organizations that directly work with rebel groups. Compliant rebels, in turn, can grow out of the interactions between rebels and international organizations.

The study also finds that international law fares better where it is compatible with local norms. Child soldiering occurs in cultural and social contexts where childhood is construed in ways that do not coincide with the international standard of recognizing adolescents as minors until they reach the age of 18. The finding that a shift to compliance occurs only among legitimacy-seeking rebels does not mean that international law will never reach legitimacy-indifferent groups. Conventional thinking is that Islamist groups are beyond hope of engagement, yet there are indications that legitimacy-seeking Islamist groups do exist. MILF is one group that responded to international law throughout the 2000s, and the Taliban is another. These groups have at times deferred to international law to further their strategic goals and to provide a basis for interactions with outside actors to boost their legitimacy.

If international law is to be relevant and effective, however, it must not ignore political realities. Not all rebel groups are attuned to the norms of international

when it came under international pressure to end this support; Sudan stopped its support for the LRA because of international pressure, especially from the United States.

law. Some are, yet rarely will non-state armed actors take the initiative to reach out for help, or to design their own in-house Action Plan, to change their behavior. This is where outside political agents come into the picture. Rebel group histories and organizational structures matter, of course, but the actions of international actors also matter in inducing compliance.

The findings in this book also have larger implications for international relations research. International relations scholars have focused on the behavior of states, but many contemporary world phenomena involve non-state actors, individuals, multinational companies, or rebel groups. This book finds that legitimacy-seeking groups aspire to be states in the international system. Some of these groups are almost quasi-states, providing social services to their constituents and conducting foreign diplomacy. This area of overlap between states and non-state actors takes us beyond the established fields of scholarship and research. Exploring it will entail pushing research into a new frontier of world politics.

More broadly, my analysis of rebel compliance speaks to the schism in the field of international relations between rationalist and constructivist traditions. It suggests that the two traditions should communicate with one another. My research shows that rebel groups' thinking is rational and strategic in weighing political benefits and costs. At the same time, my research has shown that, by responding to rebels' motivations and understanding their interests, outside humanitarian groups can be persuasive and can induce compliance – an approach often emphasized by constructivist research. Indeed, one of the key findings in this book is that outside actors/ international organizations have the potential to be very influential in shaping rebel group compliance.

What we do not yet understand very well, at this point, is the progression that adaptive rebel groups move through as they come around to compliance. Without this understanding, we cannot identify or pinpoint the particular interventions – or the mix of two or more intervention options – that are likely to be most effective at specific points in time. Would it be best to blend peacekeeping and humanitarian engagement and target this approach to just certain types of rebel groups? When would it be best to attempt humanitarian engagement instead of threatening economic sanctions or indictments from the ICC? This book represents my best efforts, given the available evidence, to enhance our understanding of the dynamics of rebel compliance, and to begin to sketch a framework for answering these kinds of questions. I am acutely aware that, at this point, this framework has some gaps.

Future studies can address some of these lacunae. We do not yet know much about the relative efficacy of different forms of targeted humanitarian engagement. Efficacy needs to be rigorously assessed using program evaluations if possible. We also do not know much about the behaviors and decision logic of weak rebel groups, given that much less information is usually available for weaker groups than for strong and prominent ones. As well, there is a need to know more about black markets for the financing of rebel groups. This is an important area for research, given that the financial portfolio of rebel groups has implications for their compliance behavior. If our goal is to see the ranks of compliant rebels grow, we also have to pay more attention to intransigent rebels that look like they will never change their behavior. As I have explained, extremist groups are unlikely to respond to diplomatic engagement. Yet we also know that such groups are not easily deterred or controlled with force or the threat of force. New approaches – or new adaptations or combinations of existing approaches – are needed.[100] My contribution in this book has been to suggest ways of bringing legitimacy-seeking groups into the fold of compliant groups. Discovering ways to influence the behaviors and choices of extremist groups remains an immense challenge for the future.

[100] Trager and Zagorcheva (2005).

APPENDIX 1

Data Appendix

This appendix describes the variables in the RGIL database that were used in statistical analyses in the book. The brief description of the RGIL database is given in Chapter 4. The data were collected by utilizing existing datasets and by adding more information. The primary sources are the NSA dataset[1] and the OSV dataset.[2] The sources and collection methods are discussed in the current as well as the next section, "Notes on Data." Additional materials are available at the project website at: http://hyeranjo.wix.com/compliantrebels.

Civilian Killing by Rebel Groups: The number of civilians killed by a specific rebel group (Source: UCDP OSV dataset).

Use of Child Soldiers: Whether (1) or not (0) a rebel group used child soldiers (Source: Child Soldier International, various years; Lasley (2012); Blattman and Beber (2013)).

Detention Visit Granted by Rebel Group to the ICRC: The indicator of whether a rebel group granted full visit (2), partial visit (1), or no visit (0) to the ICRC in their detention centers. Full visit cases are where the ICRC received unimpeded access; partial visit cases are where visits were restricted to non-security detainees; no visit cases are where no visit occurred to the rebel detention centers. These involve the situations where rebel group did not detain, rebel groups refused the visit, governments denied access to the whole country, or where the ICRC failed to visit because of security situations. The full descriptions are in Jo and Thomson (2013). (Source: ICRC Annual Reports, various years.)

Legally Allowed Rebel Political Wing: Whether (1) or not (0) a rebel group has a legally allowed political wing (Source: NSA dataset, Cunningham *et al.* (2013)).

Secessionist Conflict: Whether (1) or not (0) a rebel group was engaged in secessionist conflict (Source: NSA dataset, Cunningham *et al.* (2013)).

[1] Cunningham *et al.* (2013). [2] Eck and Hultman (2007).

Number of Human Rights Organizations in Foreign State Sponsor: The number of secretariats of human rights organizations in a foreign sponsor country supporting a rebel group (Source: Salehyan *et al.* (2014)).

Rebel Strength: An ordinal measure indicating the strength of a rebel group relative to the government: much weaker (1), weaker (2), parity (3), stronger (4), and much stronger (5) (Source: NSA dataset, Cunningham *et al.* (2013)).

Strength of Central Command and Control: An indicator for the strength of the central command-and-control structure of a rebel group organization: low (1), moderate (2), and high (3) (Source: NSA dataset, Cunningham *et al.* (2013)).

Lootable Resources: Whether (1) or not (0) a rebel group operates in the region with lootable resources, such as minerals or drugs (Source: Fearon (2004); Lujala (2010)).

Territorial Control: Whether (1) or not (0) a rebel group controls some territory (Source: NSA dataset, Cunningham *et al.* (2013)).

Civilian Killing by Government: The number of civilians killed by government side (Source: UCDP OSV dataset).

Use of Child Soldiers by Government: An ordinal measure of the government recruiting children aged less than 18 into the armed forces: no (0), rare or exceptionally (1), and not uncommon (2). If more than 1 percent of the military are under 18, then coded as "not uncommon" (Source: Simmons (2010)).

Detention Visit Granted by Government to the ICRC: An indicator of whether a government granted full visit (2), partial visit (1), or no visit (0) to the ICRC in their detention centers. Full visit cases are where the ICRC received an unimpeded access; partial visit cases are where visits were restricted to non-security detainees; no visit cases are where no visit occurred to the detention centers run by governments. (Source: Jo and Thomson (2013); ICRC Annual Reports, various years).

SUMMARY STATISTICS

Variables	Observations	Mean	Std Deviation	Minimum	Maximum
Civilian killing by rebel groups	1,126	86.1590	880.9028	0	27,445
Use of child soldiers	1,127	0.5768	0.4943	0	1
Detention visit	779	0.2837	0.6652	0	2
Legal political wing	1,307	0.3481	0.4766	0	1
Secessionist conflict	1,296	0.3218	0.4673	0	1
No of HRO in foreign sponsorship	892	1.1420	5.2310	0	71
Rebel strength	1,314	1.6712	0.7312	1	5
Strength of command	1,176	2.0196	0.6315	1	3
Lootable resources	1,125	0.3911	0.4882	0	1
Territorial control	1,308	1.3784	0.4852	1	2
Government killing of civilians	1,127	210.6886	4505.816	0	150,964
Government use of child soldiers	603	2.2670	0.7945	1	3
Government detention visit	613	0.6819	0.3929	0	1

CORRELATION MATRIX

	Civilian killing by rebels	Use of child soldiers	Detention visit by rebels	Legal political wing	Secessionist conflict	HRO	Rebel strength	Central control strength	Lootable resources	Territorial control	Government civilian killing	Government use of child soldiers	Government detention visit
Civilian killing by rebels	1.000												
Use of child soldiers	−0.0374 (0.2134)	1.000											
Detention visit by rebels	0.0071 (0.8437)	0.0408 (0.2586)	1.0000										
Legal political wing	−0.0444 (0.1417)	0.0582 (0.0546)	−0.0885 (0.0145)	1.000									
Secessionist conflict	−0.0463 (0.1280)	0.0534 (0.0800)	−0.0808 (0.0268)	−0.0837 (0.0026)	1.000								
HRO	−0.0125 (0.7125)	−0.0162 (0.6354)	0.1574 (0.0001)	−0.0482 (0.1536)	−0.0163 (0.6323)	1.000							
Rebel strength	0.1061 (0.0004)	0.0004 (0.9888)	0.3268 (0.0000)	−0.0397 (0.1517)	−0.2326 (0.0000)	0.0210 (0.5351)	1.000						
Central control strength	0.0248 (0.4364)	−0.0371 (0.2465)	0.1639 (0.0000)	−0.0041 (0.8894)	0.0529 (0.0713)	0.1070 (0.0028)	0.2404 (0.0000)	1.000					
Lootable resources	0.0349 (0.2420)	0.0666 (0.0268)	0.0510 (0.1551)	0.0568 (0.0600)	−0.0790 (0.0093)	0.1112 (0.0010)	−0.0068 (0.8221)	0.0604 (0.0581)	1.000				
Territorial control	0.0511 (0.0901)	0.0854 (0.0047)	0.3940 (0.0000)	0.1970 (0.0000)	0.1158 (0.0000)	0.0397 (0.2407)	0.2137 (0.0000)	0.0494 (0.0906)	0.1493 (0.0000)	1.000			

Government civilian killing	0.0293	−0.0329	−0.0004	−0.0250	−0.0286	−0.0082	0.1126	0.0460	−0.0240	−0.0128	1.000		
	(0.3259)	(0.2734)	(0.9908)	(0.4079)	(0.3464)	(0.8096)	(0.0002)	(0.1487)	(0.4222)	(0.6719)			
Government use of child soldiers	0.0336	−0.0320	0.2166	0.1309	−0.2767	0.0973	0.1727	−0.0152	0.1123	0.1400	0.0466	1.000	
	(0.4099)	(0.4358)	(0.0000)	(0.0014)	(0.0000)	(0.0308)	(0.0000)	(0.7293)	(0.0059)	(0.0006)	(0.2540)		
Detention visit by government	0.0487	0.1461	0.1037	−0.0062	−0.0716	0.0142	0.1184	0.1171	0.0287	0.1010	0.0309	−0.0437	1.000
	(0.2283)	(0.0003)	(0.0102)	(0.8791)	(0.0813)	(0.7496)	(0.0036)	(0.0059)	(0.4780)	(0.0131)	(0.4452)	(0.4147)	

APPENDIX 2

Notes on Data

The study on rebel groups using a quantitative approach is new and developing. Because of this early effort, I feel it is necessary to put forth a note on the difficulties and challenges of collecting such data. The hope is that this kind of discussion will be useful in improving future research on a related topic. With this aim in mind, this section introduces the main sources of the RGIL database, outlines the challenges that my research team faced in constructing the database, and discusses efforts to address those data limitations and drawbacks.

The current note only deals with general issues in making the RGIL database. For specific information and issues related to each empirical measure used in Chapters 5, 6, and 7, readers are advised to consult with each chapter. For example, for readers who are interested in the civilian killing count by rebel groups, Chapter 5 will provide detailed information on that data. In the following note, for descriptions of the data collection stage, I use "my research team" or "we" to recognize the collective efforts of the students that contributed to the making of the RGIL database. For descriptions of data pertaining to the analysis stage, however, I use "I" to denote the individual effort as the author of this book.

SOURCES

The main sources of the RGIL database include academic books, journal articles, newspapers, think-tank reports, and official/unofficial reports from governments, international organizations, or NGOs. For academic books, the research team relied on historical books or journal articles on a specific rebel group. Newspaper and magazine sources include credible news channels such as Reuters, the BBC, the *New York Times*, CNN, *The Economist*, Agnes Frances, *Foreign Affairs*, and *Foreign Policy*. For recent rebel groups, the sources are often restricted to journalistic sources as well as reports from think-tanks.

International organizations also produce reliable reports on human rights violations. For instance, the reports from the United Nations Special Office of the Children and Armed Conflict served as valuable sources for building the child soldier section of the database. Various Truth and Reconciliation Commission reports, as in Sierra Leone, El Salvador, or South Africa, contained independently verified third-party information at the end the conflict, which provided views and facts on human rights violations of internal conflicts.

Non-governmental organizations were also main sources as some of them specialize in collecting and monitoring one issue area. Again, in constructing the database on child soldiering by rebel groups, the reports from Child Soldiers International and Watchlist were useful for providing the details of child soldiering practices by rebel groups. Also, "Their Words," the database constructed by Geneva Call to archive the commitments made by rebel groups, was essential in the analysis of rebel commitment to international law. Some of the unofficial documents from NGOs were acquired during interviews with the author and are noted as such in the footnotes.

For resources from think-tank and research institutes, the research team relied heavily on the reports from the Uppsala Conflict Encyclopedia for conflict narratives and backgrounders from the Council of Foreign Relations. For the rebel groups that were also classified as terrorists, the database from the Study of Terrorism and Responses to Terrorism (START) at the University of Maryland, as well as the Mapping Militant Organizations project at Stanford University served as reliable go-to sources.

The quantitative dataset was built on the following existing datasets:

(1) armed conflict datasets that define the rebel actors and developments in internal conflicts developed by Uppsala University in Sweden;
(2) NSA dataset that focuses on the rebel groups and their characteristics developed by Cunningham *et al.* (2013);
(3) OSV dataset that records the counts of civilians killed by each warring party, including rebel groups, in internal conflicts (Chapter 5);
(4) child soldier dataset in Africa developed by Lasley (2012); and Beber and Blattman (2013) (Chapter 6); and
(5) detention visit records in Jo and Thomson (2013) (Chapter 7).

These sources and adaptations of measures are discussed in the relevant chapters in full.

CHALLENGES

The three main challenges of collecting rebel group behaviors and characteristics can be summarized as:

(1) poor quality of the data (unreliable data);
(2) missing data (lack of data, or completely or partially missing data); and
(3) issues of attributing violations to a certain rebel group.

Poor quality of the data primarily comes from poor sources. Often, the details of rebel behaviors are not sufficiently known for us to determine whether those behaviors constitute violations of international law. In many uncertain cases where we did not have full circumstantial evidence, we classified them as no violations, to avoid wrong attribution of violations to a certain rebel group. Additionally, the research team encountered a lot of unreliable data, mostly unfounded allegations, produced by individual blogs or journalistic sources. We made careful efforts to avoid using those unreliable sources and relied on credible sources.

Missing data problems are generally rebel group-specific. Small and obscure groups often have missing data. There are also time trends as well. Recent rebel groups, say groups in the 2000s, receive more media attention than older, say, 1990s groups. This gave us more information for recent rebel groups than older groups. The time trend was especially evident in the case of detention visits, where the ICRC reports become more detailed over time. As a result, fewer missing values were created for recent years than for older years. However, the link between recent groups and more information does not necessarily mean that the quality of information is better for recent rebel groups than for older ones. The information about older groups is sometimes more coherent with quality information, as the information has been vetted by historians or institutions like truth commissions or other third-party verifiers.

Whether we can attribute international law violations to a certain group was another issue the research team faced in constructing the RGIL database. Particularly, attribution challenge was the greatest in the case of multiple rebel groups in one country. Many sources only say "armed groups in country X did Y." In those cases, it is not certain which group the source is specifically referring to, among many rebel groups in that country. Cross-checking was the best available option for this research team. For example, when multiple sources mentioned that the Afghan Northern Alliance, composed of five armed groups, used child soldiers, we checked whether each group used child soldiers and found out that Junbish was the only one that did not use child soldiers. In the case of insufficient sources, we opted to code conservatively and coded "no use."

EFFORTS TO ADDRESS DATA LIMITATIONS

As the author, I tackled the above-mentioned data issues several ways. I did so by focusing on the general picture of rebel compliance in accordance with the proposed theory, by relying on crude-but-correct rather than specific-but-imperfect measurements, and by dealing with the problem of missing data head-on in some cases.

The first approach was to pay close attention to the "test" of the theory proposed in this book. The data problems are acute when the data threaten our inferences about the theory. I made several efforts to ward off these inferential threats due to measurement difficulties. Amid these efforts, poor quality of information or questionable reliability of data necessitated some coarsening of measures. Rather than using detailed measures, the quantitative data are constructed at the basic level, leaving the detailed picture in the qualitative reports of the RGIL database. Given the lack of information or missing information, I chose a more crude measure that could be measured consistently. One example is the measure of rebel groups' political wings. Although I tried to uncover the political and military organizational structures of rebel groups, it is impossible to assess whether a political wing had complete control over the military wing and whether that relationship changed over time. Facing these difficulties, I settled with the measure of "presence" of a political wing. The alternative measure was the indicator as to whether the rebel political wing was "legalized" to build some political relationships with domestic constituencies. In some cases, this kind of measurement strategy required some sacrifice in validity in order to retain reliability.

The second effort was to analyze the missing or poor quality data to better understand the patterns of rebel compliance. When the missing data problems were serious, I made an effort to deal with the problem head-on. One such effort was highlighted in my analysis of the detention issue. By investigating what might have caused the data to be missing, I have analyzed rebel compliance behavior, taking into account the political processes that generated the missingness. Interested readers can refer to Chapter 7 as an example.

The third approach was to augment the data analysis with qualitative case studies. The primary goals of case studies are to illustrate the key causal mechanisms. In the course of specifying the relationships between rebel characteristics and rebel behaviors, I was able to get more of a handle on the measures closer to the intended theoretical concepts in case studies, compared with the quantitative analysis. In general, to quantify a valid concept, we need a detailed understanding of the ins and outs of the concept regarding a certain group. This was better done in the case studies where I was able to obtain more detailed information about a particular rebel group under study, so readers are encouraged to read into the qualitative measurements in the case studies as well.

Rebel data are often uncertain, but this should not deter us from studying an important phenomenon. Understanding rebel activities and characteristics is part of a growing scholarly effort, both at the micro- and macro-level. The hope is that the RGIL database provides some basis for future research efforts on the topic of civil wars, rebel groups, and international law.

APPENDIX 3

Rebel Groups and Humanitarian Violations, 1989–2009

This appendix lists the violations of international humanitarian law and human rights law as recorded in the RGIL database. The rebel group list is from the NSA dataset (v.2012). The civilian killing counts are from the OSV dataset (v.4.3, 2012). Child soldier use data are mainly from the Global Report (various years) published by the Child Soldiers International. Detention access data are from Jo and Thomson (2013). NA denotes not available. Readers should consult with each chapter about the details of those measurements and note the data limitations discussed in Appendix 2.

	Treatment of civilians 1	Treatment of civilians 2	Treatment of children	Treatment of detainees
Rebel group (country)	Yearly average killing counts	Total civilian killing counts	Used child soldiers?	Accepted ICRC visit to detention centers?
ABSDF (Myanmar)	0	0	No	No
ABSU (India)	0	0	No	No
ADF (Uganda)	87	693	Yes	No
AFDL (Democratic Republic of the Congo)	147	29,593	Yes	No
AFRC (Sierra Leone)	0	0	Yes	Yes
Al-Gamaa al-Islamiyya (Egypt)	30	181	No	No
Al-Itahad al -Islami (Ethiopia)	0	0	No	No
Al-Mahdi Army (Iraq)	23	117	No	No

(*continued*)

(*continued*)

	Treatment of civilians 1	Treatment of civilians 2	Treatment of children	Treatment of detainees
Rebel group (country)	Yearly average killing counts	Total civilian killing counts	Used child soldiers?	Accepted ICRC visit to detention centers?
Al-Shabaab (Somalia)	22	43	Yes	No
Al-Qaeda (Yemen)	NA	NA	No	No
ALF (Ethiopia)	NA	NA	NA	No
AMB (Israel)	41	124	Yes	No
Ansar al-Islam (Iraq)	30	118	No	No
APFP (Soviet Union)	0	0	No	No
AQAP (Yemen)	0	0	No	No
AQIM (Algeria)	9	102	Yes	No
ARDUF (Ethiopia)	0	0	No	No
ARIF (Myanmar)	0	0	Yes	No
ARS/UIC (Somalia)	0	0	No	No
ASG (Abu Sayyaf) (Philippines)	16	251	Yes	Yes
ASWJ (Nigeria)	0	0	No	No
ATNMC (Mali)	0	0	No	No
ATTF (India)	14	124	Yes	No
Autonomous Province of Western Bosnia (Bosnia)	0	0	No	Partial
Bakassi Boys (Nigeria)	NA	NA	No	No
Baluch Ittehad (Pakistan)	0	0	No	No
Baluchistan Republican Army (Pakistan)	0	0	No	No
BDK (Democratic Republic of the Congo)	0	0	No	No
BDSF/NDFB (India)	31	367	No	No
BLA (Pakistan)	0	0	Yes	No
BMA (Myanmar)	0	0	No	No
Boko Haram (Nigeria)	0	0	No	No
BRA (Papua New Guinea)	0	0	Yes	No
CNDD (Burundi)	267	2,124	Yes	No
CNDP (Democratic Republic of the Congo)	86	171	Yes	No
CNR (Chad)	38	115	No	No

(*continued*)

(*continued*)

Rebel group (country)	Treatment of civilians 1: Yearly average killing counts	Treatment of civilians 2: Total civilian killing counts	Treatment of children: Used child soldiers?	Treatment of detainees: Accepted ICRC visit to detention centers?
Cobras (Republic of the Congo)	NA	NA	No	No
Cocoyes (Republic of the Congo)	0	0	Yes	No
CPI-Maoist (India)	157	785	Yes	No
CPJP (Central African Republic)	0	0	No	No
CPN-M/UPF (Nepal)	111	1,217	Yes	Yes
CPP (Philippines)	6	115	No	No
CRA (Niger)	0	0	No	No
Croatian Irregulars (Croatia)	NA	NA	No	No
Croatian Republic of Bosnia and Herzegovina (Bosnia and Herzegovina)	66	132	No	No
CSNPD (Chad)	0	0	No	No
Democratic Republic of Yemen (Yemen)	0	0	No	No
Devrimci Sol (Turkey)	0	0	No	No
DHD (India)	35	35	Yes	No
DKBA (Myanmar)	NA	NA	No	No
Dniester Republic (Moldova)	0	0	No	No
EIJM (Eritrea)	0	0	No	No
ELN (Colombia)	10	149	Yes	Yes
EPL (Colombia)	0	0	No	No
EPLF (Ethiopia)	0	0	No	No
EPR (Mexico)	0	0	No	No
EPRDF (Ethiopia)	0	0	No	No
EPRLF (Sri Lanka)	0	0	No	No
ETA (Spain)	0	0	No	No
Exile and Redemption (Algeria)	0	0	No	No
EZLN (Mexico)	0	0	No	No
Faction of François Bozizé (Central African Republic)	0	0	No	No

(*continued*)

(*continued*)

	Treatment of civilians 1	Treatment of civilians 2	Treatment of children	Treatment of detainees
Rebel group (country)	Yearly average killing counts	Total civilian killing counts	Used child soldiers?	Accepted ICRC visit to detention centers?
Fatah (Israel)	0	0	Yes	No
FAPC (Democratic Republic of the Congo)	NA	NA	No	No
FARC (Colombia)	48	1,001	Yes	No
FARF (Chad)	15	30	Yes	Yes
FARS (Niger)	0	0	NA	No
FDLR (Rwanda)	NA	NA	Yes	No
FDN/Contras (Nicaragua)	0	0	No	No
FDR (Niger)	0	0	No	No
FDU (Republic of the Congo)	0	0	No	No
FIAA (Mali)	96	96	No	No
FIS (Algeria)	0	0	Yes	No
FLAA (Niger)	0	0	No	No
FLEC-FAC (Angola)	0	0	Yes	No
FLRN (Haiti)	0	0	No	No
FMLN (El Salvador)	0	0	No	No
FN (Côte d'Ivoire)	0	0	No	No
FNI (Democratic Republic of the Congo)	0	0	Yes	No
FNT (Chad)	0	0	No	No
Forces of George Athor (Sudan)	0	0	No	No
Forces of the Caucasus Emirate (Russia)	0	0	No	No
FPR (Rwanda)	192	960	No	Yes
FRETILIN (Indonesia)	0	0	Yes	No
FROLINA (Burundi)	0	0	Yes	No
FRUD (Djibouti)	0	0	No	No
FUCD (Chad)	0	0	No	No
FUNCINPEC (Cambodia)	0	0	No	No
GAM (Indonesia)	26	230	Yes	Yes
GIA (Algeria)	101	1,109	Yes	No
GICM (Morocco)	0	0	No	No

(*continued*)

(*continued*)

Rebel group (country)	Treatment of civilians 1 Yearly average killing counts	Treatment of civilians 2 Total civilian killing counts	Treatment of children Used child soldiers?	Treatment of detainees Accepted ICRC visit to detention centers?
God's Army (Myanmar)	0	0	Yes	No
Government of Armenia and ANM (Soviet Union)	0	0	NA	No
Hamas (Israel)	33	359	Yes	No
Harakat Ras Kamboni (Somalia)	0	0	No	No
Hezb-i-Islami (Afghanistan)	0	0	Yes	Yes
Hezb-i-Wahdat (Afghanistan)	0	0	Yes	Partial
Hezbollah (Israel)	0	0	Yes	No
Hizbul-Islam (Somalia)	0	0	No	No
Husseinov Military Faction	0	0	No	No
IMU (Uzbekistan)	NA	NA	No	No
INPFL (Liberia)	0	0	Yes	No
IRA (United Kingdom)	0	0	No	No
ISI (Iraq)	671	4,026	No	Yes
Islamic Legion (Chad)	0	0	No	No
Jamaat al-Muslimeen (Trinidad)	0	0	No	No
Jamiat-i-Islami (Afghanistan)	0	0	Yes	Yes
Janjaweed (Sudan)	NA	NA	No	No
JEM (Sudan)	10	69	Yes	No
JIG (Uzbekistan)	0	0	No	Yes
Jondullah (Iran)	0	0	No	No
JSS (Bangladesh)	50	199	Yes	No
Junbish-I Milli-yi Islami (Afghanistan)	0	0	No	Yes
JVP (Sri Lanka)	199	397	No	No
Kamajors (Sierra Leone)	0	0	Yes	No
Kashmir Insurgents (India)	143	2,997	Yes	No
KCP (India)	0	0	Yes	No
KDP (Iraq)	0	0	No	Yes
KDPI (Iran)	0	0	No	No

(*continued*)

(*continued*)

	Treatment of civilians 1	Treatment of civilians 2	Treatment of children	Treatment of detainees
Rebel group (country)	Yearly average killing counts	Total civilian killing counts	Used child soldiers?	Accepted ICRC visit to detention centers?
Khmer Rouge (Cambodia)	67	667	Yes	Partial
KIO (Myanmar)	0	0	Yes	No
KLA (Yugoslavia)	0	0	Yes	Yes
KNF (India)	0	0	Yes	No
KNPP (Myanmar)	0	0	Yes	No
KNU (Myanmar)	2.5	52	Yes	No
KPNLF (Cambodia)	0	0	No	No
Lebanese Army Aoun (Lebanon)	0	0	No	No
Lebanese Forces (Lebanon)	0	0	No	No
LRA (Uganda)	325	6,814	Yes	No
LRM (Laos)	0	0	No	No
LTTE (Sri Lanka)	100	2,089	Yes	Yes
LURD (Liberia)	0	0	Yes	Yes
Mahaz-e Milli (Afghanistan)	0	0	No	No
Mai Mai (Kenya)	NA	NA	Yes	No
MCC (India)	6	77	Yes	No
MDD (Chad)	0	0	No	No
MDJT (Chad)	0	0	Yes	No
MFDC (Senegal)	16	221	No	No
MILF (Philippines)	13	263	Yes	Yes
Military Faction: Forces of Amsha Desta and Merid Negusie (Ethiopia)	0	0	No	No
Military Faction: Forces of Andre Kolingba (Central African Republic)	0	0	No	No
Military Faction: Forces of General Rodriguez (Paraguay)	0	0	No	No
Military Faction: Forces of Himmler Rebu and Guy François (Haiti)	0	0	No	No

(*continued*)

(*continued*)

	Treatment of civilians 1	Treatment of civilians 2	Treatment of children	Treatment of detainees
Rebel group (country)	Yearly average killing counts	Total civilian killing counts	Used child soldiers?	Accepted ICRC visit to detention centers?
Military Faction: Forces of Honasan, Abenini, and Zumel (Philippines)	0	0	No	No
Military Faction: Forces of Hugo Chávez (Venezuela)	0	0	No	No
Military Faction: Forces of Maldoum Bada Abbas (Chad)	0	0	No	No
Military Faction: Forces of Moisés Giroldi (Panama)	0	0	No	No
Military Faction: Forces of Raol Cédras (Tajikistan)	0	0	No	No
MIU (Uzbekistan)	0	0	Yes	No
MJCDPJ (Guinea-Bissau)	0	0	Yes	Yes
MJP (Côte d'Ivoire)	0	0	Yes	Yes
MKP (Turkey)	0	0	No	No
MLC (Democratic Republic of the Congo)	0	0	Yes	Yes
MNDAA (Myanmar)	0	0	Yes	No
MNJ (Niger)	0	0	No	No
MNLF (Philippines)	0	0	Yes	No
MODEL (Liberia)	0	0	No	Yes
MOSANAT (Chad)	0	0	No	No
Movement for Peace in Tajikistan (Tajikistan)	0	0	No	No
MPA (Mali)	0	0	No	No
MPCI (Côte d'Ivoire)	103	103	Yes	Yes
MPIGO (Côte d'Ivoire)	33	65	Yes	Yes
MPS (Chad)	0	0	No	No
MQM (Pakistan)	0	0	Yes	No
MRTA (Peru)	0	0	No	No
MTA (Myanmar)	0	0	Yes	No
Mujahideen e Khalq (Iran)	0	0	No	No

(*continued*)

(*continued*)

	Treatment of civilians 1	Treatment of civilians 2	Treatment of children	Treatment of detainees
Rebel group (country)	Yearly average killing counts	Total civilian killing counts	Used child soldiers?	Accepted ICRC visit to detention centers?
National Salvation Front (Romania)	0	0	No	No
NDFBNARD (India)	25	25	No	No
NDPVF (Nigeria)	0	0	No	No
Ninjas (Republic of the Congo)	0	0	No	No
NLFT (India)	28	333	Yes	No
NMSP (Myanmar)	0	0	No	No
NPFL (Liberia)	301	601	Yes	No
NRF (Sudan)	0	0	No	Yes
NSCN (India)	35	318	Yes	No
NSCN-K (India)	0	0	Yes	No
Ntsiloulous (Republic of the Congo)	23	116	Yes	No
OLF (Ethiopia)	0	0	Yes	No
ONLF (Ethiopia)	5	82	No	No
OP Lavalas (Haiti)	0	0	No	No
OPON Forces (Azerbaijan)	0	0	No	No
Opposition Alliance (Rwanda)	513	3,592	Yes	No
Palipehutu-FNL (Burundi)	48	381	Yes	No
Patani Insurgents (Thailand)	197	1,376	No	No
PFLP (Israel)	0	0	Yes	No
PFLPNAGC (Israel)	0	0	No	No
PFNR (Chad)	NA	NA	No	No
PIJ (Israel)	7	61	Yes	No
PKK (Turkey)	57	1,205	Yes	Yes
PLA (India)	0	0	Yes	No
PLO (Israel)	0	0	Yes	No
PNA (Israel)	0	0	Yes	No
POLISARIO (Morocco)	0	0	No	No
Popular Resistance Committees (Israel)	0	0	Yes	No
PREPAK (India)	0	0	Yes	No
Presidential Guard (Comoros)	0	0	No	No

(*continued*)

(*continued*)

	Treatment of civilians 1	Treatment of civilians 2	Treatment of children	Treatment of detainees
Rebel group (country)	Yearly average killing counts	Total civilian killing counts	Used child soldiers?	Accepted ICRC visit to detention centers?
PUK (Iraq)	0	0	No	Yes
PULF (India)	0	0	Yes	No
PWG (India)	3	47	Yes	No
RAFD (Chad)	0	0	No	No
RCD (Democratic Republic of the Congo)	1,070	4,279	Yes	Yes
Real IRA (United Kingdom)	0	0	No	No
RENAMO (Mozambique)	356	1,424	Yes	No
Republic of Abkhazia (Georgia)	37	74	No	Yes
Republic of Chechnya (Russia)	18	219	No	Yes
Republic of Croatia (Yugoslavia)	0	0	No	No
Republic of Nagorno-Karabakh (Azerbaijan)	32	161	No	Yes
Republic of Slovenia (Yugoslavia)	0	0	No	No
Republic of South Ossetia (Georgia)	0	0	No	No
RFDG (Guinea)	0	0	No	No
RJF (Iraq)	0	0	No	No
RSO (Myanmar)	0	0	Yes	No
RUF (Sierra Leone)	136	1,357	Yes	Yes
SCIRI (Iraq)	0	0	No	Yes
Sendero Luminoso (Peru)	51	714	Yes	No
Serbian Irregulars (Croatia)	0	0	No	No
Serbian Republic of Bosnia and Herzegovina (Bosnia and Herzegovina)	3,114	12,454	Yes	Partial
Serbian Republic of Krajina (Croatia)	0	0	No	Yes

(*continued*)

(*continued*)

	Treatment of civilians 1	Treatment of civilians 2	Treatment of children	Treatment of detainees
Rebel group (country)	Yearly average killing counts	Total civilian killing counts	Used child soldiers?	Accepted ICRC visit to detention centers?
Sikh Insurgents (India)	270	1,348	No	No
SLM/A (Sudan)	9	63	Yes	Yes
SLM/ANAMM (Sudan)	72	72	Yes	Yes
SLM/ANA Unity (Sudan)	0	0	Yes	No
SNM (Somalia)	0	0	No	Yes
SPLM (Sudan)	85	1,362	No	Yes
SPM (Somalia)	0	0	No	Yes
SRRC (Somalia)	0	0	Yes	No
SSANAS (Myanmar)	0	0	No	No
Taliban (Afghanistan)	60	534	Yes	Yes
TNSM (Pakistan)	0	0	Yes	No
TTP (Pakistan)	220	439	Yes	No
UFDD (Chad)	0	0	No	No
UFDR (Central African Republic)	0	0	Yes	No
UFLA (India)	21	407	Yes	No
UFR (Chad)	0	0	Yes	No
UFRA (Nigeria)	0	0	No	No
UIFSA (Afghanistan)	33	200	Yes	Yes
UNITA (Angola)	178	2,496	Yes	Yes
UNLF (India)	0	0	Yes	No
UNRF II (Uganda)	57	57	No	No
UPA (Uganda)	10	40	No	No
URNG (Guatemala)	0	0	Yes	No
USC (Somalia)	25	50	No	Yes
UTO (Tajikistan)	0	0	Yes	Yes
UWSA (Myanmar)	0	0	Yes	No
Wahhabi Movement of the Buinaksk District (Russia)	0	0	No	No
WNBF (Uganda)	0	0	Yes	No
WSB (Sierra Leone)	NA	NA	No	No
Zviadists (Georgia)	NA	NA	No	No

APPENDIX 4

Rebel Groups and Legal Commitments

This appendix provides a non-exhaustive list of rebel groups' commitments to international law.

UNITED NATIONS ACTION PLANS

United Nations Action Plans are conducted between rebel groups and the UN Special Representative of the Secretary-General for Children and Armed Conflict to end the use of child soldiers.

Forces armées des forces nouvelles (FAFN)	Côte d'Ivoire	2005
Sudan Liberation Army–Minni Minawi (SLA-MM)	Sudan	2007
Moro Islamic Liberation Front (MILF)	Philippines	2009
Sudan People's Liberation Movement (SPLM)	Sudan	2009, 2012
Unified Communist Party of Nepal (UCPN-M)	Nepal	2009
Convention of Patriots for Justice and Peace (CPJP)	Central African Republic	2011

DEED OF COMMITMENT

The Deed of Commitment is provided by Geneva Call as a commitment to end the use of anti-personnel mines.

Moro Islamic Liberation Front (MILF)	Philippines	2000
Patriotic Union of Kurdistan (PUK)	Iraq	2002
Somalia Reconciliation and Restoration Council (SRRC)	Somalia	2002
United Somali Congress (USC)	Somalia	2002
Arakan Rohingya Islamic Front (ARIF)	Myanmar	2003
National Council for the Defense of Democracy–Forces for the Defense of Democracy (CNDD-FDD)	Burundi	2003
Nationalist Socialist Council of Nagaland (NSCN)	India	2003
Rohingya Solidarity Organisation (RSO)	Myanmar	2003
Kurdistan Workers' Party (PKK)	Turkey	2006
Popular Front for the Liberation of Saguia el-Hamra and Río de Oro (POLISARIO)	Morocco	2006
Kurdish Democratic Party of Iran (KDPI)	Iran	2007
Sudan People's Liberation Movement (SPLM)	Sudan	2009
Kurdistan Democratic Party (KDP/DPK)	Iraq	2010
Party of Free Life of Kurdistan (PJAK)	Iran	2010
Karenni National Progressive Party (KNPP)	Myanmar	2012

UNILATERAL DECLARATIONS

Unilateral declarations are issued by rebel groups to publicize their decision to abide by international laws. These commitments can be addressed in respect to the Geneva Conventions, the ICRC, or UN bodies focusing on particular norms or on broad aspects of human rights law. Groups can issue declarations orally, such as the FMLN in 1985, through public statements, such as the CPN-M, or by private letters to the ICRC, such as the FPR.

Farabundo Martí National Liberation Front (FMLN)	El Salvador	1985, 1988
Nicaraguan Democratic Force – Contras (FDN/Contras)	Nicaragua	1987
National Liberation Army (ELN)	Colombia	1994
Rwandese Patriotic Front (FPR)	Rwanda	1994
Zapatista Army of National Liberation (EZLN)	Mexico	1994
Declaration of War of the Zapatista National Liberation Army		

(*continued*)

(*continued*)

Kurdistan Workers' Party (PKK) *PKK Statement to the UN*	Turkey	1995
Túpac Amaru Revolutionary Movement (MRTA) *Communique No. 4*	Peru	1996
Liberation Tigers of Tamil Eelam (LTTE) *Letter to the UN Commission on Human Rights*	Sri Lanka	1998
National Liberation Army (NLA)	Macedonia	2001
Moro National Liberation Front (MNLF)	Philippines	2002, 2006
Communist Party of Nepal-Maoist (CPN-M) *Appeal of the Communist Party of Nepal*	Nepal	2004
Karenni National Progressive Party (KNPP)	Myanmar	2006, 2007
Karen National Union (KNU)	Myanmar	2007
Justice and Equality Movement (JEM) *Statement by the Opposition Movements*	Sudan	2008
Sudan Liberation Movement/Army (SLM/A) *Statement by the Opposition Movements*	Sudan	2008
National Transitional Council of Libya (NTC)	Libya	2011

BILATERAL AGREEMENTS

Bilateral agreements are between governments and their rebel counterparts, usually on the issues concerning human rights law and/or international humanitarian law.

Farabundo Martí National Liberation Front (FMLN) *Agreement on Human Rights*	El Salvador	1990
Serbian Republic of Krajina *Memorandum of Understanding of November 27, 1991*	Croatia	1991
Guatemalan National Revolutionary Unity (URNG) *Comprehensive Agreement on Human Rights*	Guatemala	1994

(*continued*)

(continued)

Revolutionary Armed Forces of Colombia (FARC) *Government–FARC Humanitarian Exchange Accord*	Colombia	2001
Moro Islamic Liberation Front (MILF) *Implementing Guidelines on the Humanitarian, Rehabilitation, and Development Aspects of the GRP–MILF Tripoli Agreement on Peace of 2001* *Agreement on the Civilian Protection Component of the International Monitoring Team (2009)*	Philippines	2002, 2009
Sudan People's Liberation Movement (SPLM) *Agreement on the Protection of Civilians and Civilian Facilities*	Sudan	2002
Justice and Equality Movement (JEM) *Agreement on Humanitarian Ceasefire on the Conflict in Darfur*	Sudan	2004
Sudan Liberation Movement/Army (SLM/A) *Agreement on Humanitarian Ceasefire on the Conflict in Darfur*	Sudan	2004

Bibliography

Abuza, Zachary 2003a. "Funding Terrorism in Southeast Asia: The Financial Network of Al Qaeda and Jemaah Islamiyah," *Contemporary Southeast Asia* 25: 169–199.

2003b. *Militant Islam in Southeast Asia: Crucible of Terror*. Boulder, CO: Lynne Rienner.

Acuña, Tathiana Flores 1995. *The United Nations Mission in El Salvador: A Humanitarian Law Perspective*. The Hague: Martinus Nijhoff.

Adamson, Fiona 2013. "Mechanisms of Diaspora Mobilization and the Transnationalization of Civil War," in Jeffrey T. Checkel (ed.), *Transnational Dynamics of Civil War*. Cambridge University Press.

Advocates for Human Rights 2009. "A House with Two Rooms: Final Report of the Truth and Reconciliation Commission of Liberia Diaspora Project," CreateSpace Independent Publishing, available at: www.theadvocatesforhumanrights.org/final_report.

Aeschlimann, Alain 2005. "Protection of Detainees: ICRC Action Behind Bars," *International Review of the Red Cross* 87: 83–122.

African National Congress 1998. "ANC Submission to the TRC in Reply to the TRC's 'Findings on the ANC'," ANC Submissions, South Africa's National Liberation Movement, October 28, available at: www.anc.org.za/show.php?id=2667.

Akhavan, Payam 2009. "Are International Criminal Tribunals a Disincentive to Peace?: Reconciling Judicial Romanticism with Political Realism," *Human Rights Quarterly* 31: 624–654.

Akol, Lam 2005. "Operation Lifeline Sudan: War, Peace and Relief in Southern Sudan," in *Choosing to Engage: Armed Groups and Peace Processes*. Conciliation Resources. Accessed at: www.c-r.org/accord-article/operation-lifeline-sudan#sthash.m9u8XbeU.dpuf.

Al-Abdeh, Malik 2013. "Rebels, Inc.," *Foreign Policy*, December 3.

Al-Gama'ah al-Islamiyah 2014. *Initiative to Stop the Violence: Sadat's Assassins and the Renunciation of Political Violence*, trans. Sherman Jackson. New Haven, CT: Yale University Press.

Allen, Tim and Koen Vlassenroot 2010. *The Lord's Resistance Army: Myth and Reality*. London: Zed Books.

Allison, Michael 2006. "Leaving the Past Behind? A Study of the FMLN and URNG Transitions to Political Parties," PhD dissertation, Florida State University.
Alonso, Rogelio and Ferdinando Reinares 2005. "Terrorism, Human Rights and Law Enforcement in Spain," *Terrorism and Political Violence* 17: 265–278.
Alston, Philip and Ryan Goodman 2012. *International Human Rights*. Oxford University Press.
Alston, Philip, Ryan Goodman, and Henry J. Steiner 2007. *International Human Rights in Context: Law, Politics, Morals*. Oxford University Press.
Alvarez, Alberto Martin 2010. "From Revolutionary War to Democratic Revolution: The Farabundo Marti National Liberation Front (FMLN) in El Salvador," Berghof Transitions Series No. 9, Berghof Conflict Research.
Aly, Heba 2014. "Islamic Law and the Rules of War," Integrated Regional Information Networks, IRIN News, April 24, available at: www.irinnews.org/report/99987/islamic-law-and-the-rules-of-war.
Amnesty International 2013a. "Rule of Fear: Isis Abuses in Detention in Northern Syria," December 19, available at: www.amnesty.org/en/library/info/MDE24/063/2013/en.
2013b. "Syria: Harrowing Torture, Summary Killings in Secret ISIS Detention Centers," December 19, available at: www.amnesty.org/en/news/syria-harrowing-torture-summary-killings-secret-isis-detention-centres-2013-12-19.
2011. "The Battle for Libya: Killings, Disappearances and Torture," September 13, available at: www.amnesty.org/en/library/info/MDE19/025/2011.
1995. "Sudan, the Tears of Orphans: No Future without Human Rights," January 1, 1995, p. 87, available at: www.amnesty.org/en/library/info/AFR54/002/1995.
Anderson, Kenneth 2000. "The Ottawa Convention Banning Landmines, the Role of International Non-Governmental Organizations and the Idea of International Civil Society," *European Journal of International Law* 11: 110–119.
Arendt, Hannah 1970. *On Violence*. New York: Harcourt, Brace & World.
Asian Center for Human Rights 2013. "India's Child Soldiers: A Shadow Report to the UN Committee on the Rights of the Child on the Involvement of Children in Armed Conflict," New Delhi, India.
Auber, Tamar 2013. "Africa: UN Security Council Charcoal Ban Poses Serious Environmental, Humanitarian Risks for Somalia," *AllAfrica*, August 28, available at: http://allafrica.com/stories/201308291082.html.
Autesserre, Séverine 2010. *The Trouble with the Congo: Local Violence and the Failure of International Peacebuilding*. Cambridge University Press.
Baaz, Maria Eriksson and Maria Stern 2009. "Why Do Soldiers Rape? Masculinity, Violence, and Sexuality in the Armed Forces in the Congo (DRC)," *International Studies Quarterly* 53: 495–518.
Bakke, Lina 2007. "The Iranian Mojahedin's Struggle for Legitimacy," MA thesis, University of Oslo.
Bale, Tim 2007. "Are Bans on Political Parties Bound to Turn out Badly? A Comparative Investigation of Three 'Intolerant' Democracies: Turkey, Spain, and Belgium," *Comparative European Politics* 5: 141–157.
Bangerter, Olivier 2012. "*Internal Control: Codes of Conduct within Insurgent Armed Groups*." Geneva: Small Arms Survey.
2011. "Reasons Why Armed Groups Choose to Respect International Humanitarian Law or Not," *International Review of the Red Cross* 93: 353–384.

2010. "Disseminating and Implementing International Humanitarian Law within Organized Armed Groups: Measures Armed Groups Can Take to Improve Respect for International Humanitarian Law," in *Non-State Actors and International Humanitarian Law: Organized Armed Groups: A Challenge for the Twenty-First Century*, International Institute of Humanitarian Law. Milan: FrancoAngeli.

Bapat, Navin 2012. "Understanding State Sponsorship of Militant Groups," *British Journal of Political Science* 42: 1–29.

Barnard, Anne 2014. "Dual Threat Has Mainstream Syrian Rebels Fearing Demise: Facing Both ISIS Militants and Bashar Al-Assad's Forces in Syria," *New York Times*, August 15.

Bassiouni, Cherif 2013. *The Shari'a and Islamic Criminal Justice in Time of War and Peace*. Cambridge University Press.

2012. *Introduction to International Criminal Law*, 2nd edn. Dordrecht: Martinus Nijhoff.

Bassiouni, Cherif and Amna Guellali (eds.) 2010. *Jihad and its Challenges to International and Domestic Law*, Hague Colloquium on Fundamental Principles of Law. Hague Academic Press.

Bates, Robert 2008. *When Things Fell Apart: State Failure in Late-Century Africa*. Cambridge University Press.

BBC 2014. "Syria Profile – Timeline," September 16, available at: www.bbc.com/news/world-middle-east-14703995.

2013a. "DR Congo's M23 Rebels: Rwandan Support 'Falling'," July 5, available at: www.bbc.com/news/world-africa-23198141.

2013b. "Leading Syrian Rebel Groups Form New Islamic Front," November 22, available at: www.bbc.com/news/world-middle-east-25053525.

2012. "DR Congo: US Sanctions M23 Rebel Leader Sultani Makenga," November 14, available at: www.bbc.com/news/world-africa-20325993.

Beber, Bernd and Christopher Blattman 2013. "The Logic of Child Soldiering and Coercion," *International Organization* 67: 65–104.

Beck, Colin and Emily Miner 2013. "Who Gets Designated a Terrorist and Why?" *Social Forces* 91: 837–871.

Beetham, David 1991. *The Legitimation of Power*. Houndsmill: Macmillan.

Bell, Christine 2008. *On the Law of Peace: Peace Agreements and the Lex Pacificatoria*. Oxford University Press.

2003. *Peace Agreements and Human Rights*. Oxford University Press.

Bellal, Annyssa and Stuart Casey-Maslen 2011. "Rules of Engagement: Protecting Civilians through Dialogue with Armed Non-State Actors," Geneva Academy of International Humanitarian Law and Human Rights, October.

Betancur, Belisario, Reinaldo Figueredo Planchart, and Thomas Buergenthal 1993. "From Madness to Hope: The 12-Year War in El Salvador: Report of the Commission on the Truth for El Salvador," Commission on the Truth for El Salvador. Truth Commission Digital Collection, United States Institute of Peace, available at: www.usip.org/sites/default/files/file/ElSalvador-Report.pdf.

Bixler, Amanda 2002. "Private Enforcement of International Human Rights Laws: Could a Small Church Group Successfully Combat Slavery in the Sudan," *Chicago Journal of International Law* 3: 511.

Blanchard, Christopher and Amy Belasco 2014. "Proposed Train and Equip Authorities for Syria: In Brief," Congressional Research Report No. 43727, Congressional Research Service, Washington, DC, September 16.

Blattman, Christopher and Jeannie Annan 2010. "The Consequences of Child Soldiering," *Review of Economics and Statistics* 92: 882–898.

Blaydes, Lisa and Lawrence Rubin 2008. "Ideological Reorientation and Counterterrorism: Confronting Militant Islam in Egypt," *Terrorism and Political Violence* 20: 461–479.

Bloom, Mia and Roy Licklider 2007. *Living Together after Ethnic Killing*. London: Routledge.

Bloom, Rebecca 2007. "Backgrounder: Ogaden National Liberation Front (ONLF)," Council on Foreign Relations, November 1, available at: www.cfr.org/ethiopia/ogaden-national-liberation-front-onlf/p13208.

Bøås, Morten and Kevin Dunn 2007. *African Guerrillas: Raging Against the Machine*. Boulder, CO: Lynne Rienner.

Bob, Clifford 2005. *The Marketing of Rebellion: Insurgents, Media, and International Activism*. Cambridge University Press.

Boghardt, Lori Plotkin 2014. "Saudi Funding of ISIS," Policywatch 2275, Washington Institute, June 23, available at: www.washingtoninstitute.org/policy-analysis/view/saudi-funding-of-isis.

Bollen, Kenneth 2002. "Latent Variables in Psychology and the Social Sciences," *Annual Review of Psychology* 53: 605–634.

Bond, James 1971. "Protection of Non-Combatants in Guerrilla Wars," *William and Mary Law Review* 12: 787–804.

Boot, Max 2013. *Invisible Armies: An Epic History of Guerrilla Warfare from Ancient Times to the Present*. New York: Liveright.

Booth, John and Mitchell Seligson 2009. *The Legitimacy Puzzle in Latin America: Political Support and Democracy in Eight Nations*. Cambridge University Press.

Booth, Martin 1996. *Opium: A History*. New York: St. Martin's Press.

Boutellis, Arthur 2012. "In the DRC Communications Wars, Rebels Learn PoC Language," International Peace Institute, July 25, available at: http://theglobalobservatory.org/2012/07/in-the-drc-communications-war-rebels-learn-poc-language.

Brabazon, James 2003. "Liberia: Liberians United for Reconciliation and Democracy (LURD)," Armed Non-State Actors Project Briefing Paper No. 1, Royal Institute of International Affairs, Africa Programme, February 2003.

Bradbury, Mark, Nicholas Leader, and Kate Mackintosh 2000. "The 'Agreement on Ground Rules' in South Sudan," in *The Politics of Principle: Principles of Humanitarian Action in Practice*. London: Overseas Development Institute.

Branch, Adam 2011. *Displacing Human Rights: War and Intervention in Northern Uganda*. Oxford University Press.

Bukay, David 2004. *Muhammad's Monsters: A Comprehensive Guide to Radical Islam for Western Audiences*. Green Forest, AR: New Leaf Publishing.

Byman, Daniel, Peter Chalk, Bruce Hoffman, William Rosenau, and David Brannan 2001. *Trends in Outside Support for Insurgent Movements*. Santa Monica, CA: RAND Corporation.

Cammett, Melani 2014. *Compassionate Communalism: Welfare and Sectarianism in Lebanon*. Ithaca, NY: Cornell University Press.

Capizzi, Elaine, Helen Hill, and Dave Macey 1976. "Fretilin and the Struggle for Independence in East Timor," *Race and Class* 17: 381–395.

Caris, Charles and Samuel Reynolds 2014. "ISIS Governance in Syria," Middle East Security Report No. 22, July, Institute for the Study of War, Washington, DC.

Carter, Jimmy 2005. "The Case for Engagement: An Interview with President Carter," Conciliation Resources, London.

Casalin, Deborah 2011. "Taking Prisoners: Reviewing the International Humanitarian Law Grounds for Deprivation of Liberty by Armed Opposition Groups," *International Review of the Red Cross* 93: 743–757.

Cassese, Antonio 2008. *International Criminal Law*, 2nd edn. Oxford University Press.

Cederman, Lars-Erik, Kristian Gleditsch, and Halvard Buhaug 2013. *Inequality, Grievances, and Civil War*. Cambridge University Press.

Central Intelligence Agency 1993. "Religious Groups and Their Ties to the FMLN," CIA, unclassified document by Freedom of Information Act, available at: www.foia.cia.gov/sites/default/files/document_conversions/89801/DOC_0000049389.pdf.

Chalk, Peter 2013. "The Bangsamoro Islamic Freedom Fighters: The Newest Obstacles to Peace in the Southern Philippines?" *CTC Sentinel*, Combating Terrorism Center at West Point, New York.

Chandra, Uday 2014. "The Maoist Movement in Contemporary India," *Social Movement Studies: Journal of Social, Cultural and Political Protest* 13(3): 414–419, dx.doi.org/10.1080/14742837.2013.845730.

Charity and Security Network 2012 "Safeguarding Humanitarianism in Armed Conflict: A Call for Reconciling International Legal Obligations and Counterterrorism Measures in the United States," June 5, available at: www.charityandsecurity.org/SafeguardingHumanitarianism.

Charron, Andrea 2013. *UN Sanctions and Conflict: Responding to Peace and Security Threats*. London: Routledge.

Chaulia, Sreeram 2011. *International Organizations and Civilian Protection: Power, Ideas and Humanitarian Aid in Conflict Zones*. London: Tauris.

Cheney, Catherine 2012. "Ethiopia's Oromo Liberation Front Shifts from Violence to Politics," *World Politics Review*, January 4.

Chenoweth, Erica and Maria Stephan 2012. *Why Civil Resistance Works: The Strategic Logic of Nonviolent Conflict*, Columbia Studies in Terrorism and Irregular Warfare. New York: Columbia University Press.

Child Soldiers International 2008a. "Child Soldiers Global Report 2008 – Occupied Palestine Territory," Coalition to Stop the Use of Child Soldiers, available at: www.child-soldiers.org/chapter_reader.php?id=212.

2008b. "Child Soldiers Global Report 2008 – Ethiopia," Coalition to Stop the Use of Child Soldiers, available at: www.refworld.org/docid/486cb0fec.html.

2008c. "Child Soldiers Global Report 2008 – Côte d'Ivoire," Coalition to Stop the Use of Child Soldiers, available at: www.refworld.org/docid/486cb0f72.html.

2004. "Child Soldiers Global Report 2004 – Sudan," Coalition to Stop the Use of Child Soldiers, available at: www.child-soldiers.org/global_report_reader.php?id=281.

2001. "Child Soldiers Global Report 2001 – Colombia," Coalition to Stop the Use of Child Soldiers, available at: www.child-soldiers.org/global_report_reader.php?id=281.

Christia, Fotini 2012. *Alliance Formation in Civil Wars*. Cambridge University Press.

Clapham, Andrew 2010. "The Rights and Responsibilities of Armed Non-State Actors: The Legal Landscape and Issues Surrounding Engagement," Geneva Academy of International Humanitarian Law and Human Rights, available at: http://ssrn.com/abstract=1569636.

2006. *Human Rights of Non-State Actors*. Oxford University Press.

Clapham, Christopher (ed.) 1998. *African Guerrillas*. Bloomington, IN: Indiana University Press.

Clark, Phil 2011. "Chasing Cases: The ICC and the Politics of State Referral in the Democratic Republic of Congo and Uganda," in Carsten Stahn and Mohamed M. El Zeidy (eds.), *The International Criminal Court and Complementarity: From Theory to Practice*, vol. II. Cambridge University Press.

Clark, Roger 1980. "The 'Decolonization' of East Timor and the United Nations Norms on Self-Determination and Aggression," *Yale Journal of World Public Order* 7: 2–44.

Clemons, Steve 2014. "'Thank God for the Saudis': ISIS, Iraq, and the Lessons of Blowback," *The Atlantic*, June 23, available at: www.theatlantic.com/international/archive/2014/06/isis-saudi-arabia-iraq-syria-bandar/373181.

Cohen, Dara 2013. "Explaining Rape during Civil War: Cross-National Evidence (1980–2009)," *American Political Science Review* 107: 461–477.

Cohen, Dara and Ragnhild Nordås 2014. "Sexual Violence in Armed Conflict: Introducing the SVAC Dataset, 1989–2009," *Journal of Peace Research* 51: 418–428.

2013. "Sexual Violence in Armed Conflict (SVAC) Dataset: Codebook and User Instruction Guide," Version 1.0, last revised, October 23, 2013, available at: www.sexualviolencedata.org.

Cole, Wade and Francisco Ramirez 2013. "Conditional Decoupling: Assessing the Impact of National Human Rights Institutions, 1981 to 2004," *American Sociological Review* doi:10.1177/0003122413492762.

Collier, Paul and Anke Hoeffler 2000. "Greed and Grievance in Civil War," *Oxford Economic Papers* 56: 563–595.

Cronin, Audrey Kurth 2011. *How Terrorism Ends*. Princeton University Press.

Cunningham, David, Kristian Gleditsch, and Idean Salehyan 2013. "Non-State Actors in Civil Wars: A New Dataset," *Conflict Management and Peace Science* 30: 516–531.

Dabone, Zakaria 2011. "International Law: Armed Groups in a State-Centric System," *International Review of the Red Cross* 93: 395–424.

Dai, Xinyuan 2005. "Why Comply? The Domestic Constituency Mechanism," *International Organization* 59: 363–398.

Davenport, Christian and Allan Stam 2009. "What Really Happened in Rwanda?" *Pacific Standard*, October 6, available at: www.psmag.com/navigation/politics-and-law/what-really-happened-in-rwanda-3432.

De Zayas, Alfred 2005. "Human Rights and Indefinite Detention," *International Review of the Red Cross* 87: 15–38.

Devi N., Rebecca 2008. "Conflict Situations and Children's Education in Manipur," *Journal of Indian Education* 34: 25–31.

Dickinson, Elizabeth 2013. "Playing with Fire: Why Private Gulf Financing for Syria's Extremist Rebels Risks Igniting Sectarian Conflict at Home," Saban Center Analysis Paper Series, No. 31. Washington, DC: Brookings Institution.

Dietrich, Christian 2000. "UNITA's Diamond Mining and Exporting Capacity," in Jakkie Cilliers and Christian Dietrich (eds.), *Angola's War Economy: The Role of Oil and Diamonds*. Pretoria: Institute for Security Studies.

Donohue, William and Moty Cristal 2012. "Growing Out in Organization," in William Zartman and Guy Olivier Faure (eds.), *Engaging Extremists: Trade-Offs, Timing, and Diplomacy*. Washington, DC: United States Institute of Peace Press.

Downes, Alexander 2008. *Targeting Civilians in War*. Ithaca, NY: Cornell University Press.

Downs, George and Michael Jones 2002. "Reputation, Compliance and International Law," *Journal of Legal Studies* 31: S95–S114.

Doyle, Michael, Ian Johnstone, and Robert Orr (eds.), 1997. *Keeping the Peace: Multidimensional UN Operations in Cambodia and El Salvador*. Cambridge University Press.

Doyle, Michael and Nicholas Sambanis 2006. *Making War and Building Peace: United Nations Peace Operations*. Princeton University Press.

Drumbl, Mark 2012. *Reimagining Child Soldiers in International Law and Policy*. Oxford University Press.

2007. *Atrocity, Punishment, and International Law*. Cambridge University Press.

Dudouet, Veronique 2012. "Intra-Party Dynamics and the Political Transformation of Non-State Armed Groups," *International Journal of Conflict and Violence* 6(1): 96–108.

Eck, Kristine and Lisa Hultman 2012. "UCDP One-Sided Violence Dataset V.1.4–2012, 1989–2011," Uppsala Conflict Data Program, Uppsala University, Department of Peace and Conflict Research.

2007. "One-Sided Violence against Civilians in War: Insights from New Fatality Data," *Journal of Peace Research* 44: 223–246.

Economist Intelligence Unit 2013. "Spain: Political Forces at a Glance," July 25, available at: http://country.eiu.com/article.aspx?articleid=1320764116&Country=Spain&topic=Summary&subtopic=Political+forces+at+a+glance.

Eichstaedt, Peter 2009. *First Kill Your Family: Child Soldiers of Uganda and the Lord's Resistance Army*. Chicago Review Press.

Espejo, Edwin 2014. "Philippine Gov't, MILF End Crucial 10-Day Peace Talks in Agreement," *Asian Correspondent*, August 11.

European Sudanese Public Affairs Council 1998. "The SPLA and Human Rights in Sudan," ESPAC Briefing Paper No. 2, London, May.

Evans, Martin 2004. "Senegal: Mouvement des Forces Démocratiques de Casamance (MFDC)," Chatham House Briefing Paper, Africa Programme, Armed Non-State Actors AFP BP 04/02, December.

Ewumbue-Monono, Churchill 2006. "Respect for International Humanitarian Law by Armed Non-State Actors in Africa," *International Review of the Red Cross* 88: 905–924.

Fabienne, Peter 2010. "Political Legitimacy," in Edward N. Zalta (ed.), *Stanford Encyclopedia of Philosophy*. Stanford, CA: Metaphysics Research Laboratory, Center for the Study of Language and Information.

Fair, Christine 2007. "The Sri Lankan Tamil Diaspora: Sustaining Conflict and Pushing for Peace," in Hazel Smith and Paul Stares (eds.), *Diasporas in Conflict: Peacemakers or Peace Wreckers?* Tokyo: United Nations University Press.

Fajardo, Nonoy 2003. "Children in the Crossfire: Prevention and Rehabilitation of Child Soldiers," presentation at the Conference on Child Soldiers organized by the United States Department of Labor, available at: www.dol.gov/ilab/programs/iclp/childsoldiers/event_overview.htm.

Farmer, Ben 2011. "Taliban Use of Improvised Explosive Devices (IEDs) Reaches Record High in Afghanistan," *Telegraph*, August 8, available at: www.telegraph.co.uk/news/worldnews/asia/afghanistan/8689408/Taliban-use-of-IEDs-reaches-record-high-in-Afghanistan.html.

Fast, Larissa 2013. *Aid in Danger*. Philadelphia, PA: University of Pennsylvania Press.

Fazal, Tanisha 2013. "Secessionism and Civilian Targeting," paper presented at the American Political Science Association Annual Meeting, Chicago, IL, August 29–September 1.

Fearon, James 2004. "Separatist Wars, Partition, and World Order," *Security Studies* 13: 394–415.

Fisher, Max 2012. "Of Course this Congolese Rebel Group Has a Facebook Fan Page," *Washington Post*, October 29, 2012, available at: www.washingtonpost.com/blogs/worldviews/wp/2012/10/19/of-course-this-congolese-rebel-group-has-a-facebook-fan-page.

FMLN (Farabundo Martí National Liberation Front) 1988. *The Legitimacy of Our Methods of Struggle*. Berkeley, CA: Inkworks Press.

Franck, Thomas 1990. *The Power of Legitimacy among Nations*. Oxford University Press.

Gahr Støre, Jonas 2012. "In Defense of Dialogue," TED talk, available at: www.ted.com/talks/jonas_gahr_store_in_defense_of_dialogue.html.

Gambhir, Harleen 2014. "Dabiq: The Strategic Messaging of the Islamic State," ISW Backgrounder, Institute for the Study of War, Washington, DC, August 15.

Gandhi, Jennifer and Ellen Lust-Okar 2009. "Elections under Authoritarianism," *Annual Review of Political Science* 12: 403–422.

Gazagne, Philippe 2009. "Engaging Armed Non-State Actors on the Issue of Child Recruitment and Use," in David Nosworthy (ed.), *Seen, but Not Heard: Placing Children and Youth on the Security Governance Agenda*. Geneva: Center for the Democratic Control of Armed Forces.

Gberie, Lansana 2005. *A Dirty War in West Africa: The RUF and the Destruction of Sierra Leone*. Bloomington, IN: Indiana University Press.

Geneva Academy 2013. "Reaction to Norms: Armed Groups and the Protection of Civilians," Policy Briefing, Geneva Academy of International Humanitarian Law and Human Rights.

Geneva Call 2012a. "Annual Report 2012," available at: www.genevacall.org/wp-content/uploads/dlm_uploads/2014/06/2012-Geneva-Call-Annual-Report.pdf.

2012b. "Burma/Myanmar: Two Armed Groups Undertake Not to Use Child Soldiers," Press Release, August 6, available at: http://reliefweb.int/report/myanmar/two-armed-groups-undertake-not-use-child-soldiers-first-sign-geneva-call%E2%80%99s-deed.

2010a. "Communique: Iranian Kurdish Organizations Prohibit the Use of Anti-Personnel Mines," April 21, available at: www.genevacall.org/iranian-kurdish-organizations-prohibit-use-anti-personnel-mines.

2010b. "Fact Finding During Armed Conflict: Report of the 2009 Verification Mission to the Philippines to Investigate Allegations of Anti-Personnel Landmine Use by the Moro Islamic Liberation Front, " available at: www.genevacall.org/wp-content/uploads/dlm_uploads/2013/12/Report-of-the-2009-Verification-Mission-to-the-

Philippines-to-Investigate-Allegations-of-Anti-Personnel-Landmine-Use-by-the-Moro-Islamic-Liberation-Front.pdf.

Gilley, Bruce 2009. *The Right to Rule: How States Win and Lose Legitimacy*. New York: Columbia University Press.

2006. "The Meaning and Measure of State Legitimacy: Results for 72 Countries," *European Journal of Political Research* 45: 499–525.

Gillioz, Christophe 2012. "On ICRC Engagement with Non-State Armed Groups: Recent Developments," Program on Humanitarian Policy and Conflict Research, available at: www.hpcrresearch.org/blog/hpcr/2012-04-02/icrc-engagement-non-state-armed-groups-recent-developments.

Gleditsch, Kristian, Simon Hug, Livia Isabella Schubiger, and Julian Wucherpfennig 2011. "International Conventions and Non-State Actors: Selection, Signaling, and Reputation Effects," paper presented at the Fourth Conference on the Political Economy of International Organizations, Zurich, January 27–29.

Gleditsch, Nils, Peter Wallensteen, Mikael Eriksson, Margareta Sollenberg, and Strand Havard 2002. "Armed Conflict 1946–2001: A New Dataset," *Journal of Peace Research* 39: 615–637.

Goodhand, Jonathan 2006. *Aiding Peace?: The Role of NGOs in Armed Conflict*. Boulder, CO: Lynne Rienner.

Gorur, Aditi 2012a. "Striking While the Iron's Hot: The Case for Humanitarian Engagement with M23 after Goma," *Spotlight*, Stimson Center, Washington, DC, December 21.

2012b. "Turning Talk into Action: Encouraging M23 to Uphold Human Rights," *Spotlight*, Stimson Center, Washington, DC, October 31.

Graver, Ane Broch 2005. "ANC – a Legitimate Giant? The Legitimacy of the ANC Government in South Africa," Thesis, Oslo University.

Guardian 2012. "Al-Qaida-Linked Islamists in Mali Threaten French Citizen after UN Move," October 13, available at: www.theguardian.com/world/2012/oct/13/al-qaida-islamists-mali-french-citizens-un.

Gunter, Michael 1996. "The KDP–PUK Conflict in Northern Iraq," *Middle East Journal* 50: 224–241.

Gurr, Ted 1969. *Why Men Rebel*. Princeton University Press.

Guzman, Andrew 2008. *How International Law Works*. Cambridge University Press.

Hafner-Burton, Emilie 2013. *Making Human Rights a Reality*. Princeton University Press.

Hamberg, Stephan 2013. "Transnational Advocacy Networks, Rebel Groups, and Demobilization of Child Soldiers in Sudan," in Jeffrey Checkel (ed.), *Transnational Dynamics of Civil War*. New York: Cambridge University Press.

Harmer, Adele 2004. "Aid to Poorly Performing Countries: Sudan Case Study," Background Paper No. 5, ODI Study on Poor Performing Countries, Overseas Development Institute, London.

Hazen, Jennifer 2013. *What Rebels Want: Resources and Supply Networks in Wartime*. Ithaca, NY: Cornell University Press.

Healy, Joseph and Donald Sybertz 1996. *Towards an African Narrative Theology*. New York: Orbis.

Henckaerts, Jean-Marie and Louise Doswald-Beck 2005. *Customary International Humanitarian Law*. Cambridge University Press.

Herbst, Jeffrey 2004. "African Militaries and Rebellion: The Political Economy of Threat and Combat Effectiveness," *Journal of Peace Research* 41: 357–369.

Hersh, Joshua 2013. "Syrian People Struggle to Survive Humanitarian Disaster Hidden From Western Eyes," *Huffington Post*, December 17, available at: www.huffingtonpost.com/2013/12/17/syria-aleppo-humanitarian-crisis_n_4455694.html.

Hill, Daniel W., Will H. Moore, and Bumba Mukherjee 2013. "Information Politics Versus Organizational Incentives: When are Amnesty International's 'Naming and Shaming' Reports Biased?" *International Studies Quarterly* 57: 219–232.

Hofmann, Claudia and Ulrich Schneckener 2011. "Engaging Non-State Armed Actors in State- and Peace-Building: Options and Strategies," *International Review of the Red Cross* 93: 603–621.

Hogg, Jonny and Louis Charbonneau 2013. "UN's Gamble in Eastern DRC," *Independent on Sunday*, September 1.

Horstmann, Alexander 2011. "Sacred Networks and Struggles among the Karen Baptists across the Thailand–Burma Border," *Moussons* 17: 85–104.

Hovil, Lucy and Erik Werker 2005. "Portrait of a Failed Rebellion: An Account of Rational, Sub-Optimal Violence in Western Uganda," *Rationality and Society* 17: 5–34.

Howse, Robert and Ruti Teitel 2010. "Beyond Compliance: Rethinking Why International Law Really Matters," *Global Policy* 1: 127–136.

Huang, Reyko 2013. "Rebel Diplomacy in Civil Wars," paper presented at the Annual Meeting of the American Political Science Association, Chicago, IL, August 29–September 1.

2012. "The Wartime Origins of Postwar Democratization," PhD dissertation, Columbia University.

Hudson, Valerie, Bonnie Ballif-Spanvill, Mary Caprioli, and Chad Emmett 2012. *Sex and World Peace*. New York: Colombia University Press.

Hultman, Lisa, Jacob Kathman, and Megan Shannon 2013. "United Nations Peacekeeping and Civilian Protection in Civil War," *American Journal of Political Science* 57(4): 875–891.

Human Rights Watch 2014a. "Child Soldiers Worldwide," available at: www.hrw.org/node/105699.

2014b. "Maybe We Live and Maybe We Die: Recruitment and Use of Children by Armed Groups in Syria," June 23, available at: www.hrw.org/reports/2014/06/22/maybe-we-live-and-maybe-we-die.

2014c. "Syria: Armed Groups Send Children into Battle," June 23, available at: www.hrw.org/news/2014/06/22/syria-armed-groups-send-children-battle.

2012. "No Place for Children: Child Recruitment, Forced Marriage, and Attacks on Schools in Somalia," February 20, available at: www.hrw.org/reports/2012/02/20/no-place-children.

2010. "ICC: Q&A on the Trial of Jean-Pierre Bemba," November 22, available at: www.hrw.org/news/2010/11/18/bemba-qa.

2008a. "Collective Punishment: War Crimes and Crimes against Humanity in the Ogaden Area of Ethiopia's Somali Region," available at: www.hrw.org/reports/2008/ethiopia0608.

2008b. "Killings in Kiwanja: The UN's Inability to Protect Civilians," December 12, available at: www.hrw.org/reports/2008/12/12/killings-kiwanja.

2004. "Sri Lanka: Tamil Tigers Forcibly Recruit Child Soldiers," available at: www.hrw.org/news/2004/11/09/sri-lanka-tamil-tigers-forcibly-recruit-child-soldiers.

Humphreys, Macartan and Jeremy Weinstein 2008. "Who Fights? The Determinants of Participation in Civil War" *American Journal of Political Science* 52: 436–455.

IHS Jane's Terrorism & Insurgency Center 2013. "Analysis: Syria's Insurgent Landscape," September, available at: www.ihs.com/pdfs/Syrias-Insurgent-Landscape-oct-2013.pdf.

Iliopoulos, Katherine 2009. "Sierra Leone Rebels Guilty of Crimes against Humanity," Crimes of War, available at: www.crimesofwar.org/commentary/sierra-leone-rebels-guilty-of-crimes-against-humanity.

Immigration and Refugee Board of Canada 2012. "Democratic Republic of the Congo: Movement for the Liberation of Congo (Mouvement de Libération du Congo, MLC), Including Leadership and Treatment of Party Members (2009–2012)," available at: www.refworld.org/docid/4f9e58782.html.

Integrated Regional Information Networks 2013. "Engaging with Philippine Armed Groups," *IRIN News*, April 25, available at: www.irinnews.org/report/97918/engaging-with-philippine-armed-groups.

2011. "Philippines: Moves to End Use of Child Soldiers, but Problem Persists," *IRIN News*, April 8, available at: www.irinnews.org/report/92416/philippines-moves-to-end-use-of-child-soldiers-but-problem-persists.

2002. "DRC: Rights Group Condemns Beating of Activists," *IRIN News*, March 20, available at: www.irinnews.org/fr/report/30809/drc-rights-group-condemns-beating-of-activists.

Inter-American Commission on Human Rights 1993. "Irregular Armed Groups and Human Rights," available at: www1.umn.edu/humanrts/iachr/indig-guat-ch11.html.

International Committee of the Red Cross 2013. "Annual Report 2012," available at: www.icrc.org/eng/resources/documents/annual-report/icrc-annual-report-2012.htm.

International Council on Human Rights Policy 2000. "Ends and Means: Human Rights Approaches to Armed Groups," available at: www.ichrp.org/files/reports/6/105_report_en.pdf.

International Institute of Humanitarian Law 2010. *Non-State Actors and International Humanitarian Law. Organized Armed Groups: A Challenge for the 21st Century*. Milan: FrancoAngeli.

Irrawaddy 2000. "KNU Chairman Padoe Saw Ba Thin Sein Interview: Every Karen Must Be Involved in Political Destiny," *Irrawaddy News*, June 1, available at: www2.irrawaddy.org/print_article.php?art_id=3573.

Jackson, Ashley and Antonio Giustozzi 2012. "Talking to the Other Side: Humanitarian Engagement with the Taliban in Afghanistan," Humanitarian Policy Group, Overseas Development Institute, London, December.

Jackson, Sherman 2009. "Beyond Jihad: The New Thought of the Gama'a Islamiyya," *Journal of Islamic Law and Culture* 11: 52–69.

Jahate, Lamin 2013. "Senegal Rebels Alienate Those They Fight For," Al Jazeera, January 13.

Jalabi, Raya 2014. "Who Are the Yazidis and Why Is Isis Hunting Them?" *Guardian*, August 11, available at: www.theguardian.com/world/2014/aug/07/who-yazidi-isis-iraq-religion-ethnicity-mountains.

Jardin, Matthew 2010. "East Timor, the United Nations, and the International Community: Force Feeding Human Rights into the Institutionalized Jaws of Failure," *Pacifica Review* 12: 47–62.

Jenkins, P. Nash 2014. "The Vast Majority of Syrians are Opposed to an Islamic Caliphate," *Time*, July 9.

Jo, Hyeran and Josiah Barrett 2014. "Commitment and Compliance by Rebel Groups: Case of United Nations Action Plans," unpublished manuscript, Texas A&M University.

Jo, Hyeran and Beth Simmons 2014. "Can the International Criminal Court Deter Atrocity?" 18 December, available at: SSRN: http://ssrn.com/abstract=2552820 or http://dx.doi.org/10.2139/ssrn.2552820.

Jo, Hyeran and Catarina Thomson 2013. "Legitimacy and Compliance with International Law: Access to Detainees in Civil Conflicts 1991–2006," *British Journal of Political Science* 44: 323–355.

Kahl, Colin 2007. "In the Crossfire or the Crosshairs? Norms, Civilian Casualties, and US Conduct in Iraq," *International Security* 32: 7–46.

Kahler, Miles 2000. "Conclusion: The Causes and Consequences of Legalization," *International Organization* 54: 661–683.

Kalyvas, Stathis 2008. "Promises and Pitfalls of an Emerging Research Program: The Microdynamics of Civil War," in Ian Shapiro, Tarek Masoud, and Stathis N. Kalyvas (eds.), *Order, Conflict, and Violence*. Cambridge University Press.

2006. *The Logic of Violence in Civil War*. New York: Cambridge University Press.

Kalyvas, Stathis and Laia Balcells 2010. "International System and Technologies of Rebellion: How the Cold War Shaped Internal Conflict," *American Political Science Review* 104: 415–429.

Kaplan, Eben 2005. "Child Soldiers Around the World," CFR Backgrounder, Council on Foreign Relations, available at: www.cfr.org/human-rights/child-soldiers-around-world/p9331.

Kay, Joseph 2013. "Behind Rebel Lines: Living with the M23 in DR Congo," Think Africa Press, August 29, available at: www.thinkafricapress.com/drc/living-m23-taxes.

Keen, David 2012. *Useful Enemies: When Waging Wars is More Important than Winning Them*. New Haven, CT: Yale University Press.

1998. *The Economic Functions of Violence in Civil Wars*. Oxford University Press.

Keenan, Paul 2012a. "The Karen National Union Negotiations, 1949–2012," Burma Center for Ethnic Studies, Chiang Mai University, Thailand.

2012b. "Karenni (Kayah) State: The Situation Regarding the Peace Process in Karenni (Kayah) State," Briefing Paper No. 9, July, Burma Center for Ethnic Studies, Chiang Mai University, Thailand.

Kelman, Herbert 2001. "Social and Psychological Processes of Legitimization and Delegitimization," in John T. Jost and Brenda Major (eds.), *The Psychology of Legitimacy: Emerging Perspectives on Ideology, Justice and Intergroup Relations*. Cambridge University Press.

Kinsella, Helen 2011. *The Image before the Weapon: A Critical History of the Distinction between Combatant and Civilian*. Ithaca, NY: Cornell University Press.

Kleffner, Jann 2012. "The Law and Policy of Complementarity in Relation to 'Criminal Proceedings' Carried out by Non-State Organized Armed Groups," in Carsten Stahn and Mohamed M. El Zeidy (eds.), *The International Criminal*

Court and Complementarity: From Theory to Practice, vol. II. Cambridge University Press, 707–720.

Kok, Naomi 2013. "The International Conference on the Great Lakes Region," *African Studies Review* 22: 277–281.

Krieger, Heike (ed.) forthcoming. *Patterns of Inducing Compliance – Ensuring Respect for International Humanitarian Law in War-Torn Areas of Limited Statehood*. Cambridge University Press.

Kuperman, Alan 2008. "The Moral Hazard of Humanitarian Intervention: Lessons from the Balkans," *International Studies Quarterly* 52: 49–80.

Laitin, David 2007. *Nations, States, and Violence*. Oxford University Press.

Lake, David 2007. "Building Legitimate States: Order, Authority, and International Trusteeship," unpublished manuscript, University of California, San Diego.

Lamb, Robert 2014. "Rethinking Legitimacy and Illegitimacy: A New Approach to Assessing Support and Opposition across Disciplines," a Report of the Center for Strategic and International Studies (CSIS) Program on Crisis, Conflict, and Cooperation.

Landmine and Cluster Munition Monitor 2013. "Myanmar/Burma Mine Ban Policy," Regional Profiles, October 30, available at: www.the-monitor.org/index.php/cp/display/region_profiles/theme/2870.

2004. "Afghanistan," *Landmine Monitor Report 2004: Toward a Mine-Free World*, available at: www.the-monitor.org/index.php/publications/display?url=lm/2004/afghanistan.html.

Lasley, Trace 2012. "Creed vs. Deed: Secession, Legitimacy, and the Use of Child Soldiers," PhD dissertation, University of Kentucky.

Lessa, Francesca and Leigh Payne 2013. *Amnesty in the Age of Human Rights Accountability: Comparative and International Perspectives*. Cambridge University Press.

Lidow, Nicholai 2008. "Feeding Civil War: Markets, Resources, and Rebel Organizations," unpublished manuscript, Stanford University.

Lipset, Seymour Martin 1983. *Political Man: The Social Bases of Politics*. London: Heinemann.

Lujala, Päivi 2010. "The Spoils of Nature: Armed Civil Conflict and Rebel Access to Natural Resources," *Journal of Peace Research* 47(1): 15–28.

Lund, Aron 2013. "The Non-State Militant Landscape in Syria," Combating Terrorism Center at West Point, New York, August 27.

Magone, Claire, Michael Neuman, and Fabrice Weissman 2011. *Humanitarian Negotiations Revealed: The MSF Experience*. London: Hurst.

Makinano, Merliza 2001. "Child Soldiers in the Philippines," International Labor Affairs Service, Department of Labor and Employment, Philippines.

Mampilly, Zachariah 2011. *Rebel Rulers: Insurgent Governance and Civilian Life during War*. Ithaca, NY: Cornell University Press.

Mantilla, Giovanni 2015. "Coerced Empires Strike Back: The Political Origins of the International Law of Internal Conflicts," Unpublished typescript, Princeton University.

Markakis, John 1996. "The Somali in Ethiopia," *Review of African Political Economy* 23: 567–570.

Maslen, Stuart 2001. *Anti-Personnel Mines under Humanitarian Law: A View from the Vanishing Point*. Cambridge: Intersentia.

Masters, Jonathan 2014. "Mujahadeen-e-Khalq (MEK)," CFR Backgrounder, Council on Foreign Relations, available at: www.cfr.org/iran/mujahadeen-e-khalq-mek/p9158.

Mattiaci, Eleonora and Benjajmin Jones 2014. "140 Characters for a Manifesto: Social Media's Impact on the Libyan Civil War 2011," paper presented at the International Studies Association Annual Meeting, Toronto, April 2–4.

Maxwell, David 2004. "Operation Enduring Freedom – Philippines: What Would Sun Tzu Say?" *Military Review*, May–June.

McCubbins, Mathew and D. Roderick Kiewiet 1991. *The Logic of Delegation*. University of Chicago Press.

McDowall, David 2004. *A Modern History of the Kurds*, 3rd edn. London: Tauris.

McGreal, Chris 2012. "Banned Iranian Terror Group Lobbies for Legitimacy on Capitol Hill," *Guardian*, May 22, available at: www.theguardian.com/world/2012/may/22/iranian-terror-group-lobbies-capitol-hill.

McHugh, Gerard 2009. "Strengthening Protection of Children Through Accountability: The Role of the UN Security Council in Holding to Account Persistent Violators of Children's Rights and Protections in Situations of Armed Conflict," *Conflict Dynamics International*, March, available at: www.cdint.org/Conflict_Dynamics-UNSC_Actions_CAC_Report_MASTER_March_2009_PR.pdf.

McHugh, Gerard and Manuel Bessler 2006. "Guidelines on Humanitarian Negotiations with Armed Groups," UN Office for the Coordination of Humanitarian Affairs, East Jerusalem.

McHugh, Gerard and Simar Singh 2013. "Preserving the Integrity of Humanitarian Negotiations," *Humanitarian Exchange Magazine*, No. 58, July, available at: www.odihpn.org/humanitarian-exchange-magazine/issue-58/preserving-the-integrity-of-humanitarian-negotiations.

McKenna, Thomas 1998. *Muslim Rulers and Rebels: Everyday Politics and Armed Separatism in the Southern Philippines*. Berkeley, CA: University of California Press.

Memorial Institute for the Prevention of Terrorism 2013. "Group Profile: Moro Islamic Liberation Front (MILF)," MIPT Terrorism Knowledge Database, Oklahoma City.

Merari, Ariel 1993. "Terrorism as a Strategy of Insurgency," *Terrorism and Political Violence* 5: 213–251.

Minorities at Risk 2015. "Chronology for Kurds in Iran," Center for International Development and Conflict Management, University of Maryland, available at: www.cidcm.umd.edu/mar/chronology.asp?groupID=63007.

Modirzadeh, Naz 2006. "Taking Islamic Law Seriously: INGOs and the Battle for Muslim Hearts and Minds," *Harvard Human Rights Journal* 19: 191–233.

Modirzadeh, Naz, Dustin A. Lewis, and Claude Bruderlein 2011. "Humanitarian Engagement under Counter-Terrorism: A Conflict of Norms and the Emerging Policy Landscape," *International Review of the Red Cross* 93: 623–647.

Morrow, James 2014. *Order within Anarchy: The Laws of War as an International Institution*. Cambridge University Press.

2007. "When do States Follow the Laws of War?" *American Political Science Review* 101: 559–572.

Murdie, Amanda and Tavishi Bhasin 2011. "Aiding and Abetting? Human Rights INGOs and Domestic Anti-Government Protest," *Journal of Conflict Resolution* 55: 163–191.

Murphy, Jim 1993. *The Boys' War: Confederate and Union Soldiers Talk About the Civil War*. Boston, MA: Houghton Mifflin Harcourt.
Murphy, Sean 2002. *United States Practice in International Law*, vol. 1. Cambridge University Press.
Muthoo, Abhinay 2000. *Bargaining Theory with Applications*. Cambridge University Press.
National Transitional Council 2011. "Press Statement on the Laws of Armed Conflict," available at: ntclibyaus.files.wordpress.com/2011/08/ntc-ps-laws2.pdf.
Nilsson, Desirée 2012. "Anchoring the Peace: Civil Society Actors in Peace Accords and Durable Peace," *International Interactions* 38: 243–266.
Nindorera, Willy 2012. "The CNDD-FDD in Burundi: The Path from Armed to Political Struggle," Berghof Transitions Series No. 10, Resistance/Liberation Movements and Transition to Politics.
O'Bagy, Elizabeth 2013. "The Free Syrian Army," Middle East Security Report No. 9, Institute for the Study of War, Washington, DC.
Okamba, Louis 1996. "Angola – Politics: Child Soldiers Die in a War No One Talks About," Inter-Press Service News Agency, May 24, available at: www.ipsnews.net// 1996/05/angola-politics-child-soldiers-die-in-a-war-no-one-talks-about.
Olson, Mancur 2000. *Power and Prosperity: Outgrowing Communist and Capitalist Dictatorships*. Oxford University Press.
Osiel, Mark 2009. *The End Reciprocity: Terror, Torture, and the Law of War*. Cambridge University Press.
Otto, Sabine 2013. "Coding One-Sided Violence from Media Reports," *Cooperation and Conflict* 48: 556–566.
Özerdem, Alpaslan, Sukanya Podder, and Eddie L. Quitoriano 2010. "Identity, Ideology and Child Soldiering: Community and Youth Participation in Civil Conflict: A Study on the MILF, Mindanao, Philippines," *Civil Wars* 12: 304–325.
Patel, Atish 2013. "Report: India's 3,000 Child Soldiers," *Wall Street Journal*, May 12.
Peterman, Amber, Dara Kay Cohen, Tia Palermo, and Amelia Hoover Green 2011. "Rape Reporting During War: Why the Numbers Don't Mean What You Think They Do," *Foreign Affairs*, August 1.
Petrasek, David 2005. "Vive la Différence? Humanitarian and Political Approaches to Engaging Armed Groups," Conciliation Resources, London.
Pipes, Richard 2011. *The Russian Revolution*. New York: Random House.
Plett, Barbara 2013. "UN 'Plans to Fight Rebels in DRC'," *BBC News Africa*, January 25.
Podder, Sukanya 2013. "Non-State Armed Groups and Stability: Reconsidering Legitimacy and Inclusion," *Contemporary Security Policy* 34: 16–39.
2012a. "Legitimacy, Loyalty and Civilian Support for the Moro Islamic Liberation Front: Changing Dynamics in Mindanao, Philippines," *Politics, Religion & Ideology* 13: 495–512.
2012b. "From Spoilers to Statebuilders: Constructive Approaches to Engagement with Non-State Armed Groups in Fragile States," OECD Development Co-operation Working Papers, WP 5/2012, October.
Podder, Sukanya and Alpaslan Özerdem 2012. "Grassroots and Rebellion: A Study on the Future of the Moro Struggle in Mindanao, Philippines," *Civil Wars* 14: 521–545.
Potz-Nielsen, Carly 2013. "Peace Process and Rebel Fragmentation," paper presented at the Summer Research Academy, Texas A&M University.

Price, Megan, Anita Gohdes, and Patrick Ball 2014. "Updated Statistical Analysis of Documentation of Killings in the Syrian Arab Republic," Commissioned by the Office of the UN High Commissioner for Human Rights, Human Rights Data Analysis Group, August.

Public Radio International 2014. "ISIS? ISIL? The Islamic State? We Really Still Can't Decide?" September 18, available at: www.pri.org/stories/2014-09-18/isis-isil-islamic-state-we-really-still-cant-decide.

Radtke, Mitch and Hyeran Jo 2013. "Fighting the Hydra: Rebel Groups and Economic Sanctions," unpublished manuscript, Texas A&M University.

Rakove, Jack 2010. *Revolutionaries: A New History of the Invention of America*. Boston, MA: Houghton Mifflin Harcourt.

Rao, Raghunath, Rajesh Chandy, and Jaideep Prabhu 2008. "The Fruits of Legitimacy: Why Some New Ventures Gain More from Innovation than Others," *Journal of Marketing* 72: 58–75.

Ratner, Steven 2011. "Law Promotion Beyond Law Talk: The Red Cross, Persuasion, and the Laws of War," *European Journal of International Law* 22: 459–506.

Raustiala, Kal and Anne-Marie Slaughter 2006. "International Law, International Relations and Compliance," in Walter Carlsnaes, Thomas Risse, and Beth A. Simmons (eds.), *Handbook of International Relations*. London: Sage.

Regan, Patrick 2008. *Sixteen Million One*. Boulder, CO: Paradigm.

Regan, Patrick and Aysegul Aydin 2006. "Diplomacy and Other Forms of Intervention in Civil Wars," *Journal of Conflict Resolution* 50: 736–756.

Renders, Marleen and Ulf Terlinden 2010. "Negotiating Statehood in a Hybrid Political Order: The Case of Somaliland," *Development and Change* 41: 723–746.

Reno, William 2011. *Warfare in Independent Africa*, New Approaches to African History. Cambridge University Press.

Reusse-Decrey, Elisabeth 2005. "The Struggle against Landmines: An Opening for Peace Talks in Colombia," Conciliation Resources, London.

2000. "Engaging Non-State Actors in a Landmine Ban: A Pioneering Conference: Full Conference Proceedings," Swiss CBL, International Conference Center, Geneva, Switzerland, March 24–25, available at: www.peacepalacelibrary.nl/ebooks/files/357157931.pdf.

Reuters 2013. "Free Syrian Army Fighters Being Trained According to International Humanitarian Law in Turkey," May 12.

Rice, Xan and Tania Branigan 2009. "Sudanese President Expels Aid Agencies," *The Guardian*, March 5, available at: www.theguardian.com/world/2009/mar/05/sudan-aid-agencies-expelled.

Ricigliano, Robert 2005. "Engaging Armed Groups in Peace Processes," Conciliation Resources, London.

Riedel, Bruce 2007. "Al Qaeda Strikes Back," *Foreign Affairs* 86: 24–40.

Rigual, Christelle 2013. "Armed Groups' Holdings of Guided Light Weapons," Research Note No. 31, Small Arms Survey, Geneva.

Risse, Thomas, Stephen Ropp, and Kathryn Sikkink 2013. *The Persistent Power of Human Rights: From Commitment to Compliance*. Cambridge University Press.

1999. *The Power of Human Rights: International Norms and Domestic Change*. Cambridge University Press.

Roberts, Adam and Richard Guelff 2000. *Documents on the Laws of War*. Oxford University Press.

Roberts, Anthea and Sandesh Sivakumaran 2012. "Lawmaking by Nonstate Actors: Engaging Armed Groups in the Creation of International Humanitarian Law," *Yale Journal of International Law* 37: 107–152.

Rogers, Steven 2004. "Beyond the Abu Sayyaf: The Lessons of Failure in the Philippines," *Foreign Affairs* 83: 15–20.

Romano, David 2006. *The Kurdish Nationalist Movement: Opportunity, Mobilization and Identity*. Cambridge University Press.

Ross, Michael 2004. "What Do We Know About Natural Resources and Civil War?" *Journal of Peace Research* 41: 337–356.

Rudolph, Rachael M. 2013. "Transition in the Philippines: The Moro National Liberation Front (MNLF), the Moro Islamic Liberation Front (MILF) and Abu Sayyaf's Group (ASG)," in Rachael Rudolph and Anisseh Van Engeland (eds.), *From Terrorism to Politics*, Farnham: Ashgate, 151–170.

Sabliere, Jean-Marc de la 2012. "Security Council Engagement on the Protection of Children in Armed Conflict: Progress Achieved and the Way Forward," UN Office of the Special Representative of the Secretary-General for Children Affected by Armed Conflict.

Salehyan, Idean 2011. *Rebels without Borders: Transnational Insurgencies in World Politics*. Ithaca, NY: Cornell University Press.

Salehyan, Idean, Kristian Gleditsch, and David Cunningham 2011. "Explaining External Support for Insurgent Groups," *International Organization* 65: 709–744.

Salehyan, Idean, David Siroky, and Reed Wood 2014. "External Rebel Sponsorship and Civilian Abuse: A Principal–Agent Analysis of Wartime Atrocities," *International Organization* 68: 633–661.

Sànchez-Cuencaa, Ignacio 2007. "The Dynamics of Nationalist Terrorism: ETA and the IRA," *Terrorism and Political Violence* 19: 289–306.

Sanín, Francisco Gutiérrez and Elisabeth Jean Wood 2014. "Ideology in Civil War: Instrumental Adoption and Beyond," *Journal of Peace Research* 51: 213–226.

Santos, Soliman and Paz Verdades Santos 2010. "Primed and Purposeful: Armed Groups and Human Security Efforts in the Philippines," a joint publication of the South–South Network for Non-State Armed Group Engagement and the Small Arms Survey, Small Arms Survey, Geneva.

Sassoli, Marco 2010. "Taking Armed Groups Seriously: Ways to Improve Their Compliance with International Humanitarian Law," *International Humanitarian Legal Studies* 1: 5–51.

Schabas, William 2011. *An Introduction to the International Criminal Court*, 4th edn. Cambridge University Press.

Scheffer, David 2013. *All the Missing Souls: A Personal History of the War Crimes Tribunals*. Princeton University Press.

Schiavo-Campo, Salvatore and Mary Judd 2005. "The Mindanao Conflict in the Philippines: Roots, Costs, and Potential Peace Dividend," World Bank Social Development Papers, Conflict Prevention and Reconstruction, Paper No. 24, February.

Schmitt, Michael N. 2010. "Military Necessity and Humanity in International Humanitarian Law: Preserving the Delicate Balance," *Virginia Journal of International Law* 50: 795–839.

Scott, James 1990. *Domination and the Arts of Resistance: Hidden Transcripts*. New Haven, CT: Yale University Press.

1984. *Everyday Forms of Peasant Resistance*. New Haven, CT: Yale University Press.
Shane, Scott and Ben Hubbard 2014. "ISIS Displaying a Deft Command of Varied Media," *New York Times*, August 30.
Sierra Leone Truth and Reconciliation Commission 2004. *Witness to Truth: Sierra Leone Truth and Reconciliation Commission Report*, vol. 2. Accra, Ghana: GPL Press, available at: www.sierra-leone.org/Other-Conflict/TRCVolume2.pdf.
Sikkink, Kathryn 2011. *The Justice Cascade: How Human Rights Prosecutions Are Changing World Politics*. New York: W. W. Norton.
Simmons, Beth 2010. *Mobilizing for Human Rights: International Law in Domestic Politics*. Cambridge University Press.
Singer, Peter 2006. *Children at War*. Berkeley, CA: University of California Press.
Sinjab, Lina 2013. "Syria Crisis: Guide to Armed and Political Opposition," BBC News, December 13.
Sivakumaran, Sandesh 2013. "Command Responsibility in the Sierra Leonean Conflict: The Duty to Take Measures to Prevent Crimes and Punish the Perpetrators," in Charles Chernor Jalloh (ed.), *The Sierra Leone Special Court and its Legacy: The Impact for Africa and International Criminal Law*. Cambridge University Press.
2012. *The Law of Non-International Armed Conflict*. Oxford University Press.
2011. "Lessons for the Law of Armed Conflict from Commitments of Armed Groups: Identification of Legitimate Targets and Prisoners of War," *International Review of the Red Cross* 93: 1–20.
2009. "Courts of Armed Opposition Groups: Fair Trials or Summary Justice?" *Journal of International Criminal Justice* 7: 489–513.
Slim, Randa 2011. "Meet Syria's Opposition," *Foreign Policy*, November 2.
Smith, David 2013. "US Blocks Military Aid to Rwanda over Alleged Backing of M23 Child Soldiers," *Guardian*, October 4.
Soames, Christopher, Rt Hon Lord 1980. "From Rhodesia to Zimbabwe," *International Affairs* 56: 405–419.
Sobek, David and Caroline L. Payne 2010. "A Tale of Two Types: Rebel Goals and the Onset of Civil Wars," *International Studies Quarterly* 54: 213–240.
Somer, Jonathan 2012. "Engaging Armed Non-State Actors to Protect Children from the Effects of Armed Conflict: When the Stick Doesn't Cut the Mustard," *Journal of Human Rights Practice* 4: 128–140.
Song, Sang-Hyun 2013. "Preventive Potential of the International Criminal Court," *Asian Journal of International Law* 3: 203–213.
South, Ashley 2011. "Burma's Longest War: Anatomy of the Karen Conflict," Transnational Institute, Burma Center, the Netherlands.
Spittaels, Steven and Filip Hilgert 2008. "Mapping Conflict Motives: Eastern DRC," International Peace Information Service Report. Antwerp, Belgium.
Staniland, Paul 2012a. "Organizing Insurgency: Networks, Resources, and Rebellion in South Asia," *International Security* 37: 142–177.
2012b. "States, Insurgents, and Wartime Political Orders," *Perspectives on Politics* 10: 243–264.
Stanton, Jessica 2013. "Terrorism in the Context of Civil War" *Journal of Politics* 75: 1009–1022.
Stearns, Jason 2012. "From CNDP to M23: The Evolution of an Armed Movement in Eastern Congo," Rift Valley Institute, London.

2011. *Dancing in the Glory of Monsters: The Collapse of the Congo and the Great War of Africa*. New York: Public Affairs.

Stearns, Jason, Ben Shepherd, and Bronwen Manby 2012. "M23 and the Challenges to Peace in the Eastern DRC," transcript, Chatham House, London.

Steinberg, David 2011. "Myanmar's Perpetual Dilemma: Ethnicity in a 'Discipline-Flourishing Democracy'," Politics, Governance, and Security Series, No. 22, East–West Center, Honolulu.

Stewart, Rory and Gerald Knaus 2012. *Can Intervention Work?* New York: W. W. Norton.

Swiney, Gabriel 2005. "Saving Lives: The Principle of Distinction and the Realities of Modern War," *The International Lawyer* 39: 733–758.

Talmon, Stefan 2011. "Recognition of the Libyan National Transitional Council," *Insights, American Journal of International Law* 15: 16.

Tambo, Olivier 1980. "Statement on Signing Declaration, on Behalf of the ANC and Umkhonto We Sizwe, Adhering to the Geneva Conventions of 1949 and Protocol 1 of 1977," speech made in Geneva, November 28.

Tancos, Kathryn and Mohamed Amiin Adow 2012. "Somali Islamist Militia Defends Recruiting Teen Soldiers," CNN, February 22.

Tarrow, Sidney 2007. "Inside Insurgencies: Politics and Violence in an Age of Civil War," *Perspectives on Politics* 5: 587–600.

Thakur, Ramesh and Thomas Weiss 2009. "R2P: From Idea to Norm – and Action?" *Global Responsibility to Protect* 1: 22–53.

Themner, Lotta and Peter Wallensteen 2012. "Armed Conflicts, 1946–2011," *Journal of Peace Research* 49: 565–575.

Thomas, Jakana 2014. "Rewarding Bad Behavior: How Governments Respond to Terrorism in Civil War," *American Journal of Political Science* 58: 804–818.

Tilly, Charles 1978. *From Mobilization to Revolution*. Reading, MA: Addison-Wesley.

Trager, Robert and Dessie Zagorcheva 2005. "Deterring Terrorism: It Can be Done," *International Security* 30: 87–123.

Trefon, Theodore 2013. "Uncertainty and Powerlessness in Congo 2012," *Review of African Political Economy* 40: 141–151.

Truth and Reconciliation Commission 1998. "Truth and Reconciliation Commission of South Africa Report," available at: www.justice.gov.za/trc/report/index.htm.

Tuck, David 2011. "Detention by Armed Groups: Overcoming Challenges to Humanitarian Action," *International Review of the Red Cross* 93(883): 759–782.

Tyler, Tom 2010. "Legitimacy and Rule Adherence: A Psychological Perspective on the Antecedents and Consequences of Legitimacy," in Ramona Bobocel, Aaron Kay, Mark Zanna, and James Olson (eds.), *The Psychology of Justice and Legitimacy: The Ontario Symposium*, vol. 11. London: Psychology Press.

2006. *Why People Obey the Law*. Princeton University Press.

United Nations 2014a. "Report of the United Nations Joint Human Rights Office on Human Rights Violations Committed by the Mouvement du 23 Mars (M23) in North Kivu Province," April 2012–November 2013, Joint Human Rights Office, available at: www.ohchr.org/Documents/Countries/CD/UNJHROOctober2014_en.pdf.

2014b. "Action Plans with Armed Forces and Armed Groups," United Nations Office of the Special Representative of the Secretary-General for Children and Armed Conflict, November 10, available at: http://childrenandarmedconflict.un.org/our-work/action-plans.

2014c. "Report of the Secretary-General to the Security Council," May 15, A/68/878-S/2014/339, available at: https://childrenandarmedconflict.un.org.
2013a. "The Six Grave Violations against Children during Armed Conflict: The Legal Foundation," Office of the Special Representative of the Secretary-General for Children and Armed Conflict, Working Paper No. 1, available at: https://childrenandarmedconflict.un.org/publications/WorkingPaper-1_SixGraveViolationsLegalFoundation.pdf.
2013b. "Children and Armed Conflict," Report of the Secretary-General, May 15, A/67/845–S/2013/245, available at: www.protectingeducation.org/sites/default/files/documents/unsc_children_and_armed_conflict_report_2013.pdf.
2011a. "After Much Wrangling, General Assembly Seats National Transitional Council of Libya as Country's Representative for Sixty-Sixth Session," General Assembly, Sixty-Sixth General Assembly, Plenary 2nd Meeting, available at: www.un.org/News/Press/docs/2011/ga11137.doc.htm.
2011b. "Report of the Secretary-General on Children and Armed Conflict in the Sudan," July 5, S/2011/413, available at: www.smallarmssurveysudan.org/fileadmin/docs/documents/HSBA-Sec-Gen-2011-413.pdf.
2009. "Child Soldiers: UN Official Welcomes Action Plan by Philippine Rebel Group," United Nations News Center, July 31, available at: www.un.org/apps/news/story.asp?NewsID=31643%.Uc7HcPm87bw.
2008. "Supplemental General Order for General Order Nos. 1 & 2; and in support of the Action Plan between the MILF and the United Nations in the Philippines Regarding the Issue of Recruitment and Use of Child Soldiers in the Armed Conflict in Mindanao," available at Geneva Call's "Their Words" database at: theirwords.org.
2002. "Adult Wars, Child Soldiers: Voices of Children Involved in Armed Conflict in the East Asia and Pacific Region," UN Children's Fund (UNICEF), available at: www.unicef.org/sowc06/pdfs/pub_adultwars_en.pdf.
United States Department of State 2012. "The Lord's Resistance Army," Fact Sheet, Office of the Spokesperson, Washington DC, March 23, available at: www.state.gov/r/pa/prs/ps/2012/03/186734.htm.
United States Department of Treasury 2012. "Treasury Designates Congolese Militant Leader: Sanctions Target Leader of Mouvement du 23 Mars for Using Child Soldiers and Violating Arms Embargo," Press Center, November 13, available at: www.treasury.gov/press-center/press-releases/Pages/tg1763.aspx.
Valentino, Benjamin 2004. *Final Solutions: Mass Killing and Genocide in the Twentieth Century*. Ithaca, NY: Cornell University Press.
Valentino, Benjamin, Paul Huth, and Sarah Croco 2006. "Covenants Without the Sword: International Law and the Protection of Civilians in Times of War," *World Politics* 58: 339–377.
Van Amstel, Nelleke 2012. "In Search of Legal Grounds to Detain for Armed Groups," *Journal of International Humanitarian Legal Studies* 3: 160–191.
Van Den Bosch, Esmeralda 2013. "Non-State Governance in Eastern Democratic Republic of Congo: A Case Study of the M23 Administration," MA thesis, Catholic University of Leuven.
Van Engeland-Nourai, Anicee 2010. "The Challenges of Fragmentation of International Humanitarian Law Regarding the Protection of Civilians: An Islamic Perspective,"

in Cherif Bassiouni and Amna Guellali (eds.), *Jihad and its Challenges to International and Domestic Law*. Hague Academic Press.
Van Kessel, Ineke 2001. "Legitimacy and Generational Conflict in the UDF: The Struggle Behind the Struggle," *Transformation* 46: 32–52.
Verhey, Beth 2001. "The Demobilization and Reintegration of Child Soldiers: El Salvador Case Study," World Bank, Washington, DC.
Veuthey, Michel 2002. "Learning from History: Accession to the Conventions, Special Agreements, and Unilateral Declarations," paper presented at the Proceedings of the Bruges Colloquium, Relevance of International Humanitarian Law to Non-State Actors, October 25–26.
Voice of America 2013. "UN Charcoal Ban Crucial to Somalia Survival," November 19, available at: www.voanews.com/content/un-charcoal-ban-crucial-to-somalia-survival/1793038.html.
Wallace, Geoffrey 2012. "Welcome Guests, or Inescapble Victims? The Causes of Prisoner Abuse in War," *Journal of Conflict Resolution* 56(6): 955–981.
Wallace, Marion and John Kinahan 2011. *A History of Namibia: From the Beginning to 1990*. London: Hurst.
Walter, Barbara 2011. "Conflict Relapse and the Sustainability of Post-Conflict Peace," *World Development Report 2011*, World Bank, Washington, DC.
2009. *Reputation and Civil War: Why Separatist Conflicts are So Violent*. Cambridge University Press.
Washburne, Sarah Lykes 2010. "Legitimacy, Identity and Conflict: The Struggle for Political Authority in Southern Sudan, 2005–2010," PhD dissertation in Arab and Islamic Studies, University of Exeter.
Watchlist 2013. "Action Plans to Prevent and End Violations against Children: The Role of Action Plans in the UN's Children and Armed Conflict Agenda," Watchlist Discussion Paper, April 2013, available at: www.watchlist.org/wordpress/wp-content/uploads/final-discussion-paper-action-plans.pdf.
Weatherford, Stephen 2002. "Measuring Political Legitimacy," *American Political Science Review* 86: 149–166.
Weber, Max 1964. *The Theory of Social and Economic Organization*, ed. Talcott Parsons. New York: Free Press.
Wedeen, Lisa 1999. *Ambiguities of Domination: Politics, Rhetoric, and Symbols in Contemporary Syria*. University of Chicago Press.
Weinberg, Leonard, Ami Pedahzur, and Arie Perliger 2009. *Political Parties and Terrorist Groups*, 2nd edn, Studies in Extremism and Democracy. London: Routledge.
Weinstein, Jeremy 2006. *Inside Rebellion*. Cambridge University Press.
Weiss, Edith and Harold Jacobson 2000. *Engaging Countries: Strengthening Compliance with International Environmental Accords*. Cambridge, MA: MIT Press.
Weiss, Thomas 2012. *Humanitarian Intervention*. Cambridge: Polity.
Werth, Nicolas, Karel Bartošek, Jean-Louis Panné, Jean-Louis Margolin, Andrzej Paczkowski, and Stéphane Courtois 1999. *The Black Book of Communism: Crimes, Terror, Repression*. Cambridge, MA: Harvard University Press.
Whippman, David 2001. "Kosovo and the Limits of International Law," *Fordham International Law Journal* 25: 129–150.
Willms, Jan 2012. "Justice through Armed Groups' Governance – an Oxymoron?" SFB-Governance Working Paper Series, No. 70, University of Berlin.

Witt, John Fabian 2012. *Lincoln's Code: The Laws of War in American History*. New York: Free Press.

Wood, Elisabeth Jean 2009. "Armed Groups and Sexual Violence: When is Wartime Rape Rare?" *Politics & Society* 37: 131–161.

2008. "Sexual Violence during War: Toward an Understanding of Variation," in Stathis Kalyvas, Ian Shapiro, and Tarek Masoud (eds.), *Order, Conflict, and Violence*. Cambridge University Press.

2003. *Insurgent Collective Action and Civil War in El Salvador*. New York: Cambridge University Press.

Wood, Reed 2010. "Rebel Capability and Strategic Violence against Civilians," *Journal of Peace Research* 47: 601–614.

World Bank 2014. "Migration and Remittances: Recent Developments and Outlook," Migration and Development Brief, No. 22, World Bank Migration and Remittances Team, Development Prospects Group, Washington, DC.

Yildiz, Kerim and Susan Breau 2010. *The Kurdish Conflict: International Humanitarian Law and Post-Conflict Mechanisms*. London: Routledge.

Zahar, Marie-Joëlle 2001. "Protégés, Clients, Cannon Fodder: Civil–Militia Relations in Internal Conflicts," in Simon Chesterman (ed.), *Civilians in War*. Boulder, CO: Lynne Rienner, 43–65.

Zartman, William and Guy Olivier Faure 2011. *Engaging Extremists: Trade-Offs, Timing, and Diplomacy*. Washington, DC: United States Institute of Peace Press.

Zegveld, Liesbeth 2002. *Accountability of Armed Opposition Groups in International Law*. Cambridge University Press.

Zelditch, Morris, Jr. 2001. "Theories of Legitimacy," in Brenda Major and John T. Jost (eds.), *The Psychology of Legitimacy: Emerging Perspectives on Ideology, Justice and Intergroup Relations*. Cambridge University Press.

Zelin, Aaron 2014. "ISIS Is Dead, Long Live the Islamic State," *Foreign Policy*, June 30.

2013. "Al-Qaeda in Syria: A Closer Look at ISIS (Parts I and II)," Policywatch 2137–8, Washington Institute for Near East Policy, September 10–11.

Zinko, Robert, Gerald R. Ferris, Fred R. Blass, and Mary Dana Laird 2007. "Toward a Theory of Reputation in Organizations," in Joseph J. Martocchio (ed.), *Research in Personnel and Human Resources Management*, vol. 26. Bradford: Emerald Group Publishing.

Index